the new zealand project

the new zealand project

max harris

BRIDGET WILLIAMS BOOKS

First published in 2017 by Bridget Williams Books Ltd, PO Box 12474,
Wellington 6144, New Zealand, www.bwb.co.nz, info@bwb.co.nz

ISBN 9780947492588 (Paperback), ISBN 9780947492595 (EPUB)
ISBN 9780947492601 (KINDLE), ISBN 9780947492618 (PDF)
DOI https://doi.org/10.7810/9780947492588

Acknowledgements
This book has been published with the support of the Bridget Williams Books
Publishing Trust.

The support of the New Zealand Law Foundation for the research and
writing of the book is acknowledged. The New Zealand Law Foundation
is an independent charitable trust that supports the dissemination of legal
research and scholarship through its grants programme. The views expressed
in this book should not be attributed to the Foundation.

Image credit: Visible Earth, EOS Project Science Office, NASA

A catalogue record for this book is available from the National Library of
New Zealand. Kei te pātengi raraunga o Te Puna Mātauranga o Aotearoa te
whakarārangi o tēnei pukapuka.

Edited by David Cohen
Cover and internal design by Base Two
Typesetting by Tina Delceg
Printed by Printlink, Wellington

contents

1   the new zealand project

Two unexpected turns in my life set me on the path to writing these words.

In August 2014, I was having the time of my life as an intern in former prime minister Helen Clark's executive office at the United Nations Development Programme in New York. The work was fascinating. I was writing a report on how UNDP might better anticipate future trends, researching speeches and helping out as best I could. And after work and on the weekends I was watching outdoor movies on the banks of the Hudson River, and going to gigs in different parts of Manhattan and Brooklyn, including one the previous month by New Zealander Liam Finn at Poisson Rouge over in Greenwich Village. I drifted through op-shops in the Lower East Side, second-hand bookstores in Brooklyn and cafés near where I was living at the time in Harlem.

Then one Sunday morning, after a night out with New Zealanders at a downtown bar, it happened.

I was in my apartment anxiously hunched over my computer, looking online for possible explanations about fleeting chest pains I'd been experiencing. About nine months earlier, a Kiwi doctor friend had said I should ask a specialist about an unusual medical condition that matched several features of my physical appearance and was known to cause heart problems. I was doing what every doctor says you shouldn't do: browsing the internet to see whether my situation matched what my friend had described. I convinced myself that I had the condition, and that I might have already experienced some kind of serious heart episode.

When I got up for a glass of water, I felt dizzy. The light around me dimmed quickly. The next thing I knew I'd hit the floor.

Forty-five minutes later I was in a taxi to Mt Sinai Hospital – though only after several calls to my health insurance provider to double-check I'd be covered.

At Mt Sinai I learned that I had a potentially life-threatening aortic aneurysm: an expansion of the aorta, the blood vessel that carries oxygen from the heart. What was more, I was told, it could tear at any moment. Surgery to fix the aneurysm would carry a mortality risk. I was also told that it was likely that I had Loeys-Dietz syndrome, a connective tissue disorder. I read online that the average life expectancy of those with the condition was 26.1 years.

I had just turned 26.

In the months that followed, events took a turn for the better. I was told that the online material for Loeys-Dietz that I had looked at was out of date. If my aneurysm was corrected through 'valve-sparing aortic root replacement' surgery, which could be done in the United Kingdom where I was living, I could lead a relatively long, normal life.

While awaiting surgery, I was reminded of an annual examination at the University of Oxford known as the All Souls Prize Fellowship. I'd heard it described as one of the hardest exams in the world. That was all hype and hyperbole – there is plenty of that around in Oxford – but it's certainly a challenging test. It involves six hours of writing on a specialist subject, six hours of answering general questions, an interview in front of 50–60 academics for shortlisted candidates, and then, for the one or two or three lucky people who pass, seven years of open-ended funding for research and writing. I first heard about it while I was studying law and public policy at Oxford, mainly through tour guides who told tall tales about the questions, process and candidates. At one time I had thought it might be fun to sit it before returning to New Zealand, but I'd decided against it. With pre-op time on my hands, though, I changed my mind and signed up.

I sat the exam in October. At the time I was gripped with fear. I'd been told that my aneurysm could dissect at any moment, with possibly fatal consequences. Almost every physical twinge and pain in my body worried me: was that squeeze in my chest my aorta stretching to breaking point? Was that numbness in my foot a sign that my circulation was cutting off and the aneurysm tearing? Every night before I went to sleep I asked for reassurance from my girlfriend that I would make it through to the morning – but I felt as if I couldn't hug her too tightly in case it put fatal pressure on the aneurysm.

All of that meant that I wasn't able to fully concentrate as I sat down by the door for the exam in the dusty Old Library. I noticed there was no invigilator after the first fifteen minutes. Would I wreck the exam for everyone else if my aorta decided to tear halfway through?

Luckily, it held out. And the questions in the exam matched my interests perfectly. I wrote about subjects in law that I had explored at university and in my later work. In the general papers there were questions I already felt passionately about: prisoner voting, the merits of worker cooperatives, whether the teaching of economics should be overhauled. (There were some more unusual questions that I answered, too: 'Postmodernism is sooo last century. Discuss.')

One question in particular dovetailed with my experiences of the previous months. It posed an Epicurus quotation, 'Death is nothing to us, since so long as we exist, death is not with us; but when death comes, then we do not exist.' I wrote about how death had been anything but distant for me since my episode in New York. I explained my heart condition and Loeys-Dietz syndrome. I argued that Epicurus's wisdom came across as a little too cool and detached for anyone who had come close to death.

To my surprise, the examiners liked my answers. I was called back for an interview in late October. To my even greater surprise, after an interview that I thought had gone badly, I was one of two people offered the seven-year fellowship.

I didn't have much time to celebrate: my surgery was scheduled for the following week. My family – Mum, Dad, and my brother and sister – travelled from New Zealand to be with me. The operation took some eight hours. A masterful surgeon at the John Radcliffe Hospital, in Oxford, removed the portion of my aorta that was dilated, and replaced it with a new dacron tube he'd fashioned, re-sewing it to ensure a normal flow of blood. I can't remember any of what immediately followed the surgery. But I was told that, when I awoke, I bowed my head to the nurses around me and cupped my hands together in instinctive gratitude. I have notes that I wrote as soon as I came to that I scrawled in lop-sided handwriting to my family, girlfriend and the medical team. 'You're all champs,' one said. Another: 'I'm so happy to be alive.'

I had always been scared of death. But the thought of dying in surgery in 2014 (only a 2–3 per cent risk, but still), and the fact of being told that my life ahead would be if not foreshortened then at least more complicated, made me think about the contribution I wanted to make.

At the same time, I was given the privilege of no-strings-attached funding from All Souls for seven years to work on topics that were meaningful to me. The ancient institution – it was established in 1438 – is one of thirty-eight colleges in Oxford, each a kind of mini-university with academics, students and classrooms. It has no students apart from the Fellows who pass the annual examination. It's made up primarily of senior academics, most of whom don't have to do any teaching. And it has its own rituals and traditions, which are peculiar even by Oxford standards: a speech in Latin that the youngest Fellow has to give every year, for instance, and a College 'mallard song' that honours a wild duck supposedly found when the college was built. My All Souls funding included optional accommodation, meals and PhD funding if I wanted to pursue an academic route.

What would you do if you came this close to death and were then offered seven years of funding to do anything you wanted?

When I told an audience at an early discussion of this project that my answer to this question was 'write about New Zealand politics', they laughed. But to me it made sense.

I didn't grow up in a particularly political household. But I was fortunate to grow up around books. My family talked about ideas. My parents encouraged me to learn. I went to a primary school, Clyde Quay, in Wellington, that provided a context for political thinking, grounded pupils in an understanding of values and got us thinking about the New Zealand system. My school experiences, in Indonesia and at Wellington College, brought me into contact with inspiring teachers, and nudged me towards historical and political books, such as James Belich's *Making Peoples: A History of the New Zealanders*, which I first discovered during my final year at school.

Then at the University of Auckland, where I was from 2006 until 2010, I studied law, history and politics, which deepened my interest in New Zealand's culture, past, and present. After university, while finishing my honours thesis, I worked for 18 months in the New Zealand Supreme Court as clerk to Chief Justice Sian Elias. Elias spoke and wrote eloquently about values and principles – and the values and principles unique to Aotearoa New Zealand. My time working for her made me think about the direction of the country, and about how through law one has the privilege of understanding activities that have left a permanent mark on the political landscape.

Other things were just as important in drawing me to New Zealand politics. I have always felt a deep connection to the peoples, causes and contours of our land. I am not tangata whenua, or one of the first peoples of Aotearoa New Zealand. I am a Pākehā New Zealander, born in London while my parents were living there, and my family has not been here all that long. My mother's parents moved to New Zealand from the UK after the Second World War; my father arrived as an adult. But what little kapa haka and Māoritanga I experienced at primary school spoke to my soul.

When I travelled with my family to Indonesia in 2000, my connection to

New Zealand grew stronger: I felt the risk of losing a sense of belonging, and I encountered international students who didn't have a home. I didn't want to be like that. I was, and wanted to be, a New Zealander. And my sense of social debt to the country only increased as I benefited from publicly funded education at primary school, high school and university (to say nothing of publicly funded health care, transport and other institutions).

I found myself drawn back to New Zealand after commencing studies at Oxford in 2012. I started a blog, *The Aotearoa Project*. I continued to check New Zealand news websites first thing each morning. I wrote about New Zealand issues for Oxford assignments. I organised several events for Kiwis in London on the future of New Zealand. All in all, thinking about the country – and thinking about the many New Zealands that exist across these islands under one long white cloud – has never been far from my mind.

Why, though, write a *book* about New Zealand – and why *this* book?

This work was born out of an instinct that something is not right in New Zealand society, that politics is partly to blame for this, and that collective political action might be able not only to address these challenges but to create new ways of thriving together. (I understand politics here to mean action and activities that concern how power is exercised.) In conversations I was having, in New Zealand and elsewhere, prior to 2014 – and not just in my circle of friends or acquaintances – there was a growing sense of discomfort with the direction of the country, whether this related to issues of child poverty or housing or resource management or other problems. Some felt a deeper malaise and believed that New Zealand had been cast adrift for a long time. I worked with people who felt this way on various campaigns in criminal justice, law and climate change, especially between 2011 and 2012. I heard disagreement over whether there was anything seriously wrong, but almost everybody suggested that things could be better. People of all persuasions wanted a greater sense of ambition in the political realm, new ideas and fresher language.

I wanted to investigate these hunches and opinions and to speak with people who had reflected deeply on them.

I wanted to offer some hope and concrete ideas for people – especially those of my own generation – who were organising themselves in an effort to build a better politics. And I had an inkling that some of our challenges, whether relating to inequality or the need for decolonisation or mass incarceration were shared by other countries. I wanted to reflect on whether these challenges in New Zealand and elsewhere were the same, and if they were, to consider whether we might be able to lead the way in developing imaginative responses.

I felt that only a book, drawing on research from overseas as well as interviews in New Zealand, could provide the space to explore the gravity of problems facing us and to sketch out solutions in a global context.

There were also individuals I encountered (not just young people) who were not engaged with politics, who thought it was unimportant to their lives. They had opinions – perspectives that could improve the state of the country – but they had been left behind by our political system. That felt wrong to me, because, as the election of Donald Trump later confirmed, politics matters. I wrote with them in mind, too. I hope this writing can start conversations that will make politics more appealing to them.

On one level, then, I was eager to widen and deepen political debate. There is widespread disaffection with mainstream politics in our country. I discuss this in more detail in Chapter 11. There is also a lack of depth in debate, especially in the sphere of electoral politics. There are few institutions that can sketch out new political frameworks or propose fresh policy ideas. There is a paucity of think tanks, too. Academics attempt to contribute to political debates, but this responsibility is often seen as secondary. Partly as a result of this disaffection and lack of depth, partly as a result of past political decisions, New Zealand's 'Overton window' – the space for what is seen as politically possible – has narrowed. I wanted to bring more people into political conversations, to improve the quality of analysis in those conversations and to expand our notions of what is realistic and achievable through political action.

But this book isn't neutral. It also develops a narrative about why New Zealand has lost its way and how we might regain a sense of collective direction.

The story I tell centres around four connected themes, one primary and three supporting. The main theme is the lack of a values-based politics at the electoral level and the need for a politics grounded in cornerstone progressive values of care, community and creativity. This is elaborated here with reference to the need for a rejuvenated role for the state in the economy and in social policy; the need for that state, and our broader society, to be decolonised; and the need for the state to be driven by genuine people power.

It is difficult to define values. I understand them to be principles that we hold dear that contribute to a life well led. A values-based politics, then, is a politics (in the activist and electoral spheres) that is motivated by values and that seeks to give effect to values through political action. It is related to, and inspired by, Māori approaches to ethics, life and collective action, which place values at the centre of behaviour and decision-making. A core claim of this book is that New Zealand politics is not motivated sufficiently by values or giving sufficient effect to values. This is not to denigrate all politicians or activists. Some people involved with politics are motivated by values, while others want to be motivated by values but are held back by broader pressures.

Three interconnected forces have stood in the way of a values-based politics, especially since the mid-1980s. First, there's been a rise of selfishness and self-interest in society at large, mainly due to economic reforms. Second, the framework for determining the purpose of politics has been lost. Third, there's been a continued emphasis on a technocratic approach to political activity: an approach to politics that sees it as technical and value-free.

As I discuss in Chapter 4, and elsewhere, the economic reforms that started in the mid-1980s have created a more self-interested society, and chipped away at the idea of a society with a shared destiny. Those reforms cut taxes on the wealthy, privatised or semi-privatised public institutions, and loosened regulation of markets. As citizens, we have been more willing to see ourselves as isolated, competitive individuals who should pursue our own self-interest. As voters, we are more willing to be motivated by self-interest. And political campaigners and politicians may have become more guided by self-interest, too – even if there remain campaigners and some politicians who have resisted such trends.[1] The reforms of the 1980s were not free of values – values such as freedom, private property, efficiency and others were championed by politicians. But the rise of self-interest did crowd out some space for values-based politics. And to the extent that there were values at all, they were inconsistent with the values of care, community and creativity (to which I return below).

There has also been the loss of any moral framework for determining what politics is for. Here again the economic ideas of the 1980s are partly to blame. Criticisms of the role of the government in the economy led to a retreat of the state and a view that politics should largely be a delivery device for particular kinds of markets that are 'free' to at least some participants and relatively unregulated, except for basic contract law and other legal protections. That created a vacuum of thinking.

But others must shoulder some responsibility. There has been a general failure by academics and intellectuals to propose the possible goals of political activity. This failure has partly to do with the structural features of New Zealand's political landscape. Some responsibility should be shared, too, by successive politicians who have clung to an unimaginative British-style pragmatism as the guiding principle of their work. Being practical is important, but pragmatism has too often merely been a code for muddle-through politics.

Third, pressures towards a technocratic approach to politics, especially at the parliamentary level, have undermined the ability for values to be central. As far back as the 1930s, writers lamented the way that politics had been flattened into a specialised activity involving technical cost–benefit calculations without open-ended moral or ethical judgments.[2] But there has been a resurgence in technocratic discourse since the 1990s, with the rise of Third Way politics, especially in the UK and the US, on the watch of Tony Blair and Bill Clinton, respectively. This type of politics, discussed in more depth in Chapter 12, demands a focus on 'what works', and has had the effect of draining politics to a large extent of any moral or values-based content. (I see values as related to morals, but less cold or hard-edged.)

Discussion of values should not detract from the fact that evidence is important. Policy should, wherever possible, be informed by evidence, albeit with a clear understanding of its limits, and I try to be guided by this principle. But it is still the case that the move towards technocratic politics has contributed to the neglect of a values-based framework.

My call is for values to be central to New Zealand political practice, in the electoral sphere, in campaigning, and in activism and all forms of political conversation. This is a strategic intervention, a plea for this moment and our time.

Because it is a strategic intervention, it should be clear that values do not exhaust what is needed. But a greater role for values, an injection of values as a basis for political action, could allow New Zealand to regain a sense of direction and imagination and political progress.

Values connect to the heart as well as to the head, as academic George Lakoff has pointed out, and so a values-based politics can help people to be more engaged politically.[3] As well, my notion is inspired by Māori world views, and therefore has the potential to be a model for politics that is grounded in this place, in Aotearoa New Zealand. It is not enough to exhort activists, campaigners and politicians to be motivated by values. We need to undo the structural changes that have blocked the way. We also need to believe that politicians and other political actors are capable of being motivated by values. Finally, we need to believe that, while people might be driven by basic economic interests, those interests are not immutable – and we can reshape and reconstruct those interests using values.[4]

I want to be specific and constructive, to make an effort to help to fill the vacuum that has been left by the absence of thinking about the purpose of politics in New Zealand – so my analysis also focuses on what I call 'cornerstone progressive values'. In my research, I attempted to list all possible progressive values: freedom, equality, community, identity, dignity, security, responsibility, inclusiveness, creativity and integrity.[5] I then worked to synthesise, condense and distil these values into a set of 'cornerstone' values from which all other values flowed. I was especially interested in formulating the values in new ways, to find fresh language to move people towards political action.

But I also wanted to capture key values that ought to form part of a progressive project that does not view history as linear or always improving, but assumes that we can do better. Out of this exercise, I gathered freedom, equality, dignity and integrity under *care*. I rearranged the values of community, identity, security, responsibility and inclusiveness under an expanded notion of *community*. I kept *creativity* separate as the final cornerstone progressive value.

This is not an academic political theory book. But it is worth saying a little more about the meaning of these 'three Cs'.

I understand care to mean a concern for the wellbeing of others. Put another way, it's about looking out for each other and looking after each other. It is different from pity or charity: it should involve not patronising offers of help but support, interest and empathy directed from one person to another on an equal footing. Care contributes to a person's dignity and security in a society. It's the value we demonstrate when we stop to help someone who has fallen. It's the value that the state can demonstrate through, for instance, the provision of free public health care.

The Māori concept of manaakitanga is the obvious analogue of care in te ao Māori. But the notion of care I am putting forward here is closer to the Māori concept of aroha, which hints at ideas of love, kindness and goodwill, and helps to highlight the constellation of related values surrounding care.[6] Feminist political theory work on 'the ethics of care' (first developed by Carol Gilligan and others) has also deepened our understanding of care as a virtue. Some theorists claim that care is a feminine ethic. Others emphasise the relationship-based foundation of care.[7]

Community is a more complex value. It recognises the connectedness and interdependence of people. Our strengths are developed through the work of others as well as our own efforts; our identities are the product of how we are recognised as well as how we want to be seen; and we rely on others to live and thrive. The value of community gives rise to a responsibility to be aware of the effects of actions on others, in the moment and into the future (which prompts us to reflect on our impact on the natural world). It demands, as with care, that we look outside ourselves.

Again, Māori practices and concepts deepen this idea. In the practice of mihimihi, a speaker's family and tribal background (often including ancestral and tribal names, as well as important geographical features associated with their tribal area) is recounted as a formal introduction. Mihimihi is designed to reveal connections between people – to underscore, in one sense, the way we are all entangled and interconnected within a community. The notion of whanaungatanga – often translated more broadly as kinship, or the building of family-like relationships – is also akin to this. It gestures at the warmth that we should feel towards each other. Community is opposed to exclusion (though some people would say that exclusion is inherent in community), and should move us in the direction of inclusiveness. My focus is on the national community, but the value of community is also realised in local neighbourhood connectedness and in attachments that form across national boundaries.

The third cornerstone value of creativity is rarely referred to in discussions of progressive politics. I think that's a mistake. Creativity is key to the progressive project. It involves an emphasis on imagination. It is the value that is invoked when discussing the need for innovative new solutions to social challenges. It is in tension with the value of tradition. Creativity is about fashioning things of value. It is connected to the practice of the arts, and associated values of play, fun and spontaneity. (It has an analogue in the Māori concept of auahatanga.)[8] The inclusion of creativity in a set of cornerstone progressive values is a useful corrective to the tendency for progressive politics to be overly earnest: it takes us towards concerns of the heart as well as of the head. Towards playfulness, lightness and variety. We need more of it in New Zealand politics.

Care, community and creativity are cornerstone progressive values. They make sense of progressive practice. They are appealing. They have resonance for Aotearoa New Zealand.[9] However, I try not to apply these values in a mechanical way. This book is not only concerned with values-based politics, but values constitute the foundations of what I am putting forward. In some chapters, one value is given particular prominence; in others I refer to all three.

These values can conflict. As far as possible I attempt to realise them harmoniously. To take one example: 'creativity' can be given an individualistic interpretation, and can be used to support self-interested economic activity (which might be thought of as 'creative'). However, because such self-interested economic activity can undermine the two other cornerstone values, care and community, my suggestion is that this is not the right way to understand 'creativity'. Creativity must be advanced in a way that is consistent with care and community. In a similar way, care and community must each be pursued in a way that does not undermine the other cornerstone progressive values.

To call for a values-based politics is to assume that the state (along with other political actors) can pursue values through action. It requires more explanation of what a state is capable of doing and what a state should do. This connects to the second supporting theme in this book: the need for a rejuvenated account of the state within politics. There were many critiques of the state in the twentieth century, some more justified than others. It has been variously seen as an oppressive, totalitarian force (especially in the aftermath of the Second World War); a bureaucratic, inefficient body; and a monolith that stifles the vitality of the free market (an argument that came to the fore in economic reforms around the world in the 1980s).

These critiques did not always lead to the state's downsizing. But they left discussion of the state in tatters in the early twenty-first century, as much in New Zealand as elsewhere. The state – that collection of actors that falls within the three branches of executive, legislature (Parliament) and judiciary (courts) – has a different history and character in different parts of the world. Here, we have lost a sense of what it is good at. This has resulted in ignorance of active redistribution, robust regulation and steering within the economy. It has reinforced the tendency of politicians to muddle through rather than follow a framework for appropriate action. Getting clear on the advantages and singular capabilities of the state (even if only as part of an account of how it can be used strategically) is necessary in figuring out what role it should play in the overlapping spheres of the economy, social policy, foreign policy and justice policy.

However, the state, in the New Zealand context, can reasonably be seen as having dubious origins, particularly given that our contemporary institutions were established through an oppressive process of British colonisation. The state has perpetrated wrongs against iwi, hapū and Māori individuals, especially through the police and the justice systems. Is it possible to pursue a values-based politics and advocate for an active state even when historical wrongs have not yet been completely rectified and the state and parts of society remain mired in colonial ways of thinking? An answer lies in the third theme of this book: an ongoing decolonisation process needs to take place, at the level of state and of society, alongside the pursuit of a values-based politics.

Decolonisation involves undoing the effects of colonisation in all its forms: economic, political, cultural, social and intellectual. As a Pākehā who has not experienced the consequences of structural or everyday racism, I am less well-equipped than others to write authoritatively on the effects of colonisation. I am not the best placed, either, to say how decolonisation should happen, and to dictate this may also be to perpetuate colonial notions about the superiority of European perspectives. But I do aim to support those Māori who *have* had experience of racism or prejudice, and have demanded ongoing decolonisation. I draw on the writing of Ani Mikaere and the ideas of people I have interviewed, such as Moana Jackson and Kim Workman. Their views suggest that decolonisation of political practice must be a constitutive part of building a values-based politics in Aotearoa New Zealand.

Some might say all this sounds awfully top-down: a set of directions for what the state should do to all of us below it. State institutions have been criticised in the past for being overly detached from the public. I might also be challenged for proposing grand solutions in a way that sounds 'top-down' or akin to social engineering: with the author at the top, readers at the bottom. My fourth theme is relevant in this context: a decolonised, values-based politics – and the New Zealand project as a whole – must be driven by genuine people power.

Many people and groups in Aotearoa New Zealand are demoralised and desensitised. I look at this in Chapter 11. There is a need to reverse these trends. Structural changes are needed, in education, the public sector and elsewhere. These changes will help ensure that people power, a fuller realisation of the ideal of democracy, drives and disciplines the state.

One of my hopes – an exciting, not frightening, hope – is that, once the conditions for this genuine people power are created, there will be developments beyond what can easily be foreseen today. I offer only ideas to be debated here, not a fully costed programme of policies that must be enacted.

These four themes make clear the story I am telling. Rediscovering New Zealand's lost direction is the aim of *The New Zealand Project*. The themes are not laid out in a linear way; instead, they suffuse the remainder of the book, and I loop back around them in the course of exploring specific points in New Zealand politics and policy.

The eight middle chapters are flanked by an introductory and a closing chapter. In the next chapter, I set out key features of New Zealand's political context. In Chapters 3 to 10 I explore major challenges for the future in foreign policy, the economy, 'race relations', social infrastructure, justice, work, the environment and gender. These chapters do not, of course, provide an exhaustive list of the areas of priority for political action in this country.

I don't claim expertise in all of these areas. But I have drawn on interviews with activists, academics, writers and others to enrich the analysis, and have moved across these areas so that interconnections between them can be underscored. I adopted this broad approach because too much fine policy detail can obscure the wider picture.

Chapter 11 reflects on how some of these ideas might be turned into action, in part through changes to structures of political participation. Chapter 12 connects the debates in the book more explicitly to global debates about the Third Way and social democracy, and points to how the New Zealand project might be taken forward.

This is a personal book; I am not completely absent in the narrative, and some of my views will not be shared by others. But it is not meant to be an egotistical manifesto. I hope it is read in the spirit in which it is written: as an attempt to amplify others' voices, and an invitation to debate. Any personal book has limits. Other people might disagree with my proposals – and I'd welcome that disagreement. Everyone can have their own New Zealand project. Yours might not take the form of a book; it might be a story, a work of art, a piece of music. It might focus on different subjects that I do not discuss here. If what I've written leads people to produce different New Zealand projects, then – far from being disappointed – I'll be pleased: we'll have more debate about the future of the country. I think we need more of that.

This book also has its limits in another sense. I was fortunate to grow up in a financially comfortable Pākehā family. My background means there are experiences I will be unable to describe, injustices that I may not be able to capture as compellingly as I would like and blind spots in my line of sight. My relative youth also means I do not have the life experience of some readers.

Nevertheless there is at least one advantage of writing this book as a relatively young person: I have the imagination and impatience that I think characterise many young New Zealanders. That sense of imagination and impatience underpins this book.

I haven't lived long enough yet to have lost a sense of hope or a sense of the possible. But I've lived long enough to know that things are moving too slowly for those of us with hope, who want to make the impossible possible. And I've lived close enough to death to feel like we have no time to lose.

2 winds from the north, south, west and east: global forces and frictions shaping new zealand politics

New Zealand is not an isolated set of islands. It is a country buffeted and boosted by global trends. People bring in products, services and thinking from overseas. Businesses and organisations are influenced by international practices. Governments consider policy examples from other countries. And now, more than ever, the online world allows for a continuous exchange of opinions, news and ideas.

In Chapters 3–10 (and to some extent Chapter 11) I examine New Zealand-specific trends that have shaped our contemporary political environment. For example, in Chapter 6, I discuss the rise of contracting out and how that has affected social policy. I also discuss other global trends that have had particular effects on spheres of policy: I pay close attention to neoliberalism's impact on economic policy in Chapter 4.

This chapter concerns global forces and frictions that have some impact on policy-making and politics in New Zealand. I have selected six that I think are of particular importance: challenges to fundamental political ideas, technological transformations, the rise of 'the national' (again), resurgent attention to colonisation and structural racism, the consolidation of celebrity culture, and shifting global dynamics of power.

My choice undoubtedly involves value judgments. What these overlapping trends have in common is that they have been the subject of significant political discussion, and either have already been shown to be influential for New Zealand, or have the capacity to change the trajectory of our politics. I explain each trend below, in brief, and some implications for the country.

challenges to fundamental political ideas

At the end of the 1980s, as the Berlin Wall fell and the Cold War was concluded, there was a widespread belief that major political questions were settled. Capitalism – a system based on free enterprise and market economies – seemed to have triumphed over communism as a political and economic model.

'Liberal' principles – such as the need to protect free speech, and the view that the individual is the key unit of society – appeared to be all-important. Democracy (political systems based on free and fair elections, and some underpinning principles such as minority and individual rights) had prevailed over alternative political forms. This led Francis Fukuyama, a political scientist, to declare 'the end of history'.[1] The idea, first expressed shortly before the Wall fell, was that battles of fundamental political ideas, which have stretched out across the ages, were over. Politics would no longer need to evolve towards anything better.

In the last 20–30 years that Holy Trinity of capitalism, liberalism and democracy has come under renewed challenge. Fukuyama's pronouncement now looks misguided, certainly a little rash. In particular, since the 2008 global financial crisis (GFC), new questions have been asked about whether capitalism, liberalism and democracy are the best guiding principles for politics.

Two high-profile books about capitalism attracted a lot of debate among activists, campaigners and politicians while I was writing this chapter. One was Paul Mason's *PostCapitalism: A Guide to our Future*, the other Wolfgang Streeck's *How Will Capitalism End?*.[2] In relation to liberalism, British journalist and commentator David Goodhart wrote a widely read essay in 2014 entitled 'A Postliberal Future?'.[3] After the election of Donald Trump, musician Brian Eno said: 'Welcome to the post-Liberal world.'[4] When it came to democracy, debates about alternatives were not confined to political essays or radical tracts. Occupy Wall Street, a protest movement started in New York in 2011, raised public concern about the structure of representative democracy. In particular, it focused attention on inequality and the corporate influence on elections. *The Economist*, usually a pretty sober periodical, published a long essay in 2014, 'What's Gone Wrong with Democracy'.

There are many possible reasons why capitalism, liberalism and democracy have been called into question. Real defects or gaps in these 'isms' and systems of thought have been identified in recent years. The GFC made people wonder not just whether financial markets needed more government oversight; it also made people wonder whether capitalism was a sustainable system. The ongoing significance of group identity in people's lives – whether ethnic identity, gender identity or something else – has resulted in a querying of whether liberalism, which sees the world mostly in individualistic terms, provides the right framework for political and social action. Disaffection with politics –

exemplified by low voter turnout in many countries, and disillusionment with politicians and 'the political class' – has caused some to consider alternatives to democracy. In addition to these evident defects or gaps, some countries that have not adhered to liberal, capitalist democratic principles have performed well, at least in terms of conventional economic metrics: China is one example (though some would claim that China is a capitalist country with streaks of liberalism). Whatever the explanation, what is clear is that big debates have been reopened. It remains hard to think beyond liberalism, capitalism or democracy: Frederic Jameson once said that 'it is easier to imagine the end of the world than the end of capitalism'.[5] But at the very least, discussions are beginning about the need to develop alternatives.

These debates have been in evidence in New Zealand, too. Concerns about the levels of inequality, discussed further in Chapter 4, have prompted doubts to be expressed about the capitalist system in operation. In early 2017, the writer David Hall asked whether the wave of post-liberal feeling globally might shift approaches to trade or immigration in New Zealand.[6] Unhappiness with the current state of democracy was one reason a group of young New Zealanders set up Loomio, an online decision-making tool that aims to redress the gaps in offline democracy.[7] The debates about capitalism, liberalism and democracy might not cause these systems to be abandoned. They might lead to these systems being refined or revised. But these emerging debates, whether in this country or elsewhere, highlight the need for the window of political possibility to be prised open. They also should encourage us to look more deeply into the failings of capitalism, liberalism and democracy, to test the failings and to think about alternatives where needed. These points are picked up further in Chapters 4 and 11 in particular.

technology

Loomio is one example of a political tool that has been developed through technology. But all around the world there is an explosion of technological innovation that has a bearing on how politics can and should operate. Two areas of technological transformation that are particularly significant are automation in the workplace and shifts in information and communication technology.

A 2015 report by the Committee for Economic Development of Australia, to take just one example of research on automation, suggested that as many as 40% of Australian jobs could be replaced by robotics and computers within a decade or two.[8] These shifts have focused commentators' attention on the workplace, and whether there is a need to rethink employment. In relation to information and communication technology, global mobile phone penetration is 96%, according to the World Economic Forum.[9] Internet access remains uneven globally, but the spread of the internet has the capacity to affect how people gather information, interact socially, organise politically and travel, among other things.

New Zealand has seen the influence of technological transformation in recent years, including within politics. The Labour Party's Future of Work Commission has attempted to grapple with the effect of automation on employment.[10] Internet usage has mushroomed in New Zealand. Eighty per cent of New Zealand households were connected to the internet in 2012.[11] New Zealand is fourth in the world – behind Malaysia, the US and the UK – in terms of the percentage of people over the age of 18 who are constantly logged into Facebook. 1.9 million New Zealanders use Facebook each day, on average 14 times per day, with 2.5 million New Zealanders using this site in a given month.[12]

It is possible to get overly excited about the impact of technological change. The language of 'disruption' has become something of a buzzword. There is some evidence that labour productivity in the last four or five decades is no greater, and perhaps slower, than earlier periods of the twentieth century.[13] It is important, therefore, that technological transformation is discussed with some measure of balance and perspective.

Nevertheless it is worth asking what this technological shift means for politics. Later chapters develop the specific implications of technology for work (Chapter 8) and of social media for activism (Chapter 10). But for now it's worth noting that technological change simultaneously brings insecurity and opportunity. Threats to work from automation create further stress for those in insecure employment. There is also a risk that automation might worsen inequality, by increasing profits for managers and owners and reducing salaries or eliminating jobs for the most vulnerable. It's possible, too, that those who are most educated are best equipped to weather the storm of automation.

However, in some areas technological change may create power for previously marginalised groups. A New Zealand blogger has said, of social media and online commentary: 'Social media allows for the harmful actions of the privileged, which usually are left unchallenged because of the power these people hold socially, to be aggressively interrogated.'

'In New Zealand,' the blog continues, 'Twitter has been used to shift our conversation on rape culture … [and] has democratized which issues get covered in mainstream media.' And: 'Online activism … can be impolite and spoken in discordant tones at times, but ultimately it represents a major kind of resistance which cannot exist offline.'[14]

Whether the benefits of some of these technological shifts outweigh the risks is a matter for further inquiry. But it is clear that, at the very least, concerns about technology will be a central feature of future political debate. Discussion about the future of New Zealand politics and policy-making cannot ignore these developments.

the rise of 'the national' (again)

In the 1990s, there was much talk of 'globalisation': the idea that national boundaries were becoming less important, and that the world was becoming 'flat'.[15] Globalisation was not without its critics, who said it flattened cultural difference, transferred power to multinational corporations, and undermined national regulatory sovereignty. As well, there were some who questioned whether globalisation was as 'new' or as significant as people claimed: for example, Kevin O'Rourke and Jeffrey Williamson showed global flows of information and economic activity were more intensive at other times in the nineteenth and twentieth century.[16] But there was a widely held view, at least in the 1990s, that the world was converging in economic policy and cultural practices like never before.

That momentum began to stutter during the 2000s and early 2010s. Talks about the lowering of trade barriers through the World Trade Organization's (WTO's) Doha Development Round faltered. The GFC in 2008, which saw US bank and housing market failures have a ripple effect on much of the rest of the world, led to some countries seeking to insulate themselves from future crises. Then, in 2016, the UK voted in a referendum to leave the European Union, and the US elected Donald Trump to the presidency, on the back of a campaign in which he used racist, anti-immigrant language and promised to withdraw from international agreements, including the Paris Agreement on climate change. Other countries had also begun to move in a more xenophobic direction, such as India after the election of Narendra Modi in 2014 and the Philippines after the election of Rodrigo Duterte in 2016. The xenophobic One Nation Party, led by Pauline Hanson, made a return to the Australian Parliament in 2016.

And challenges to international law and international institutions were seen elsewhere, for example in promises by South Africa and Burundi to withdraw from the International Criminal Court. The humanitarian crisis in Syria also caused a massive displacement of people, sparking further debates about appropriate levels of migration, especially in Europe. Overall, the world in 2017 found itself 'in a kind of interregnum between the era of nation-states and whatever comes after them', in the words of political theorist Wendy Brown.[17]

New Zealand was undoubtedly affected by globalising trends in the 1990s and 2000s. Successive governments were strong supporters of the WTO free trade agenda (and the WTO was led by ex-New Zealand prime minister Mike Moore from 1999–2002), and New Zealand law incorporated international agreements: for example, the New Zealand Bill of Rights Act 1990 gave domestic effect to the International Covenant on Civil and Political Rights. But New Zealand has been slower to follow the worldwide trend towards protectionism and insularity since the GFC. There have been occasional stirrings of anti-migrant rhetoric from New Zealand politicians: from the National-led government, with its adoption of a law authorising detention of migrant group arrivals in 2013; from the Labour Party, in its scaremongering about 'Asian' homeowners in Auckland in 2015; and periodically from Winston Peters's New Zealand First party. However, New Zealand has – for now at least – largely resisted the virulent xenophobia that has been seen elsewhere.

This book, as its title suggests, uses a national frame – because it proceeds on the premise that couching political action in national terms can be an effective way to mobilise people towards realising the public good. But this book also acknowledges that nationalism can be a dangerous, exclusive force.[18] It is therefore imperative that national-level action is combined with openness: in foreign policy (discussed in Chapter 3) and immigration policy (mentioned in Chapter 5) in particular. As well, New Zealand must remain mindful of international obligations, for example in the area of climate change action (outlined in Chapter 9).

resurgent attention to colonisation and structural racism

In the mid-2010s, there was a renewed focus on the ongoing effects of colonisation and structural racism around the world. Colonisation and racism were not new subjects of activism: movements have struggled against these forces for centuries, and across many continents. But in the mid-2010s colonisation and institutional racism became the subject of heightened protest, media attention and political comment.

The 2014–15 period was crucial to this shift. In 2014, US police murders of young black men caused a surge of public outcry. Eric Garner's death at the hands of New York police (using a chokehold) in July 2014 and the shooting of unarmed Michael Brown in Ferguson, Missouri, in August 2014 drew particular attention. These were followed by the deaths of Tamir Rice (at just 12 years of age), Freddie Gray and Sandra Bland, among others. Black Lives Matter, formed after George Zimmerman was acquitted of the murder of Trayvon Martin in 2012, increased its profile over 2014–15 through a combination of effective Twitter activism (using the hashtag #BlackLivesMatter) and mass protest. Black Lives Matter highlighted institutional racism in the police, the prison system, the workforce and elsewhere – and it influenced similar movements around the world.

During the same period, student movements in Africa, the Americas and Europe shone a light on the effects of colonisation at universities – and called for decolonisation, a concept we have already discussed in Chapter 1. South African students led the charge, with the establishment of the #RhodesMustFall movement at the University of Cape Town (UCT) in 2015. This movement called for the removal of a statue of imperialist Cecil Rhodes, and a wider reconsideration of the UCT curriculum. A Rhodes Must Fall group formed in Oxford in 2015, inspired by #RhodesMustFall in South Africa,[19] and a group at the School of Oriental and African Studies (SOAS) in London pushed for decolonisation of the curriculum; related movements to replace symbols of colonisation also gained traction in the city of Bristol, Queen Mary University in London, and the University of Cambridge. In the United States, students pushed for curriculum review and the relocation of emblems of slavery and colonisation at Georgetown, Harvard, Princeton, Amherst, and Yale, and other institutions. These movements were significant because they helped to spark wider debates about the long shadow of colonisation and slavery, especially in the US and the UK, and the ongoing economic advantages procured in those places through colonisation and slavery. Along with Black Lives Matter, these movements highlighted that racism and anti-blackness remain live problems in many parts of the world – and connected racism today to histories of colonisation and slavery.

Why all this resurgent attention to colonisation, slavery, and racism? At the surface level, new technology helped messages to be disseminated broadly, building support for various movements. Cellphone cameras captured police violence and Facebook allowed the viral sharing of these videos; social media facilitated collaboration between student activists around the world. But this does not explain why there was an underlying interest in these videos, or an underlying interest in activist collaboration. An obvious point is that police violence, colonial influence and racism remained patent problems around the world in 2014–15; these movements merely drew attention to years of political inaction on these issues. Considerable credit should also go, however, to activists in the US (involved with Black Lives Matter) and South Africa (involved with #RhodesMustFall) for using messages with widespread resonance, and for picking focal points that allowed observers to easily understand their aims and goals. A further hypothesis is that these movements were ultimately about who has power – in struggles with police, within university spaces – in contemporary democracy. That focus on the skewed distribution of power may have developed out of the discomfort expressed with current political structures in the aftermath of the GFC and the Occupy movement.

The activity did not go unnoticed in New Zealand. Of course, campaigners and commentators – especially those with an understanding of the history of Māori – have long pointed out (and been affected by) the ongoing existence of colonial or quasi-colonial or racist policies and ways of thinking in New Zealand. But, to take just one example, from 2014–15 students underscored everyday racism at the University of Auckland through the 'I, Too, Am Auckland' online video series, where students recounted racist comments experienced as part of university life. In 2016, Dame Tariana Turia, who has fought against institutional racism for decades in and out of parliamentary politics, wrote that 'it was time to tackle institutional racism'.[20] There were New Zealand-specific reasons for this renewed attention, not least the persistent disparities between Māori and non-Māori in incarceration figures, unemployment rates and other measures of social deprivation. Demographic changes – the fact, for example, that Asian, Pasifika and Māori populations are growing faster than the rest of the New Zealand population[21] – also highlighted the need to act. These population increases underscored that New Zealand could not but deal with residual prejudice and rethink its own identities.

This trend forms an important part of the contemporary political context in New Zealand. It is addressed at length in Chapter 5, but other chapters –

notably Chapters 6 and 7 – touch on institutional racism, too. And the need for decolonisation of state and society, as discussed in Chapter 1, is a theme that runs through the book.

celebrity culture

The cult of the celebrity is nothing new. It is at the heart of entertainment industries in Hollywood, Bollywood and elsewhere. It is a part of the 'society of the spectacle', described in 1967 by Guy Debord: a society that celebrates the image, the advertisement, the significance of fame.[22] The idolisation of good-looking celebrities has been a constant in the history of commercial film, music and the mass media.

But our social media-savvy generation faces a supercharged and supersized celebrity culture. On top of customary gossip and paparazzi surveillance, coverage of celebrity activity has become more intense and all-encompassing in today's 24-hour news cycle, in New Zealand as elsewhere. The definition of celebrity has also been widened: in New Zealand, it means not just royalty (the Queen), politicians, actors, and musicians, but also family members of all of these people (for example, Max Key). Moreover, there has been the emergence of a new kind of celebrity: the everyday celebrity, the ordinary-person-turned-celebrity, spotlighted on shows like *The Bachelor* and *The Apprentice*. Connected to this new kind of celebrity, a new kind of show has become prevalent, exemplified by *Survivor* – a show that involves a competitive pressure to perform, a ranking of people, and voting people off.

The heightened intensity of celebrity coverage, the widening of the definition of a 'celebrity', and the popularity of new kinds of competitive shows could well have far-reaching effects. It's not far-fetched to suggest that more intrusive surveillance of celebrities, along with the ubiquity of smartphones, could lessen the general public's expectations of privacy. The rise of the everyday celebrity could entrench a false egalitarianism: a version of the American Dream that claims that it is possible for anyone to become famous, to succeed, at least temporarily. Shows such as *New Zealand's Next Top Model* could normalise among the general public the warped way in which celebrities are talked about and followed. In March 2015, *X Factor* judges Willy Moon and Natalia Kills lashed out at an *X Factor* contestant, calling him 'disgusting' and 'creepy' (and admittedly facing a significant public backlash). This sort of pernicious personal attack was once reserved for celebrities (but may have never been defensible in that context either). Everyday celebrity shows, and shows in the competitive and hierarchical mould, make it possible for that judgmental mean-spiritedness to seep into the mainstream. They crowd out space for generosity and goodwill.

It is too soon to say definitively whether celebrity culture has changed expectations of privacy, created a false egalitarianism or made everyone more mean-spirited. These effects take time to materialise. But what we do have evidence about is some general shift in values possibly precipitated by celebrity culture. Writer George Monbiot has cited a study in the journal *Cyberpsychology* that tracked the values documented by popular 'tween' television from 1967 to 2007.[23] The study – completed by academics at the University of California, Los Angeles – picked the most popular tween television shows at ten-year intervals (*Growing Pains* in 1987, *Sabrina the Teenage Witch* in 1997, *America's Next Top Model* in 2007) and asked survey participants to describe key themes in these shows. The findings? '[F]ame, financial success, and other individualistic values, notably achievement, rose in importance across the decades.' Moreover, 'communitarian values, as predicted, declined in relative importance over time.' Interestingly, community feeling was the top-ranked value in 1967 and dropped to a number 11 ranking out of 16 by 2007. The authors of the study conclude that:

> early adolescents are not watching characters in everyday environments; instead they are watching and likely identifying with youth who have enormously successful careers to the point of becoming famous. If tweens observe characters they admire succeeding and achieving wide public recognition and material success with little effort or training, they are likely to believe that this success is entirely possible and easy to achieve.[24]

The strong suggestion is that the strain of celebrity culture that is now dominant venerates values that are individualistic and uncaring, encourages judgmental and hierarchical thinking, and sets people up for anxiety and disappointment.

Politics has contributed to this values shift in the entertainment world, through the widespread adoption of neoliberal policies, which I discuss further in Chapter 4. My argument, summarised earlier, is that politics has become drained of values – and to the extent that values remain, residually, in the sink that is our politics, they are values of individualism and competitiveness. I say that we need to fill up our sink with values, and in particular to fill up that sink with progressive values – of care, community and creativity – that provide a common pool for political action.

But this supercharged, supersized, individualised celebrity culture is not just a product of neoliberal policies. It could also be a cultural barrier to the project in this book, since this strain of celebrity culture feeds back into politics. In other words, moves towards a more individualistic values set have contributed to celebrity culture, but celebrity culture has also reinforced those values. This two-way relationship between individualistic values and celebrity culture may help to explain the success of Donald Trump in the US election in 2016.[25] Trump, of course, starred in *The Apprentice*: the paradigmatic example of the new mould of competitive, judgmental, mean-spirited TV show. His election to the most powerful office in the world just years later – after a campaign of obnoxious comments and prejudiced sloganeering – shows the popularity of celebrity culture values, and points to the risks of these values becoming further entrenched in US society.

There's a lot of reflexive, ironic engagement with celebrity culture; celebrity culture is clearly not all menacing or mean-spirited. But we still need to reckon with this globalised culture, in particular its celebration of individualistic and materialistic values, as we consider how to build a more caring, communal and creative politics in New Zealand.

shifting global power dynamics

We've already discussed how the global position in the arena of political ideas appeared to be settled around 1990 but has unravelled since. A similar story could be told about global power dynamics.

At the end of the Cold War, to put it crudely, the Soviet Union crumbled, and the US and Western Europe appeared in the ascendancy. But who holds power in the world today appears to be much more unsettled. Different answers could be given depending on whether the question concerns military, economic or moral power. In economic (and, perhaps, moral and military) terms, the US is on the decline. Since 1990, the American share of global gross domestic product (GDP) has dipped markedly. At the same time, as Xiaoming Huang and Jason Young have said in a paper for the New Zealand Contemporary China Research Centre, 'China's share of global economic activity … [increased] from just over

2% in 1980 to over 14% in 2011.'[26] The fastest growing economies in the world are largely in Africa and Asia, according to the World Economic Forum.[27] The 'global South' – the group of countries with lower overall levels of economic development – is also expanding, notwithstanding the ongoing problem of sovereign debt. The United Nations Development Programme's 2013 Human Development Report predicted a 'global rebalancing', and projected that the combined output of China, India and Brazil would surpass the aggregate production of the US, Germany, the UK, France, Italy and Canada by 2020.[28]

In terms of political and strategic influence, it is problematic and perilous to attempt a snapshot of a world in flux. What will follow the UK's 2016 decision to exit the European Union – whether a reinvigorated Commonwealth, or a steady decline in UK global influence – is hard to tell. What can be said is that since 1990, non-state actors – terrorist groups (such as al-Qaeda and ISIS), multinational corporations and global philanthropic foundations (such as the Gates Foundation) – have either maintained or increased their levels of political influence. At the same time, cities and connections between cities have become more important. By 2025, 600 cities (including 440 in emerging economies) will generate 65% of the world's economic growth.[29] And city-level policy groupings, such as the C40 Cities Climate Leadership Group, are becoming increasingly common and prominent.

What does all this mean for New Zealand? In the realm of foreign policy, the country has a choice to make about whether it pivots back to traditional partners (such as the UK and the US) or seeks to forge new partnerships.[30] Regardless of which route it pursues, New Zealand needs to take the economic consolidation of China seriously. And we must think strategically – with foresight – about how to approach possible increases in Chinese migration to New Zealand, expanded Chinese influence in the Pacific and human rights concerns in China. I say a little more about this in Chapter 3. But these global developments don't just affect foreign policy. The crossroads in global power dynamics should prompt us to ask what kind of country we want to be in the world. And that question involves considering what kind of example we want to set for others. In domestic policy, for example, will New Zealand make decolonisation more of a priority, possibly bringing us closer to other countries (including those in Latin America) who have adopted a decolonisation agenda? I set out one possible answer to that question in Chapter 5. I address further how the New Zealand project might contribute to a new model of 'public democracy' beyond social democracy, relevant to other countries, in Chapter 12.

conclusion

Not all of the global forces and frictions described here have to be accepted. As should be clear – for example, in my discussion of celebrity culture – some of these trends might need to be challenged. And it is important to underscore that these trends do not just travel from overseas to New Zealand, where we passively receive them; New Zealanders have contributed – and will continue to contribute – to these trends worldwide. We have the power to shape them.

How do we decide which trends to harness? Which trends to confront? We need to have an understanding of how deeply embedded these trends are to figure out the extent to which we can arrest them. But once we have grasped their significance, one answer is that we might use the filter of progressive values, asking whether these trends advance or undermine the cause of care, community and creativity.

Outlining these trends serves several other purposes. *The New Zealand Project* is, in part, an attempt to widen political debate. Having an understanding of global trends helps us to recognise the current borders of what is perceived to be realistic or possible. With an understanding of where those borders are, we can work out where and how we might push them back.

Furthermore, discussing these trends is a reminder of how broad the influences on politics are in New Zealand. Politics is affected by the state of ideas (as in the first trend discussed in this chapter), the state of the economy and technology, political developments in other countries (the rise of the national and the resurgent attention to colonisation and racism), cultural patterns and international relations. All of us contribute to the landscape of our politics every day, through our conversations and actions. And all of us can contribute to changing that landscape.

Let's now turn to how we can do that.

3 new zealand and the world

When I tell people abroad that I'm from New Zealand, I'm usually met with friendly nods and warm smiles. The images people associate with New Zealand are often either broadly benign New Zealand icons – *Lord of the Rings*, Lorde or Flight of the Conchords – or unthreatening features: New Zealand's environmental beauty or its sheep. We're generally seen as kind people from a good country.

It's easy to forget that not all foreign nationals are met with such warmth when they reveal where they are from. In the mix of cultural and political generalisations that crop up when countries of origin are mentioned, Australians can be viewed as aggressive or insensitive, Americans tainted by their governments' interventionist foreign policy, the Brits caricatured as overly class-conscious or old-fashioned.

The positive reception Kiwis like me get is partly a result of the role New Zealand has played in world affairs. As one international relations expert has put it, 'Reputation is important in foreign policy.'[1] New Zealand has tended to act collaboratively and constructively on the global stage. But as with other areas of policy examined in this book, it is not inevitable that New Zealand's strong record will be maintained into the future. In recent years, New Zealand has lost a sense of direction in its foreign policy decisions – and government actions have lacked a consistent underlying theoretical framework.

This chapter aims to provide a stronger framework for how New Zealand thinks about its place in the world, and applies it to problems that are likely to arise in the future. The first section examines the idea of an independent foreign policy. I look at what this phrase means and has meant. I explain how New Zealand foreign policy (the ideas and actions pursued by government officials that relate to affairs abroad) has departed from an 'independent' approach, especially in the last 20 years, and argue for its reassertion. The remainder focuses on specific issues and proposals in the foreign policy realm, applying an independent foreign policy perspective.

an 'independent' foreign policy?

During the Second World War, in 1944, New Zealand and Australia agreed to what became known as the Canberra Pact, which strengthened formal security arrangements between the two countries. John Beaglehole writes that it was in this pact that New Zealand 'most clearly announced its independence of mind', setting a course that was distinct from Britain and the United States. This was developed further in New Zealand's strong role in the creation of the United Nations in 1945.[2] It was during this period, perhaps, that the idea of an 'independent foreign policy' was born. Sir Alister McIntosh, the Secretary of the Department of External Affairs, also traced the establishment of an independent foreign policy to the 1935 election of Michael Joseph Savage's Labour government.[3] It is simplistic to tie the idea to the mid-1940s, of course, and it should be noted that at this point New Zealand had not yet adopted the Statute of Westminster, which ended the ability of the British Parliament to pass laws for New Zealand; that would not occur until 1947. It should also be added that, after this period, New Zealand would move closer to Britain and the US, in fits and starts, in for example the signing of ANZUS in 1951. (ANZUS was the Australia, New Zealand, and United States Security Treaty, which agreed that these countries would cooperate on military matters.) But the strongest stirrings of an independent role for New Zealand were felt during this period.

The idea of an 'independent foreign policy', along with the associated concepts of New Zealand as a 'good international citizen' doing its 'fair share' in the world, has continued to be invoked in New Zealand foreign policy under successive governments. In a March 2015 interview about New Zealand involvement in fighting the Islamic State (ISIS) in Iraq, Prime Minister John Key said, 'We run independent foreign policy in New Zealand'.[4] In 2007, his predecessor, Helen Clark, described New Zealand's nuclear-free stance as 'a cornerstone of our independent foreign policy'.[5]

But what does independent foreign policy mean? In a 1975 article, the academic Juliet Lodge said this was 'indeterminate'. It has hardly become any more determinate since then (except, perhaps, in some academic work reconstructing how politicians understand the concept, especially the work of David Capie). We might ask today whether New Zealand still has an independent foreign policy, or if there is a gap between foreign policy language and foreign policy practice. Is the idea still relevant and defensible?

We can answer these questions together by interpreting the history of how New Zealand politicians and decision-makers appear to have understood the concept, which can be broken down into three parts: foreign policy that is justified in ethical terms, flexibility in New Zealand's alignment and creativity in advancing policy goals. I discuss each of these factors below.

justifying foreign policy in ethical terms

Foreign policy is often justified in terms of a country's interests or values.[6] Broadly speaking, an interest relates to a benefit or a setback for a country in economic or military terms. Values, as I have noted elsewhere, are principles we hold dear, individually or collectively, because of the contribution they make to a life (or lives) well led. The distinction between promoting interests and promoting values is in some ways unhelpful, because a country that promotes values (such as human rights) may also have an interest in promoting those values. But it is possible to argue that all countries fall on a spectrum, which, put crudely, has at one end countries that seek to advance their own power and self-interest on the global stage, and at the other countries that aim to give prominence to ethical ideals. The latter group is inclined to support multilateral institutions such as the UN; the former tends to favour countries that strike out on their own.

No country is purely interest-based or purely ethically grounded, but a feature of New Zealand's independent foreign policy has been the justification of foreign policy decisions in terms of ethical precepts. Norman Kirk famously said that New Zealand foreign policy needs a 'sound moral basis'.[7] But an even more pertinent case in point is David Lange's 1985 speech at the Oxford Union on nuclear disarmament – often mentioned in passing, rarely closely analysed.

In his speech, Lange approvingly quotes the US president as having said that nuclear weapons are 'immoral' and that a nuclear build-up 'cannot be sustained morally'. Lange goes on to say that there is 'no moral case for nuclear weapons', and that 'their very existence corrupts the best of intentions'.[8] What is notable is Lange's reliance on ethical language and argumentation. He speaks not of the place of nuclear weapons in the power politics of the world, but of the rightness and wrongness of nuclear weapons and those who use them. Some might say that New Zealand can afford to avoid realpolitik reasoning and can retreat to ethical language, because of the country's size. Regardless of the reason, it's clear that successive New Zealand political leaders have understood an independent foreign policy to have this dimension.

In case it's thought that ethical reasoning in foreign policy is only characteristic of New Zealand politicians on the centre-left, it should be noted that there are rich instances of foreign policy being justified in the same way by National Party premiers. To take just one example, National Prime Minister Jim Bolger, who held office from 1990 until 1997, acted boldly at the 1995 Commonwealth Heads of Government Meeting, hosted by New Zealand, when evidence came to light that the Nigerian government had been complicit in the murder of environmental activists. Bolger pushed for Nigeria to be suspended from the Commonwealth. 'If the actions of the Nigerian government were acceptable inside the Commonwealth, then I for one didn't know that I wanted to be inside the Commonwealth,' Bolger recalled later. 'If Commonwealth leaders were going to allow that sort of judicial killing to go on, because leaders or countries didn't like people taking an activist role and pointing out the errors of the government's policy,' he recounted, 'then what value did the Commonwealth have?'[9]

Bolger notes that two countries, Malaysia and Zimbabwe, were 'uncomfortable' about the Commonwealth 'looking behind a nation's borders and making judgments on various actions', and he points out that he and the then South African President, Nelson Mandela, brought them around to ensure unanimous agreement on Nigeria's suspension.[10] Some might disagree with the notion that Nigeria should have been suspended from the Commonwealth. But this strong ethical stance on extrajudicial killing, taken in concert with Mandela in the knowledge that 'judgment' was involved and that the Commonwealth was 'taking an activist role', is an example of ethical justification as part of New Zealand's foreign policy.

True, New Zealand has acted in a more interest-based fashion at various points during its diplomatic history. When Britain requested support from New Zealand in Malaya in 1955, Prime Minister Sidney Holland agreed, saying that New Zealand needed to pull its weight 'in the British boat'. That, he added, 'is a British thing to do'.[11] This was a foreign policy move based on historical ties and New Zealand's interests, rather than ethics. And as researcher Bruce Vaughn has pointed out, interests as well as high-minded ideals have driven New Zealand military intervention in the wider Pacific region: in Bougainville (beginning in 1997), Timor-Leste (in 1999 following a referendum on independence from Indonesia), the Solomon Islands (in 2003, due to civil strife) and Tonga (in 2006 following riots). New Zealand has been intent on preventing the emergence of 'failed state[s]', in Vaughn's words, since this 'could adversely affect New Zealand security' and result in 'opportunities for transnational crime, money laundering, arms trafficking, piracy or ... illegal immigration or safe havens for terrorist elements'.[12] There has not, then, been exclusive use of ethical reasoning in the foreign policy sphere. But my claim is more limited than that: it is only that ethical reasoning has played a prominent role in New Zealand foreign policy, and has been a key component of New Zealand's independent foreign policy.

flexibility in new zealand's alignment

At the heart of New Zealand's independence in foreign policy has been a commitment to flexibility in the country's alignment with other nations. New Zealand governments have resisted intractable alliances, preferring to come to decisions on foreign policy free of prior strategic commitments. New Zealand has aimed to be unaligned, with some exceptions that I discuss below – yet it is not part of the Non-Aligned Movement, a group of over 100 states that gathers at international conferences in opposition to dominant power blocs. (New Zealand did, however, attend – under a National government – the 1955 Bandung Conference, where the Non-Aligned Movement began to take shape.)

New Zealand politicians have been willing to sacrifice alliances where they have obstructed the ability for the country to pursue an independent foreign policy. The most high-profile incident of this sort was the 1985 departure from ANZUS. The Labour government had made it clear, upon winning office in 1984 after a strong citizen-led campaign, that it would make New Zealand nuclear-free. This meant that New Zealand would not use nuclear energy and also that, among other things, it would refuse entry to vessels carrying nuclear material. Following several exchanges between officials and heads of state, the US sought to test this policy by sending a naval vessel, the USS *Buchanan*, to New Zealand in early 1985. It was thought this vessel was nuclear-capable, although it was unclear whether it was carrying nuclear material. Amid some ambiguity, the Labour government rejected the visit.

America suspended its defence obligations and ties to New Zealand. The 1985 ANZUS meeting was postponed. The American government confirmed the end of security obligations in 1986, but this did not shift the New Zealand position. In 1987, legislation was passed confirming New Zealand's nuclear-free status. American international relations scholar Amy Catalinac notes that, while this end of an alignment was possible because of a lack of threat to New Zealand's interests, the best explanation of this episode was that New Zealand had 'a desire to assert autonomy'.[13] It goes without saying that these actions required considerable courage.

Other similar episodes, before and after the 1980s, include New Zealand's resistance to military action by the Southeast Asian Treaty Organisation (SEATO) in Laos in 1961, and New Zealand's unwillingness to go to war in Iraq in 2003. What is clear in all of them is that New Zealand politicians and foreign policy decision-makers have often been forthright in asserting the right to make autonomous decisions, away from the forces of traditional alignments.

Some have claimed this is foolhardy. As Juliet Lodge notes in her perceptive 1975 article, in a world of interdependence, complete autonomy for a country is unrealistic, and New Zealand has always been influenced by economic and cultural relationships in foreign policy decision-making.[14] New Zealand has had strong informal and formal alliances throughout its history. Yet New Zealand has generally avoided rigid alignment, even with Britain; this resistance has strengthened over time; and autonomy and independence have been largely valued in the rhetoric and reality of New Zealand foreign policy.

creativity in advancing policy goals

A third part of New Zealand independent foreign policy has been the use of creative tools to advance ethical objectives. Almost every country is resourceful in its diplomatic efforts: diplomats are encouraged to be lateral, creative thinkers who use unusual methods to achieve their ends. But New Zealand's approach to independent foreign policy has involved particularly novel and unconventional means of promoting a New Zealand agenda. It is noteworthy that New Zealand's campaign for a seat on the United Nations Security Council in 2015–16 contained three key words – integrity, independence, innovation – each of which roughly maps onto the three characteristics of independent foreign policy discussed here: ethical reasoning, a resistance to alignment and creativity.[15]

On the issue of French nuclear testing in the Pacific, there are several examples of creative or innovative foreign policy across different prime ministers' premierships. Under Norman Kirk's government, in 1973, when France did not appear to be complying with the International Court of Justice (ICJ) injunction to stop testing, two frigates were sent to the edges of the Mururoa test zone – with a cabinet minister on board. This was a vivid form of protest that underscored New Zealand's commitment to end nuclear testing. The move also arguably contributed to the French decision to move its testing underground in 1974.[16]

In 1995, under Jim Bolger's leadership, New Zealand resumed a case against France at the International Court of Justice (ICJ) in The Hague. France had said it would conduct a series of tests of nuclear weapons in the Pacific that year. Bolger said that New Zealand saw nuclear testing as 'totally unacceptable' and 'looked, therefore, to every possible avenue to challenge the testing, including legal means'.[17] New Zealand lost its application to reopen the case. But as Geoffrey Palmer has written, the case 'brought political pressure to bear on France on the nuclear issue'.[18] Bolger said that the 'case received great attention and this without doubt added to the pressure on France to cease testing'.[19] New Zealand's move to resume this case was undoubtedly a creative one. International law was here used in an effort to draw attention to French nuclear testing, and the (attempted) use of law highlighted the ethical dimension of the New Zealand campaign against nuclear testing for the world to see.

This, then, has been part of New Zealand's independent foreign policy over the years: resort to unlikely institutions and the staging of attention-commanding protest in order to showcase foreign policy issues. Nothing has been said about the innovative work done by citizens and NGOs – for example, in opposition to the 1981 Springbok tour – to influence the foreign policy agenda. But these individuals and groups have also formed part of the foreign policy process (the focus in this chapter thus far has been on prime ministers, politicians and officials because they are the primary actors in foreign policy decision-making), and have used creative methods to draw attention to issues. Taken together, these tactics bear some resemblance to what the American international relations scholar Joseph Nye has described, in the context of his far more powerful nation, as 'smart power' – the thoughtful application of diplomatic skills and principles in order to achieve global change.[20]

does new zealand still have an independent foreign policy?

In recent years, there appears to have been a drift away from the notion of an independent foreign policy – or at least some evidence that New Zealand is no longer pursuing foreign policy that is ethically grounded, resists alignments and is diplomatically creative.

At the beginning of 2015, when discussing whether New Zealand troops should be sent to Iraq to fight Islamic State, Prime Minister John Key described military intervention as 'the price of [being in] the club', referring to New Zealand's membership of the Five Eyes intelligence network, which also includes Canada, Australia, the US and the UK.[21] Key did later try to offer more substantive reasons for intervention. But such reasoning for foreign policy action is hardly ethical in its terms. And New Zealand has become more closely aligned with the US since 1999. As Paul Buchanan has noted, the Labour government from 1999–2008 'started the rapprochement', and the US–NZ Wellington Agreement in 2010, followed by the Washington Declaration in 2012, have converted informal understandings into a strategic partnership. This falls short of a formal alliance, but will lead to more joint training, possibly enhanced equipment for the New Zealand military and exposure to US strategic doctrine.[22]

As for creative foreign policy tactics, New Zealand has continued to remain engaged in interesting ways on foreign policy issues in the past decade or two, and at times has acted boldly, too. In 2009, New Zealand established a Global Research Alliance for Agricultural Greenhouse Gases, a network for the sharing of best practice on agriculture and greenhouse gas emissions. But the fruits of this alliance have not been prominent – and generally, New Zealand seems not to have acted as creatively in foreign policy decision-making as in the past. New Zealand has by and large avoided raising foreign policy issues in innovative ways, and has not engaged with a wide variety of institutions or actors in developing foreign policy messages – although its success in winning a seat on the United Nations Security Council deserves plaudits.

All of these developments are unfortunate, because there is, perhaps now more than ever, still a case for New Zealand to pursue an independent foreign policy. Sure, the world is more interdependent, which means that New Zealand cannot isolate itself. Yes, New Zealand has to be hard-nosed and realistic, and cannot be so creative that it is not seen as a credible international actor. However, New Zealand retains the leverage it needs to advance ethically grounded foreign policy goals. Avoiding fixed alignments, say with the US, is important as both China and the US seek to exert influence in the Pacific; New Zealand can enhance its bargaining power if it holds back from formalised alignments. And being creative in pushing a foreign policy agenda is also even more necessary, given that non-state actors are proliferating in the foreign policy space, making it difficult for governments to be heard clearly. The remainder of this chapter addresses select foreign policy topics on which New Zealand might focus in the coming years. The analysis that follows shows in practice how New Zealand could be ethically grounded, non-aligned and creative in aspects of its foreign policy – and sketches some parts of an independent foreign policy for New Zealand in the twenty-first century.

the case of ioane teitiota and climate change refugees

One specific area where New Zealand's independent foreign policy could result in a shift in emphasis is climate change advocacy, in particular regarding the position of Pacific states. New Zealand has not played a significant role in publicly advocating for Pacific nations, many of whom are being significantly affected by climate change – and has not itself partnered with Pacific nations to address the problems more directly.

Take climate change 'refugees'. I put 'refugees' in quotation marks because individuals fleeing countries due to climate change are not considered refugees under traditional legal interpretations of the 1951 Refugee Convention. (There is generally a requirement of persecution by a state or human actor, which is difficult to prove in the instance of climate change; refugees also have to show a particular threat that they face, and people affected by climate change confront the difficulty of a rather indiscriminate threat.) Climate displacement is likely to be a global problem – it has been suggested that between 50 and 200 million people will be affected by climate displacement by 2050.[23] Pacific countries may be a major site of such change. Tuvalu's Prime Minister, Enele Sopoaga, has likened climate change to 'a weapon of mass destruction'.[24] Kiribati, the tiny Pacific country of 110,000 people that sits an average 2 metres above sea level, is also threatened by erosion and rising tides.

New Zealand is not oblivious to this problem. The threat of climate change in the Pacific has been raised by numerous NGOs and organisations, including Oxfam and Greenpeace, and a court case involving a Kiribati man moved through the New Zealand court system before being concluded in 2015. Ioane Teitiota had argued that he was a climate change refugee, because he was unable to return to Kiribati due to fears about the impact of climate change, but he had his arguments rejected in the Immigration and Protection Tribunal, the High Court and the Court of Appeal, with the Supreme Court refusing to hear his case in full in 2015. The Supreme Court said that its decision not to hear the Teitiota case 'should not be taken as ruling out [the] possibility [that climate change might create a pathway into the Refugee Convention] in an appropriate case'.[25] Yet the case has received little mainstream media coverage, only gar-nering some attention when Teitiota was deported in September 2015.

It has been left to other countries to lead. Following a June 2011 meeting in Oslo on climate change and displacement, and a December 2011 meeting with the UN high commissioner for refugees, Norway and Switzerland undertook to develop a coherent approach to climate displacement issues.[26] In October 2012, the Nansen Initiative was launched as a series of consultations with affected states – including in Latin America, the Pacific and the Horn of Africa – in order to attempt to seek a consensus on a framework for climate displacement. Australia sat on the steering group of the Nansen Initiative, but New Zealand was not heavily involved. The secretariat was based in Geneva, and the work was driven by Norway and Switzerland. In 2016, the Nansen Initiative became the Platform on Disaster Displacement, overseen by Germany and Bangladesh. Fourteen countries were on the steering group. New Zealand was again nowhere to be seen.

New Zealand could do so much more on the specific issue of climate change refugees and climate advocacy. New Zealand is close to Pacific countries that are affected by climate change, and New Zealand has skills and ties with other countries that – if harnessed in the right way – could be useful for climate advocacy. The proposal I want to focus on here is how New Zealand should push on multiple fronts for a global legal framework on climate displacement.[27]

At the 2015 Paris conference on climate change, a coordination facility for climate displacement was mooted. But a stronger legal framework, which might impose obligations on states in relation to individuals displaced by climate change, was not explicitly under review at Paris – and one has not emerged since. To advance this proposal, New Zealand diplomats and politicians could provide support to the Platform on Disaster Displacement, and even at this late stage offer to join the steering group. New Zealand could speak at global climate conferences specifically about the issue and raise general awarenesss of climate refugees in media outlets in the lead-up to such gatherings. Norwegian Foreign Minister Jonas Gahr Støre, who would later become the leader of the Norwegian Labour Party, wrote an article in April 2011 in the *New York Review of Books* about the need for dialogue with the Taliban in Afghanistan, entitled 'Why We Must Talk'[28] – and he also gave a popular TED talk in November 2011, In 'Defense of Dialogue'.[29] Is it so inconceivable that a New Zealand prime minister or foreign affairs minister might write an article in a leading international publication or deliver a major TED talk? New Zealand could, at the same time, seek to establish opportunities for Pacific heads of state and others to speak at global conferences on climate displacement and gaps in the existing international law framework. We could also convene a meeting of interested states in the Pacific to discuss short-term management of emerging climate displacement problems.

New Zealand could only do all these things, of course, if it were addressing the climate refugee problem, by taking some climate refugees from the Pacific and working with Pacific countries to understand their needs and preferred solutions.

This proposal could be ethically justified – it is concerned with the protection of vulnerable individuals displaced by climate change. It also involves non-aligned action, driven by New Zealand's own initiative, and could capitalise on creative media tools. The proposal might also facilitate global action on climate displacement – especially since New Zealand, positioned close to countries affected in the Pacific, would be perceived by other nations as having some authority on the subject.

Undoubtedly there are risks to be managed. It is important that New Zealand is not seen as paternalistic. New Zealand would have to consult closely with Pacific nations to ensure it is not speaking over or above the voices of those directly affected by climate change. (Some small states are reluctant about using the term 'climate refugee', since it could delay action to try to mitigate or prevent climate change; New Zealand would have to pay particular attention to the views of Pacific states on this point.) Notwithstanding these considerations, it is clear that we could advance the cause of a global legal framework for climate displacement. Such a move would be consistent with an independent foreign policy for New Zealand, properly construed.

Governments would not want to cut across the progress made by the Platform on Disaster Displacement. Indeed, we could also do more to support the platform. In late 2015 in Oslo, I sat down with Jan Egeland, secretary-general of the Norwegian Refugee Council, a globally recognised NGO, to talk about this and related matters.

Egeland is something of a celebrity in Norway: he has been head of the Norwegian Red Cross, played major roles in the UN, and even has a tribute song named after him by a Norwegian band. He was cautious in speaking about New Zealand, and noted that the Norwegian Refugee Council is politically independent and nonpartisan. At the time, it was the Nansen Initiative that was still in place, before becoming the Platform on Disaster Displacement. Nevertheless, Egeland said that there was a 'great need' for the cause of climate displacement to be 'brought forward with more energy'. Work on climate displacement was often dominated by states in the north-western corner of the world, Egeland told me: Scandinavian states, for example, or the UK and Canada. But New Zealand would have an important role, positioned as it is in the Pacific. New Zealand would do well to heed these words, and to support the cause of Pacific states (some of which have different views on climate displacement) through the Platform on Disaster Displacement.

who we aid and how we aid

A clear example where New Zealand foreign policy has shifted away from an independent approach is in the operation of the New Zealand Aid Programme (NZAID), the public sector agency responsible for allocating overseas development assistance, or aid overseas. NZAID was established in 2002 as a semi-autonomous body of the Ministry of Foreign Affairs and Trade (MFAT).

In 2009, the Foreign Minister, Murray McCully, released Cabinet materials indicating a shift in direction for NZAID – a shift that had been anticipated due to the National-led government's views on the nature of aid. One Cabinet paper mentioned three specific changes. NZAID's goal was to change, from 'the elimination of poverty' to 'the support of sustainable economic development in developing countries'. New Zealand's aid was to become more focused on the Pacific: it was proposed that an increased proportion of overseas development assistance go to Pacific countries. And a certain type of work was to be prioritised: 'interventions that have self-sustaining measurable impacts with demonstrable value for both recipient and donor'.[30]

There are two important ideas nestled within this thicket of bureaucratic verbiage. First, NZAID was to focus, from 2009, on evidence-based interventions with sound justifications – impacts would have to be 'measurable', and the value of the interventions would have to be 'demonstrable'. So far, so good: NZAID's money should not be spent wastefully. But the second aspect of the sentence is more controversial. NZAID was to move towards interventions with 'value for *both recipient and donor*' (my emphasis). Of course, New Zealand's self-interest was never entirely ignored in past efforts to eliminate poverty. (Aid can always be justified, in part, as an attempt to prevent crises that might ripple back to affect the donor country.) But the phrase 'both recipient and donor' signalled a new outlook that focused on New Zealand's own benefit. It meant that if there were a choice between an aid intervention that could exclusively help a recipient country, and an aid intervention that could help both a recipient country and New Zealand, the second of these options would be preferred. The changes were implemented in 2009. NZAID was also folded back into MFAT and renamed the New Zealand Aid Programme, as a symbol of the shift in mandate for the agency.

One might think that the move to consider New Zealand's benefit in aid-giving was entirely appropriate policy: the New Zealand Aid Programme is spending taxpayers' money, and should seek to benefit New Zealanders (and others) wherever possible. The major problem is that this misconstrues the purpose of aid – and in so doing, undermines New Zealand's tradition of independent foreign policy. My own view, based on research and brief stints working with the United Nations Development Programme in New York, is that the purpose of aid is to address unmet needs, in for instance nutrition, sanitation, health care and education, and to build the long-term institutional conditions necessary for a country to support citizens in leading healthy, happy, safe and secure lives. To achieve these goals, emergency and humanitarian aid is necessary, along with dedicated development aid that is directed towards social protection systems, the protection of the environment, gender empowerment and the strengthening of civil society.[31]

The 2009 changes to the New Zealand's Aid Programme meant that it could no longer focus only on conditions in recipient countries; the agency was also now required to think about value for the donor (i.e. New Zealand). The likely result of this is less money spent on emergency and humanitarian aid that does not provide value for New Zealand, and reduced long-term investment in institutions. The programme was also directed to emphasise 'sustained economic development' – one narrow aspect of development in a recipient country. The changes meant that New Zealand aid policy could not be justified purely in ethical terms – and would have to be justified in terms of self-interest. This represented another drift from the ideal of independent foreign policy that is ethically justified, cautious about alignments and creative in pursuing goals.

The 2009 changes ought to be reversed. Sustainable economic development is just one part of development. It should not be the primary goal of the aid programme. Increasing investment in the Pacific might be necessary to address unmet global needs, but it does not need to be an explicit objective. Highlighting such investment tethers New Zealand aid too closely to collective self-interest. Most importantly, the New Zealand Aid Programme should no longer be charged with providing value to both recipient and donor countries. The emphasis on demonstrable, measurable impact from aid interventions can be maintained, and it is useful for the programme to have sharp strategic goals. But the other changes overseen in 2009 need to be jettisoned. Whether the New Zealand Aid Programme and MFAT should be institutionally separated is more of an operational question, and might not be necessary if MFAT as a whole clarifies its aim to pursue ethical, relatively non-aligned and creative foreign policy.

The amount New Zealand gives in overseas development assistance should be reviewed, too. In 1969, the Pearson Commission on International Development proposed that countries' aid contributions be, at minimum, 0.7 per cent of gross national product (GNP). The figure was calculated by considering how developing countries could achieve satisfactory rates of growth and development, and was adopted by the UN in a resolution in 1970.[32] However, since 1970, New Zealand's aid has languished well below this target figure. In 2014, New Zealand gave NZ$605.65m in aid, or 0.27 per cent of GNP, which put New Zealand below the average amount given by countries in the Development Assistance Committee (DAC), the main forum of international donors.[33] The 0.7 per cent figure is a little arbitrary, but it represents a symbolic commitment to the importance of aid and could guarantee tangible improvements in the lives of people in developing countries.

New Zealand should consider lifting its overseas development assistance to 0.7 per cent of GNP, which (on 2014 figures) would require us to give NZ$1.57 billion in total, an increase of NZ$906.55 million. Increasing this figure would provide a symbolic commitment, and would be consistent with New Zealand's tradition of ethical foreign policy.

How would this be done? How would the commitment be funded? And what risks would have to be monitored? The UK provides a model: it increased its own aid contribution over a series of years, and then passed the International Development (Official Development Assistance) Target Act 2015 under a Conservative government. The Act imposed a duty on the relevant minister to achieve the 0.7 per cent target each year. The relevant minister – the secretary of state for international development – is required, if the target is not met in any given year, to lay a statement to Parliament explaining why not.

Total core Crown revenue in 2013/2014 was NZ$67.3 billion.[34] On current revenue (and notwithstanding predicted increases in revenue that are discussed in Chapter 4), lifting New Zealand's aid contribution would amount to use of 1.35 per cent of annual revenue. This is not unaffordable.

One final challenge here would be to ensure that creative accounting is not used to artificially inflate what constitutes overseas development assistance. But this could be addressed through legislation that requires clear itemising of investments considered part of 'overseas development assistance', and through strong evaluation by the New Zealand Aid Programme.

What is needed, however, is pressure 'from below' – from ordinary New Zealanders – to ensure this figure is lifted. Jan Egeland confirmed this, when describing why Norway has had such a strong tradition of giving more than 0.7 per cent of GNP in development assistance. 'You need to have strong currents in the population that are built on the compassion tradition or the solidarity tradition or the internationalist tradition,' Egeland told me.

New Zealand has traditions of compassion, solidarity and internationalism, as I have discussed in this chapter and as I examine elsewhere. But there is a need for these traditions to be strengthened and mobilised. That is partly, of course, the project of building up the power of progressive values of community, care and creativity – the project of this book and beyond.

new zealand and asia

Talk of New Zealand's relationship with 'Asia' is almost too broad for anything meaningful to be said. Asia has a population of 4.393 billion as of 2015, according to UN estimates – more than half the world's population – and comprises countries with vastly different cultures, politics and religions.[35] So sweeping references to 'Asia' are unsatisfactory and the term needs to be handled delicately.

I use 'Asia' here partly because policy documents use the term, but I attempt in what follows to break down the word and concept a little more. New Zealand's policy towards 'Asia' lacks vision. MFAT's *Statement of Intent: 2011–2014* focuses on building economic and export performance through foreign policy. But it is short-term in perspective: a major part of the report discusses how opportunities might be leveraged from the 2011 Rugby World Cup, though this was a one-off event. (Admittedly, the document was centred around the 2011–2014 period, and the Rugby World Cup was a significant chance for New Zealand to showcase its strengths to the world.) Asia does not feature in a big way in the statement, though readers are directed to the statement under the heading 'Key Documents on Asia' on the MFAT website. Mention is made of the need to support New Zealand businesses in China and India, and of growth prospects in Asia. There is also an oblique reference to 'rebalancing of global influence'.[36] However, there is little analysis of how New Zealand's tilt towards the US, discussed already in this chapter, might pose risks for relations with Asia. (A charitable interpretation of this is that such risks are discussed elsewhere, in a confidential security document that has not been made public.) There is no deliberate strategy for building strong relationships with Asia.

Perhaps this is unfair on the ministry. The statement is, after all, meant to be a general document. Does New Zealand's strategy for ASEAN (Association of Southeast Asian Nations), released in 2013, offer more? This strategy is only concerned, of course, with South-East Asian countries. But it is also disappointingly superficial.[37] It describes an 'NZ Inc' strategy, but the glossy, image-heavy, sparse document is just 10 pages long, with the actual strategy only described from pages 6–10 (with several of these pages taken up with quotations in giant text that appear only to pad out the document). Three goals are set out: New Zealand becoming better connected and more influential within ASEAN; New Zealand becoming better integrated within the ASEAN community; and New Zealand boosting trade investment. It is not clear how the first two goals would be measured or how they are different from each other, though some specific targets are set out for the third goal. There is, to give ministry officials credit, a separate strategy document on New Zealand's relationship to India, with more measurable aims outlined in areas such as migration and exports.[38] More recently, as well, MFAT developed the China Capable public sector programme to ensure the public sector has stronger knowledge of China. But there is no up-to-date Asia-wide strategy document at the time of this writing, and the absence of an MFAT strategy document on China is also striking.

Successive governments have taken promising steps towards ensuring New Zealand engages strategically with Asia. In 2007, under Helen Clark's government, a White Paper on New Zealand and Asia, *Our Future with Asia*, was produced (drawing on Seriously Asia, a 2003 forum held in Wellington). The White Paper used some of the same buzzwords as the more recent ASEAN strategy, talking of 'better integrating' without fully elucidating this phrase, but it did place some emphasis on New Zealand becoming 'more Asialiterate'.[39] This was said to require, in particular, better Asian language skills, and improved reporting about Asia in the media. It is not clear how these thoughtful recommendations were taken forward.

In thinking about practical proposals for improving New Zealand's relationship with Asia, New Zealand could draw lessons from Australia's White Paper on Asia, *Australia in the Asian Century*, released in 2012.[40] While the length of a document is no proxy for substance or quality, it is telling that this one ran to 320 pages, compared with New Zealand's 11-page ASEAN strategy. A section of the Australian paper is dedicated to building Asia-relevant capabilities,[41] which is useful for New Zealand's thinking about improving the media's Asia literacy and strengthening Asian language learning. *Australia in the Asian Century* focuses on attracting Asian migration to Australia (through, for example, a quality education system) as well as improving Australian opportunities in Asia; New Zealand would benefit from a similar two-way perspective on its Asian partnership. The Australian White Paper points to school centres for Asian language excellence as useful ways to support language learning, and proposes that 'Asia and Australia's Engagement with Asia' be embedded within the Australian school curriculum as a cross-curriculum priority. The paper also recommends that all schools give students access to learning Chinese (Mandarin), Indonesian, Hindi or Japanese. On the media front, the paper calls for more exchange programmes, and collaboration with national broadcasters to ensure more in-depth coverage of Asia.

What emerges from this is a sense that New Zealand should redouble its efforts to build cultural, as well as economic, links with Asia. A specific China strategy is needed, which takes into account the place of China in the Pacific at a time when – as noted – China and the US are jostling for influence in the region.[42] As the global balance of power shifts towards China, New Zealand must ensure that it does not remain wedded to the US and Europe for purely historical reasons; it at least needs to prepare for how it should interact with China on trade, culture and human rights. A strategy should contain costed commitments and measurable goals.

The two strong recommendations from the 2007 New Zealand White Paper, having to do with language learning and improved media awareness of Asia, should also be taken seriously. Following Australia, 'New Zealand and Asia' could be made a core part of the New Zealand curriculum, perhaps as a part of social studies in secondary schools. New Zealand schools should each endeavour to offer one Asian language; a starting aim could be to develop centres of language-learning excellence around the country.[43] Meanwhile, in relation to media efforts, the government could work alongside Radio New Zealand and Television New Zealand to improve Asian programming, and could sponsor additional media exchanges between Asia and New Zealand.

new zealand: an 'author of peace'?

The final idea proposed in this chapter may be less familiar: New Zealand should consider building a foreign policy comparative advantage in mediation and reconciliation for conflict.

Peace and reconciliation have been key themes in New Zealand history. The Treaty of Waitangi, signed in 1840, was in part an assurance to Māori that peace would be guaranteed in New Zealand as settlers arrived in increasing numbers. It was also an act of conciliation between two peoples. The English version of the preamble to the Treaty noted that the Crown was 'anxious to ... secure to [the Native Chiefs and Tribes of New Zealand] the enjoyment of Peace and Good Order'.[44] (It may be, of course, that assurances about peace were merely an attempt to secure Māori land, and peace certainly did not eventuate after the signing of the Treaty.)[45] Just over forty years later, Te Whiti-o-Rongomai (with Tohu Kākahi) led a group offering peaceful resistance at Parihaka, after colonial officials invaded Taranaki in 1881. Te Whiti famously said:

> Though the lions rage still I am for peace ... Though I be killed I yet shall live; though dead, I shall live in peace which will be the accomplishment of my aim. The future is mine, and little children, when asked hereafter as to the author of peace, shall say 'Te Whiti'.[46]

Pounamu, or greenstone, so often worn around the necks of New Zealanders, is a symbol of peace (and was often given as part of peace agreements historically).[47] New Zealand's nuclear-free stance was, at least partially, an effort to stand up for peace and to forestall the prospect of nuclear war. And Helen Clark's refusal to join the invasion of Iraq in 2003 is seen by many as a shining light in New Zealand's independent foreign policy.

Peace is a fundamental value underpinning international law instruments and international organisations, too. The United Nations Charter, which established the UN, with New Zealand's participation, in 1945, envisions saving 'succeeding generations from the scourge of war', noting that all states ought to 'practice tolerance and live together in peace with one another as good neighbours'.[48] Yet, apart from the UN itself, and some NGOs, there are few bodies or parties dedicated to securing peace and reconciliation at a time of conflict.

We could play a role standing up for peace. New Zealand's history of an independent foreign policy – of ethical, relatively non-aligned, creative actions on the global stage – and the country's size perfectly positions it to be an arbitrator of disputes, particularly in Asia. New Zealand is seen as a fair, friendly, relatively neutral player in international relations (although this status is in danger of shifting as New Zealand pivots back towards the US). This idea of peace and reconciliation should resonate with New Zealanders, given the country's own national history. If New Zealand adopted as a foreign policy goal the strengthening of capacity to carry out international dispute resolution, this could also further advance New Zealand's tradition of ethical action.

How could New Zealand develop this comparative advantage? Finland is a useful case study to consider. It cemented a reputation as a host for conciliatory negotiations after the 1975 Helsinki Accords, an agreement between the Soviet Union and the West to improve relations.[49] Following this agreement, Finland appears to have made a strategic choice to build its strength in this area. It has acted creatively, deploying one of the dimensions of New Zealand's independent foreign policy that I mentioned earlier. (The Finnish guideline document begins: 'To stand out from the crowd a small nation needs to be creative.')[50] Finland has assisted UN-led efforts to mediate in conflict zones, through diplomatic and financial support. In addition, high-profile Finnish politicians have led peace negotiation processes. President Martti Ahtisaari steered peace negotiations in Aceh, a Sumatran region in Indonesia, after his term as president, concluding negotiations successfully in 2005. In 2000, he set up a Finnish-based NGO, the Crisis Management Initiative, which is now partly funded by the Finnish government – and Ahtisaari won the Nobel Peace prize for his work in 2008. In 2010, a policy document reported on support for peace processes in the African Union, Nepal, East Timor and Central Asia.[51] The same document called for a move to 'strengthen Finland's role as a peace mediator', including through long-term funding for this capacity, partnerships with other 'great powers of mediation', and more education and training.[52]

There are some differences between Finland and New Zealand (Finland is closer to a cluster of other countries than New Zealand, and also has a slightly bigger population – around 5.4 million), but there are also lessons that we could learn from the Finnish experience. If New Zealand were serious about building capacity in mediation and reconciliation, it could begin by strengthening partnerships with the 'great powers of mediation': Finland, Norway, Switzerland, Sweden and Ireland. It is telling that all of these countries are European; there would seem to be an opportunity for Aotearoa New Zealand to become a positive force for dispute resolution in Asia and the Pacific.

New Zealand might then commit to investing in relevant training for its diplomats. The University of Otago established a National Centre for Peace and Conflict Studies in 2009; that centre could seek, with the support of the government, to establish a peace negotiation stream to train expert mediators for international conflicts. As noted in the Finnish government document, investments in mediation might be counted as part of overseas development assistance, meaning that much of this investment would not require further revenue if there was already an agreement to increase New Zealand's aid levels to 0.7 per cent of GNP. Jan Egeland told me that 'if you're not willing to invest some resources and some money [into building some capacity in peace-building], it will rarely become very effective.'

New Zealand might also seek to raise the profile of specific local individuals with peace credentials. In 2017, the head of a leading international organisation working on peace and mediation, the Centre for Humanitarian Dialogue in Geneva, was a New Zealander, David Harland. He is an example of the type of individual New Zealand might support and promote as a negotiator – New Zealand's Martti Ahtisaari, perhaps. New Zealand should then be willing, once capacity has been developed, to make itself available as a mediator in disputes, especially those geographically close to New Zealand, in which New Zealand might have some expertise. The dispute in the South China Sea between China and neighbouring countries (especially Brunei, Vietnam, Malaysia and the Philippines); ongoing conflicts between the Burmese government and the Rohingya people in Burma; and lingering tensions within Sri Lanka offer three possible sites of mediation.[53] But further conflicts will invariably arise. New Zealand should be alert to these and to how it might assist. If we can be proactive in this way, it is not inconceivable that we may come to be seen as not just ethical, creative, and relatively non-aligned, but also as 'the author of peace' in some regions.

That would do much to uphold the legacy of Te Whiti-o-Rongomai.

conclusion

Foreign policy is an area where New Zealand lacks a coherent vision or direction. It is also an area where self-interest – collective self-interest – has swamped values over the last 20 years in particular: a theme that will be developed across different policy areas in the chapters to come. This chapter has attempted to redress the loss of vision or direction by scrutinising the 'independent foreign policy' mantra in a principled way, considering case studies from Australia, Norway and Finland, and laying out some proposals for how New Zealand might reinvigorate an independent policy.

Not every issue of New Zealand's place in the world can be addressed in a single chapter, and I touch on other related issues elsewhere. Ultimately, the argument here has been that with a greater sense of clarity, New Zealand can embrace its status as a small state, sharpen its approach to Asia and its philosophy towards aid, and carve out an effective reputation in important areas such as climate displacement and international dispute resolution. As I write these words, New Zealand had just concluded its term on the United Nations Security Council, and had begun to develop an approach on the Security Council that was moving in this direction – including, for example, in its sponsorship of the 2016 resolution on Israeli settlements in Palestine. But the approach did not fully make the most of the idea of an independent foreign policy, or New Zealand's status as a small state.

Jan Egeland – who wrote a book in 1985 on small states[54] – told me in Oslo in 2015 that small states can overestimate or underestimate their power. Small states will never be major powers: they cannot threaten or force anybody to do anything. On the other hand, they should not underestimate what they can do. In particular, Egeland said, it is important not to 'underestimate what the consistent, well-prepared, coherent small actor can do to facilitate, encourage, host, organise international initiatives'. I have tried to show what New Zealand might be able to do – on climate displacement, in the field of aid, in Asia and on peace-building – if it becomes more consistent, well-prepared and coherent as an international actor. A major part of becoming more consistent, well-prepared and coherent is being clear on the meaning of an 'independent foreign policy', and pursuing an independent foreign policy with vigour and commitment.

4   a new framework for economic policy

Since the 1980s, a particular set of ideas has become dominant in debate and commentary about politics – in the UK and the US in particular, but also in New Zealand, much of Latin America and parts of Asia and Africa. Certain maxims have become commonplace:[1] the private sector is an engine of innovation and creativity. The pursuit of self-interest, and the presence of competition, are beneficial since they can produce that innovation and creativity. 'The market' generally functions well in setting prices. If people pay market prices, their market exchange should be respected and should not generally be interfered with ('caveat emptor': the buyer is responsible). Inequality should not be of major concern if it is the result of market interactions. Consumption and growth are useful metrics of the health of an economy. It is legitimate to view all activities and actors in a society through an economic lens. Free speech takes place within a marketplace of ideas, the collective store of human skills is human capital, citizens are clients or consumers. Governments should be slow to act in the economy, since government intervention tends to stifle innovation and disrupt market forces. Income and company taxes penalise hard-working individuals and businesses. Raising these taxes leads to the flight of skills, talent and revenue. Recipients of government support can become dependent. Well-intentioned government action can have unintended consequences. 'Fairness' is an empty concept that might be best defined by what people accept within the market. There is no such thing as society, or 'the public'.[2] Choose self-interest. Choose self-regulation. Choose markets.

These maxims have a logic. They have a consistent approach to the role of government, the operation of the market and the nature of self-interested people and businesses. This is partly because they emerged from think tanks and academics who worked to iron out inconsistencies and to sharpen earlier accounts of liberalism, including the Mont Pelerin Society, Friedrich von Hayek, Milton Friedman and James Buchanan. Hayek said in 1947 at the Mont Pelerin Society, 'Common work on the more detailed outline of a liberal order is practicable only among a group of people who are in agreement on fundamentals.'[3] (Just because the 'fundamentals' were internally consistent did not mean that they were right, of course, or that they correctly mapped onto external reality.)

The maxims also gave rise to a similar set of policy prescriptions abroad: relatively low income and company taxes, increased consumption taxes (imposed at a flat rate), deregulation (especially of finance), an end to government industrial policy, privatisation of public services, contracting out of government functions to private providers, enhanced conditions for foreign investment, and attacks on the power of unions.

Alongside these policy prescriptions, a loose collection of ideals was invoked, including freedom or liberty (generally taken to mean negative liberty, or freedom from state intervention), private property and prosperity. The combination of the maxims, policies and values resulted in economic policy being viewed as the dominant policy area. Independent social or environmental concerns were subservient to economic interests, and these social and environmental concerns were simultaneously reframed in economic language.

What I have been describing – this shift in language, ideas and policies – is often described as 'neoliberalism'. Neoliberalism is the political project that gives effect to such language, ideas and policies.[4] In New Zealand, it involved electing politicians, such as Ruth Richardson, who were committed to the cause – and building a network of think tanks and organisations (the Business Roundtable being one) to shift public debate. Paradoxically, neoliberal governments often *increased* the size of the state, though the maxims I have highlighted pushed for a reduced role for government regulation, redistribution and intervention.[5] In light of that, neoliberalism is best understood as the set of maxims, policies and values that *creates space* for the selective application of small-government politics when it suits some politicians.

The neoliberal political project has failed in Aotearoa New Zealand.[6] The Fourth Labour Government and the Bolger-led National Government advanced such an agenda. It has failed on its own terms in respect of the economic development that it brought. The agenda may have succeeded in increasing the concentration of wealth among the richest people in New Zealand. But New Zealand's economy has not undergone the promised transformation, either in terms of sectors or rates of growth, notwithstanding the inadequacies of various growth metrics.

Growth of annual gross domestic product (GDP) – a partial measure of the production and activity in the economy – dropped from 4.8 per cent in 1984 to -0.3 per cent in 1988. It recovered to a high of 6.3 per cent in 1993, but barring two strong outlier years in 1999 and 2002 (when it grew at 5.5 per cent and 4.9

per cent, respectively), the economy has mostly grown somewhat sluggishly at between 1 per cent and 4 per cent.[7] These are not terrible rates, and other countries pursuing neoliberal policies have largely had similar ones. But there has not been a flourishing of new industries or economic prosperity. More tellingly, it was after 1985 that New Zealand fell below the Organisation for Economic Development (OECD) average for GDP per capita. The gap between New Zealand's GDP per capita and the OECD average has only widened since then.[8]

Rates of exports, unemployment and productivity – all useful signals of the health of an economy – also make for uncomfortable reading if we consider the statistics since 1984. As the New Zealand Institute pointed out, New Zealand's export growth has been below the OECD average since 1973, following Britain's joining the European Economic Community in 1971. But the gap between New Zealand's export growth rate and the OECD growth rate average has expanded since 1985.[9] Neoliberalism produced no export dividend: no boom for Kiwi exporters, once trade supports were removed and the supposed logic of free trade was given more room to take hold.

Neoliberalism normalised a higher rate of unemployment, too. For much of the twentieth century in New Zealand, unemployment moved between 1 and 3 per cent. The one exception was the spike to more than 8 per cent in the 1930s, following the Great Depression.[10] In the early 1980s, New Zealand unemployment began to creep over 4 per cent for the first time since the turn of the century.

It is no coincidence that in the 1987 election the Labour government abandoned its commitment to full employment.[11] For a short three-year period between 2004 and 2007, unemployment was between 3.7 and 4 per cent. But unemployment has more consistently fluctuated between 4 per cent and 7 per cent since 1984.[12] Although different causes may have contributed to this pattern, it is nevertheless the case that unemployment rates have increased since the reforms – with governments seemingly more comfortable with 4–7 per cent unemployment, as opposed to the 1–3 per cent range of the pre-1984 years. Given the large numbers of people affected (as of June 2016, 4 per cent unemployment means almost 150,000 members of the working-age population officially without a paid job)[13] – and the significant effect of unemployment on self-esteem, family wellbeing and a person's sense of belonging in a community – these figures should give us pause.

New Zealand's productivity growth has remained low over time, in particular in the area of labour. Average labour productivity growth (growth in the amount of goods and services produced by one hour of labour) between 1976 and 2006 was 1.1 per cent, lower than Australia, Canada and the US, despite slight increases in the early 1980s and 1990s. But even the Treasury analysis identifies a shift from the early 1980s on. It has noted that the level of labour productivity was fairly steady from the mid-1960s through until the early 1980s. 'Labour productivity growth has picked up since then,' according to the Treasury, 'but has not been enough to close the gap with these comparator nations or the OECD average.' As a result, 'New Zealand's ranking of 22nd in the OECD [out of 30] in terms of level of labour productivity has been constant since the 1980s'.[14] New Zealand's low productivity is so striking as to have been described as a 'productivity paradox' by the Productivity Commission.[15]

Neoliberalism has made people more indebted. We now live in a society permanently in debt. Between 1991 and 2011, household and consumer debt in New Zealand increased sixfold. As a percentage of disposable income, household and consumer debt went from 58 per cent in 1991 to 147 per cent in 2011.[16] New Zealand's household debt-to-income ratio had reached 165 per cent in 2016.[17] That means on average New Zealand households have $165 of debt for every $100 of income. There are various connections between neoliberalism and such indebtedness: the reforms of the 1980s in New Zealand (and elsewhere) deregulated finance, making it easier for households to take out loans (for example, for mortgages), and to become indebted. Cuts to public services created greater need for loans as individuals and families were forced to pay more for basic needs. The introduction of fees for tertiary education has created a new group of debtors: students. Indebtedness produces a sense of insecurity among individuals and families. It also stifles demand, perhaps explaining New Zealand's low growth levels, since more of individuals' and families' money goes to servicing debt.

In addition to failing on its own terms, the neoliberal political project in New Zealand has created negative social outcomes. Alongside the unemployment rates discussed earlier, there was a 'large and rapid rise in household income inequality from late 1980s to early 1990s', according to the Ministry of Social Development, with levels of inequality staying largely steady since the 1990s. Population poverty – measured as the number of households on less than 60 per cent of median income (after housing costs) – more than doubled from the late 1980s to the early 1990s, though those levels of poverty were reduced in the 2000s.[18]

Research on the effects of the 1980s reforms on inequalities between Māori and non-Māori is ongoing and more needs to be done.[19] But the sharp increase in unemployment between 1986 and 1991 had a disproportionate effect on the Māori working population: the non-Māori unemployment rate increased from 5.8 per cent to 9 per cent over this period, while the Māori unemployment rate increased from 14.9 per cent to 24.2 per cent.[20] We can only speculate about the long-term negative repercussions of this wedge.

Harder to measure, but just as important, is how the neoliberal political project permanently changed views and values on these and related issues. I have already indicated that the 1980s seemed to bring a 'new normal' of higher employment rates that were not challenged. Some of the mantras I described earlier made many New Zealanders indifferent to inequality, leading to a cementing of inequality, without compensatory political action. In the early to mid-2010s, views began to shift, partly because of important advocacy and analytical work.[21] But it remains true that aspects of neoliberalism – the criticism of concepts of community and society, the querying of the idea of 'fairness' – crowded out the space for values such as community and care. Under the economic reforms described at the outset of this chapter, ideas of fairness, community and society were questioned. And the sanctioning of self-interest and selfish economic pursuits relegated care to a secondary concern. The individual occupied centre stage in this model. Other people – the rest of the community, people that might require care – faded into the background.

Defenders of the maxims, policies and values that were introduced in this period may dispute this. They could argue that some policy changes, such as the independence of the Reserve Bank (which means that interest rates for banks are set by New Zealand's central bank and not by politicians), were necessary.

Indeed, they might argue that debt, exports, productivity, unemployment and growth would have been worse but for the changes of this period. It might be said that some of the challenges facing the New Zealand economy – its reliance on agriculture and tourism, say – preceded the 1980s. Perhaps. But it cannot be denied that if there are these deeper problems with the New Zealand economy, neoliberalism represented a political programme that did not attempt to address these problems in depth. Moreover, certain consequences of the 1980s, such as the immediate sharp increases in poverty and unemployment, can now be traced back to the reforms of the years of Rogernomics and what followed under Ruth Richardson's economic stewardship in the early 1990s.

Another possible objection is that 'neoliberalism' (in general, not just in New Zealand) did not really exist, and is simply a grab-bag term used by radical left-wingers for policies they oppose. This is a weak argument. Hayek and others within the Mont Pelerin Society set out deliberately to build 'fundamentals', a new order for economic thinking: they wanted to create not only some attractive policy ideas, but a system of maxims, policies, and values. To say that neoliberalism exists is to accept that Hayek, Friedman and others succeeded, at least in part. Even three researchers from the International Monetary Fund (IMF), hardly a paragon of progressivism, have recently talked comfortably in terms of 'neoliberalism' while arguing in a discussion paper that neoliberalism has not delivered evenly on promises of increased growth.[22] Of course, it is important to define the term 'neoliberalism' with care and to use it sensibly. But it is one thing to call for precision in definition and use of neoliberalism, and quite another to claim that it does not exist at all.

Our discussion so far has been leading to one ineluctable conclusion: that a new model of economic thinking is needed in New Zealand to fill the intellectual gap left by the failure of neoliberalism.

In the 2000s and the 2010s, some constraints have been placed on the excesses of the 1980s and 1990s, in what might be described as Third Way politics, which aims to find a middle ground between capitalism and socialism. Indeed, Helen Clark's government took many steps that went beyond Third Way ideology, as in the re-nationalisation of rail and ferries, and the introduction of a more progressive tax system. But it is unclear to what extent the Third Way is really distinct from neoliberalism. And the statistics that I have presented suggest that the Third Way has failed to arrest its most concerning trends.

A Fourth Way is needed.[23] I won't describe all its aspects in this chapter; in part, it is the object of this book as a whole to do that, and I offer more detail in Chapter 12. But I will attempt to explain what might form its basis. This new consensus,[24] or new commonsense, involves a return to the role of the state in economic policy: a consideration of what the state is singularly capable of doing, and a renewed defence of certain state functions, which can lead to bold and innovative policy. It also involves a questioning of GDP as a measure of growth, in addition to ongoing debate about 'growth' itself, and a reshaping of how economic debate in New Zealand happens – so that economic debate is not seen merely as the preserve of experts.

what should the state do?

The trick of the intellectual architecture of neoliberalism is that it combined a set of values with a story about the institution that could deliver those values: the market. At the same time, neoliberalism framed another institution – the state – as a slow, unwieldy, dangerous force.

A new approach to the economy requires not only an account of key values (such as care, community and creativity), but also a strong institutional narrative about who or what can deliver these values.

This might involve a return to the market as the key institution, a turn to the community or an account in favour of the state. The neoliberal years, and Third Way policies, have shown some of the pitfalls of relying excessively on the market: inequality can be widened and economic goals might not even be fulfilled. Economists themselves have begun to highlight further limitations with markets; Nobel Prize-winning economists George Akerlof and Robert Shiller, in *Phishing for Phools: The Economics of Manipulation and Deception*, recently described how deception is inherent in market transactions and why the 'market failure' paradigm might not give an accurate view of how often markets can lead to socially sub-optimal outcomes.

There has, however, been increased faith in community provision of goods and services in recent years – through social entrepreneurship, 'the sharing economy' (exemplified, some say, by Airbnb and Uber), and local initiatives such as 'transition towns'. Could 'the community', with the state receding into the background, be the new institution for a Fourth Way? We should acknowledge the strong historical work of charities, religious groups and other community providers in providing economic goods and services in New Zealand. Nevertheless I remain unconvinced that a fall-back on 'the community' as an institution is the best route for guaranteeing progressive values. In the absence of regulation, communal delivery can result in power imbalances and large monopolistic actors benefiting behind the façade of 'the community'; some have said that Airbnb involves this domination by a small set of individuals who opportunistically use the rhetoric of community.[25] There is little evidence that community provision can succeed at scale. And claims for community control can also be co-opted by advocates for 'free' market provision of goods and services.

In my view, of the available options (primarily market, community, or state), the Fourth Way requires a renewed defence of the state in economic policy, and a realistic assessment of the strengths and weaknesses of the market and the community. Certain social and economic functions can only be carried out by the state. And the state also has the capacity to blunt the rough edges of the market, and to address the weaknesses of community provision. A central role for it in economic policy does not preclude some role for the community and the market; it simply means that the state becomes the key guiding institution in the facilitation of values in an economy.

Jane Kelsey, a professor of law at the University of Auckland who has provided some of the most far-sighted academic analysis of neoliberalism of anyone globally, offered a similar point about the state when I interviewed her in late 2015. 'We have to rethink what we want from the state,' she said in her office at Auckland's law faculty. 'The national still matters. The state still matters. The state is still the vehicle through which things happen domestically and internationally. [The rethinking] will come out of – partly – responses to crises. But my abiding concern is that if we don't have that debate before crises, then we end up with ... more of the same – as we've seen play out in the Europe context. The plea ... is to have the discussion now so that [in the event of a crisis] we have some ideas of what to do.'

It helps to begin by asking what the state is uniquely capable of doing in the sphere of economic policy. This doesn't exhaust the activities that the state should be engaged in, but it establishes a minimum case for what it should do. Following a review of the possible sites of state activity, three functions should loom large: redistribution, regulation and steering. These functions help to define the shape of a market within an economy: its direction, divisions and outer limits. These functions draw on the strengths of the state. They cannot be fulfilled in the same way by the market or community. Setting out these functions is a helpful focus for government itself. But clarity about these functions may also allow businesses, communities and individuals to plan their activities and develop a division of labour in reliance on the state. An outline of what these terms mean can lead us into a discussion of specific policies that could be adopted under 'redistribution', 'regulation' and 'steering'.

redistribution

No other body can redistribute at scale as effectively as the state.[26] Redistribution involves the acquisition of wealth, usually in monetary form, from those with considerable wealth – and the redirection of these resources towards those in need, primarily through spending on social services. Only the state can tax. Further, the state is well placed to direct money towards social services. It can borrow at lower interest rates than private individuals. Economies of scale mean that state spending can achieve better value for money. The capacity for interagency thinking in the state means that information can be pooled, while respecting individuals' privacy, in order to target spending. And while the motivation of state employees to advance the public good should not be romanticised, it is relevant that state action is not motivated by profit, meaning that more effort can be directed towards optimal social outcomes.

What is needed is not only clarity about *why* the state is best placed to redistribute, but also fresh arguments about the need for redistribution. When I interviewed the Oxford professor Tony Atkinson, one of the world's leading experts on inequality who, sadly, died before the publication of this book, he said simply, 'We have to rehabilitate taxation.'

Recent years have offered more evidence for why meaningful redistribution is essential, alongside traditional arguments about the importance of revenue. Strong spending on government services represents one response to globalisation that improves a country's resilience and does not involve restricting immigration.[27]

'[T]he twenty-first century nature of work suggests we should be even more reliant on redistribution,' said Susan St John, an economics academic at the University of Auckland Business School. She told me redistribution would reduce the volatility people are facing in contract work and insecure employment.

On a different theme, persistent inequality in New Zealand in the absence of redistribution may have impeded levels of economic development: 2014 research by the IMF concluded that lower rates of inequality are correlated with 'faster and more durable growth'. The same research found that redistribution has a 'generally benign' effect on growth, countering the claim that taxation and spending undermine economic growth.[28] (It did not explain why this was so, but it can be inferred that redistribution does not have a substantial effect on value creation in the public and private sector, and that redistribution might even support growth, by ensuring good quality public services that can be drawn upon in the creation of value in the private and public sector.)

And high levels of economic inequality – even if these levels have stayed stagnant rather than increasing over the years – produce the possibility of individuals and groups with wealth having a disproportionate political influence, at the same time that others without wealth are increasingly alienated from the political process.

Most troublingly, perhaps, inequality gives rise to 'social distance' – distance between us within Aotearoa New Zealand society, as financial inequality leads to spatial segregation and chasms between how people live their lives.[29] This kind of inequality undermines community by straining the ties that bind us together. It creates the risk that we will no longer understand each other. That erodes our ability to empathise with the plight of the vulnerable.

We have seen the political and social effects of inequality in the US and the UK in the past decade. The chaining together of economic inequality and inequality of political influence has emerged in the US, with the rise of political action campaigns ('PACs') and loose campaign finance restrictions. You need to be rich to get involved with politics in the US – and if you have wealth, you are likely to have higher levels of political influence.

Meanwhile, the dangers of social distance were revealed in the UK following the vote to leave the European Union in June 2016. Many British Remain voters responded to the decision by claiming they no longer understood their own country: the writer Zadie Smith, in a candid account, said others she knew around her 'must have been living behind a kind of veil, unable to see our own country for what it has become'.[30] Few commentators (Smith excepted) suggested that levels of wealth and income inequality may have contributed to the gap in understanding increasingly distant parts of the country. No one in New Zealand wants to become like the US or the UK in these respects. We mustn't allow deeply unequal access to political influence. We mustn't get to the point that we cannot understand each other, or our collective decisions.

This is why, in part, we so urgently need redistribution. (Predistribution – or how labour markets and other features of the economy are designed before money is initially distributed – is discussed in Chapter 8.)

What kind of redistribution? First, income tax brackets and rates should be constantly reviewed to ensure that they best reflect the values of care, community and creativity at the heart of a progressive Aotearoa. It is dangerous to say what this requires in concrete terms, since a specific proposal on tax rates could quickly become dated as policies and circumstances change. However, New Zealand's current top rate of 33 per cent for those earning $70,000 or more deserves to be scrutinised. If tax represents not only a fair chipping into a collective pot, but also an acknowledgement of the public services from which all benefit, it is debatable whether one-third of top incomes is a sufficient contribution (especially given that this is a marginal rate, paid only on income in excess of $70,000). And this rate seems especially dubious when other countries' top rates are considered.

In the UK, those earning between £32,000 and £150,000 pay 40 per cent in tax (on income above £32,000), and those earning above £150,000 pay 45 per cent on further income beyond £150,000 – even while a Conservative government has been in power since 2010. As a step towards reducing inequality – and tax is the best tool to achieve this, since it reduces the take-home income of those most well-off, and adds to the resources available to those most in need – New Zealand should consider raising its top rate. Before 2008, that rate was 39 per cent. A return to that rate is one option, but a better idea may be to review New Zealand's tax brackets altogether.

Is it fair that a person who earns $71,000 pays the same amount of tax at the top rate (on earnings above $70,000) as a person who earns $500,000? It may be that a higher rate, such as the 45 per cent figure used in Britain, is justified for those earning over $150,000. In addition to the 45 per cent figure for those earning over $150,000 and the 39 per cent figure for those earning between $70,000 and $150,000, some thought might go into the tax brackets below $70,000. At present, those earning up to $14,000 pay 10 per cent in income tax, those between $14,000 and $48,000 pay 17.5 per cent, and those between $48,000 and $70,000 pay 30 per cent. Whether a tax-free zone is justified (which would make the tax system more progressive still), along with slight tweaks to the amounts of tax paid in the two other brackets, could be the subject of a fuller review. A back-of-the-envelope calculation, using conservative Treasury estimates about how raising taxes might decrease disposable income shows that a shift of the $70,000–$150,000 and $150,000+ rates could bring in $1.688 billion in government revenue, making possible many other proposals in this book. The number of people paying this top tax rate would be small – as of 2016, those earning over $150,000 made up just 3 per cent of taxpayers – but they would pay a significant proportion of the overall tax take, given that in

2016 (with a lower top tax rate) those earning this amount already contributed around 24 per cent of the tax take.[31]

Is it unfair for those earning over $70,000 to increase their rate of tax, and for those earning $150,000 to pay still more? Haven't these individuals contributed to the economy, and don't they deserve to not be penalised for their hard work? These people have contributed to the economy – but the economy has also contributed to them, in public education, public health care, infrastructure and public transport. Tax represents an acknowledgment of this.

We should also be cautious about implying a trickle-down benefit to others from the contribution made by the wealthy; 'trickle-down economics' is now widely dismissed as a fantasy. Others might worry about the flight of wealthy individuals from New Zealand in the event of these tax changes, or the inevitability of tax avoidance. Often, wealth flight is used to blackmail governments considering tax increases; whether it actually materialises is another question for which the evidence is fuzzy.[32]

We must not be defeatist about tax avoidance. While it is true that individuals may seek to minimise their tax liability, efforts should continue to crack down on such avoidance, and it has not been shown that minor losses in avoidance outweigh increases in revenue. Such calculations are notoriously imprecise. Tony Atkinson, in his book on inequality, has said there is 'considerable uncertainty surrounding the estimate of the taxable elasticity [that is, how individuals will react to an increase in the top tax rate]'.[33] Atkinson said that an increase of the UK's top tax rate to 65 per cent may represent the optimal tax outcome.[34] Thomas Piketty, a leading contemporary economist, has said that, according to his estimates, 'the optimal top tax rate in the developed countries is probably above 80 percent'.[35] We should recall that prior to the Fourth Labour Government, the top tax rate was 66 per cent. We need not necessarily call for a return to that rate. But what is clear is that 'restoring progressive income taxation', in Atkinson's words, will not need to lead to the skies falling in.[36]

Another debate is needed, however, about forms of tax other than income tax. One of the central insights of Piketty's *Capital in the Twenty-First Century* is that with the expansion of housing and financial wealth in many countries (which he calls 'capital'), income is an increasingly weak signal of overall wealth.[37] In this new world of wealth, a focus on taxing income may be an indirect and inaccurate way of ensuring that the most wealthy pay their fair share. Piketty proposes a global tax on capital; he argues that tax cannot be confined to income and other sites of taxation should be considered.

In New Zealand, Gareth Morgan and Susan Guthrie have proposed a 'comprehensive capital tax': a flat 30 per cent tax on an assumed rate of return made every year from land, buildings, plant and equipment, intellectual property, brands and other similar assets.[38] Other proposals include the capital gains tax pushed by the Labour Party, in particular in the early 2010s, and the land tax floated by the National-led government in 2016 for foreign buyers or perhaps non-resident New Zealanders. Oxfam New Zealand and Hone Harawira have argued for a financial transactions tax[39] – a tax that might reduce financial volatility and close the current loophole that means financial services are not taxed (though they might logically be thought to be subject to GST). Capital, land and financial transactions taxes all have merit. But what is needed is a careful review of all non-income tax options, including other taxes such as an inheritance tax and a wealth tax, by a committee. It need not only consider the introduction of new taxes, but might also reflect on whether new taxes could be introduced at the same time as other taxes such as GST are decreased. Empirical estimations would be needed on the possible effects on revenue, productivity, deadweight losses and capital flight. It is also important that such a review involves the public rather than assuming these are questions that only experts can answer.

The National-led government since 2008 has made some progress in rethinking spending – one part of redistribution – by adopting a 'social investment' approach. It is worth commenting on this approach, framed as 'social investment' by Bill English during his time as Finance Minister, because it relates to how redistribution happens. Talk of 'social investment' rightly implies the need for outcomes from spending: 'distribution' is a little passive – a word that suggests a government need not consider what happens to the money it distributes. The word 'social' is also a useful reminder, in the abstract, that broader societal concerns matter – contrary to one of the neoliberal maxims mentioned earlier.

However, in addition to the technical problems with how 'social investment' has been operationalised, well outlined by economist Simon Chapple (including the fact that it does not take into account the greater need that more vulnerable people might have for money),[40] there are reasons to be cautious about the approach. As Colin James has pointed out in his thoughtful writing, 'social investment' may neglect the importance of building up stocks or assets, the value of which is not easily measurable.[41] The focus on government as investor may place insufficient emphasis on the benefits to society and other actors that might come from government spending, a point well made by economist Bill Rosenberg.[42] Excessive reliance on evidence can be a way to uphold a problematic status quo, when a lack of evidence is given as a reason for inaction; but some social challenges require urgent action, and all government action is about 'making decisions with imperfect knowledge', as commentator Keith Ng has pointed out.[43]

Most importantly, perhaps, 'social investment' might distract from the key task of defining what outcomes a government should be measuring. Selecting these outcomes requires values and value judgments, which should be made transparent. Those values drive what we are concerned about, what is measured (and what is not measured), and what action is taken. Journalist Simon Wilson has hinted that a lack of debate about values – or at least a failure to be driven by the right values – might explain why the social investment approach has not yet yielded effective results.[44]

Overall, Colin James seems right about the problems with the word 'spending', which connotes a short-term injection of government money as a 'palliative'.[45] Better language is needed. But there is also a need for caution about the social investment approach, which militates away from open discussions of values and long-term injections of government spending into projects where no immediate return is expected.

regulation

Regulation is another function that the state is uniquely capable of carrying out. Only the state can pass laws requiring that rules are followed in the economy. But this is a crude definition of what regulation is: the use of law to ensure compliance with standards in the economy. Of course, companies can self-regulate – adopting internal rules or codes of conduct – and international institutions can also indicate the direction in which regulation must move. But neither self-regulation nor the directions of international institutions have the mandatory force of state regulation.

As with redistribution, regulation must be defended in a new way. It is remarkable that the global financial crisis (GFC) of 2008 did not lead to an outpouring of support for muscular regulation. There were multiple causes of the crisis, some going far deeper than regulation, but many related to a failure of regulation. Complex financial instruments were developed in the US, in particular, such as credit default swaps, that were not regulated. Credit ratings agencies gave banks and financial institutions overly positive ratings partly because of a conflict of interest they faced – they benefited from positive ratings, since such ratings would lead to institutions re-employing the same agencies for future ratings decisions – and this conflict was never sufficiently regulated. Individuals working in finance were driven to excessive risk-taking in part due to unregulated extravagant bonuses. Deregulation of the split between retail and investment banking (in the US, represented by the repeal of the Glass Steagall Act in 1999) meant that banks faced increased incentives to over-lend; it also meant that the crisis spread more quickly across financial institutions.

Yet the connections between under-regulation and the GFC were initially denied. In 2009, I was lucky enough to attend the St Gallen Symposium in Switzerland, a conference attended by business leaders, politicians, economists and journalists. Kathleen L. Casey, the commissioner of the US Securities and Exchange Commission, spoke at the symposium. She said that regulators should be cautious about over-reacting to the crisis and dampening private sector activity. I asked her whether she seriously denied that under-regulation was a cause of the crisis. She held to her position. I remember, the following summer, walking around Canberra and being shocked to see that a 'Department of Deregulation' still existed in Australia. We were lucky never to have one in New Zealand. (The Australian department was disbanded in 2013).

A weak regulatory response followed the GFC all around the world, as a result of the ongoing dominance of neoliberal maxims and, perhaps, the influence of vested interests. In the UK, the 2011 Independent Commission on Banking recommended the ring-fencing of retail and investment banking, but only a weak version of this policy was ever implemented. In the US, the Dodd-Frank Wall Street Reform and Consumer Protection Act 2011 required increased transparency around derivatives and other financial instruments rather than banning or more strictly regulating the markets in these instruments.

Globally, then, there has arguably been a failure to appreciate the importance of regulation – and that failure extends to New Zealand, even if we were not so badly affected by the crisis. Blame for New Zealand's soft regulatory response to the GFC can be directed at the courts as well as the government. In New

Zealand in December 2010, the Supreme Court read down, or minimised the effect of, the Credit Contracts and Consumer Finance Act 2003 in a case called *GE Custodians v Bartle*. The Act prohibits contracts that are 'oppressive, harsh, unjustly burdensome, unconscionable, or in breach of reasonable standards of commercial practice'. In a unanimous decision, the court held – to simplify it somewhat – that where parties get independent legal advice and know of nothing that renders a transaction oppressive, a court should not quash that contract.[46] The contract in question in the case involved a 'fastdoc' loan offered to individuals not easily in a position to repay the loan – a kind of loan not dissimilar to those that circulated prior to the financial crisis in the US – but these matters were not mentioned in the judgment.[47]

The court's reasoning echoes a neoliberal maxim described at the beginning of this chapter ('caveat emptor': transactions should not be interfered with where they are entered into freely), and undermines the power of the Act to regulate harsh debt contracts. To be fair on the Supreme Court, its decisions have not all weakened the power of regulation of debt contracts: a later decision, *Hickman v Turner and Waverley Ltd*, offered a strong interpretation of the Securities Act 1978 with the effect of 'protect[ing] vulnerable members of the investing public'.[48] Nevertheless it is accurate to say that New Zealand's regulatory response to the GFC was as weak as many other countries. And New Zealand has faced other failures of regulation: in the leaky homes crisis, which is a result of the weakness of the Building Act 1991, and the Pike River coal mine tragedy in 2010, which led to various health and safety prosecutions after the death of 29 miners. In both cases, new regulatory regimes have been introduced, but the leaky homes crisis and Pike River remain examples of the importance of regulation – and the dangers of under-regulating certain sectors.

So what difference would it make if New Zealand's past failures of regulation were acknowledged, and if it were accepted that robust regulation is a fundamental state function? In all areas, it can still be recognised that regulation has costs, including the possibility of restricting creative business activity. Even so, there are two areas where this account of regulation might make a practical difference: the banking sector, and the negotiation of free trade agreements.

In the context of banking, in light of the evidence I have already outlined about rising private indebtedness, consideration could be given to whether there might be increased regulation of credit. The ratio of household debt to household incomes has dropped overall since 2008. But it has been steadily rising in the years following 2012. In 2016, the ratio stood at 165 per cent – far higher than the UK or the US ratio, but slightly lower than Australia's.[49] Based on a limited data set, a Reserve Bank analyst commented that New Zealand's ratio was 'towards the upper end' of the sample and 'on the high side internationally'.[50]

High levels of indebtedness are concerning for many reasons. On top of being correlated with economic crises, they can depress aggregate demand, raise house prices for everyone and make a country vulnerable to economic shocks (if indebtedness does not directly cause such shocks). Greater regulation might cover high-interest loans as well as standard loans. The Credit Contracts and Consumer Finance Amendment Act 2014 introduced a Responsible Lending Code, but the code is non-binding – it is therefore relatively toothless in its attempts to clamp down on exorbitant lending. Stronger rules might be necessary. Further, in the area of general lending, the Reserve Bank required investors to place 40 per cent deposits on house purchases (up from 30 per cent) and home buyers to place 20 per cent deposits on home purchases (increased in 2013) under its loan-to-value ratio (LVR) rules. These are moves in the right direction. However, questions should be raised about why the Reserve Bank, and not the government, is in charge of these lending regulations, especially as these regulations impact on how easy it is for individuals to own a home. It may be desirable, in light of the refreshed justification of regulation provided above, for the government to take greater charge of these regulations, while still drawing upon the Reserve Bank's advice.

The second area where a stronger view of the value of regulation could have a real effect is in how free trade agreements are negotiated and assessed. Trade is important for the ongoing health and expansion of the New Zealand economy. Some free trade agreements can be problematic, however, because they impair the ability of countries to regulate in the public interest. Sensible regulation is vulnerable to challenge on the ground that it involves some expropriation of an investment (even notwithstanding exceptions in many agreements) or on other grounds, and the threat of arbitration through Investor-State Dispute Settlement may also chill government attempts to regulate. (Investor-State Dispute Settlement is a way that investors or firms can challenge governments, and claim that governments have violated a trade agreement or other relevant agreement, in a forum outside a country's courts.) The text of the Trans-Pacific Partnership (TPP), released in 2016, contained some acknowledgments of the importance of regulation: Article 20.3 highlighted the 'sovereign right' of countries to pass laws for environmental protection, and Article 25.2(b) specifically recognised 'the role that regulation plays in achieving public policy objectives'. But the TPP also contained the risk that governments would be deterred from regulating in the national interest: notwithstanding some qualifications and a New Zealand-specific annex on government procurement, the rules on government procurement may have prevented the government adopting a position in favour of New Zealand services.

A general reassertion of the importance of regulation as a state function can lead to a more principled position being taken in free trade negotiations to prevent such risks. It could also result in more careful opposition being taken to free trade agreements that undermine the state's regulatory power.

steering

The state has a distinctive ability to steer the economy in a strategic direction. The state has a broad view of the strengths and weaknesses of an economy, and has the capacity to coordinate action. It has the power to bring together industry representatives, workers, local government and others. It has the ability to inject money into particular parts of the economy. Along with a renewed defence of redistribution and regulation, there needs to be a greater willingness for the state to acknowledge this 'steering' role – a word I have borrowed from Robert Wade, whose work I discuss below.

Mainstream economics in the 1980s and 1990s, influenced by neoliberal currents, largely rejected the idea of any role for the government in steering industrial development. But Mariana Mazzucato's recent work has shifted much economic thinking.

In her work, in particular in her book *The Entrepreneurial State*, Mazzucato argues that the state's conventional support for research and development (which is not strong in New Zealand) is insufficient if countries are seeking genuine innovation and development.[51] Mazzucato suggests that despite the rhetoric surrounding venture capital and the dynamism of the private sector, venture capitalists are often unwilling to take major risks, especially at the seed funding stage. This argument may have even greater resonance in New Zealand, where capital markets are shallow, making it possibly even more likely that venture capitalists will be risk-averse. She says that historically it is governments that have taken some of the most successful investment risks, and that this highlights that the government's role in an economy goes beyond addressing market failure.

'Not only has government funded the riskiest research, whether applied or basic,' Mazzucato has written. '[B]ut it has indeed often been the source of the most radical, path-breaking types of innovation. To this extent it has actively created markets not just fixed them.'[52] She has shown, meticulously, that the US government has been behind major innovations in nanotechnology, the internet and biotechnology, through initiatives such as the Defense Advanced Research Agency (DARPA), the Small Business Innovation Research Program and the National Nanotechnology Initiative. Mazzucato has famously pointed out that each key innovation that has contributed to the the development of the iPhone can be traced back to funding by the state.[53] Lastly, Mazzucato claims that the state must take more credit for its role in developing industries and innovation, and that it should consider taking stakes in companies and initiatives to which it has provided important funding. This would allow 'a more collective distribution of the rewards' of state-backed innovation.[54]

Mazzucato is not the only economist to have wielded this argument. Dani Rodrik has made the point that all states play some role in favouring infrastructure or certain sectors (through, among other things, funding roads); the question is not, Rodrik says, whether the state should intervene but rather how it should intervene.[55]

To talk about how these arguments apply to New Zealand, I sat down with Robert Wade in Oxford in late 2015. The New Zealand-born Wade is a prize-winning economist and political scientist at the London School of Economics and Political Science. Wade has remained engaged with New Zealand political developments. He has long argued that the state has an important steering role in economic development. He told me that we should see the government not just as 'umpire' of the market, but as a 'steward'.

In New Zealand, Wade believes, the focus should be on diversifying the economy – and upgrading products. He gave the example of Danish ham as a product that has been upgraded over time to ensure the quality of Danish exports, and the Danish turbine industry as another where government investment has resulted in successful industrial development. He agreed with Mazzucato's work showing that industrial policy, where governments direct and inject money into industry, has long existed in many countries, including developed countries, but has often been unacknowledged.

'The US tells the world ... "don't do industrial policy",' the soft-spoken scholar told me, 'but there's a great deal going on in the US that's below the radar.' The key is getting over the view, once voiced to Wade by another leading economist, that 'all governments are predatory'. And governments, he told me, need to prepare the ground for a steering role by building a 'support network' and a 'positive feedback mechanism, by which those investing in sectors or activities to be encouraged can aggregate their support and sustain the investment against resistance'. Moreover, in addition to government spending in industries, governments can play a role in 'building networks of companies which normally compete but which can all gain from cooperation on specific projects'.

How could these insights help New Zealand? First, the government might develop a more coherent strategy for the development of Crown research institutes, to maximise the benefits of research – for example, into agriculture and climate change through AgResearch – for export growth, while still respecting the intellectual independence of the institutes. Second, a more active, entrepreneurial step would be to steer certain state-owned enterprises in the direction of renewable energy, including for the purposes of building export revenue. State-owned enterprises must operate successfully as businesses, but their state ownership means that they can be run differently from ordinary businesses. And there are state-owned enterprises that already have the potential to develop their contribution to renewable energy use.

Third, the outline of the state's steering role might provide the basis for a more long-term regional development policy, which would entail targeted and monitored support for under-resourced regions. Our economy is moving towards what might be called 'Aucklandisation', a growth of and dependence on economic activity in Auckland, which renders the wider economy more vulnerable and depresses economic activity in other areas. A coherent regional development policy could address the risk of this.

Fourth, the government could work with growing areas of the economy – such as the Māori economy, the tourism and wine industry, the film industry, social enterprise, and other small- and medium-sized enterprises – in order to investigate whether partnerships can be built with government, perhaps in conjunction with export targets or other accountability mechanisms.

Partnerships could involve government support in accessing finance, government investment in venture capital funds, the establishment of government investment banks for strategic areas, or government stakes in particular companies (as proposed by Mazzucato) – the latter possibly providing an additional source of government revenue. The overall aim of this exercise would be what Robert Wade discussed: the diversification and upgrading of the New Zealand economy.

For those who claim that this might represent gross government interference with New Zealand's economic trajectory or 'picking winners', it is worth pointing out that the government already supports New Zealand industry – through law, diplomacy, public rhetoric and New Zealand Trade and Enterprise. Some of the steering described above already happens, yet in a way that lacks strategic vision. Of course, the legacy of the Think Big projects of the early 1980s looms over proposals to strengthen industrial policy in New Zealand. It would be helpful for the lessons of Think Big to be properly learned before a fortified industrial strategy is developed.

True, not all government investments will be successful. It is inevitable, too, that in New Zealand there might be some leakage of revenue overseas, perhaps as companies grow. These risks would have to be managed. Care would have to be taken to ensure that government steering is consistent with New Zealand's free trade agreement obligations – and if such steering seems inconsistent, a debate should be had about whether those obligations go too far in restricting the steering capacity of the state. The value of government steering should be borne in mind in future trade negotiations.

It is essential throughout this that the government involves individuals who have long-term thinking abilities and business savvy – and that it maintains some level of public participation in the process. We need not romanticise the capacity of government to boost economic productivity. But the experience of a range of economies, as demonstrated by economists like Mazzucato and Rodrik, is that government can, by drawing on knowledge from the private sector, and building on its capabilities, make strategic interventions to improve productivity, exports and competitiveness.

the future of the state in the economy

The three functions of redistribution, regulation and steering deserve greater attention by governments on both the right and left. This is not where state action in the economy ends. There are other functions, perhaps not exclusively carried out by the state, that require ongoing discussion: in particular, what the state owns and subsidises deserves more thought.

We should be clear about not only what the state is involved in within the economy – but also who is involved with the state.[56] One criticism of the post-Second World War governments in the UK, and the Michael Joseph Savage-led government in New Zealand, is that while they set up enduring welfare institutions, these were dominated by bureaucrats and tended to exclude workers and the most vulnerable, who were often the beneficiaries of these institutions.[57] It is crucial that decisions about ownership, steering and redistribution draw on a broad knowledge base – including the knowledge of businesses, workers and academics. Where new institutions are set up (for example, an investment bank to solidify the government's steering role), individuals in decision-making roles should reflect the variety of relevant actors. If the state is to return to a central role in economic policy, it matters that we see it not as some aloof institution, but rather as reflective of the community. I look at this again in Chapter 11.

alternatives to gross domestic product per capita

To some readers, the changes I have proposed might not seem far-reaching enough. What has been suggested here could be regarded as a tepid response to the burning problems of significant inequality, child poverty, economic stagnation and a captured public debate. But this book aims only to stir up political debate; it does not seek to provide a complete blueprint for political action. Moreover, some of the changes that have been mooted in this chapter could be seen as a bridge towards more thoroughgoing economic transformation.

Another change to economic policy, which might seem limited in isolation but can help to usher in a broader shift, is the move to adopt an alternative to gross domestic product (GDP) as a measure of economic health. GDP per capita is the total output of a country divided by the population: in other words, it measures the average output per person. The limitations of GDP are well recognised: it does not take note of distribution or inequality, it ignores important aspects of a country's health (such as environmental protection), and it does not measure activity away from the formal economy.[58] In addition to these, as I have discussed already, GDP is not meaningful to most people as a metric.[59] Arthur Grimes, former Chair of the Reserve Bank and now a senior fellow at Motu Economic and Public Policy Research, told me that GDP shouldn't be ignored – but 'the emphasis on GDP per capita clearly needs to be substantially reduced'. Yet GDP and GDP per capita are often simplistically invoked in political debates in New Zealand, most commonly to determine when a recession (defined as two consecutive quarters of negative GDP growth) has occurred.

In some ways, political practice in New Zealand, as elsewhere, is already moving beyond GDP. GDP is no longer the only gauge of economic health ever mentioned. New Zealand politicians and commentators regularly toss around statistics about debt, inflation, unemployment, productivity or exports. One way to dislodge GDP as a measure of economic health is to continue to use these alternative measures, and to explain the shortcomings of GDP when it is invoked. This could highlight the importance of multiple measures, and the fact that GDP is a problematic indicator of social progress.

Economists and commentators are likely to return to GDP, though, since it does pithily capture economic factors related to production and income. The best way to move beyond it is for an alternative to be developed, with the caveat that no single metric can be completely valid. Other existing single metrics have their own flaws. The Human Development Index is a statistically rigorous measure, but it is currently measured annually only, and may not capture enough year-to-year fluctuations to be meaningful.

The most promising alternative is a version of the New Zealand Treasury's Living Standards Framework. This was designed to capture progress in a nuanced way. It consists of five focus areas: economic growth, reducing macro-economic vulnerability, sustainability, growing social capital, and increasing equity. The framework also takes note of important stocks – financial and physical, human, social and natural – and flows such as income, leisure and freedom. It is certainly not value-free: it opts to prize social capital and equity. But it aims to make growth less of a priority, making it just one of these five focus areas. Former Treasury chief economist Girol Karacaoglu has helpfully suggested how these five areas might be translated into measurement tools, drawing on measurements such as net national income per capita, net international investment position, the World Values Survey, and the percentage of the population below the 50 per cent median income.[60] The Treasury continues to develop the framework, and to review support for it in the public sector and community – and it should be adapted in response to criticism. Arthur Grimes, who has written extensively on wellbeing economics, was 'not quite sure how you operationalise' the Living Standards Framework, and he raised concerns about the arbitrariness of the five focus areas. But he acknowledged it was 'definitely a step forward' and represented 'the right direction of travel'. It might be that if the framework can be translated into a single score, measured relatively regularly, this 'LSF score' could be preferable to GDP per capita.

A further move that would help to displace GDP is to develop a different definition of a recession. As long as it is regarded as two consecutive quarters of negative GDP growth, economists will be unable to escape keeping one eye on GDP growth rates. Instead, how about 'societal ill-health' being formally diagnosed following two quarters of dropping LSF scores, once the LSF has been converted into a single metric? This is just one idea. But economists who have already done considerable work on this front could be encouraged to continue to generate new definitions.

At the same time that all of these ideas are considered, broader debates should continue about the notion of 'growth' itself. Should growth be an economic ideal? Is it possible to reconceptualise it so that it is shorn from associations with consumption and materialism? Or is it necessary to abandon it altogether? This debate requires not just evidence but values – a sense of the principles we want to value as a society. It also requires that people feel empowered to enter the debate.

broadening debate about economic policy

In Oxford, from 2013, I became a little involved with a group called People's Political Economy. The group's name was a riff on PPE – the traditional Oxford undergraduate course in philosophy, politics and economics – and its aim was to upend Oxford's model of education: to develop shared learning groups in the Oxford community, which would involve the exchange of experience and knowledge on the subjects of politics and economics. The ethos of the group was that every person has opinions on matters of money and power, and that there is value in sharing and working through those views.

During the same period, in the early 2010s, several student groups emerged in the UK challenging the economics curriculum to engage with other disciplines: Post-Crash Economics groups at Manchester, the London School of

Economics, and elsewhere, and a broader group called Rethinking Economics. These new groups suggested that a narrow economic discipline should take some responsibility for the GFC, which was not predicted by mainstream economists and which resulted from amoral and ahistorical approaches to credit, bubbles and the free market.

In 2014, Thomas Piketty made a similar point in his book, *Capital in the Twenty-First Century*: 'For too long economists have sought to define themselves in terms of their supposedly scientific methods.'[61] Social scientists in other disciplines, he added, 'should not leave the study of economic facts to economists and must not flee in horror the minute a number rears its head'.[62] Tony Atkinson was similarly critical of economics when I met him. It has become 'too specialised' and 'too inner-regarding', he said, and 'we've got into thinking about a very narrow range of things'. Overall, he said, 'I think economics is in a pretty bad way at the moment.' The message out of the early 2010s, from Piketty and students and others, was that economics must open itself to engagement from non-economists, and that non-economists need to open themselves to engagement with economics.

There are lessons here for New Zealand. Those involved with economics, especially politicians, Treasury officials and journalists, need to acknowledge that there are many available approaches to economic policy, and that economic policy (just like economics) benefits from the input of different voices. University economics curricula should continue to be reviewed, too. Economic decision-making needs to be opened up to public participation. That is not to say that economics is simple. It isn't. But no one should dismiss in advance the possibility that any person might have a valuable view on it. We should be sceptical of anyone who claims that there is one right economic answer, or who uses economic jargon as a shield against genuine scrutiny and criticism.[63]

conclusion

Economic policy forms only one chapter in this book. But matters touching on economic policy are also discussed elsewhere, for example, in Chapter 6 on social infrastructure and Chapter 8 on those in and out of work. My decision to dedicate just one of twelve chapters to the theme was a deliberate response to one of the maxims of neoliberalism: that economic policy is all-important. Economics *is* fundamental to social change. But economics, and economic policy, is best understood within a broader framework of history and values.

One question that arises is how we can move from the realm of theory – a new framework for the state, including a different approach to taxation and regulation and industrial policy – to real change, in which policy, politics and our social world are less dominated by neoliberalism. I have discussed how some of this can be effected: through universities, through politicians being brave enough to test alternative ideas, through people participating in debate. Engagement with the ideas in this chapter is one way forward: the new framework for economic policy will only be improved if criticisms are raised and fresh proposals are suggested. But, as I say elsewhere, change will also only occur through a shift in underlying power dynamics in New Zealand politics. (More about this in Chapter 11.)

Thomas Piketty points out in *Capital in the Twenty-First Century*, 'no mathematical formula or economic estimate can tell us exactly what tax rate ought to be applied to what level of income. Only collective deliberation and democratic experimentation can do that.'[64] The point applies more broadly to economic policy. It is 'collective deliberation and democratic experimentation' that we need, ideally within a New Zealand that places the values of care, community and creativity at the core of decision-making.

5 the art of what might not seem possible at the moment: on decolonisation and constitutions

'You have the biggest mouth I've ever seen,' Whāea Raewyn told me. I had been practising co-leading the haka at Clyde Quay Primary School, aged eight or nine, trying to summon up as much energy and ferocity I could out of my puny body. I am not sure if Whāea Raewyn meant the comment as a compliment. Whatever the case, the line has stayed with me ever since.

I had my first day at Clyde Quay in 1994. My twin brother and I joined the class in the second year of primary school, when most of the kids already knew each other. I felt like a bit of an outsider. My family had lived in China for four years before coming to New Zealand. I probably sounded different. I don't know where I thought 'home' was back then.

Out of this confusion, and over the following five or six years that I was in that school in Mount Victoria in Wellington, it was the Māori dimension of life that gave me a sense of solidity. This was, of course, only one part of a busy primary school schedule. But it was a major part of the Clyde Quay community. The school principal for most of my time there was Whāea Liz, we sang waiata at regular school assemblies, and we performed in school productions that were interwoven with Māori themes.

The Māori cultural life of Clyde Quay captured me. I got goosebumps singing waiata like 'Pā Mai' and 'Matairangi E', and sang these on car trips with my family. I tried hard to pronounce te reo Māori correctly. I still remember performances telling the story of Māui, and talking about tūrangawaewae – a place to stand. The Māori dimension of cultural life at Clyde Quay, which I was encouraged to take part in, gave me a feeling of belonging and that place to stand. It was unique to Aotearoa. And – whether it was the historical stories of early explorers I was reliving, or the 'ruana te whenua!' line in one school waiata – it made me feel bigger.

While I for the most part left behind these waiata and references when living in Indonesia from age 12 to 16, I continued to come back to te ao Māori as I got older. I relished the chance to study New Zealand history in my final year at school at Wellington College. I took a course in te reo Māori at university in Auckland, was moved again by Māori stories when studying history and law, and felt a deep commitment to work with Māori to raise awareness of the Treaty of Waitangi. When I moved to the UK, I took part in a campaign about decolonisation, Rhodes Must Fall in Oxford, partly because I was struck by how little issues of colonisation were discussed in the home of Empire.

What all this shows is the value of early cultural immersion in te reo Māori for building awareness, sensitivity and understanding. It also helps to explain, from a personal perspective, why matters Māori are so fundamental to my view of the future of Aotearoa New Zealand.

Whāea Raewyn may have said I was big-mouthed, aged eight or nine. But this chapter is less about my voice and more about listening to, and amplifying, the stories and visions of others. The chapter is shaped by Māori accounts of politics and society that I have read, and by influential conversations I have had with many friends and colleagues about biculturalism and multiculturalism, including a recent interview with Moana Jackson. The chapter demonstrates, I hope, that, just as I felt bigger as a small kid at Clyde Quay by learning about Māori history and belting waiata out proudly, so we can be bigger as a country if Pākehā interacting with te ao Māori show humility, and if all of us are bold in our dreams for how a better politics on matters Māori might transform New Zealand.

decolonisation

In te reo Māori, the directional particle which means in front of, 'ki mua', is also closely related to the word for the past, 'mua'. The past is not shelved or forgotten. It is ahead, staring us in the face. That linguistic fact parallels a fact of contemporary politics: in Māori affairs, we see all around us the consequences of historical colonial policy, government action and interactions between Māori and others in Aotearoa New Zealand. Therefore it is appropriate to front up to the past and build on historical insights as we look to the future.

One way to front up to the past is to trace the effects of colonisation on Aotearoa New Zealand, and to work to undo the ongoing damage of colonisation. That's partly what the decolonisation I mentioned in the introductory chapter is about. Decolonisation has a theoretical base, in the work of Aimé Césaire and Franz Fanon, and New Zealand's Linda Tuhiwai Smith, among others.[1] It means different things in different settings. In Aotearoa New Zealand, drawing on the work of Smith and Ani Mikaere,[2] it means recognising the political, social and economic effects of colonisation, and working to redress them. It means seeing our own place in history as part of a longer story: New Zealand history did not just start two hundred years ago, of course. Decolonisation has an intellectual dimension too, because it involves understanding how colonisation might have shaped *ways of thinking*. But decolonisation is not merely a negative process of undoing. It is also a positive project. As Palestinian-Canadian writer Harsha Walia has said, 'Decolonisation is the process whereby we create the conditions in which we want to live and the social relations we wish to have.' Who is in control of that process is crucial. Decolonisation must involve what Walia calls 'a profound recentring on Indigenous worldviews'.[3]

Colonisation has had ongoing effects on contemporary New Zealand life. There are stark inequalities in outcome between Māori and non-Māori that have persisted for decades. These are partly the product of historical injustices, including land confiscation, displacement and denial of political rights. Everyday racism exists in multiple forms. To take just one example, the excellent 'I, Too, Am Auckland' project charts Māori and Pasifika students at the University of Auckland talking about experiences of racism.[4] This racism towards Māori and Pasifika is underpinned by notions of white supremacy and superiority that have significant continuities with views expressed during colonisation. Māori land ownership, as discussed in the next section, has been splintered through colonisation, and legal structures protecting Māori cultural practices – including customary rights and customary title – are difficult to access or limited.

Pākehā (a term I will return to later) and Māori have distinct roles to play in decolonisation. As Ani Mikaere notes, 'Pākehā need to own up to the truth about how they have come to occupy their position of dominance in our country – and to deal with it.'[5] In South Africa and the US, among other places, there is an increasing literature on whiteness and white privilege.[6] But much less has been written or said about white privilege, or Pākehā privilege, in New Zealand – though this is changing. Pākehā, and I include myself in this, need to identify the benefits of being perceived as Pākehā. Mikaere goes further, and with good reason. She writes: '[Pākehā] need to take ownership of their history and to take positive steps to redress the situation. Such steps will include learning to let go of some of their power.'[7]

What this means in practice is that Pākehā in positions of power 'must place their trust in Māori, not the other way around', Mikaere says.[8] Māori political actors have diverse political views. But Māori political actors with diverse views must have a greater ability than at present to shape the direction of this country: through the content of political ideas and the roles held in the political process (at both the activist and parliamentary level).

How Pākehā interact with Māori in this process of decolonisation is important. 'Decolonisation together', in Harsha Walia's words,[9] may be possible, but only if Pākehā are aware of the power they (we) have historically exercised, and that they (we) hold currently, as well as their (our) likely blind spots. Even the practice of solidarity needs to be decolonised, as Australian activist Clare Land has discussed.[10] Pākehā supporters or allies must be willing to listen to Māori and to amplify Māori perspectives, without stereotyping Māori or eliding the differences within Māori communities. This process could benefit Pākehā, too (though the benefits to Pākehā should not be the main justification): there is much to be learned from recentring Māori world views, and just as in the past colonisation harmed both oppressor and oppressed,[11] so too decolonisation can be liberating for both Pākehā and Māori. One of the greatest challenges in this process is how Pākehā, like me, strike a balance between owning the problems of racism and the effects of colonisation, and avoiding ongoing domination.

This chapter is an imperfect attempt to strike that balance. These ideas need to be supplemented by the views of others, Māori and Pākehā. Learning the lessons of history is one starting point, I suggest, for Pākehā in particular. Reopening the conversation about constitutional change may allow for discussion about how decolonisation could take institutional forms. Integrating te reo Māori into the school curriculum – in a process that ought to be guided by Māori voices – could be beneficial for the country as a whole. I point to some ways in which inequalities between Māori and Pākehā might be addressed, though the solutions require further analysis from others, and it is worth bearing in mind Mikaere's insight that 'successful lives as Māori require a good deal more than simply measuring up to a Pākehā standard'.[12] In closing, I suggest how policy affecting other ethnic groups in New Zealand, including Pasifika peoples, might be usefully guided by an approach grounded in the Treaty of Waitangi.

Values of care, community and creativity cannot be realised in a context where people are on an unequal footing. In particular, the value of community cannot be secured in full until historical injustices are righted. Decolonisation is essential to the New Zealand project. It is a process that is important for all of us.

recurring themes

There are cycles of empowerment and disempowerment of Māori in the history of Māori–government relations – sometimes during the term of the same government. This hesitation and fluctuation in commitment has contributed to gaps between Māori and non-Māori outcomes remaining across such areas as health, education, housing and unemployment.

The period following the signing of the Treaty of Waitangi, for example, saw the government-coordinated confiscation of swathes of Māori land. This occurred through wars in Taranaki, Waikato and elsewhere in the 1860s, and also through the operation of the Native Land Court, which encouraged Māori to individualise and sell land titles. But there were moments of more progressive government action, such as the establishment of the Māori parlimentary seats in 1867 (though some scholars note rightly that this was intended only a temporary measure and did not reflect any generalised goodwill on the part of the settler government towards Māori).[13]

The election of the Liberal government from 1891–1912 saw, partly through the work of effective Māori politicians such as Āpirana Ngata and James Carroll, some devolution of power to Māori. The Maori Councils Act and Maori Lands Administration Act of 1900 guaranteed regional Māori decision-making on health and social policy, and created land councils to oversee the sale or leasing of land.[14] But the same government reasserted Crown rights to buy land from Māori, in a manner that facilitated Māori loss of land, through the Lands Improvement and Native Lands Acquisition Act 1894, and directed that extensive land surveying take place in Te Urewera in 1895 without consultation with Tūhoe.[15]

The Muldoon-era government of 1975–84 attempted to sell land at Ōrākei in 1978, prompting the Bastion Point occupation, and allowed significant discharge of sewage at Waitara on the Taranaki coast as part of the Syngas Think Big project, resulting in one of the first significant Waitangi Tribunal claims, the Motunui-Waitara claim. During the same government, though, there were successful employment schemes to engage Māori (including those in gangs), such as the Temporary Employment Programme and Maori Access scheme, as well as the development of the Tu Tangata philosophy through the Department of Maori Affairs under Kara Puketapu.[16]

A similar story can be told about the respect shown for the Treaty of Waitangi by successive governments.

It is sometimes said that the Treaty was ignored from 1840 until 1975, when Matiu Rata secured the passage of the Treaty of Waitangi Act, thus creating the Waitangi Tribunal. It is true that the Treaty was publicly disparaged frequently during this period – most prominently in the *Wi Parata v The Bishop of Wellington* case in 1877, in which it was described as a 'simple nullity'.

However, this narrative about 1840–1975 inaction, followed by action on the Treaty since then, is simplistic. The Treaty was referred to in the 1840s as a 'Maori Magna Carta', with Sir Peter Buck invoking this idea again in the 1930s.[17] Moreover, the government raised its right of pre-emption (that is, its right to be the first purchaser of Māori lands) opportunistically during the nineteenth century, a right guaranteed only in the English version of Article 2 of the Treaty, illustrating that it was quite willing to enforce the Treaty where that suited its interests.[18] Māori activists made repeated attempts to secure recognition of the Treaty. There was, therefore, halting and sporadic protection of the Treaty between 1840 and 1975, even though it was also publicly dismissed during the same time.

Then, after 1975, while the Treaty was made more central to some legislation – including in 1985, when the Waitangi Tribunal was given the power to review alleged historical (pre-1975) breaches, and through the Treaty settlements that followed – it was also in other ways denigrated by political leaders. In 2000, admittedly some time after his period as prime minister, David Lange observed, 'I have to say [the Treaty] means nothing to me.' The Court of Appeal, he said, had 'absurdly' described it as a 'partnership'; he claimed it provided 'no basis for nationhood'.[19]

Nevertheless it is revealing that in Don Brash's divisive Ōrewa speech in 2004, on the subject of nationhood, he claimed that 'racial separatism' contradicted the Treaty: he even said the three main clauses of the Treaty 'must be upheld' (although he made many other criticisms about 'the Treaty process').[20] Perhaps this was just clever political rhetoric – or perhaps the speech shows a growing acknowledgment that the Treaty must be a benchmark for government action, even if the speech offered some questionable interpretations of the Treaty itself.

The history of governmental interactions with the Treaty of Waitangi reveals cycles of commitment and ignorance. It is also not just a history that can be divided bluntly into progress and regress, or good and bad; it is a history, at times, of well-intentioned government action with adverse consequences, and occasionally expediently motivated government action that has had positive consequences in the long run. All of this must be seen, of course, within the broader context of the overwhelmingly negative effects of colonisation.

In the last half-century, there have also been varying levels of political commitment to addressing inequalities between Māori and non-Māori. The Hunn Report in 1961 charted a gap between outcomes for Māori and non-Māori, but resulted in problematic proposals for 'integration'. Concern for the position of Māori resulted in the Labour Party giving the Waitangi Tribunal powers to review pre-1975 breaches of the Treaty of Waitangi in 1985, and commissioning John Rangihau's report, *Puao-Te-Ata-Tu*, released in 1986. However, the Labour government of the late 1980s did little substantively to follow up on the Rangihau report. A similar story can be told of the Labour-led government of the 1999–2008 period, which boldly launched a Closing the Gaps policy, but reduced the public support it gave to the policy following Don Brash's Ōrewa speech of January 2004 and the passage of the Foreshore and Seabed Act 2004.

Overall, there has been no linear improvement in Māori–government relations over time, but nor has there been any steady decline. Successive governments have undermined the economic base, cultural identity and political strength of Māori – but there are sporadic examples of governments attempting to support Māori development in different ways. Māori have also empowered their own communities without government involvement, whether through political self-organisation (as shown by the establishment of the Kīngitanga movement in 1858), peaceful resistance (such as at Parihaka in 1881), cultural revitalisation (think of the establishment of the Te Kōhanga Reo National Trust in 1982 to spearhead the development of Māori language immersion) or other means. In general, there can be no complacency about the future. But positive change is also possible where there is a groundswell of interest in issues accompanied by strong ideas and political leadership. A firmer foundation for Māori–government relations would be beneficial, as part of decolonisation, to ensure steadier progress in this area over time.

Two further comments are warranted. First, what my speedy review reveals is that governments in New Zealand have repeatedly ignored the lessons of history. Māori land reform is another example of this. It became apparent to many following the 1860s that government attempts to encourage economic development on Māori land, through the Native Land Court, had a far-reaching negative effect on the strength of iwi, by splintering collectives. Despite the obvious harm caused by these reforms, the Liberal government attempted similar changes in the first decade of the twentieth century. In 2015–16, the National-led government initiated reform of the Te Ture Whenua Māori Act 1993 aiming to individualise Māori land, which in proposing a concept of 'participating owners' resembles the approach to 'assembled owners' that had such atomising effects on collective land-holdings from 1909 onwards.[21] Cynical readers might say the failures of past policies in such areas are being deliberately overlooked. A charitable interpretation is that noble aims are being pursued, but that history has been marginalised in the policy-making process, with very harmful effects.

Second, throughout the history of Māori–government relations, Māori have been a diverse group with many internal differences. Some Māori have pushed for change outside of mainstream electoral politics, such as Rua Kenana's building of the community at Maungapōhatu or Iritana Tawhiwhirangi in her work with Te Kōhanga Reo National Trust from 1982 onwards. Others have worked within Parliament (Āpirana Ngata and Parekura Horomia being two examples) or the public service (Kara Puketapu). Within mainstream politics, Māori have been well-represented in political parties across the spectrum, with there also being a strong tradition of Māori forging the creation of new political parties when conventional political parties have skewed debate on Māori issues. Matiu Rata set up Mana Motuhake, Tariana Turia left Labour to establish the Māori Party, and Hone Harawira departed from the Māori Party to create the Mana Party. It should not be assumed that 'Māori' in the phrase 'Māori–government', or iwi in 'iwi–government', are a homogeneous group. It is also important not to undermine Māori agency by over-using the term 'Māori' in place of identifying specific Māori individuals or groups – say, Māori politicians, or particular iwi or hapū[22] – even though it may sometimes be necessary to talk broadly about Māori and Pākehā, or Māori and non-Māori, in order to identify social trends and patterns.

These historical snapshots are a backdrop. History must be confronted in future policy-making and politics in this space; it lies in front of the country and not behind it. Efforts must be made not to forget its lessons.

How, though, can improvements be secured in this field when there are structural, institutional and cultural barriers? Brazilian theorist Roberto Unger argues that to achieve structural change, what is needed are specific measures that, taken together, constitute a programme of radical reform.[23] I follow Unger's approach below, suggesting concrete policy actions – but acknowledging that these policy actions will only make a difference if they add up to a programme of structural transformation.

To achieve structural transformation in the position of Māori in Aotearoa New Zealand – required because of the extent of inequality, disadvantage and Pākehā misunderstanding – what is needed is redistribution of public power (including possibly through constitutional change), concerted political action to redress inequalities and strengthen Māori culture and collectives, and policies that shift Pākehā understanding (such as making te reo Māori compulsory in schools).[24] All of this must be led by Māori in the spirit of decolonisation. Moreover, it does not need to come at the expense of immigrants or Pasifika peoples; indeed, the idea of radical transformation – and values arising out of the Treaty of Waitangi – can also provide the basis for a society that shows care for immigrants and Pasifika peoples.

redistribution of public power through constitutional change

The need for greater backbone and consistency in political decision-making about Māori points to the possible value of a single written constitution for Aotearoa New Zealand.

A written constitution – an entrenched document that describes in one place the institutions of government and power in New Zealand, and the values and principles against which those institutions should be judged – could have significant benefits for Māori and non-Māori.[25]

Currently, legal scholars will say that New Zealand has a constitution – it's just not written down in one place. (It is written down, in statutes, judge-made decisions, and elsewhere.) But there is little agreement about what is in it. If 'having a constitution' means we should all be able to say what is and what is not in the constitution, there is a reasonable argument that New Zealand does not have one at all. The Constitution Act 1986 outlines the existence of the sovereign (the monarch acting through the governor-general), the executive (essentially the government, the public service and related bodies such as the police), the judiciary (courts) and the legislature (Parliament); most would agree the Constitution Act forms part of New Zealand's constitution. But beyond this legislation, there is significant disagreement about what is constitutional in New Zealand.

The governor-general's website says New Zealand's constitution 'has a number of sources, including crucial pieces of legislation, several legal documents, common law derived from court decisions as well as established constitutional practices known as conventions.' Increasingly, it adds, 'New Zealand's constitution reflects the Treaty of Waitangi'. Though one might expect this general outline to be non-specific, there is still so much vagueness in this description – and it is vagueness that is characteristic of discussions of the New Zealand constitution. If the New Zealand constitution 'includes' these things, what else is in it? Which 'crucial pieces of legislation' are part of the constitution? Which common law decisions? And if 'increasingly' New Zealand's constitution 'reflects' the Treaty, at what point will it reflect the Treaty? What does it even mean for the constitution to reflect the Treaty?

You might expect other sources to be more precise. But a Cabinet background document on the constitution has a similar structure. It talks of 'various statutes with constitutional significance' being part of the constitution. It says that 'the sources of the New Zealand constitution *include*' certain elements (my emphasis), rather than saying what the New Zealand constitution is. The document does give examples of the statutes with constitutional significance – '(e.g., the Constitution Act, the Electoral Act, the Bill of Rights Act)' – but these are illustrations, not an exhaustive description.

So no one, myself included, really knows what is in our constitution. At best, we know what is at its core, but we don't know what is at the edges. And this highlights the first set of major benefits of a written constitution: clarity, certainty and accessibility. Setting out the constitution in one place would help people in and out of politics to be aware of the rules and principles governing the exercise of power. That knowledge would provide a stable footing for people getting on with their lives, allowing them to be more capable of challenging decisions that violate constitutional rules and principles. Such security could be particularly useful for Māori, given the past volatility of policy and politics affecting te ao Māori. For example, had there been a written constitution confirming the existence of Māori customary rights, including customary title, the Labour government might have been less willing to pass the Foreshore and Seabed Act in 2004. (That said, it is always difficult to speculate about how history might have turned out differently under varied circumstances.)

More substantively, a written constitution could help to prevent abuses of political power, if judges were given the power to invalidate legislation inconsistent with the constitution, as generally occurs where a written constitution is adopted.

New Zealand Parliament can currently pass legislation that violates the New Zealand Bill of Rights Act – which protects civil and political rights such as freedom of expression, the right to a fair trial and the right to be free from torture – with no recourse for victims of that rights violation. Parliament can pass such legislation even if it has been told by the attorney-general that the legislation breaches rights.[26]

Abuses of power can occur in other ways. The main mechanisms of accountability are internal parliamentary processes – parliamentary debate and select committees being the main examples – and elections every three years. But these are inadequate. Because New Zealand does not separate the executive from the legislature (unlike, say, the United States, which has an Administration constitutionally separated from Congress), the executive or government dominates parliamentary processes such as select committees. It is very rare that a government with a majority in the House, even a slender majority, has legislation rejected by Parliament as a whole. Even extensive criticism of legislation in select committee can result in minimal changes to legislation because of political imperatives. Finally, while it is possible for governments and MPs to be voted out every three years, most people vote on a package of issues (rather than on a single piece of legislation) and one vote every three years is an indirect and weak way of preventing unconstitutional legislation. Allowing a 'second look' at legislation by independent judges, with the time and expertise to review that legislation, ensures egregious legislation is not able to stand and discourages parliaments from passing it. Those consequences are especially important for Māori, who – over the course of New Zealand history, through laws like the Foreshore and Seabed Act 2004 – have been affected disproportionately by parliamentary abuses of power. Empowering judges to review legislation in this way is not undemocratic and may give judges less power than they have presently, as I suggest below.

A written constitution could also enhance New Zealand identities. This benefit is dependent on the process of constitution-making and the substance of the constitution, points I return to below, and it is the most speculative of the benefits discussed in this section. 'New Zealand identity' is also a concept that has been used in the past to undermine different minority groups and to assert dominant ideas of what it means to be a New Zealander, which is partly why I have referred to 'New Zealand identities'.[27] The logic behind a constitution being supportive of identities should be clear. At the moment in New Zealand, our national values, and the principles that should be benchmarks for judging exercise of public power, are up for grabs. Influential commentators can argue that we have a nation based on freedom, or a country concerned with equality, or a legal system founded on the rule of law. However, there remains a lot of fuzziness about what New Zealand's national values and principles are or ought to be. As long as we are fuzzy about our national values and principles, it is difficult to extend or deepen these principles. A written constitution, if properly developed (with decolonisation at its heart), could help to establish the norms that we want to govern society, culture and politics. Naturally, there will be disagreement about those norms. A written constitution provides a starting point for further conversations about shared norms, and it could be the basis for a modest measure of national pride and unity.

Four good questions are often raised about having a written constitution. Would it give judges too much power? Aren't we better off remaining flexible and allowing our constitution to adapt to changing social values? Could the making of the constitution prize some voices over others, leaving some perspectives permanently excluded? And what would be in the constitution?

Concerns about judicial power are understandable. Judges are unelected, although they are appointed by elected MPs and can be removed in the event of serious misconduct. But judges are already given significant responsibilities – which appears acceptable to the New Zealand public. They can make and develop the common law (i.e. 'judge-made law'). They make choices between possible interpretations of statutes, and review laws for consistency with the New Zealand Bill of Rights, in the process of which they can question whether alternative approaches could have been adopted by Parliament to achieve certain goals. A written constitution would give judges the power to have a second look at legislation, and to respond strongly where that legislation is unconstitutional. It would allow them to put a cross, rather than just a question mark, over legislation – and Parliament would still be able to pass legislation which would be more consistent with the constitution following a dialogue with the courts. This would be, arguably, merely an incremental extension of judges' existing powers, to the extent those powers are known.

The second, more counter-intuitive response is that the status quo should make us more worried about judicial power. In the absence of a written constitution, and any real clarity about what is in the constitution, judges are deciding what the constitution is for New Zealand, when this arises in particular cases. Judges also have the power to determine the scope of their own powers, arguably creating a conflict of interest. The orthodoxy is that Parliament is sovereign and that judges must uphold the laws of Parliament. But even that orthodoxy is ambiguous: some judges have asked whether laws that exceed the competence of Parliament are laws at all.[28]

In a law journal article, I argued that there are existing resources in New Zealand law that would allow judges to strike down legislation in certain cases, if they were of a mind to do so.[29] In another example of the ambiguity over the extent of judicial power, in 2015, a High Court judge, Justice Paul Heath, decided that judges have the power to declare laws inconsistent with the New Zealand Bill of Rights Act (to issue 'declarations of inconsistency'), after some confusion about whether judges had this declaratory power.[30] Overall, judicial power might be better clarified and legitimated through a nationwide consultative process determining the extent of what judges can do under a single written constitution. Judicial power could also be clearly circumscribed by the words of that written constitution. All in all, having a single written constitution might give greater confidence to those concerned about putting limits on judicial power.

The concern that a single written constitution might undermine flexibility is overblown and ignores the dangers of flexibility. Law-making is not completely flexible as it stands in New Zealand: laws have to be made in a way consistent with parliamentary processes and convention. Laws have to be passed within accepted parameters. The same would remain true with a written constitution – laws would have to be consistent with broad constitutional parameters – with the main difference being that those parameters would be clearer to all. There is a risk that a written constitution would cement particular legal positions, which might become outdated; to avoid this, careful thought would need to go into rules around constitutional amendment. Overall, this point about amending the constitution aside, to the extent that some flexibility will be lost, it may only be the flexibility for Parliament to pass laws inconsistent with human rights or key constitutional concepts – and is that a flexibility that we really want to be prizing?

What those constitutional parameters are depends on the content of a single written constitution and the process of constitution-making – and it is much more difficult to settle these points. Indeed, in some ways it would be inappropriate for me to lay down in advance in this book how the constitution should be developed, and what should be in the constitution. To do that might be seen as condescending. But is it possible to come up with principles for thinking through the issue? In 2015, I spoke with lawyer, academic and campaigner Moana Jackson about this.

Jackson invited me to his home in Naenae, in Lower Hutt, and greeted me warmly. He had just helped to complete the report of Matike Mai Aotearoa, a product of the Independent Working Group on Constitutional Transformation. This was a project that he had convened around the same time that the government (as part of the National Party and the Māori Party's 2011 confidence-and-supply agreement) had launched its Constitutional Review Panel. The project was Māori-led, having been first promoted at the Iwi Chairs' Forum in 2010, and resulted in 252 hui with Māori between 2012 and 2015 on the subject of constitutional transformation. It was chaired by Margaret Mutu, and a major role in the project had been played by a rangatahi (young people's) group, which organised 70 youth wānanga. Jackson was at pains to point out that while he helped to facilitate the project, it was a collaborative effort.

Drawing on the conversation with Jackson, the report of Matike Mai Aotearoa, and the government-led report arising out of the Constitutional Review Panel – and reviewing this material in light of the cornerstone values of this book and the idea of decolonisation – it is possible to sketch the principles that should frame what is in a future single written constitution.[31]

A written constitution should be reflective of Aotearoa New Zealand, said Jackson. 'A constitution has to belong here,' he insisted. The Constitutional Review Panel report mentions similar themes. In the discussion held as part of its constitutional conversation – and the panel received 5,259 submissions – people were 'keen to look for unique solutions to local issues', and sought a constitution that reflected a 'sense of belonging'.[32] This ethos is tied to community – one of my three Cs. Community requires not just a sense of solidarity and unity across different groups, but also proper representation. In the context of constitutions, the ethos suggests that a single written constitution should not just be another version of the UK constitution or an edited copy of a constitution from somewhere else. Work must be done to think through how Aotearoa New Zealand is different and how that might be captured in constitutional form.[33]

But how can a constitution reflect a New Zealand that is constantly changing? This question suggests a second principle for New Zealand's future constitution-making: the constitution should be shaped for the long term, and should be capable of accommodating diverse views and changing circumstances. One way to achieve this is to ensure that it is clearly grounded in durable values.

Moana Jackson elaborated on this in our conversation. More than half of the discussions he helped to coordinate (with Margaret Mutu) as part of the Matike Mai Aotearoa report revolved around 'governing values', and trying to ensure that a 'common base of understanding' exists beneath any specific constitutional model. This long-term outlook in constitutional drafting – using open-ended values that can be applied as circumstances change – respects the will of future generations. It is a good check that ensures the constitution will not become outdated. In this way the emphasis on the long term might be connected to another one of the three Cs: care. A commitment to an enduring constitution that is workable over a long period of time requires care in drafting, but also demonstrates care for all those living with that constitution.

Further, the constitution should be ambitious for the future of the country. The Matike Mai Aotearoa report speaks of 'constitutional transformation'. Another way to put the point is to say that a constitution should hope to set New Zealand in a direction that allows us all to be better and to aspire to be bigger. Discussions of constitutional change are often framed around whether there are problems to be patched up – parts of our constitution that are 'broke' or not 'broke', and ought to be fixed. But this makes constitutional change sound like a small-scale activity – like hammering in nails to fix the deck on a bach. Constitutional change should involve much more. It's not just about making sure some planks of wood are sturdy. It's about making an architectural decision about what kind of house we want to live in. As Moana Jackson has said, that requires considering the kawa (protocol) or values of that house or whare; it also requires reflection on the important structural features that allow that house or whare to fit its environment and last over time. It is a project that should be ambitious and imaginative; otherwise it represents a lost opportunity to improve how we all can live and be together as a community. This is consistent with the third of the three Cs: creativity. Constitution-making should reflect what people think, but if it is to honour what a constitution is, it should also be a creative and imaginative process.

Do these principles lead us in the direction of possible content for a constitution? The make-up of the New Zealand constitution is for the people to decide. But some ideas should be on the table, if we are to build a constitution that is reflective of this place, long-term in approach, and ambitious.

Whether the Treaty of Waitangi should be in the written constitution is controversial; it is New Zealand's founding document, but Moana Jackson's 252 hui on constitutional transformation suggested 'a pretty clear majority' of Māori are opposed to entrenching the Treaty. One possible compromise position is allowing the Treaty to sit behind the constitution, perhaps alongside the 1835 Declaration of Independence, with the constitution referring to values that can be seeded out of the Treaty. The Declaration of Independence was a document signed in 1835 by Māori chiefs constituted as 'the Confederation of United Tribes' and British representative James Busby, which underscored the chiefs' sovereign power in exchange for protection from the British. I have written elsewhere about how the English and Māori texts of the Treaty might seed numerous values, including peace and order, human rights, respect for property, the rule of law, good governance, self-determination, equality, deliberation and consensus.[34] These values could be expressed in the constitution, in addition to core tikanga values. Interestingly, some of the key tikanga values discussed in the Matike Mai Aotearoa report – such as the value of whakawhanaungatanga and community, the value of conciliation and the value of tikanga – overlap with the cornerstone progressive values discussed in Chapter 1.[35]

It will also be worth considering, in addition to an elaboration of the key political institutions in New Zealand (such as the executive, legislature and judiciary) and the incorporation of the New Zealand Bill of Rights Act 1990, whether economic, social, cultural and environmental rights should be included in the written constitution.

The government's Constitutional Review Panel report recommended setting up a process to explore in more detail adding economic, social and cultural rights to the New Zealand Bill of Rights Act, including environmental rights.[36] Geoffrey Palmer and Andrew Butler's proposed draft written constitution for New Zealand contains a right to education, and includes other social and economic rights as 'non-justiciable principles' (principles that cannot be enforced directly by the courts).[37] Judges have been capable of interpreting rights such as the right to education, housing and health care in other countries, including South Africa, and these rights would reflect the priorities of New Zealanders, and 'this land', in Moana Jackson's words.

Alongside these suggestions, options to consider should include new institutions, that depart from the UK's standard Westminster model. New Zealand is not the UK. We should not be frightened to at least think about institutions that go beyond the traditional tripartite separation. Could iwi be a fourth branch of government?[38] Are there ways that iwi sovereignty might be acknowledged or taken forward as part of this process?[39] Or does local government need distinct constitutional recognition? The constitutional position of local government was specifically referred to in the Constitutional Review Panel report.[40] The Matike Mai Aotearoa report also offers several models (although these models are expressly subservient to constitutional values or ethos) that propose an assembly of iwi and hapū, possibly alongside Parliament. It is suggested by Matike Mai Aotearoa that this iwi and hapū assembly could reflect Article Two of te Tiriti (with its protection of te tino rangatiratanga), with Parliament reflecting Article One (with its reference to kāwanatanga or government), and a further 'relational sphere' allowing interaction between the two spheres. Could another option (not mentioned in the Matike Mai Aotearoa report) be an elected executive to fulfil Treaty obligations, alongside a more diverse legislative assembly, perhaps including iwi and hapū, to hold the executive to account? The Treaty, after all, refers only to the government (kāwanatanga) or executive, and arguably leaves open what form the legislature should take. All of these proposals, regardless of how novel they sound, warrant serious consideration.

There is a need for sensitivity in the process that takes us from where we are now. It shouldn't be rushed. The Constitutional Review Panel's report indicated that there was not yet majority support in New Zealand for a written constitution that gives judges strike-down powers. It may be that with further education – such as through the civics, Treaty and citizenship education suggested in that report – views may change (though engagement with constitutional issues from Māori is already very strong).[41] Successive governments need to be committed to continuing the conversation, through innovative tools such as citizens' assemblies (where a representative sample of the broader population gathers to consider information and make recommendations on policy issues).

And throughout the process, it is important that Māori voices are given central weight. As Moana Jackson has said, there is a strong view – especially from Māori perspectives – that the current Parliament lacks legitimacy, because of the way power was assumed over time despite commitments in the Treaty. The legitimacy problem has not completely disappeared with Treaty settlements. The way forward, then, is for Māori to lead the constitutional conversation. If Māori, as the original people of this land, do not support moves for constitutional change, those moves cannot be pursued. The suggestion of a Māori Constitutional Convention in the Matike Mai Aotearoa report deserves support and further debate. The broader conversation must then draw in other key voices.

The end point of progressive constitutional change may appear unrealistic. But there is an 'ineffable hope in this land', in Jackson's words. I've seen it in the increasing number of young people engaging in debates about our constitutional future. I'm not saying that New Zealand should under all circumstances adopt a written constitution. What I have tried to say is that the debate needs to continue, led by Māori, and with a wider frame of ideas considered. Written constitutions matter. They provide backstop protections when things go wrong. They help to provide clarity on values and the protections that do exist in our laws. And they could help to structure and harness the ineffable hope to which Moana Jackson refers.

addressing inequality, realising rangatiratanga

New Zealand is becoming a two-track society, where on average Māori have worse outcomes than non-Māori. To take a few examples: Māori comprise 51 per cent of the prison population, while numbering only 15 per cent of the population overall.[42] The infant mortality rate for Māori is 7 per 1,000 births, compared to 5.5 per 1,000 births for non-Māori (and non-Pasifika) individuals.[43] In 2012, Māori unemployment was approaching 15 per cent, whereas it was around 5.5 per cent for the non-Māori population.[44] In 2013, 20 per cent of Māori were on income-tested benefits, compared to 6.2 per cent of non-Māori (and non-Pasifika).[45]

Care should be taken with these statistics. They can hide wide variation within groups. Statistics comparing Māori and Pākehā can suggest wrongly that it is Pākehā standards that Māori should be measuring up to, as Mikaere has cautioned. And they can create a false, simplistic deficit-based picture of Māori people. What these statistics do broadly illustrate, however, is apparent systemic neglect of inequalities between Māori and non-Māori. These figures should reflect badly on the government, not on Māori. We should not resile from criticising the government for this neglect.

That point is reinforced by the fact that many of these inequalities have worsened over time. Although across some indicators, including participation in tertiary education, the gap in outcomes between Māori and non-Māori is narrowing,[46] Lisa Marriott, an associate professor of taxation, and Dalice Sim, a statistical consultant – both at Victoria University in Wellington – noted in their 2014 research that 'the majority of indicators suggest worsening outcomes for Māori ... in the form of increasing gaps in indicators when compared to the European population'. The authors add that 'significant inequality not only remains in New Zealand, but is also escalating as measured by growing gaps in many inequality indicators'.[47] They point out that data are also limited – there are no 'multiagency attempts to monitor progress of these social measures.' Their conclusion: 'New Zealand's strategy to address inequality as it relates to Māori and Pacific people has not been successful, [and it] warrants greater government attention if the gaps are not to continue increasing into the future.'[48]

It is a common claim in political debate that the gaps between Māori and non-Māori are to do with poverty, not ethnicity or history, and that it is therefore misleading to view statistics through the lens of ethnicity. Using these statistics suggests an incorrect narrative, some say, and will lead to the wrong policy solutions. The problem is need, not race, to put the contrast in other terms. This overlooks decades of historical injustices faced specifically by Māori. It also ignores the contemporary prejudice faced by Māori in the media, in casual conversation and elsewhere. Ethnicity matters in modern New Zealand (even if some people would like it to matter less, and even if there is nothing biologically essential about race or ethnicity). Policy responses should acknowledge this.

Others might say that even if there is a problem in correlations between ethnicity and outcome, policy tailored to Māori is not the answer. But the

New Zealand government has a duty of reparation. Moreover, as Marriott and Sim point out, redistribution based on need (and use of the tax and transfer system) has not worked in addressing ethnic inequalities. As well, New Zealand law and policy has many examples – women's hospitals in the field of health, for instance – where approaches vary based on a group's distinguishing circumstances. Tailoring policy to address particular outcomes for particular groups is a normal part of the policy-making process.

So what should politicians and policy-makers do to address glaring inequalities? Elsewhere, I have mentioned some of the steps that might be taken: for example, I mention the Māori economy in Chapter 4, I refer in Chapter 6 to concerted action on rheumatic fever, and Chapter 7 proposes an alternative approach to imprisonment that might have beneficial outcomes for Māori offenders. In some instances, these specific policy measures are what is needed. For example, in the sphere of imprisonment (the subject of a Waitangi Tribunal claim at the time this book was being written), a provision like section 718(2)(e) of the Canadian Criminal Code might be adapted to the New Zealand context; the Canadian provision notes that 'all available sanctions other than imprisonment that are reasonable in the circumstances should be considered, with particular attention to the circumstances of aboriginal offenders'. The Canadian Supreme Court has interpreted this provision as a 'direction to members of the judiciary to inquire into the causes of the problem' of indigenous over-representation in the Canadian justice system, 'and to endeavour to remedy [the problem], to the extent that a remedy is possible through the sentencing process'.[49] This statutory amendment, if tailored to New Zealand (with a reference to 'indigenous' as opposed to 'aboriginal' offenders) could provide one way to address Māori over-representation in prisons.

In addition to specific policy measures, changes are needed to the structure of political leadership to ensure there is commitment to preventing the emergence of a two-track society in Aotearoa New Zealand. This is where decolonisation can really take effect. Real mana must be given to ministers of Māori development so that, for example, they are ranked among the top three ministers and meet regularly with the prime minister. That minister must be given significant resources and a broad remit. (Changing the name of the minister to the minister of Māori affairs, and altering the name of Te Puni Kōkiri accordingly, is a cosmetic move but would be a symbolic indication that Māori policy needs to go far beyond economic development.) A special unit could be set up within the prime minister's office, as existed for a time during Helen Clark's time as premier, to address the different outcomes experienced by Māori and non-Māori. Significant efforts must go into the recruitment of Māori in courts, politics and public service.

Action in this area cannot be led by government alone. The government has a duty to address inequalities in this sphere, since past government action has been a contributing cause of the problem. However, there is a danger that well-intentioned government action may come to be seen as illegitimate in future. Māori groups – including iwi and hapū – must be supported by the government, as part of a process of decolonisation, to decide how inequalities in outcomes are addressed.

Māori are a diverse group. But Māori are more likely – because of connections to iwi or more informal links – to understand the position of those Māori that have fared less well in spheres such as employment and health. Māori are more likely to have faced the ongoing reality of institutional racism. This heightened awareness of the position of the marginalised, and the experience of prejudice provides an important basis for addressing inequalities. It should also be underscored that the Crown undertook in the Treaty of Waitangi/te Tiriti to give Māori space to protect and promote their own interests. Article Two of te Tiriti guaranteed to 'rangatira', 'hapu', and 'tangata katoa o Nu Tirani' [all people of New Zealand] 'te tino rangatiratanga' – the fullest extent of chieftainship – over their 'wenua' [whenua, land], 'kainga' [villages], and all their 'taonga' [treasures]. (The Māori version of the Treaty is to be preferred, according to presumptions under international law and on the grounds that it was this version with which many rangatira were presented.)[50] It is not a stretch to claim that the welfare of Māori people is a taonga, and that fully fledged powers of chieftainship require Māori to have the ability to steer policy on their affairs. In short, it is a Treaty duty incumbent upon the Crown and a Treaty right for Māori to be given space and support to direct policy to address inequalities between Māori and non-Māori.

This means several things in the short term at least. First, the Whānau Ora model of family-focused, Māori-led, community-centred approaches to social policy might be extended to other relevant areas of policy. There has been some criticism of Whānau Ora. But it is a relatively new initiative, and it is not clear that its alleged weaknesses run deep. It is even less clear that its weaknesses outweigh its benefits.

Second, iwi, hapū and urban Māori authorities need to be sufficiently resourced so that they are able to lead. In particular, iwi and hapū should be given assistance so that they can help Māori lacking knowledge of their family background to trace their whakapapa. According to the 2013 census, around 110,000 Māori – out of a total of 598,000 in the broader population – do not know their iwi.[51] While some iwi and hapū have stronger records than others, a major challenge (something mentioned to me by Māori friends and colleagues) is to gather together individuals with iwi and hapū connections who might be scattered around the country or abroad, especially in Australia. It would seem appropriate for the government to provide further funding for this task, since reimmersion in Māori culture will give many individuals a sense of security and belonging that will enable beneficial participation in society. That funding should also be available to urban Māori authorities, if they would like to use it. Such an attempt to link Māori back to iwi and hapū is nothing new. And Māori political action can occur without government resourcing. But a public commitment to this initiative could be redoubled.

Third, government should be willing to support iwi projects to address Māori policy challenges, such as Ngāti Kahungunu's proposed alternative approach to imprisonment discussed in the Matike Mai Aotearoa report. Government must, as far as possible, avoid restricting or supervising such projects, if it is to be truly committed to tino rangatiratanga. Where Māori cultural programmes are being delivered by government, it is also crucial that Māori are given the flexibility to determine the content and approach of these programmes. Riki Mihaere's research on the individualisation of Māori cultural programmes in prisons is a reminder of the risks involved in this field: it demonstrates that when delivered in an individualised manner, Māori culture can be distorted.[52] Partnerships and co-management of resources between iwi and government may be appropriate – seemingly successful co-management arrangements have been set up in relation to freshwater lakes in Rotorua, and the Waikato River – but caution needs to be exercised by government, since the co-management of natural resources and other taonga falls short of respect for rangatiratanga under Article 2 of the Treaty of Waitangi.[53]

Fourth, iwi and hapū and other Māori community groups must be given room and assistance to represent their own stories. This is occurring in part already through Treaty settlements.[54] Aroha Harris has asked, 'What will it take for our history writing to become not only the nation's reading but also the nation's memory?' She adds: 'What will it take to have our key messages about the past occur in every day lives and events?'[55] While it is for Māori to decide how these messages are communicated – online, through documentaries or writing – it may be that the government should also be willing to reflect on how public symbols and public holidays might reflect Māori narratives and Māori figures. Rachel Buchanan has suggested that statues of figures such as Te Whiti-o-Rongomai (one of the leaders of Parihaka's peace movement, discussed in Chapter 4) could be added to the statues of Pākehā – like Edward Gibbon Wakefield or Richard Seddon – that hold pride of place in Wellington and elsewhere.[56] Symbols matter. They say something about a community's values and aspirations. And they help to ensure, as Aroha Harris has said, that 'key messages about the past occur in everyday lives and events'.

In addition to these short-term measures, which are more easy to implement, tino rangatiratanga requires that serious thought be given to new institutional forms such as an iwi and hapū assembly – already discussed above – to give constitutional expression to Articles One and Two of the Treaty. In all of these endeavours, the government needs to be prepared not to lead, but to listen.

This is what a 'post-Treaty settlement era' might look like. A journey towards a Treaty-centred constitution. A government committed to adopting policy and changing political structures to address inequalities between Māori and non-Māori. Iwi, hapū, and Māori more generally being given support and space to address Māori policy. A continuing commitment to Treaty relationships and redressing imbalances in power, rather than an attempt to move on. Too often the phrase 'post-Treaty settlement era' seems to be used to mean 'post-Treaty era' by those who see the Treaty as an inconvenience.

Moana Jackson summed up the challenge of addressing power and persistent inequalities in our conversation when he told me: 'Treaties don't get "settled". They get honoured. You can't honour the Treaty until colonisation is "settled". You can't "settle" colonisation with money and an apology. [And] you can only "settle" colonisation by doing something about the power that the colonisers took.'

integrating te reo māori more fully into the national curriculum
One might think at this point that no government would ever be brave enough to take such far-reaching steps to addressing inequalities – these ideas seem unrealistic. A couple of responses are available.

First, we should all expect more from governments. We need to expand our ideas about what is 'realistic'. When we say something is 'politically unrealistic', we do not mean that a proposal is physically impossible to achieve. We mean something different from saying it's unrealistic for somebody to climb Mt Everest. We mean, instead, that a proposal does not seem to have a real chance of being implemented, because of what we know about politics. But we can change what we think has a real chance of being implemented. As citizens we have the power to decide what is 'realistic' when we choose how we react to policy announcements and when we choose how to vote. We can reward political parties that offer more imaginative ideas and be more open to visionary suggestions – if we decide that imagination and vision are values we want in our political sphere.

Second, of course it is true (as I try to show elsewhere) that ambitious policy change must be preceded and accompanied by a shift in underlying attitudes, values and culture. A proposal can seem unrealistic, but can be made more realistic by the build-up of a groundswell of support for particular attitudes or values. In the field of race relations and policy on Māori affairs, I would suggest that an idea supported by then National Party trade minister Tim Groser in 2012 might help pave the way for more ambitious policy change: namely, extending the teaching of te reo Māori as part of the national curriculum for all New Zealanders. There are diverse views within the Māori community on this proposal, as there are on any political issue. My view is that comprehensive teaching of te reo Māori in schools – which improves pronunciation, and knowledge of Māori concepts, proverbs and thought – could lay the foundations for a commitment to improved Māori policy. It should also reduce narrow-minded stigma and basic misunderstandings about te ao Māori, or the Māori world.

Before describing the benefits of expanded te reo Māori, it is important to set out the context of existing te reo Māori provision in New Zealand schools. Te reo Māori has a slightly uncertain place in the New Zealand curriculum at present. The country's official languages, which also include sign language, are discussed in the curriculum, with the suggestion being that they have a special place; and 'learning languages' is one of eight key learning areas, yet there is no specific reference to Māori. The Treaty of Waitangi, alongside inclusion and cultural diversity, is a core principle of the curriculum, but this does not necessitate teaching of the language. What I suggest here is that the teaching of te reo Māori becomes a key learning area, in addition to other areas such as English, the arts and technology. This could require schools to include the language at primary, intermediate and early secondary level (up until Year 10), but would leave schools significant discretion to determine how te reo Māori would be delivered, subject to minimum quality standards. Often this debate is couched in terms of making te reo Māori 'compulsory'. But public education involves a curriculum that is required to be taught to all students. A better way of phrasing the question is whether te reo Māori should be a part of the curriculum, which is a guide for all public schools in New Zealand.

There are many reasons why te reo Māori should be given this pride of place in the national curriculum, which can be drawn from the history of efforts to improve the speaking of the reo, the Waitangi Tribunal's 1986 report on te reo Māori, the Tribunal's 2011 Wai 262 report on broader aspects of Māori culture (including te reo), and public debate about te reo Māori in recent years.

Teaching te reo Māori in a more thorough way, from Years 1–10, would reduce the gap between the rhetoric of Māori being an official language (enshrined in 1987 in the Māori Language Act) and the reality. An 'official' language should not just be a language that is accepted when it is spoken; it should be a language that is encouraged and promoted. Existing promotion is positive, but does not go far enough.

A stronger teaching of te reo Māori avoids self-satisfied tokenism. One of the Waitangi Tribunal claimants said in the hearings for its 1986 report that it is 'intolerable that a Maori should be treated like a mascot'.[57] The same holds true today. Sometimes te reo Māori can appear to be a mascot when used in an insincere or inappropriate way. Having more New Zealanders capable of speaking te reo Māori competently will ensure that the language is given respect, and is not just treated as a souvenir or feel-good badge.

Learning te reo Māori would be valuable for the learning of other languages. Language-learning is more limited in New Zealand schools than in many European countries. The learning of one second language makes it easier to learn more languages, thereby enriching language-learning culture. This could make New Zealanders more amenable to learning languages such as Indonesian or Chinese, assuming they do not already speak these languages, which could be fruitful for economic opportunities. Former National Party politician Tim Groser, academic and public intellectual Ranginui Walker and Race Relations Commissioner Susan Devoy have made similar points. Walker noted that people who are inducted into bilingualism in early childhood 'have an intuitive understanding of languages and they have no problem learning a third and fourth language'.[58] Devoy has said being bilingual (which would require strong immersion in Māori) would give New Zealanders 'a real added advantage'.[59]

Te reo Māori is a unique part of New Zealand, too. As noted in the tribunal's 1986 report, '[w]ithout the language this new dimension of life from which New Zealand as a whole may profit would be lost on us'.[60] Uniqueness alone is not a reason to hold on to anything. But te reo Māori grounds Aotearoa New Zealand in the Pacific, and creates a positive bridge between the present and the past. The 2011 Wai 262 report made this point: 'As we become an increasingly diverse society, how will our shared values and nationhood be expressed and celebrated? We cannot know for certain, but it is quite possible that our greater heterogeneity will mean we rely more and more upon Māori culture to mark our unique place in the world and give us a common bond of identity.'[61] The report expressed a 'deep fear for the survival of te reo',[62] recording that language use among Māori is increasing at a rate slower than population growth of Māori.[63] It also noted David Williams's account of how much te reo Māori has declined historically: 90 per cent of Māori spoke te reo in 1913, just 55 per cent in 1950, and a mere 5 per cent in 1975.[64]

The argument that te reo Māori is not useful in a modern society was addressed fully in the Waitangi Tribunal's 1986 report, and does not need to be amplified again here. The argument trades on damaging stereotypes of Māori as a primitive language, when it is clear that Māori may be useful in today's world as a medium of cross-cultural contact and, if we are to turn to economic arguments, as a way to engage with the burgeoning Māori economy. Revitalising te reo Māori might spur more people to develop an interest in Māori literature, which is distinctive to this country.[65]

I have already said that Pākehā cultural understanding will be improved by understanding of te reo Māori. But there is a crucial connection between language and culture for Māori, too. The 1986 Tribunal report talked of the 'loss of mana' and 'humiliation' felt by Māori when they could not speak te reo Māori on the marae. When these feelings are experienced, 'it is natural and understandable that [individuals not speaking te reo] should seek to put the blame for their deficiency on someone or something other than themselves', including the education system. Teaching te reo Māori through years 1–10 can begin to address this loss of mana, and bring some Māori back to their cultural ancestry, which can improve a sense of belonging and security. A wider social benefit – in terms of heightened social inclusion and participation – might follow from this.

The government has some responsibility for loss of mana felt by Māori. At the very least, it has approached the language with 'benign neglect' in the past; in some cases it has actively suppressed the language, too.[66] The 2011 Waitangi Tribunal Report expressed 'deep unease' about the government's response to the growth in Māori language speaking in the 1980s and 1990s. The government did not do enough to support the emergence of kōhanga reo (preschool Māori language nests) and kura kaupapa (Māori immersion primary schools), according to the Tribunal.[67] These failings give rise to a reparative duty on the government to address the wrongs it perpetuated in the past. That has been effectively acknowledged in section 6 of Te Ture mō Te Reo Māori 2016 (New Zealand's first fully bilingual piece of substantive legislation).

Three further reasons relate to Māori campaigns, other cultural progress and quasi-legal obligations. Māori have long pushed for te reo Māori to be taught in schools; a 1972 petition led by Hana Jackson called for this change. Teaching te reo Māori more wholeheartedly across the national curriculum would at least partially address these strong demands. Advances have been made by government in other support for Māoritanga in recent years: the creation of Māori Television and funding for Māori radio are examples of this. It could be said that the benefits of these cultural investments cannot be fully realised – viewer and listener numbers cannot be seriously boosted – until there is a corresponding commitment to investment in te reo Māori. Māmari Stephens has written about how non-Māori learning te reo helped her to have more conversations in te reo; this argument could be extended to claim that having a larger group of non-Māori and Māori speaking te reo in future (through te reo Māori learning in all schools) will ensure that the language is used and practised more regularly.[68] And integrating the language into all schools from Years 1–10 helps to discharge quasi-legal obligations. The Privy Council said that, in light of 'the vulnerable state' of te reo Māori, 'especially vigorous action' should be taken for its protection.[69] The 2011 Waitangi Tribunal Report said that there was an 'urgent need to reinvigorate the Māori language sector'.[70] Neither of these legal statements is binding or specific about the need for te reo to be taught in all New Zealand schools; indeed, it is worth noting that the 1986 Waitangi Tribunal report declined to make such a recommendation. These are statements made by legal bodies, but they do not make action mandatory. Nevertheless these bodies have used muscular language to recommend far-reaching action, and incorporating te reo Māori into the national curriculum would seem to satisfy these recommendations.

Finally, there is a sense of arbitrariness currently in how well people speak Māori when they leave primary or secondary school. I was lucky to go to a school that treasured Māori; that gave me an interest in the reo, which I have pursued. Other schools have voluntarily pushed for further te reo teaching, including King's College in Auckland. But if the learning of te reo Māori gives individuals a cultural, and possible economic, advantage, should we really make fluency dependent on where that person's parents live or the whims of the local school – factors outside of that individual's control? The teaching of te reo Māori across schools can ensure greater consistency, and reduce the arbitrariness that currently exists.

It is for governments and Māori to decide on the detail of any roll-out of te reo Māori. But in this book's practical spirit, and given that one of the major objections to compulsory te reo Māori is practical – how could enough teachers be provided and how could teaching be done well? – it is useful to look at how the idea could be realised.

The implementation of the idea can learn some lessons from the experience of Wales, which decided in 1988 (through the Education Reform Act) to make the Welsh language compulsory in schools. This came after years of declining language use. In 1990, within two years, schools were required to teach Welsh from Key Stages 1–3 (from ages 5–14), with Welsh being made compulsory at Key Stage 4 (for ages 15–16) in 1999.[71] The move has appeared to stall the steep decline in the speaking of Welsh, and while there have been significant voices in opposition (and some misleading reporting), by 2015, 58 per cent supported some form of compulsory Welsh, at least through primary school.[72] Fewer Welsh people say they speak no Welsh, and the number of young children speaking Welsh had increased by 2011.[73]

Drawing on this experience, and suggestions made in policy documents and public debate in New Zealand, it seems appropriate that implementation of this idea should be phased in, with clear explanations given of the rationales of the move and its benefits for all.

What kind of phase-in period is needed? To get to a position where te reo Māori is taught in all schools, teacher training will need to be changed at all major New Zealand universities so that all teachers have minimal te reo literacy – and with special focus placed on those who are seeking to become te reo Māori teachers. Further scholarships could be funded for these teachers. Teaching resources will need to be improved. Importantly, iwi and hapū ought to be engaged (on their terms), since iwi and hapū can lead and support the teaching of te reo Māori in most regions. A valuable by-product may be closer relationships between schools and local iwi and hapū.

All of this requires time. A government could announce that te reo Māori will begin to be fully integrated, say, six years from any initial decision. The six-year period allows for new teachers to be recruited, curricula ideas to be honed, and iwi and hapū to prepare. As occurred in Wales, the introduction could happen in two waves, with te reo Māori being taught in Years 1–5 six years after an initial decision, through Years 1–10 nine years after the initial decision. This further three years for more senior students acknowledges that it may take more time to train te reo Māori teachers at a higher level of proficiency. The overall nine-year phase-in process is akin to the eleven-year period in Wales.

The move will require government support, including through Te Mātāwai, the statutory entity set up in 2016 to promote the health of the Māori language. Increased funding will be required to fund new teachers. Further funding could be given to Māori immersion schools. The task will be easier if that funding is combined with other forms of support. (Such funding might be able to diminish over time: as more children grow up learning te reo, they will also become the next generation of teachers and will require less additional training.)[74] If the government continues the conversation about the future of the constitution, and the role of Māori values within that conversation, and also takes some measures towards addressing inequalities between Māori and non-Māori, it seems more likely that prospective Māori teachers will see learning Māori as a decision for the future. Having leading politicians who speak Māori will also help to set an example of the importance of te reo Māori. In nineteenth-century New Zealand, leading judges and politicians – such as Chief Justice William Martin and Governor George Grey – spoke Māori. That is less common now. The government must also articulate the widespread benefits and work actively to counter misconceptions.

With a well-considered phase-in process, proper resourcing and other support, it seems plausible that sufficient teachers will be recruited. As Willie

Jackson has said: 'For many years we haven't been able to find enough teachers to roll out te reo competently in mainstream schools and in fact that will be the case for the next 100 years if we don't make the language compulsory. If it's made compulsory then the government will prioritise it and the necessary resources will be made available so that we can train and find the teachers who can roll out te reo Māori programmes.'[75]

The overall funding commitment needed is difficult to estimate. It is likely that some of the investment will pay for itself, since improved te reo Māori in young people may reduce the costs incurred from welfare issues, suspensions and exclusions; the Waitangi Tribunal has hinted at this in noting that Māori-medium schools produce much 'lower levels of truancy, suspensions and unjustified absences' relative to Māori in mainstream education. Moreover, funding may be able to taper off over time, as an increase in individuals speaking Māori through their school training will lessen the need for scholarships and incentives for people to learn it later in life.

Along with all this, it is important that the public sector maintains accurate statistics about the use of te reo Māori. The Wai 262 report suggests that some statistics may lack accuracy and may be designed to reflect well on the public sector.[76] It may be that clear targets, such as those contained in the existing Māori Language Strategy, will aid in holding the government to account. However, as the Wai 262 report noted, these targets must be carefully calibrated so that they do not simply reflect the existing position of the Māori language.[77]

future migration

How do recent immigrants fit into this vision?

There is a theoretical concern that recent immigrants, such as those from Asia, are threatened by talk of biculturalism. Biculturalism usually is taken to mean Māori and Pākehā, with Pākehā often used interchangeably with 'European New Zealander'. Non-European New Zealanders, or non-European recent immigrants, are therefore left wondering what room is left for them in this model.

This concern loses some of its force once we have reviewed the text of the Treaty/te Tiriti and the meaning of the term 'Pākehā'. The Treaty does not necessarily create a special relationship between Māori and European New Zealanders. Te Tiriti, the Māori text, gives government to the Queen, protects the chieftainship of Māori (referred to in Article Two as the people of New Zealand, 'nga tangata katoa o Nu Tirani'), and then notes that the Queen will protect 'all the ordinary people of New Zealand' (a reference that seems to be to Māori, if we are to be consistent with Article Two, but which could apply to others) in the same ways as British subjects are protected. The rights and duties of citizenship of British people (or English people, to use the language of te Tiriti) provide the standard for citizenship in New Zealand, but there is no further special notion of European-ness. The English version of the Treaty, which should be given less weight, mentions 'rapid extension of Emigration from both Europe and Australia' in the preamble; but no great weight should be placed on this contextual description of what was occurring at the time of the signing of the Treaty. The English version does speak of the native population and the Queen's subjects in the preamble, but this does not seem to exhaust the scope of the Treaty.

Further, the word 'Pākehā' is of uncertain linguistic origins. It is not clear that it should be limited to referring to those of 'European background'. 'Pākehā' seems to have originally referred either to gods of fish with the form of fish and humans (Paakehaakeha) or mythical beings with fair skin and hair (Pakepakeha).[78] The latter definition might encourage a fair-skinned limitation to the meaning of Pākehā. But there is debate about the etymological root of the word, and at any rate, the word does not necessarily need to be shackled to its original use or meaning. Language is fluid. It changes over time. A further reason to avoid defining Pākehā as 'European background' or 'fair-skinned' is that these terms are difficult, if not impossible, to apply: European background comprises various ethnic or identity groups, and 'fair-skinned' is hopelessly vague. The more attractive view of Pākehā is that Pākehā means non-Māori New Zealander.[79] Viewed this way, Pākehā could encompass Asian immigrants and other recent arrivals who seek to identify as New Zealanders. Bicultural-ism can be seen as a basis for multiculturalism, since biculturalism refers to Māori and Pākehā – with the latter being a compound term for multiple other cultural groups.

Governments would do well to clarify this understanding. The Treaty might also be cited as the basis for the protection of recent immigrants: in its time, the Treaty guaranteed recent immigrants the standard of protection given to British subjects – and that same standard of protection should be seen to continue over time.

These imaginative restatements of the meaning of 'Pākehā' are consistent with the progressive values of care, creativity and community (defined inclusively). They may also provide further security to immigrants, particularly those who in recent decades have been the subject of scaremongering and stereotyping by the National, Labour and New Zealand First parties. The Labour Party's 2015 efforts to stir up debate about the legitimate issue of foreign ownership of housing were a further example of this. The party used Asian-sounding surnames as a proxy for foreign ownership, but in the process made inaccurate assumptions and entrenched the notion that Asian immigrants constituted a threat to other New Zealanders.

That action was widely criticised – and such prejudice has no place in New Zealand politics. Politicians do not advance the values of care or inclusive community when they offer mean-spirited, narrow-minded attacks on immigrants. Politicians are also ignoring the major benefits brought generally by both low-skilled and high-skilled immigrants (to the extent that the distinction carries any weight). While it is difficult to generalise, research on immigrants reveals that, because of the effort required, immigrants tend to be more entrepreneurial on average, and are networked to other places.[80] And rarely is the notion of immigrants 'stealing jobs' accurate; in most cases immigrants bring resources and spending into an economy, thereby boosting aggregate demand and overall consumption and growth.

Political parties should consider in future a bipartisan commitment to relatively open immigration policies and rhetoric, across the political spectrum. Bipartisan commitments have been given in the past on the likes of New Zealand's nuclear-free status. A commitment of this kind would involve an agreement not to scaremonger about immigrants, an undertaking to err on the side of keeping borders open, a willingness to speak out when other countries such as Australia take part in scaremongering, and a consistent and generous approach to refugees. (At the time of writing, New Zealand's intention to take 1,000 refugees annually could not be described as generous, especially in light of the number of refugees per capita taken by other countries.) The bipartisan commitment to relatively open immigration would be grounded in the Treaty/te Tiriti and the expansive notion of what it means to be Pākehā.

decolonisation and the pacific

New Zealand is closely connected, geographically and culturally, to countries in the Pacific. Moreover, just as the New Zealand government has a reparative duty in relation to te reo Māori because of past wrongs, so too the government has a reparative duty towards Pasifika people because of its perpetration of past wrongs: in particular, its role in the dawn raids on alleged overstayers in the 1970s, which spread stigma and undermined Pasifika families. Some form of reparative duty was perhaps acknowledged when Helen Clark apologised to Samoa for historical injustices in 2002.[81] The government needs a concerted effort, akin to the effort to redress inequalities between Māori and others, to address Pasifika outcomes in health, education and other fields. Alongside these measures, support by government (through arts funding, for example) of Pasifika stories is necessary, just as the government should amplify Māori voices and symbols.

I spoke to Pala Molisa in Paramount Cinema's café in Wellington in early 2016 about education, inequality and Pasifika issues. Molisa is an academic at Victoria University of Wellington. But he is not a typical academic: he works on critical accounting studies, and while completing his PhD he competed for Vanuatu in the 2010 Commonwealth Games.

In our conversation, Molisa emphasised the importance of Pasifika stories within New Zealand culture. 'One of the ways [this society] keeps the structural inequalities between white people … and Māori and other non-white indigenous Pasifika peoples is by making sure our voices and our histories and our identities are completely written out of the mainstream.' Molisa said, 'The struggle now is to look for ways of bringing in these Pacific histories.' He focused on the connections between Māori and Pasifika people. 'Māori are part of the Pacific,' he averred. 'Aotearoa is part of the Pacific. But one of the things colonial culture has done is to break a lot of those links, to the point where a lot of Maori and Pacific Islanders – we don't look at each other as brothers and sisters. But we are. There's a shared whakapapa there.'

Molisa spoke about the value of sport and the arts as a bridge between Pasifika peoples and other communities, including Māori. It is clear that the media has a role to play, too, in avoiding stereotypical depictions of Pasifika. The documentary *Dawn Raids* highlights the influence the media had (particularly through cartoons) in encouraging fear and mistrust of the Pasifika community in the lead-up to the dawn raids in the 1970s.[82] Ensuring a greater number of Pasifika media voices would be one way to acknowledge the diversity of experiences of Pasifika peoples in New Zealand.

Molisa encouraged me, rightly, to think of the experiences of Pasifika peoples, Māori, and others in structural terms. In other words: the topics discussed in this chapter are not isolated wrongs or mistakes that are merely the result of particular bad governments or individuals. They are a product of patterns of thinking about ethnicity, and the inferiority of certain ethnic groups, that have persisted over New Zealand history, a structural and institutional racism originating in colonialism. 'This is still a colonial, colonising settler culture,' he told me.

Some of the proposals offered in this chapter – including the comprehensive teaching of te reo Māori in schools, and the creation of space and support for iwi and hapū to realise tino rangatiratanga – address this culture and the decolonisation of state and society. But what is also required is an honest conversation about the dynamics between ethnic groups in Aotearoa New Zealand. Those in New Zealand who have not been a victim of racism or prejudice need to strive, humbly, to understand the position of others who have experience of racism or prejudice, and to listen to experiences that they have not had. They then need to work to redistribute power to prevent those experiences from recurring.

conclusion

Some of the ideas in this chapter require imagination: for example, the idea of an iwi and hapū assembly alongside Parliament (taken from the report of the Matike Mai Aotearoa Independent Working Group on Constitutional Transformation). Partly they require imagination because the frame for political debate in New Zealand is so narrow. But the ideas are also imaginative because they are drawn from creative thinkers and sources – and because they have to be this way to respond to the scale of the challenges in the field of race relations.

Moana Jackson quietly reminded me as we talked that summer afternoon in Naenae of why imagination in politics is so important.

He asked me if I remembered the 2011 election. I nodded. 'I remember Peter Dunne [the United Future Party leader] being interviewed. He was asked, "What's your vision?" And he said: "I'm not into visions."' Moana smiled. 'I thought: *what a pathetically sad response*. Because if politicians don't have vision, who will?

'You know,' he continued, 'they have this saying that politics is the art of the possible. Well, unless it's also about the art of what might seem not possible at the moment, then it's not a visionary politics.' Perhaps this is what is needed, then, in the field of biculturalism and decolonisation: a little tentativeness, a bit of humility, but also an openness to vision, and a willingness to see politics as 'the art of what might not seem possible at the moment'.

6 social infrastructure: health, education and housing

Health care, education and housing are 'social infrastructure', in the words of Philippa Howden-Chapman, a professor of public health at the University of Otago whom I interviewed. Just as roads and bridges and ports form the infrastructure that underpins our economy, so too health care, education, and housing form the infrastructure that underpins our society. When we have a healthy body and mind, support for the development of learning and skills, and a roof over our heads, we can be secure enough to build bonds with workmates, neighbours and others in the community. When we have good quality health care, education and housing, we can also develop skills and make ourselves useful to the community.

It is easy to take for granted publicly funded health care, free primary and secondary education and state housing for those that need it. But each of these interlocking parts of New Zealand's social infrastructure was an achievement built through hard thinking, effort and political courage. As well, aspects of this social infrastructure – in particular, publicly funded health care and state housing – have been threatened since the 1980s. Experiments with privatisation of health care began in the 1980s, and parts of the state housing stock were privatised by the National-led government from 2014.

In this context, it is helpful to return to the principles that should undergird health care, education and housing. To ensure that social infrastructure continues to serve its functions, we should think creatively about specific improvements that could be made to the provision of these goods and services. This chapter highlights select issues in health, education and housing that require the attention of politicians and policy-makers. It draws on interviews with a socially committed doctor, a prominent ex-principal and others. It discusses rheumatic fever, school zoning and homelessness. I focus, finally, on how whether 'contracting out' bolsters or weakens our social infrastructure, and how a more entrepreneurial state in social policy could be the way forward. It isn't possible to address all policy priorities in the fields of health care, education and housing. I have chosen ones that are a microcosm of broader challenges within social infrastructure, and policy areas that have been neglected.

principles for social infrastructure

In addition to the recurrent principles of care, community and creativity, there are three considerations that should underpin how governments approach health care, education and housing.

If governments are truly committed to public provision of these things, they should focus on comprehensive provision. This means something slightly different in each area. But if governments believe that all New Zealanders deserve high-quality public health care, education and housing, then fairness requires that they work hard to address inequalities in health care, education and housing outcomes. Comprehensive public provision also requires that government identifies and attempts to remove hidden costs where it has claimed that it is providing these services for free. These costs undermine public provision, but also make it more likely that provision is not comprehensive, since New Zealanders with lower incomes will find it harder to pay for hidden costs.

Across health care, education and housing, public provision must strike a balance between central government oversight and community devolution through local government. Communities often have knowledge of local needs in these spheres, and community support in providing this social infrastructure can build bonds between people. On the other hand, central government oversight allows for information to be collated and economies of scale to be harnessed. Politicians and policy-makers should have regard to the value of both forms of provision of social infrastructure. As well, politicians and policy-makers should be aware of the multiple levels of provision that are possible. It is not a simple choice between centralised administration in Wellington and provision at the level of local government. Regional oversight is used in the health care system, and community provision 'beneath' local government is also common in the housing sector.

Further, there is a need for the connections and overlaps between these policy areas to be identified. Poor housing can have an impact on health. Inadequate health care can affect a child's education. Difficult experiences in education can create or worsen health problems, including mental health problems. These are just a few examples of the interrelationships between health care, education and housing. Governments must avoid treating them in an overly narrow way. This is not a new cry, of course. Talk of avoiding 'silo' thinking, adopting a 'whole-of-government' approach, or delivering 'joined-up' policy is almost clichéd in the public service. But – though this chapter divides up health care, education and housing for the purposes of analytical clarity – governments must be alert to how interventions, or the absence of interventions, in one area can have ripple effects on another area. Seeing these three areas as 'social infrastructure' is one way to understand them together. These are interconnected pillars; social infrastructure can only be strong if each is maintained and the connections reinforced.

buxton popoali'i, rheumatic fever and health care

Buxton Popoali'i played rugby for the New Zealand Schools team, the New Zealand Sevens team, the Wellington Lions and the Highlanders. Popoali'i was a promising fullback and wing who had scored 22 tries for his school, including 44 points in one match. But in 2014, aged 24, Popoali'i was forced to retire from his rugby-playing career after undergoing major heart surgery. It was his second cardiac operation, having had his heart valve replaced while at school in 2006. 'It is tough but at the same time I'm just grateful to be alive,' he said afterwards. 'If they didn't find out then [about the heart problem], I probably would have died out on the field. Anything could have happened.'[1]

Popoali'i and I both attended Wellington College. I remember his name and rugby exploits being read out in school assemblies. But we shared more than just the same secondary school. We also faced a similar heart problem: a dilated aorta. The aorta is the largest blood vessel in the body, which carries blood and oxygen away from the heart to the rest of the body. A dilated aorta is an expanded aorta, which gets so big that it is at risk of tearing ('dissecting'). I discovered mine in 2015, the year after Popoali'i.

Our respective surgeries were successful. But while I was recovering, I read about Popoali'i's health difficulties, and realised that a major difference between us (apart from his rugby skills) was that his heart condition was preventable, whereas mine was somewhat random. I have a connective tissue disorder due to a gene that unluckily cropped up, and that connective tissue disorder created a risk of a dilated aorta.

In contrast, Popoali'i required a heart valve replacement and then further surgery because of rheumatic fever. He contracted rheumatic fever while living in Cannons Creek, one of the areas of New Zealand with the highest rates of rheumatic fever.[2] Rheumatic fever is a 'disease that can develop as a complication of inadequately treated strep throat or scarlet fever', which results in damaged heart valves and in some cases heart failure – rheumatic heart disease. Risk factors include poverty, malnutrition and overcrowded housing. Rheumatic fever can be treated to avoid development into rheumatic heart disease, and is 'rare in … developed countries'.[3] So although my dilated aorta was a possibility because of my genes, Popoali'i's heart complications (while possibly partly a result of genetic predisposition) could have been prevented through improved policy and public health response to rheumatic fever: through better government attempts to address poverty, malnutrition and overcrowded housing. With a different approach to rheumatic fever at a policy and public health level, Popoali'i might still be playing rugby.

That is unjust.

Buxton Popoali'i is far from the only person affected by this condition in New Zealand, which has much higher rates of rheumatic fever than most other developed countries,[4] with 92 per cent of rheumatic fever cases involving Māori and Pasifika children.[5] It is a problem that has been neglected by New Zealand governments for far too long.

In December 2015, I arranged to meet with Diana Lennon, one of New Zealand's rheumatic fever experts, at Starship Hospital in Auckland. We wandered down the corridors trying to find a room to chat in. The hospital was extremely busy before Christmas and no rooms were free. We ended up finding a space in the crowded downstairs cafeteria.

Lennon (her colleagues call her 'Dinny') spoke passionately about her struggle to get rheumatic fever addressed by successive governments. She shared research with me showing that by the 1960s, rheumatic fever was eliminated in Denmark because of concerted government action. Yet in New Zealand, rheumatic fever remains a serious problem, though medical professionals have been trying to raise awareness of the issue for decades. In 1984, cardiologists J.M. Neutze and P.M. Clarkson wrote an article in the *New Zealand Medical Journal*, 'Rheumatic Fever: An Unsolved Problem in New Zealand'.[6] Although figures over time are not perfectly comparable, there was roughly the same number of hospital admissions for acute rheumatic fever among young people in 2010 that there were in 1980–81: just over 15 admissions per 100,000. Admissions rates in Northland, Auckland and the East Coast have been particularly high for some time.[7] Put simply, rheumatic fever rates have been worryingly high for 30 years.

The National-led government has attempted to take some action on rheumatic fever since 2010. In 2012, as part of the ten Better Public Services targets, a goal was announced of reducing hospital admission rates for rheumatic fever by two-thirds from 4.2 per 100,000 to 1.4 per 100,000 by 2017. The government claimed to be focusing on school-based clinics, home visits and community events, and improved housing in high-incidence areas. However, by 2013, admission rates had increased to 4.3 per 100,000. Progress appeared to be made by 2015: hospital admissions were down to 2.1 per 100,000.[8] But there were disputes about the figures: in unchallenged comments in Parliament, it was claimed that there was just a 14 per cent reduction in 'first episode' rheumatic fever hospitalisations, when the interim target was a 40 per cent reduction.[9] In July 2015, a group of doctors still called rheumatic fever 'perhaps the most extreme example of an avoidable health disparity in this country'.[10]

The government must ensure that it continues to press towards its targeted reduction in first-episode hospitalisations. This might require additional investment in housing and education, too, since some of the major causes of rheumatic fever are overcrowded houses, malnutrition, poverty and a lack of knowledge about the treatment of strep throat. There is also a need for targeted interventions in highly affected communities, many of which are majority-Māori and -Pasifika – and questions should be asked about why rheumatic fever rates have not been addressed for so long. Government must ensure that it is genuinely engaged with these communities, too. One early evaluation of government progress towards its rheumatic fever targets suggested that greater action could be taken to enable 'community ownership' of rheumatic fever campaigns – and the public health service should be more mobile in how it interacts with affected communities.[11]

Why should the government act on rheumatic fever when there are a host of health challenges facing Aotearoa New Zealand? The National-led government has acknowledged the need to address it by including a rheumatic fever target in its ten Better Public Services targets. Rheumatic fever is clearly a serious health issue. It can affect individuals' careers, livelihoods and life expectancies. But beyond this, the issue should be tackled because it is a microcosm of the biggest challenges facing health care in this country. It highlights the extent of disparities of outcome in health care (especially between some members of Māori and Pasifika communities, and the rest of the country), the need for community engagement in delivering public health services, the value of addressing health while also intervening in areas such as housing and education, and a failure of care – since a concerted effort to address poverty, malnutrition and overcrowding could have had a significant impact on the number of people affected by rheumatic fever.

a 'time bomb': educational inequality and school zoning

School zoning is another area of policy that has been the subject of significant public criticism. Parents, policy-makers and even students are aware of some of its major shortcomings. I knew of it at secondary school, where terms like 'out of zone' needed no translation. Yet the oft-discussed problems with school zoning have not been translated into government action, let alone a government-led debate. As this book was being completed, the National-led government announced a review of the decile funding system in education.[12] School zoning should form part of that review, and it is important that certain considerations are taken into account. It is not the only area of education policy where action is required; but it reveals some of the core challenges in education as a whole.

The expression 'school zoning' comes from the Education Act 1989. All students in the 'home zone' of a school are entitled to enrol at a school, but if a person lives outside of that zone and a school is over-subscribed, a special procedure is used to determine which students are accepted; this is the enrolment scheme. The aim is to avoid overcrowding in a 'fair and transparent' way. Schools themselves define the 'home zone'. The only limits are: there must be clear geographic boundaries for the zone, the zone must make it 'reasonably convenient' for students to attend, and schools can exclude areas to allow best use to be made of the 'existing network' of public schools or where another school is reasonably convenient.

The legislation provides guidance for how enrolment schemes ought to work. First priority is given to people who apply for a 'special programme' at the school – a programme approved by the Secretary of Education that either provides specialised education (including Māori language immersion or education to overcome disadvantage) or takes a 'significantly different' approach and needs to draw on students outside of a catchment area. Next, priority must be given (in this order) to: siblings of a current student, siblings of a former student, children of a former student, and children of employees or board members of the school. A ballot must be used within these groups if there are more applicants in each group than places available. A school must develop an 'enrolment scheme' if the secretary deems that there is, or is likely to be, overcrowding at the school. For special schools, integrated schools (formerly private schools integrated into the public system), kura kaupapa and designated character schools, there is no need for a zone to be specified, but where the number of applicants is likely to exceed places, priority must be given to students for whom the school is reasonably convenient.[13]

In 1991, changes were made to give schools entire control over how 'enrolment schemes' operated, but after some discontent about how this was operating (with students allegedly not able to go to local schools because of exclusionary practices), greater guidelines were reintroduced in 1998.[14] The legislative framework has remained largely unchanged since then.

But objections to school zoning have been voiced by commentators from across the political spectrum. Home buyers have suggested that zoning has increased the cost of housing, especially in Christchurch and Auckland.[15] It may be that school zoning has contributed to the upward trend of house prices in Auckland: it is the logic of the market (especially if unregulated) that overheated demand for housing in a school zone pushes prices up. The head of the Secondary Principals' Association, Patrick Walsh, said in 2012 that he had heard that some schools were manipulating their home zones to exclude poorer students.[16] The Post-Primary Teachers Association (PPTA) has said that the current zoning system results in 'persistent middle class advantage', since giving priority to students to do 'special programmes' can be a way to ensure selection by stealth. The PPTA has also talked of 'educational apartheid', because of evidence of 'growing segregation and polarisation' and 'some evidence which suggests that Māori and Pacific Island students are less likely to be accepted in an out-of-zone enrolment, unless they have a particular strength, such as sport, where a scholarship could be offered'.[17] One might even wonder, extending the PPTA's point, whether high house prices in some school zones in Christchurch, Wellington and Auckland produce the de facto privatisation of public schools, since the cost of living in these school zones is prohibitive except for the financially privileged.

Steve Thomas, of the conservative Maxim Institute, has also suggested that zoning allows wealthy parents to have too much influence. 'School zones,' he has written, 'reinforce access to popular schools for the privileged.'[18]

Christopher Lubienski, an American Fulbright scholar, appeared to provide concrete evidence to support these claims in 2012 in his review of 49 Auckland schools. The research found that 36 schools appeared to have tweaked their zones to include affluent suburbs that would not otherwise have been within zone, presumably because of assumptions about the link between affluent suburbs and the talent of students.[19]

Despite this chorus of criticism, there is little acknowledgment by politicians or policy-makers that the system is flawed. Perhaps that is because the concerns are exaggerated – that they are based more on perception than reality. Some secondary school principals suggested as much after the release of Lubienski's research in 2012, with one Auckland principal saying they were 'offended' by the research.[20] It seems unlikely that there is no basis for any of these claims. A more cynical explanation is that, since some property developers and some schools stand to benefit from the current system (if zoning pushes prices up, it increases developers' profits, it and allows some schools to select students from particular suburbs), there is political reluctance to change it. A further possibility is that school zoning is complex, and that solutions are not easy to devise, much less implement. Maxim's Steve Thomas appeared to adopt this perspective when saying that school zoning is one of 'the difficult, "undiscussable" topics' in education policy.[21]

This book is premised on the idea that there is value in trying to address 'undiscussable' topics. It seeks to expand what politicians see as 'realistic' in politics, and to think constructively about solutions for problems that politicians have shied away from too long. In that spirit, we should ask: what, if anything, can and should be done about school zoning?

One option is to revert to a system that places greater weight on parental choice and allows students to enrol in any public school. 'Home zones' could be abolished and schools could be free to take students from any area. The problem with this 'free choice' option is that choice would become nothing more than illusion once the model was applied. Some schools would become even more popular and overcrowded. Wealthier parents would be more capable of enabling their children to commute long distances. And there would still be a need for a system to sift through students seeking to enrol in over-crowded schools. Ultimately some students and parents would not get their first choice of school. The issues of fairness that arise under the present school zoning system would simply re-emerge in a different form.

A more promising approach is to get at root causes.

Educational inequality is a major driver of the difficulties. It is at least partly because there is a gap opening up in the quality of public schools that certain public schools have falling rolls, while others are over-subscribed. Successful public schools should not be criticised for attracting students, although it would be helpful to know what their strategies have been, and whether there is – for example – excessive use of marketing and greater reliance by some schools on discretionary school donations in an increasingly competitive schooling environment. It is important, too, to clarify how much the over-subscription problem is caused by perceived differences in quality that are not borne out by evidence. The review of the decile system will help to settle this point, since it may reveal that incorrect conclusions are drawn about schools' perceived quality based on their decile rankings. But future governments must establish the extent to which educational inequality is responsible for zoning bottlenecks, and respond accordingly. There could be a need for significant policy change to lift the average quality of public schools, so that a chasm does not emerge between the best and worst public schools. This might entail increased funding for struggling schools. For now, an independent inquiry into school zoning, enrolment schemes and educational inequality would be a useful start.

Bali Haque has had considerable experience in the educational sector within schools and at a policy level. Haque has been principal of Pakuranga College, Tamatea College and Rosehill College, president of the Secondary Principals' Association, and deputy chief executive of the New Zealand Qualifications Authority. He also wrote the book *Changing our Secondary Schools*, based on his experience. He sounded like someone I needed to talk to about the school zoning problem. We met at a hotel in Wellington.

Haque told me he was 'very ambivalent' about the Tomorrow's Schools reforms of the late 1980s, which 'devolved a lot of apparent power to schools and boards', but also created an undesirable level of competitiveness between schools. He said that New Zealand lacked a 'mediating layer' between local schools and the Ministry of Education: there is no real 'regional structure', of the kind that exists with district health boards in the health care sector. Partly as a result of these factors, there is now a 'drift to higher-decile schools', he told me, with 'those students left in lower-decile schools [being] increasingly the most vulnerable, the least mobile, the most in need'. This 'drift' was a 'time bomb ticking away'. Schools are becoming increasingly segregated, and the government's failures to address inequalities are 'an abdication' of responsibility.

'Although we've had the talk,' Haque said with feeling, 'the inequalities that started in the 1980s are still there.' One response to this might be creating larger schools and merging schools. Another policy move suggested by Haque is improving the funding given to lower-decile schools. Finally, he proposed a more contentious option, which he predicted might not be supported by all educational unions: paying teachers at low-decile schools more to help to lift educational quality. Teachers in lower-decile schools, so long as they exist, should get paid 'a hell of a lot more' than teachers in higher-decile schools, he said. 'These teachers at higher-decile schools are fantastic. But the job that they do is a very different job from those in lower-decile schools – and [in lower-decile schools] it's harder.'

This conversation provided a spur for the questions that might be addressed by an inquiry into school zoning, enrolment schemes and educational inequality:

- Have the Tomorrow's Schools reforms caused excessive competitiveness between schools, resulting in socially harmful decile drift?
- Why are some schools over-subscribed?
- Are 'home zones' being drawn up by schools in a way that is compliant with the law, with sufficient oversight from the Ministry of Education?
- Are some schools disproportionately excluding students from certain ethnic or socio-economic backgrounds?
- Are the 'enrolment scheme' procedures in the Education Act 1989 still fit for purpose? For example, does it remain appropriate to give some priority to children of alumni of a school?
- Is school zoning contributing to rising house prices in major urban centres?
- Should schools with dropping rolls be given increased government funding, either through the decile system or some other mechanism?
- Should teachers at low-decile schools be paid more?

The questions require careful investigation. For example, whether teachers at low-decile schools should be paid more turns on not only the nature of work at low-decile schools, but also whether increased pay for these teachers might stigmatise low-decile schools, and how these higher salaries might be perceived by other teachers. (The stigma question might be settled, in part, by the fact that low-decile schools are already marked out as requiring more support by their decile ranking. Paying teachers more for teaching in these schools might add no additional stigma to the stigma created by the decile system itself.) It would help to include people with diverse backgrounds, so that the inquiry is able to identify delicate issues and address them thoughtfully. At the very least, the inquiry should include unions, teachers, principals, parents, students, economists and lawyers.

As with rheumatic fever, school zoning is not the only challenge facing New Zealand's education system. But, like rheumatic fever, it is a significant challenge that has not been sufficiently addressed – and analysis of the challenge reveals the kinds of approach that need to be taken in the sector as a whole. Attention needs to be paid to the history of education policy, how educational issues interact with other policy areas (such as housing), inequalities within educational policy, and the varying responsibilities of local, regional and national actors. Taking these matters into account can ensure that we have educational policies that are caring, supportive of community and creative.

affordable housing and homelessness

The first full-length album released by Tono and the Finance Company contains the song, 'Marion Bates Realty'. It's a cracker.[22] The track begins with an upbeat cooing voice over a clean guitar and drums, and then Tono – aka the Dunedin-raised musician Anthonie Tonnon – comes in with a clever, casually delivered, carefully enunciated vocal. 'Well, here comes Marion now,' he drawls, 'nailing in the real estate sign.' The music video has a sharply dressed Tono driving down an Auckland highway, spliced together with symbols of suburbia: a fruit bowl, pruned flowers, plunger coffee, a letterbox down a long drive. And Tono sings:

A condescending email on Wednesday
And an offer we couldn't afford
We had to sign by Thursday night, or she'd be taking through people
After the weekend
Marion, it must be great to be a real estate agent
You decide who stays and goes on the street

Tono has long been interested in political themes – his first EP was titled *Love and Economics* – and 'Marion Bates Realty' is no different. It expresses the discomfort of a generation – my generation – with unaffordable housing, and the growing resentment felt by some communities towards property developers and owners.

There has been considerable attention paid to the housing crisis in Auckland, and soaring house prices across New Zealand. Indeed, affordable housing has become a global issue in middle- and high-income countries, in New York, Vancouver, London and Sydney, as well as Auckland. McKinsey, the global consulting firm, has written a report on tackling 'the world's affordable housing challenge'.[23] There are competing explanations, and solutions. Some, like the National-led government and the New Zealand Initiative think tank, have claimed that affordable housing is generally a 'supply-side' problem: that is, a problem caused by regulation and land-use restrictions that have choked housing supply.[24] This perspective prescribes a loosening up of regulation and land restrictions as a way to address the problem.

Others, in particular the Labour Party, have focused on the demand-side causes of housing affordability, often arguing that immigration and speculation have pushed up housing prices. Their proposed solutions include a capital gains tax to dampen demand, large-scale construction of new houses and increased monitoring of immigration.

Shamubeel Eaqub and Selena Eaqub in *Generation Rent: Rethinking New Zealand's Priorities* combine both explanations, and explain the affordability crisis with reference to cultural influences on demand, changing demographics, speculation and immigration, as well as factors such as infrastructure costs and financing for the building industry.[25] Some solutions have been given more airtime than others; there has been comparatively little analysis of rent controls, used successfully in Germany, or the development of housing co-operatives, though Philippa Howden-Chapman does consider mixed tenure communities in passing in *Home Truths: Confronting New Zealand's Housing Crisis.*[26] But the causes of, and solutions to, unaffordable housing have now been relatively well ventilated. What has been less well traversed is the impact of unaffordable housing on homelessness – on decisions about who 'goes on the street', in Tono's words.

Anecdotally, the last few years seem to have brought increased numbers of rough sleepers to the streets of Auckland or Wellington. It is difficult to confirm this authoritatively, since the government only adopted an agreed definition of homelessness in 2009 (updated slightly in 2015) and does not seem to keep a definitive record of the number of rough sleepers. But academics have attempted to highlight the worsening of housing deprivation over time: Kate Amore, of the University of Otago, has shown that the numbers of severely housing deprived increased by 15 per cent between 2006 and 2013. Amore has shown that as of 2013 there were 41,000 homeless New Zealanders – 1 in every 100 people – and that Māori were disproportionately represented among them.[27] And reports from major urban centres appear to support the idea that the number of homeless people has gone up in the first half of the 2010s. In 2014 the Auckland City Mission counted 147 rough sleepers in a three-kilometre radius of Auckland's Sky Tower, a 116 per cent increase on the year before.[28] In post-earthquake Christchurch, perhaps unsurprisingly, 50 per cent more people were living in temporary accommodation in 2015 compared to 2006.[29] In Marlborough, the coordinator of John's Kitchen (which provides meals to the needy) spoke in 2016 of a concern about increasing homeless numbers.[30]

It reflects another failure of a caring community for anyone to be homeless in New Zealand, where homelessness means 'a living situation where people with no other options to acquire safe and secure housing are: without shelter, in temporary accommodation, sharing accommodation with a household, or living in uninhabitable housing'.[31] Care, one of the cornerstone progressive values, involves genuine attentiveness to basic needs – and housing is one of those. People who live in insecure, uninhabitable or inadequate housing are not receiving that care. They are likely to face additional health concerns, including asthma, eczema, bedbugs, and possibly rheumatic fever.[32] Children growing up in these circumstances may not be able to focus on their education. And rough sleepers lack the sense of privacy that is guaranteed by a shelter or home. As the size of the homeless population increases, it takes more effort – more care – for individuals in the general population to get to know people sleeping rough. In this way, a neglect of care on the part of government, which leads to an increase in the homeless population, can make it more likely that people in the population neglect everyday care.[33]

For several years, I have been involved with a voluntary initiative in the UK to support rough sleepers. While the situation in the UK is different from New Zealand (the UK is a lot colder, for one thing), there are some things I have learned from conversations with homeless people that are likely to apply to New Zealand.

People sleeping rough have spoken to me about the shame of finding themselves on the street after relationship breakdowns, job losses or substance abuse. They talk about their anxiety that family or acquaintances will discover they are homeless. Others talk about loneliness and a loss of social connection. One told me that he would walk into a pub occasionally just to find conversation, to talk to someone. Another talked to me about being assaulted and physically intimidated. No one should have go to sleep worrying about their safety. Yet that is the position of many.

A typical response to this, which I've heard on talkback radio and in other casual conversations, is that these people have made bad choices and should be responsible for the effects of their actions. A caring approach to the homeless might usually be required (this argument goes), but where people have made choices resulting in their own deprivation, they are not deserving of significant care. A softer version of this claim is that there are many people in need of care in our community – including the elderly and the disabled – and only scarce resources to be dedicated to care. In light of those scarce resources, it would be legitimate for the government to withhold resources from individuals whose own choices have caused some measure of suffering.

One problem with this type of argument is that it pushes us to be less caring. Within New Zealand's existing public health care system, we do not cut off care or resources because a person's own choices might have led them to come into hospital. When I was in New Zealand in early 2016, I broke my arm after slipping on a steep ridge and ended up in Wellington Hospital; the person in the bed next to me needed a minor procedure undertaken on his ears because he'd put toilet paper in his ears at a New Year's Eve rave. Neither of us was turned away because our own choices had got us there. In fact, in general, no questions are asked by doctors or nurses in New Zealand hospitals about the link between personal choices and a medical condition, except where those questions are relevant to the medical condition. This explains a key part of the value of care: it should be extended as widely as possible, without qualification or exception.

Some might argue (often from the anonymous corners of blogs and in online responses to media items) that New Zealand is currently too generous in its provision of health care. They say greater restrictions could be based on choice: for example, smokers, say, should pay for their own treatment for lung cancer. But most New Zealanders agree that the value of care is of utmost importance when a person faces a sudden or significant health deprivation. The same should be true of a sudden or significant housing deprivation.

Though people might make a choice to move into some form of insecure housing following a series of difficult life events (and homeless people's agency should not be denied here), in almost all cases it is wrong to describe this as a 'bad choice'. The evidence on homelessness, and my experience with the homeless, suggest that this choice is often the last option available to people, after they have leaned on what friends they might have, drawn on what savings are available, and thought about what they can do. Homeless people may make a choice to enter insecure housing, but this choice is often constrained by circumstances, and it may be a choice with no meaningful alternative.

Well, it might be said, perhaps this final choice is constrained (rather than being a 'bad choice'), but didn't these individuals make bad choices earlier – to be dependent on alcohol, say, or drugs? We all make decisions that we come to regret. But the question is whether care should be withheld from people who face a conjunction of difficult circumstances – often the combination of relationship troubles, personal challenges and background socio-economic deprivation (a lack of family financial support and employment). My view is that they remain deserving of our care.

Viewing homelessness as a product of bad personal choice is inaccurate and stigmatising. Focusing only on how an individual might be to blame ignores causes in the broader economy, such as low levels of affordable housing (as Tono reminds us), structural unemployment or welfare benefits that are difficult to access. Those who are homeless often internalise the view that their homelessness is entirely their fault, which further undermines their sense of self-worth, making mental health problems more likely. It is therefore empirically wrong and practically damaging to allow this falsehood to stand.

When recommending action on homelessness, we need to remember both the urgent needs of those without permanent shelter and the structural causes of homelessness. Change can happen on multiple levels.

A government definition of homelessness was accepted in 2009 and revised in 2015. What is surprising is that despite this shared understanding of homelessness, government figures for individuals who are homeless in New Zealand (including rough sleeper figures) are not readily available. The numbers that are available, such as those that I have cited earlier, have been gathered by non-governmental organisations like the Auckland City Mission and academics. A first step towards reducing homelessness is to ensure that public data are collected on rough sleepers and the homeless population as a whole, and made public. Certainly, only approximate estimates can be made, and the task is not easy. But it is possible, as demonstrated abroad, and there is no good reason why the government should not release these figures. Good information on homelessness can help to track what is causing it to increase or decrease, and can allow civil society and political groups to hold governments to account.

At a slightly different level, new policy tools need to be experimented with and applied (consistent with values of care, community and creativity) to find secure accommodation for those facing severe housing deprivation or homelessness, which are likely to number at least 41,000 people. Auckland Council has invested more in emergency housing in recent years, and has a target to end rough sleeping by 2020. But some new ideas are also needed.

Housing research suggests that one of the most effective models for dealing with rough sleepers is the Housing First model. I first saw this model at work in South Australia when I was there in 2008, where a version known as Common Ground was applied. In South Australia and the US the model has produced good results. The idea is that, rather than moving rough sleepers through different stages of housing, they should be moved quickly into permanent accommodation with wrap-around services nearby. For example, one floor of an apartment block might be dedicated to mental health and employment services. The model aims to give individuals who have been sleeping on the street a sense of responsibility and choice about how to manage their housing. Housing First could be a way to reduce New Zealand's homeless population.

New Zealand is somewhat unusual in not imposing statutory responsibilities on government authorities to reduce the homeless population. Our housing policy lacks what Bali Haque called in the context of education a 'mediating layer' of regional governance, a layer of oversight of national policy at the regional level. That balance has not been struck because the regional level is simply non-existent. In the case of housing, local leadership has been made difficult in part by 2012 reforms of the Local Government Act 2002, which deleted one of the purposes of local government, which had been to promote social, cultural, economic and environmental wellbeing. These reforms have hampered the ability of local government to partner with central government in the delivery of social policy. A further policy change worth considering is the reversal of this reform, and the introduction of legislation akin to the UK's Homelessness Act 2002, which imposes a duty on local government to formulate a homelessness strategy. There is a danger that the exercise becomes formulaic, and some councils in New Zealand have a strategy of this kind already, including Auckland's council. However, the duty would create legal pressure to reduce homelessness, and would at least create some degree of transparency around government actions.

Ultimately, addressing homelessness requires more than just technocratic tweaks or exhortations for more 'care'. Homelessness is caused by a variety of factors, including economic policy, and part of the task of addressing it involves understanding them. Homelessness can be the result of family violence, which pushes (in most cases) women out of secure accommodation; it can also be the result of an uncaring approach to prisoners upon release. It is the product of a society that has blunt, sometimes unhelpful, ways of treating those with mental health challenges. It arises out of political indifference to those who are unemployed and those who receive benefits. Eliminating homelessness in New Zealand will require coordinated action through economic policy, criminal justice and family violence reform, and investment in mental health.

Many New Zealanders have also come to accept the sight of rough sleepers. The sharp deprivations of homelessness have become normalised; we have become numb to the pain and misery faced by people without secure housing. Homeless people are dehumanised when other New Zealanders walk by, without listening, without reacting to a plea for help. This needs to change.

Political leadership that proclaims the value of care, emphasises the variety of people (including the homeless) in our community, and calls for creative responses, can make a contribution. But that will be made easier if there is a strong popular movement against homelessness. Auckland Action Against Poverty has raised some awareness, the Labour, Green and Māori parties launched a cross-party homelessness inquiry in 2016, and the New Zealand Coalition to End Homelessness has made some national progress. More needs to be done. The media can help people who are not homeless to relate better to homeless people – to see them as people, and not as 'addicts' or 'scroungers'.

In the same way that being able to relate to prisoners is the key to a more empathetic public response to prisons, so too it will be harder for a harsh or mean-spirited attitude to be adopted towards homeless people if others can relate to them. Artists, activists and commentators can play their part, drawing attention not only to rising house prices but also those who are negatively affected – sometimes invisibly – by these rising prices, because they are priced out of the housing market and state housing is not plentiful enough to support those priced out.

'I understand supply and demand/But I also know what's right,' Tono sings in 'Marion Bates Realty'. Let's hope we can say the same thing about our politicians and policy-makers. Let's help them to understand what's right by continuing to build a popular movement to end homelessness in New Zealand.

how social infrastructure is delivered

There has been some debate in recent years over privatisation in New Zealand, especially in light of the National-led government's partial privatisation of state-owned enterprises in the early 2010s, and the sale of state housing in 2015. The arguments have been well rehearsed. It is often claimed that privatisation will lead to more efficient provision of services (because of the discipline of the market and competition), more innovation, and opportunities for investment; on the other hand, worries are expressed about decreased quality of service provision (because of pressures towards cost-cutting), reduced public accountability and inequities in provision.

Less discussed is government 'contracting out' of services, sometimes to not-for-profit organisations and sometimes to private providers. This has been particularly prevalent in government provision of education, health care and housing, since the reforms to New Zealand's public service beginning in the late 1980s. As Jane Kelsey told me, New Zealand is 'unique' in its use of contracting.[34]

Contracting out – which involves the government deciding that it will bring on board another organisation or company to deliver a service, stipulating expectations in a contract, and often paying for the service – is a key part of New Public Management, an ethos of public service operations implemented from the late 1980s. New Public Management borrowed ideas from the private sector, embracing market forces in the public sector and adopting tools such as targets in order to achieve more efficient public service outcomes. This topic sounds boring: 'contracting out' is a vague, legalistic phrase. But of course the label has been developed partly because it is unthreatening. And the use of contracting-out has far-reaching negative consequences for government accountability, rights protection and getting things done.

A review of contracting out in health care, housing and education could be valuable. Contracting out is more prevalent in health care and housing, but exists across these policy spheres. In the justice sector, Serco was contracted to provide prison services at Mt Eden Prison from 2010, but did not have its contract renewed in 2015 after allegations of physical violence and substance abuse in the prison. Some would say that the non-renewal of Serco's contract demonstrates a positive aspect of contracting-out: if targets or standards are not met, a relationship with a provider can be ended. However, there is also a convincing case to be made that the problems with Serco reveal the shortcomings inherent in contracting out. Governments ought to be especially cautious when dealing with the pillars of social infrastructure.

One shortcoming of contracting out is that the legal mechanism of a contract is not an efficient way of managing public projects. Sometimes concrete targets can be set and monitored. But often it is only possible to use relatively open-ended language. For example, the contract with Serco for management of Mt Eden Prison said, 'The Contractor must have effective safety management systems in place.'[35] What does 'effective' mean here? To some extent, all laws contain such imprecise language. But the problem in contracting-out is the need to supervise the contractor. If performance assessment language is open-ended, contractors can flex away from admitting failures. It may be that this contributed to Serco's flaws in managing Mt Eden Prison only coming to light late in 2015. There is also some evidence that this weakness in the mechanism of contracting might explain repeated failures of large infrastructure projects to be finished on time and within budget.[36] Add to this worry the fact that contracting out often incurs significant transaction costs – high legal fees to draft complex contracts, and consultants to manage the process – and it can be seen that it may not live up to its billing.

Another shortcoming here is that the legal framework for holding contractors to account is uncertain and appears to result in less accountability for contractors. The government, when undertaking ordinary activities, is subject to 'judicial review' – which means that it must act within the law, respect principles of good procedure and avoid outright unreasonable decisions, among other things. The government must also comply with the New Zealand

Bill of Rights Act 1990. In short, the government must adhere to 'public law': a special body of law that attaches to government and holds government to higher standards than private actors. When the government contracts services out, the courts have been uncertain about the extent to which 'public law' still applies. For the most part, the courts have decided that lower standards of behaviour apply to contractors.

I know about this from my law studies, but also because during a summer working at a corporate law firm, I was given a research project to examine how contractors should be dealt with in New Zealand under the law of judicial review.

The firm I was working with had been employed to do work on the *Lab Tests* case. The case challenged the Auckland District Health Board's tendering of a pathology testing contract to a company whose team included a member of the Auckland District Health Board. Concerns were raised about bias and the consultation process. The decision of the Court of Appeal remains the leading decision in New Zealand on public law and contractors, but it highlights the uncertainty of the legal position. The main judgment in that 2008 case noted: 'The changes to the public sector over the last 20 years have presented a considerable challenge to the courts. Some commentators suggested that there would be a reduced role for judicial review in the new environment. As will become apparent in the discussion which follows, the courts have not yet finally grappled with the full implications of the changes in the context of judicial review.'[37] The Court ended up deciding that some traditional judicial review obligations applied, but that 'the courts will intervene by way of judicial review in relation to contracting decisions made by public bodies in a commercial context in limited circumstances', which will vary with context.[38]

Thus, currently under New Zealand law, courts will be less stringent in ensuring that contractors stay within the law, respect principles of good procedure, avoid flat-out unreasonable decisions, and uphold other duties under judicial review. The reason for this is clear: courts assume that because governments and Parliament have opted to contract out services, they have intended to impose less accountability on these services. The limited law on the New Zealand Bill of Rights Act 1990 and other public law also suggests that obligations under these parts of the law will be attenuated for contractors.

The upshot: contractors have to adhere to lower standards of conduct and behaviour under the law than the government. That might appear to be a legalistic point. But this should be a cause for wider concern for anyone keen to ensure transparency, respect for human rights and fairness in the provision of services.

There are some specific harms of contracting-out, something that was borne out by the leaky homes crisis in New Zealand that followed the contracting-out of building regulation. (These include the possibility of businesses developing excessive influence over government policy.) There are also certain harms of contracting-out when it involves non-governmental organisations or not-for-profit providers. Applying for government contracts can take valuable time away from research and service provision. It can undermine the stability needed for a long-term approach to social policy. Perhaps more perniciously, many NGOs under contract to provide government services are fearful of making public comment about policy lest their contract is not renewed. The research of Sandra Grey and Charles Sedgwick has confirmed this point; it talks of a 'climate of fear and risk-aversion created by the neo-liberal contract state'.[39] This is a point I return to in Chapter 11.

Those supportive of government contracting argue that contracting secures certain benefits. On the Serco contract, for example, the Department of Corrections website says that it 'use[s] private sector innovation as well as international experience ... to improve ... quality, efficiency and cost effectiveness' and to have 'the opportunity to inject new ideas and new innovations'. The Department goes on to talk about how the 'move to contract management is primarily about improving performance ... and delivering value for money'.[40] The arguments above call into question whether contracting out improves cost-effectiveness and performance. It is not clear that expertise and innovation cannot be delivered by government, with appropriate people recruited and more creative policy tools adopted. Ultimately whether contracting out could be more effective is an empirical question for which there appears to be little supporting evidence.

What is the best response? One would be for governments to be extremely cautious in adopting new contracting-out arrangements – possibly even adopting a moratorium on contracting out – with governments also undertaking to do what they can to withdraw from existing contracting-out arrangements where necessary. That would have to be done consistently with legal obligations; governments could not withdraw from contracts that have already been signed without incurring major costs.

A softer response would be for a government to initiate a review of the benefits and drawbacks of existing contracting-out arrangements, especially within core social policy (such as housing, health care and education). The review could be managed by the Treasury, or the State Services Commission, or perhaps by a select committee; a 2014 report to the UK House of Commons Committee of Public Accounts, albeit on contracting out to the private sector (a narrower topic), provides one model.[41] The 'softer' response may not be sufficiently independent for those opposed to contracting out, but will allow more information to be gathered; the hard response may avert some negative outcomes, but may be seen as a rash move by others. At minimum, there should be further discussion about it. There was a surge of interest in public sector contracting in the early and mid-1990s,[42] but since then the evidence base on contracting out has been a little thin. Further discussion would consolidate that evidence base, and allow politicians and the public sector to tweak practices as needed.

The debate should also be about 'social bonds', or 'social impact bonds', a variant of contracting out. These involve an external investor offering financing for a project; the external investor agrees to pay for the project if the project's results are not achieved. A provider, such as a youth offending organisation or for-profit housing organisation, contracts with the government to achieve certain ends. If the provider delivers, the external investor is reimbursed and is paid an additional sum. The National-led government announced a social bonds pilot in 2015 in mental health and employment, and has indicated three further projects (youth offending, adult reoffending and management of chronic illnesses) where almost $30 million has been set aside to be used if the projects are successful.

Public discussion about social bonds has been limited. A favourable report was written by The New Zealand Initiative,[43] and a witty, critical assessment of social bonds was offered by 'White Man Behind a Desk', an online satirical series on New Zealand politics.[44] Several other short articles have appeared. In favour of social bonds, it could be said that the government loses no money if a social bond experiment fails, and that they are an example of innovative policy-making. On the other hand, social bonds rely on the profit motive in the delivery of social services, and are susceptible to the same critiques – cost-cutting, decreased quality, inequitable provision – as privatisation. Vulnerable people, such as those with mental health challenges, should not be the guinea pigs for this novel mode of delivering social policy. Overall, the use of social bonds should be closely monitored. As even the sympathetic New Zealand Initiative said in its report, it is clear that their success as a tool for achieving better social outcomes in a cost-effective manner is 'yet to be established'.[45]

There is a persuasive case, I think, for a more muscular role for the state in the delivery of social infrastructure. This would involve less contracting out, an end to the piloting of social bonds, an abandonment of privatisation and a commitment to state ownership and state provision (at a local and national government level) of social infrastructure.

For the most part, housing, health care and education are provided for by the state in New Zealand. But state housing is becoming more and more marginal (and became especially so under the Key-led National government), and experiments such as with social bonds show doubt about the capacity of the state to deliver services. We would do well when discussing social infrastructure to remember the major benefits of state provision. It can provide economies of scale: in other words, funding is more efficient because it is one large funder spending at scale. As discussed in Chapter 4, the state can borrow more cheaply than private providers, because interest rates are lower for state borrowing. The state can ensure interagency policy, especially useful in social infrastructure, whereas private provision is more likely to be disconnected. The state, because it is motivated by a sense of public good, can show greater concern for the most vulnerable, whereas the most vulnerable might be ignored by a provider driven by the profit motive. (More work might need to be done, however, to ensure that supposedly accessible public services are not made inaccessible to the most vulnerable by seemingly minor charges, such as prescription fees in health care or school donations at public schools.) Put another way, the state might be able to better deliver on the value of care in social infrastructure.

Concerns are often raised about whether the state is as efficient or innovative as the private sector. But with the right personnel and partnerships, the state can lead innovative projects, and, as I have suggested, the private sector itself can also be inefficient.

No firm conclusions can be drawn for now. But I want to reiterate a point already made in Chapter 4: a rejuvenated New Zealand politics will involve a rejuvenated state. This requires not just policy choices but a shift in mentality – and a cultural treasuring of state institutions such as public health care, public schools and state housing. In the UK, the National Health Service (NHS) is a cultural icon. The public health care system in New Zealand is not viewed in the same light. If we were to seek a rejuvenated state to steer social infrastructure, the public would also have to get behind state institutions that act in the name of the public – and state institutions would have to be made more participatory in order to secure that public backing.

In at least the sphere of social infrastructure, the state could well be the most effective vehicle for the delivery of care. The state, especially if its institutions are designed to facilitate participation, reflects the community and can consolidate a sense of community. State provision of social infrastructure, without contracting out, might also enable more community freedom through non-governmental organisations that feel less muzzled when it comes to criticising policy. Finally, the state can deliver solutions that are more creative than, or at least *as* creative as, those offered by other providers. On the whole, state ownership and provision of social infrastructure best realises the cornerstone values of care, community, and creativity.

conclusion

I have shuttled between theoretical discussion of how social infrastructure should be provided, and specific examples of how social infrastructure might be improved.

It is wrong to say that there is no debate on any of these issues in Aotearoa New Zealand today, or to say that there are no signs of care, community and creativity in how governments have attempted to address some of the issues. There have been stirrings of action by government, and individuals and groups have worked to raise awareness of these challenges.

Rugby player Buxton Popoali'i has done his bit to highlight rheumatic fever through television appearances, interviews and openness about his experiences. Musician Tono has drawn attention to housing that leaves people 'on the street' in his own way, through his music. Diana Lennon and Bali Haque use their work to attempt to make a policy difference.

Governments, politicians, policy-makers and the general public must stand on the shoulders of the work done by Bali, Dinny, Tono and Buxton, among others. We need to expand and improve our social infrastructure in a way that recognises the interconnectedness of policy areas, aspires to comprehensive provision, partners with local government, and respects cornerstone values of care, community and creativity.

7 justice means more than revenge

In 2011, Kim Workman called a meeting for young people interested in criminal justice at the offices of Rethinking Crime and Punishment in Wellington. At the time, Workman was the executive director of the group that he had established to improve criminal justice debate and to encourage the adoption of a more humane criminal justice policy. That same year he decided Rethinking Crime and Punishment needed a youth wing. At the meeting, Judge Andrew Becroft, Principal Youth Court Judge, spoke about areas of the criminal justice system and youth justice system that required more debate.

Judge Becroft, an inspirational man who overcame a speech impediment in his youth to become a charismatic lawyer and outspoken judge, told the young people in the audience (including me) that he thought there might be too much inertia in our generation for change to occur. Was our generation, he asked, too distracted and too self-involved to make a difference in justice policy?

We responded strongly. The fifty or so people in the room felt that we could intervene in justice policy debates, to widen the circle of participants beyond the Sensible Sentencing Trust and politicians. Out of this gathering, JustSpeak was formed – a youth-based criminal justice advocacy group – and over the following year I worked with a team of other organisers (with great assistance from Kim Workman) to coordinate monthly forums, a camp, media interviews and publications.

I sat down with Workman in 2015. We met in the Stout Research Centre at Victoria University of Wellington, where he was undertaking research as a Stout Fellow. Workman began his career as a policeman, moved into the public service (where he worked in the Ombudsman's office and as assistant secretary, penal institutions), and then shifted into social service provision with Prison Fellowship, before setting up Rethinking Crime and Punishment. In addition to being an eloquent advocate, thinker and writer, he is a Christian, of Ngāti Kahungunu and Rangitāne descent, committed to his wider whānau and engaged with everyone.

He spoke about Māori and the criminal justice system – the subject of the book he's currently writing. He began by talking about imprisonment and the culture of punishment in New Zealand. In 1989, at the time of a major inquiry into prisons in New Zealand (which resulted in *Te Ara Hou: The New Way*, or the Roper Report), there was a 'general consensus' that 'prisons weren't working' and that 'we need to find something else', Workman said. But the report did not achieve the change that many had hoped for. When I asked whether New Zealand had progressed in its thinking today compared to 1989, he looked glum. 'I don't think we have,' he replied. '[W]e do want to see people punished.'

Of particular concern to him are trends in criminal justice policy between 2009 and 2015, especially in relation to race. Though there have been positive developments – Māori focus units in prisons, tikanga Māori frameworks in the Department of Corrections and police–iwi liaison positions – Workman worries that these are 'cultural window-dressing'.

The policy has been to 'invisibilise' issues of racism, Workman said, and 'not to discuss them at all. In countless reports to the United Nations, we say we're "doing stuff". But they keep coming back and say, "Yes … but what are you doing about race discrimination?"' He looked thoughtful. 'There's no response. The only time you get a response is: "We don't think it exists." If there was no structural, institutional discrimination in New Zealand, that would make New Zealand the only country in the world not to have such discrimination.' At this point, Workman stood up to take off his jersey and to hang it over the door. As his jersey covered his face, I could hear him mutter, 'So … get real.'

This chapter aims to 'get real' about the challenges facing New Zealand's justice system. The first part discusses the surge of 'penal populism' in New Zealand between 1985 and 2015, and explains how this has caused some confusion in how criminal justice issues have been addressed by politicians and policy-makers. It teases out the principles of a sound justice system. The remainder applies these principles to overlapping problems in the sphere of justice: prisons, sexual and family violence, legal aid and diversity in the judiciary. (Some issues relevant to justice, such as New Zealand's constitutional future, are discussed in other chapters, in particular Chapter 5.)

penal populism from 1985 – and skewed debates about criminal justice

From around 1985 until today, New Zealand experienced a surge in 'penal populism': a populist push for longer prison sentences for those convicted of committing crimes, and harsher treatment of those individuals.[1] This trend has not been confined to New Zealand, and has also been visible in the UK, the US and elsewhere. It is a product of many forces, including a sense of heightened insecurity and anxiety felt by the general public, in part because of increases in inequality wrought by neoliberal policy changes; the rise of victims' rights and other criminal justice lobby groups; and disenchantment with the capacity of representative democracies to respond to people's concerns, which has led to a channelling of criticism towards institutions perceived as anti-democratic, such as the courts.[2]

It is difficult to understand how this 'penal populism', which has involved the state imposing more severe restrictions on individual liberty, was seen in the 1980s as consistent with economic reforms that championed the cause of freedom from government interference. Doesn't penal populism run counter to this push? Two possible explanations reconcile these trends. First, the economic reforms of the 1980s, referred to in Chapter 2, were never concerned with the freedom of all, and merely used the rhetoric of freedom to champion the freedom of some, while other marginalised groups were excluded (including through imprisonment). Second, penal populism was the crutch, a source of security the general public needed, as the economic reforms caused rapid change in social and economic conditions.

This penal populism changed New Zealand's political landscape and prison muster, and shifted the views of the general public, between 1985 and 2015. In 1999, after successive governments had invoked similar rhetoric, 92 per cent of the New Zealand public supported a referendum proposing a host of 'tough on crime' measures. That referendum put pressure on the Helen Clark-led Labour government to pass the Sentencing Act 2002, which contributed to higher prison sentences.

In 2001, the Hawke's Bay farmer Garth McVicar set up the Sensible Sentencing Trust, a group working to protect victims' rights and to increase prison sentences and end supposedly lenient treatment of individuals convicted of crimes. In 2005, the Labour-led government passed the Prisoners' and Victims' Claims Act. This legislation restricted any compensation awarded by courts to prisoners for mistreatment under human rights or tort law, and directed that it be placed by the Secretary of Justice in a fund for victims; the law responded to populist concerns, and overturned the age-old common law principle that where there is a right violated, there must be a remedy. The law, which has not been repealed, means that in theory, if a prisoner is raped in prison, and is entitled to compensation for a breach of the New Zealand Bill of Rights Act 1990 or for a tortious wrong having been committed, that compensation must (under section 17) go directly to a victims' account set up by the secretary of justice, once legal aid and other debts have been paid.[3]

In 2010, National MP Paul Quinn's private members' bill on prisoner disenfranchisement was supported by the National-led government. This led to all prisoners being banned from voting. By 2014, New Zealand's prison population was 208 per 100,000 people. This figure is not nearly as high as the US prison muster (698 per 100,000). But it is considerably higher than Australia's (162 per 100,000), and well over England and Wales's imprisonment rate (147 per 100,000), though England and Wales have faced their own penal populism. It is more than double Ireland's (80 per 100,000).[4] New Zealand's imprisonment rate almost tripled between 1983 and 2014, despite the fact that total crime has trended downwards since the 1990s.[5]

Two notes of caution need to be kept in mind. First, some of the developments described by penal populism can be traced back to before the 1980s; it might underestimate the issue to imply it only began in 1985. New Zealand culture has long had a retributive strain: as Kim Workman told me, 'We're such a punitive lot.' And Māori have been over-represented in prisons for decades, with such over-representation reflecting lingering racism and the ongoing effects of colonisation. Second, during the 1985–2015 period, there were also occasional policy moves in the direction of less punitive criminal justice policy. Geoffrey Palmer, as minister of justice between 1984 and 1989, experimented with policies to reduce the prison population, including by piloting 'habilitation centres' for those convicted of crimes. The Labour-led government of 1999–2008 passed the Criminal Justice Reform Act 2007, which attempted to blunt some of the effects of the Sentencing Act 2002 passed on its watch by encouraging judges to consider imposing a sentence of home detention instead of a short period of imprisonment.[6] The National government of 2008 onwards invested in prisoner rehabilitation, with then deputy prime minister Bill English calling prisons 'a moral and fiscal failure' in 2011.[7]

Nevertheless, despite these deeper causes and policy moves in an opposing direction, the broad thrust of New Zealand criminal justice policy in the past thirty years has been towards greater imprisonment and harsher treatment of those who have committed crime. That penal populism has manifested in policy and legislation, as well as in language and rhetoric, which has suggested that prisoners are a different subspecies of human beings. Politicians have not only responded to latent public moods or populism. They have also actively shaped the populism themselves and created popular resentment towards individuals who have committed crime.

This pattern in public debate has skewed how we understand the principles of our justice system in three important ways.

First, the Sensible Sentencing Trust and other commentators have implied that there is a trade-off between victims' rights and the humane treatment of individuals who have committed crime. It's a zero-sum game. This ignores the fact that it is possible to decouple the protection of victims' rights – a hugely important task for any progressive, committed to the value of care and attentive to the interests of the vulnerable – and the protection of the rights of those convicted of committing crime.

Second, penal populism (as practised by politicians, commentators and lobby groups) has suggested that public safety and victims' rights are the only significant principles in the justice system. While these principles are important, they have never been the only ones considered within the justice system: if they were, the death penalty might never have been abolished in New Zealand. Penal populism has resulted in a cramped discussion about what matters when New Zealanders think about justice. Justice has come to mean something close to revenge. A broader approach is needed.

Third, a lazy link has been made between imprisonment and public safety. The Sensible Sentencing Trust has assumed that public safety can be secured, and victims' rights protected, through higher rates of imprisonment. Prisons protect the public in one obvious way: by warehousing individuals who have been convicted of committing criminal offences. But prisons may endanger public safety in the long run, too, if they exacerbate mental illness, pose other health risks to prisoners, and surround prisoners with individuals who may have nothing in common but their criminal offending. Criminal justice debate in New Zealand needs to question the connection between imprisonment and public safety, and investigate further the most effective ways to ensure public safety.

The remainder of this chapter aims to resolve some of the confusion, at a policy level, that has arisen as a result of penal populism. Let's start by restating the important principles that ought to underpin a justice system.

the cornerstone principles of the new zealand justice system

Philosophers and others have debated the meaning of 'justice' for centuries. The English-speaking tradition usually points to Greek philosopher Aristotle as one of the earliest thinkers to explore the content of justice, but this ignores the many other cultures (including indigenous cultures) outside of Europe that developed notions of justice before Aristotle. Therefore, it is no simple task to state the principles that should guide the pursuit of justice in New Zealand, or even to define justice. I understand justice to mean a state of affairs where an ethical equilibrium has been reached: a position that is attained when everybody's ethical duties have been satisfied and do not come into conflict. The idea of an equilibrium at the heart of justice helps to explain why the iconic Lady Justice holds a set of scales that are perfectly balanced. This definition is not far from the Māori notion of utu (sometimes translated as 'balance'), which has infused Māori approaches to justice. Using this definition, and drawing on the three fundamental progressive values sketched in Chapter 1 (community, care and creativity), I outline five cornerstone principles of the justice system: a holistic approach, legitimacy, accessibility, effective policies and treating people with care.

achieving justice requires a holistic approach

The justice system is the institutional scaffolding put in place to help to achieve justice, the state of ethical equilibrium. But what is clear is that the justice system – the traditional images that come to mind of police, courts and judges – cannot alone do the work. In some cases, ethical equilibrium is best restored through actions outside of formal justice institutions, perhaps in families or schools or on marae (although we should take care to ensure that these more localised settings do not result in injustices being swept under the carpet). This is recognised already in New Zealand through restorative justice practices in schools. And the achievement of justice needs to be supported through other services. For example, victims of crime may need to be referred to health services, such as counselling. All in all, the justice system requires a holistic approach.

the justice system must be legitimate

Where mainstream institutions such as the police and courts aim to address an injustice, ethical equilibrium can only be restored if those institutions are legitimate in the eyes of all. What it means for institutions to be 'legitimate' is itself a complex question, but at a minimum it means that these institutions are acceptable to the individuals and groups with which they are dealing. If institutions are not legitimate, individuals and groups might not believe that there has been an injustice; individuals and groups might not approach those institutions in the first place (leaving an injustice unaddressed); or individuals and groups might not carry out what is necessary to restore a state of equilibrium. Institutions of justice must make especial effort to ensure that they are legitimate in the eyes of those who have been historically marginalised by the same institutions. This principle reinforces the need for decolonisation of the criminal justice system.

A concrete example of how this principle of legitimacy works in a different context is the relationship of the police with survivors of sexual violence in New Zealand. Some women justifiably view the police as illegitimate in their dealings with survivors of sexual violence, because of a number of high-profile incidents involving the police perpetrating sexual violence against women. Until the police regain their legitimacy in this area (by taking steps to address institutional misogyny, which they have begun to do through, for example, appointing sexual violence survivor Louise Nicholas as a police advisor), there is a risk that the police will not be approached where sexual violence does occur, or will not be believed or respected in their treatment of these cases. How legitimacy is achieved by institutions is a matter for each institution to determine, but it is important that external perspectives, historical mistakes and structural prejudices are taken into account.

the justice system must be accessible

Justice might be unachievable if an institution is illegitimate – but it will also be hindered if the justice system is inaccessible to those who need to use it. In this sense, legitimacy fits under the rubric of accessibility. The justice system can be inaccessible in many ways: because of the overly formal language it uses, because of alienating ceremonies or rituals, or because of how much money it costs to use. If New Zealand politicians and policy-makers are committed to achieving justice – and restoring ethical equilibrium as far as possible after it has been disrupted by injustice – they must ensure that there are no reasons for the system to be inaccessible. This may require significant changes to the existing operation of the justice system, or significant financial commitments. (I look at some of these issues below.)

the justice system requires policies that are effective

It is a truism that for justice to be achieved effective policies must be adopted. What does this deceptively simple line mean? It means that justice policies should contribute to the aims that they claim to pursue, and that those aims should themselves be tied to justice. To apply this slightly abstract point to a real-life policy: imprisonment policy should *actually* contribute to public safety, and that public safety should be tied to justice. The assumptions underlying the use of imprisonment must be tested against evidence, and the conceptual connections between imprisonment and justice must be clearly laid out. As well, for a justice policy to be effective, it must be appropriate to New Zealand culture and conditions; policies borrowed uncritically from other countries are unlikely to achieve their aims if those policies were originally designed in different conditions.

the justice system must treat people with care

Finally, while all policies must be effective, that principle is subject to another principle: that all individuals are treated by the justice system with care. Care is a fundamental progressive value discussed earlier, but it needs elaboration in this context of how the state specifically demonstrates care (as opposed to political activists or campaigners demonstrating care). I consider that where a state exercises public power, that power must be exercised in a way that treats people with care. That minimal constraint on public power prevents abuse of power, acknowledges the respect that individuals and groups deserve when they submit to state authority, and models an appropriate relationship between state and subject. Care requires thinking in advance about how individuals and groups are affected by an action, sensitivity to the needs of individuals and groups, and ongoing concern for those individuals and groups. In the sphere of justice, care is embodied in part through standards of human rights, and should be extended to all involved, including victims of crime and perpetrators.

There is a possible counter-argument that those who perpetrate horrific criminal acts are not deserving of care: they have forfeited their rights. My view is that state treatment of perpetrators in this way only creates a new injustice suffered by those perpetrators. What is more, denying care to perpetrators of crime may undermine their reintegration into society, resulting in a risk of further crime and even more injustices for new victims. Care is a crucial principle in any progressive country. It should not be waived or ignored in the justice realm, or indeed in any other part of the system, as we discussed in Chapter 6.

transforming the prison system

I visited Mt Eden Prison and what was then Auckland Central Remand Prison (ACRP) on a wintry day in 2010. I was helping to organise for a group of Auckland law students to be trained as prison volunteers, and talking to prison officers and administrators about what volunteers might usefully offer prisoners. We walked into ACRP first, and what I remember were the sterile, bone-white corridors and low ceilings. It was quieter than a hospital. The stillness made me feel claustrophobic, slightly sick. We then caught only a glimpse of Mt Eden Prison (before it was refurbished several years later), but I'll never forget it. As one of the prison administrators opened the gates of the old brick building, we were greeted with the sounds of screeching metal and shouting human beings – and a putrid smell. Prisoners shook the bars of blue cages. The place reminded me of a factory farm.[8]

Prisons are the shame of our generation – one of several blind spots in our moral vision. When the American public intellectual K. Anthony Appiah was asked what civil rights issue our society will be condemned for forgetting in future centuries, he nominated mass imprisonment.[9] Why did he suggest this? And, more broadly, what's wrong with prisons? After answering these questions, I set out how New Zealand might initiate a phased departure from a reliance on incarceration: what Angela Davis calls 'decarceration'.[10]

seven problems

First, prisons restrict social contact. They are institutions of enforced solitude, designed for individuals who, like all of us, generally desire social interaction. Prisoners can only interact with other prisoners, guards and prison officials; in New Zealand, prisoners are also entitled to one 30-minute visit a week at minimum (any further visits must be approved by individual prisons).[11]

Second, prisons suggest that prisoners are a subspecies of humanity. Prisons are separated from communities; in this way, '[t]he prisoner is detached from society … [and] leaves it', in the words of one writer.[12] Criminologist Nicola Lacey and psychologist Hanna Pickard have observed that prisoners are made to be seen as 'out-group members in society', which also harms reintegration.[13]

Third, prisons are structurally ill-equipped to deliver rehabilitation. Although the New Zealand department in charge of prisons is the Department of Corrections, achieving 'corrections' in the lives of prisoners is difficult when prisoners are only surrounded by other prisoners. One ex-prisoner recently described prisons as 'a finishing school for any upcoming [sic] prisoner'; the Principal Youth Court Judge Andrew Becroft, mentioned at the outset of this chapter, has called prisons 'universities of crime'.[14] 'Redemption scripts' (a story a person can tell themselves about the redeeming features of their life) are important if prisoners are to change – and these scripts are hard to write when individuals are identified every day in prison primarily as criminals.[15] As well, prisons are not similar to the outside world, and are therefore not conducive to rehabilitation. Indeed, they are designed to be different from the outside world in, for example, how much exercise and freedom of movement is allowed, how much social interaction and visiting is allowed, and the other deprivations of physical liberty faced by prisoners. In New Zealand, to take just one area of rehabilitative services, health services were found by an Ombudsman's report in 2012 to be inadequate, because of some of these underlying structural reasons. Mental health care was deemed to be unsuitable, dental services were unsatisfactory, and segregation of at-risk prisoners was said to be worse for prisoners' wellbeing in the long-term.[16] When I visited ACRP in 2010, the library had been closed for months because no staff were available to maintain it, meaning that prisoners had no direct access to reading materials. Overall, if rehabilitation cannot be secured through prisons, then prisons are not enhancing the cause of public safety, and leave society just as vulnerable (if not more vulnerable) when individuals are released from prison.

Fourth, prisons exclude from public view the country's most serious social problems. This might have the effect of delaying any real attempts to resolve those problems. The point is well expressed by prison abolitionist and writer Angela Davis: 'Prison relieves us of the responsibility of seriously engaging with the problems of our society, especially those produced by racism and, increasingly, global capitalism.'[17] In the New Zealand context, prisons relieve us of the responsibility of engaging with the ongoing effects of colonial disadvantage, mental health problems and drug abuse, among other problems. It has been estimated (according to 2010 figures) that, of New Zealand's approximately 8,500 prisoners, 89 per cent have been substance abusers at some point in their lives; 60 per cent of prisoners have a personality disorder; 52 per cent have experienced anxiety or psychotic disorders; and 64 per cent of male prisoners and 54 per cent of female prisoners have suffered a head injury.[18] 90 per cent of prisoners 'cannot read or write properly'.[19] It is therefore, sadly, no surprise that prisoners are 11 times more likely than the general population to commit suicide.[20]

Fifth, all around the world, prisons are ciphers for racial prejudices, with ethnic minorities invariably disproportionately represented in prison musters. In New Zealand, while Māori make up 15 per cent of the general population, they comprise 51 per cent of the prison population. In 2011, 704 out of 100,000 Māori were imprisoned;[21] this exceeds the national imprisonment rate of the US (698 per 100,000), which has the highest country-level imprisonment rate in the developed world. Such huge over-representation of Māori, which successive governments have not addressed, is partly due to the fact that – because of colonial policies of geographical dislocation, land confiscation and cultural disconnection, and the ongoing trauma of colonisation – many Māori fall into the most deprived categories of the New Zealand population, and are therefore more likely to commit crime. But other factors are at work. A 2009 report showed that 52 per cent of convicted offenders are reconvicted within five years. Māori are more likely than Pākehā to be reimprisoned after reoffending within five years: 58 per cent of Māori are reimprisoned, as opposed to 47.3 per cent of Pākehā.[22] Given that Māori have no genetic reason to reoffend, it is likely that there is some form of prejudice in play that makes police or judges or others more likely to re-imprison Māori than non-Māori; indeed, Police Commissioner Mike Bush admitted the existence of unconscious bias towards Māori within the police force in 2015.[23] It may be that there is a pernicious assumption that Māori are less capable of rehabilitation than non-Māori. While imprisonment is not the basis of racism itself, it is a particularly insidious theatre in which racist judgments are made.

Sixth, prisons are expensive. It costs $97,090 a year for a person to be incarcerated in New Zealand – far more than it costs to fund fully a year of university education for that person, or to pay them for a well-salaried job.[24] When New Zealand already has limited resources to invest in education, health care, housing and the future of its population, and when prison undermines wellbeing in the ways described above, this appears to be a questionable investment.

The investment might be justified if prisons fulfilled their aims, but the seventh and final problem with prisons is that they do not achieve their purported goals. As warehouses for human beings, they do, by dint of existing, cabin some people away from the rest of the community; they are successful, to some extent, in achieving incapacitation of offenders. But evidence shows that it is not imprisonment, but likelihood of apprehension, that deters crime

– so imprisonment does not serve a deterrent function, either in a general or a specific sense.[25] It is therefore those who champion deterrence through imprisonment – rather than those who oppose high rates of imprisonment – who are out of touch when they assume that crime happens through rational, methodical decision-making.

Prisons cannot be conducive environments for rehabilitation, for reasons mentioned above. It would be more honest, then, to rename the Department of Corrections something like the Department of Protection, although even this label would overestimate how much protection can be achieved through imprisonment. Prisons might serve some public disapproval function, but it is not clear why denunciation cannot be achieved in other forms (through court judgments and more personalised processes that allow offenders to see the harm that they have done). Overall, then, prisons undermine the fourth principle outlined in the last section of this chapter: that justice policies should be effective. They may give us a false sense of security. But they do not contribute meaningfully towards the society that we all want, a society with as little harmful offending as possible. (The Department of Corrections has acknowledged that this is an important aim by announcing publicly in its *Reducing Reoffending* 2011 strategy that it would aim to reduce reoffending by 25 per cent by 2017.) Instead, prisons represent a vengeful attempt by the state to punish – that is, to impose pain on – offenders.

It might be accepted that prisons are harmful, but perhaps, some might say, they are a necessary evil. Offenders *deserve* punishment, it could be said, for the wrongs they have committed. Victims need the closure secured by imprisonment. Some individuals need close supervision in spaces separate from society. And, after all, what are the alternatives?

Each of these arguments deserves consideration, but none overwhelms the powerful case about the harms caused by prison. On what prisoners deserve: it is true that some individuals have carried out horrific acts that require a public response and accountability. But it is not clear, as Kim Workman has said, that prisons – and the experience of solitude faced by many prisoners – do hold prisoners to account. Moreover, what is a 'fitting' or 'proportionate' response to a crime has changed over time, and prisons have only been seen as the dominant approach to serious crime since the early 1800s, when prison systems were established in the US and elsewhere.[26] Standardised prisons have only operated in New Zealand since 1876.[27]

The claim that victims require closure through imprisonment also makes intuitive sense but needs to be investigated further. While we should be careful about generalising about the needs of all victims (which is part of the problem of claiming an automatic link between victim closure and prisons), in many cases victims or survivors want to be assured of their safety and to avoid retraumatisation. Prison may sometimes provide the best assurance of a victim's safety – but it also might result in retraumatisation, including when the prisoner is inevitably released. A more direct strategy for addressing victims' needs is to provide state-funded counselling and support for victim trauma following crime. In this regard, the establishment of a National Victims Centre and Victims Code around 2011 should be applauded – although more could be done to provide direct support to victims through these mechanisms. (The Victims Centre, perhaps surprisingly, does not deliver services to victims at present, and instead refers victims to other providers in the community and elsewhere.) In all of this we should remember that, although victims' voices need to be heard and respected, the court system also exists in order to determine the appropriate response to crime, a step removed from the perpetrator and victim (if there is a victim in the case),[28] following the trauma of a crime.

Third, in relation to the protection of individuals and society, some people do indeed have deep pathologies and problems that make it possible that they will commit multiple offences over the course of a lifetime.[29] Some individuals committing violent crime seem to fit this description, as do many who commit sexual offences. Prisons that remove these individuals from society appear to offer the protection that society – and these individuals – need. However, it has already been noted above that because prisons are artificial environments, with limited social contact, prisoners may leave at least as likely (and perhaps more likely) to commit crime as when they entered. Prison does provide temporary protection. But we need to think harder, and work harder, as a society if we are to be truly committed to a society where there is no harmful offending.

Finally, it is simply wrong to assert that there are no alternatives to imprisonment: it is merely the case that alternatives to imprisonment require more imagination (or creativity, to recall a progressive value). There are already a number of effective alternatives to short-term imprisonment in place in Aotearoa New Zealand, including police-level diversion, electronic monitoring, home detention and restorative justice. Some of these alternatives have limitations, but they reveal that other policy options do exist. As for alternatives to long-term imprisonment, other countries – in particular, those in Scandinavia – have developed a number. Below I discuss in more detail what Norway has done in this field, based on a research trip I made there in late 2015. This again demonstrates that to say that there are no alternatives to imprisonment is a failure of imagination.

What this section highlights, I hope, is that prisons should not be maintained in their current form if we are committed to values of community, care and creativity; if we are committed to decolonisation; and if we want a justice system that is holistic, humane, effective and legitimate. Something must be done. But what? And how?

A useful frame for moving away from prisons in their current form is the already-mentioned 'decarceration'. Decarceration involves finding particular leverage points to target in order to reduce incarceration, and it can be supplemented by positive policy approaches that substitute for failed carceral practices.[30]

the norwegian approach

Norway's approach to criminal justice has been widely applauded. Norway's imprisonment rate is around a third of that of New Zealand: its rate in early 2017 was 74 per 100,000 (compared to New Zealand's 208 per 100,000), one of the lowest figures in the world. Norwegian prisons are known for being humane. As well, Norway has advanced victim support, including state compensation for victims of crime. With the financial support of the New Zealand Law Foundation, I travelled to Norway in late 2015 to explore how it has built this criminal justice system. I spoke off-the-record with a judge and a policeman, and had conversations with a criminal defence lawyer, a women's rights legal NGO, a legal academic and others (including many young people).

I had made inquiries about trying to visit a prison while in Norway, but with little luck. Then, after sending a message to a generic Norwegian public sector email address, I received a phone call out of the blue while I sat at a computer in downtown Oslo. A kind employee of the Norwegian Correctional Services Department, Ellen Bjercke, introduced herself. The good news, she told me, was that I would be able to visit a prison in Norway during the week I was there: Bastøy Prison. The bad news? It was a few hours away, and would require a long car trip and a ferry ride. Just as I began to worry about whether the journey was possible, though – in an act of extraordinary trust and kindness – Bjercke said she'd be happy to drive me.

A few days later, I met Ellen Bjercke on the Oslo waterfront early in the morning, and she drove me to the Bastøy ferry, cheerfully telling me en route about her experiences of the criminal justice system. When she dropped me off, she told me that the ferry was managed and operated by inmates at Bastøy Prison – one sign of the prison's thoughtful approach to developing skills in its inmates. I spoke a little to the inmates who worked as crew on the ferry, and a few minutes later, I arrived at Bastøy. It used to be called Devil's Island, because it was home to a notoriously grim boys' home. But since the 1980s the island has changed significantly, and it's now the site of an open prison, a place of wide paths, green lawns and tall trees.

In a small room, I was briefed by Tom Eberhardt, the Bastøy governor. Not a tall man, Eberhardt looked tough but friendly. He told me and several other visitors that Bastøy has a high staff–inmate ratio: 72 staff for 115 inmates (with 20–25 of the inmates being foreign nationals). There is a long waiting list for inmates wanting to transfer there. And inmates there have a choice of working in agriculture (in fields, the forest or with animals), maintenance and buildings, on the ferry, in the prison's kitchen, in the library, in carpentry, or on labour and welfare issues. One was studying for a PhD in criminology. Twenty to thirty per cent of the prison's food is grown on the island, and working with animals is seen as a way to teach inmates empathy. I took a walk around later to see the housing on the island and to have lunch. The inmates live in flats of different sizes. Inmates are placed carefully in flats to teach skills: prisoners with reduced hygiene or social skills are placed alongside those known to have greater abilities in these areas.

Tom Eberhardt explained a little bit of the philosophy that underpins the prison's operation. A key tenet is 'the principle of normality', he said, 'Everyday life in prison isn't meant to be different from everyday life outside of prison.' 'Inmates behave,' Eberhardt added, 'because they actually like being here.' Another principle is 'creating good neighbours': the prison aims to highlight that inmates are dependent on others, and that they need to be sensitive to the needs of others. When released, they 'will have to deal with other people's mindsets', he noted, so why not prepare them for this interaction within a community while in prison? He also observed, 'If you treat people badly, they will become bitter, angry – not be a good neighbor.' Helping inmates to become good neighbours therefore requires the prison to treat them well. Bastøy is a 'human ecological prison', too, based on the idea that we can take 'responsibility for ourselves by taking care of nature'. Care was clearly central to Bastøy's functioning: if you have no care for nature, Eberhardt said, you can't take care of yourselves.

Bastøy is clearly a successful prison, and the Norwegian Correctional Services Department – and Tom Eberhardt – are justifiably proud of it. There has been no violent episode there for the past 30 years. The prison helps to reintegrate its inmates into society. Eberhardt attributed this to the fact that '[t]hey're not released with hatred towards society'. As well, he told me, 'We haven't taken their hope away.' Eberhardt rejected the idea that justice should be about revenge. That cold day in December, he looked me in the eye and said: 'Revenge [in criminal justice] is like pissing your pants in Norway. It feels good. But then you start to freeze.'

How has Norway developed a criminal justice system with prisons such as Bastøy? Eberhardt: 'The culture in Norway is a forgiving culture.' In addition, he discussed the role of empathy, saying that policy-makers in Norway have asked, 'What kind of prison facility [would] you want for your son?' The point about empathy was echoed by Kari Henriksen, a Norwegian Labour MP with a deep interest in criminal justice, who told me that she could imagine herself being violent or becoming a criminal, and that such empathy was essential to policy-making. I cannot imagine a New Zealand politician being brave enough to say the same.

After returning to Oslo, I met with four representatives of KROM (the Norwegian Association of Penal Reform) to explore further the reasons for Norway's distinctive approach to criminal justice: Thomas Mathiesen, Ole Kristian Hjemdal, Sturla Falck and Kristian Andenaes. Thomas Mathiesen is a well-known Norwegian criminologist now in his 80s, the author of books such as *The Politics of Abolition* and *Prison on Trial*. Hjemdal, Falck and Andenaes have all done academic research and practical work in the criminal justice system. All four of them welcomed me warmly in a meeting room in an office block in downtown Oslo, and chatted for around two hours about their experiences and impressions.

Norway has not always been progressive in its criminal justice policy, they underscored. Key changes were made in the 1970s, and Mathiesen, Hjemdal, Falck and Andenaes emphasised three factors as being central to these shifts.

First, the climate of the 1960s and 1970s was important. 'We are children of our time,' one said. 1968 was a year of protest, especially in Europe, and the decade also brought a sense of hope and imagination to political debates. Criminal justice reforms in Norway were hence 'part of a larger change of values and basic policies'.

A second factor was the work of the Norwegian Labour Party politician Inger Louise Valle. Valle pushed hard, they told me, to introduce legislative changes in the criminal justice field that had a far-reaching effect on Norway's low prison population.

Third, I heard about the 'long-term insistence' of groups like KROM, campaigning to entrench a greater spirit of forgiveness in Norwegian society. The KROM representatives were reluctant to give themselves too much credit. But it was clear, from this conversation and the off-the-record remarks of others, that KROM had made a significant difference: including through its almost fifty-year history of annual conferences bringing together inmates, the public sector, lawyers, academics, students and judges. In sum, then: empathy (not far removed from the value of care), a broader climate of progressive values, individual political leadership and persistent campaigning were identified as the main reasons for why Norway's criminal justice system has become humane, forgiving – and largely effective.

Such was the perspective of one set of observers. Mathiesen, Hjemdal, Falck and Andenaes were at pains not to romanticise Norway, and they highlighted the return of punitive incarceration policies in recent years. Nevertheless, their insights – and my visit to Bastøy Prison – provided some hints about how a country of similar size to New Zealand (Norway has 5.2 million people) can build a justice system that is based on more than just revenge.

practical steps to transform the new zealand system

So what about New Zealand? It is helpful, as a matter of context, to outline how long most prisoners currently spend in New Zealand prisons. Unfortunately, official statistics on the average length of an imprisonment sentence that is served are not easily available. (The statistics cannot be compiled based on initial sentencing judgments following conviction, since how long a person spends in prison after sentencing is based on a range of further factors, often considered by the Parole Board.) Kim Workman noted in 2011 that 40 per cent of prisoners serve a term of only six months or less, while 85 per cent of prisoners will leave prison in under two years.[31] These figures should surprise most, in light of the media coverage, which might lead some to thinking that a majority of prisoners (or at least a sizeable proportion of them) are high-risk individuals serving long sentences. What Workman's figures reveal is that the vast majority of prisoners are in New Zealand prisons for short periods.

One response to these statistics is to say that they are evidence that prison sentences are too short in New Zealand. But we have already seen that we imprison more people than many countries in the world.

A better response to the figures, I think, is that (arguably more effective) alternatives to imprisonment could be used for a large number of offenders in New Zealand. A judge must already consider home detention where a sentence of two years' imprisonment or less is imposed.[32] But it would be possible to introduce more intensive rehabilitation for individuals who would serve short-term sentences, rather than home detention, in order to address causes of offending. My experience as a law student, and then working as a clerk (or researcher) for Chief Justice Elias at the Supreme Court for 18 months, suggested that in many cases of offending, certain factors arise: mental illness, childhood trauma (especially childhood sexual abuse), head injuries, alcoholism and drug addiction. An effort could be made to catalogue these common causes, and then to channel offenders towards centres of rehabilitative best practice that intensively address these underlying issues. As far as possible, these centres might avoid some of the pitfalls of prisons in their current form: they could be designed more like the rest of society (without uniformed prison guards), and could try to encourage social contact and to reduce social isolation. The channelling of offenders towards these centres might be overseen by 'problem-solving courts', such as the Family Violence Courts and Alcohol and Other Drug Treatment Courts piloted in New Zealand, based on successful models pioneered by the Center for Court Innovation in the US.

Restorative justice could also be used more for these offenders serving relatively short prison terms. In the Youth Court, Family Group Conferences are used before a person is charged (to determine whether there should be a prosecution) and afterwards, and anecdotal reports suggest that where an offender confronts the victim of an offence, there can be a significant sense of accountability. At the end of 2014, a legislative amendment required judges to inquire into the possibility of restorative justice in every adult criminal case.[33] The spirit of this reform could be continued to ensure that offenders with relatively short prison sentences undergo rehabilitation and, ideally, a restorative justice process.

What about prisoners with longer sentences? Does dividing 'short-term' and 'long-term' prisoners perpetuate a long-held (but scientifically unfounded) view that some individuals are capable, and others inherently incapable, of being rehabilitated? It is clear that there are some prisoners from which society needs greater protection, and that some physical separation between these prisoners and others would be necessary. I suggest that protective institutions would need to be maintained for these prisoners, but that these institutions could be designed very differently from current prisons. As with Norwegian prisons like Bastøy (even for offenders who have committed serious crime), these protective institutions might use plain-clothed officials, encourage social contact and offer rehabilitative services. The hope that individuals might be rehabilitated should be maintained, even if this is very difficult in some cases.

It could be argued, as Kim Workman noted in his interview with me, that the absence of mixing between offenders who have committed more serious crime and individuals serving shorter-term sentences would be detrimental to offenders. But this can be addressed by ensuring adequate social contact is provided to both groups; furthermore, the reality is that prisons in New Zealand today are segregated at a national level through the use of high-security prisons, and locally within prisons through the use of at-risk units. Thus, this objection does not seem to be a major concern for the establishment of protective institutions. With rehabilitative centres and protective institutions in place, it would make sense to have a moratorium on the building of traditional prisons.

These ideas might seem radical to some, but they have been proposed and – in part – implemented before. In 1989, retired judge Clinton Roper led a Ministerial Committee of Inquiry into the Prisons System, written up in a report entitled *Te Ara Hou: The New Way*. The report (mentioned by Kim Workman at the outset of this chapter) proposed dividing humane sites of containment from rehabilitation centres, which the report called 'habilitation centres', since many prisoners were never 'habilitated' before they could be 'rehabilitated'. Some pilot Habilitation Centres were set up, as Kim Workman told me, but political will was lacking and no effort was made to ensure the pilots were sufficiently resourced.

How could a transformed system of protection and correction work in New Zealand today, and how could we move from the politics of today to this new vision of criminal justice? A moratorium on building new prisons might be announced, at the same time that a (re)habilitation centre and protective institution pilot is funded and established (which might include restorative justice for those directed towards rehabilitation or habilitation centres). It would seem possible for this to be cost-neutral, given the current costs involved with maintaining prisons; the legislative framework for this move would also need to be carefully designed. There is no need for further inquiries and reports on prisons, but as part of these reforms, consideration should be given to serious steps that can be taken to reduce Māori over-representation in the criminal justice system,[34] and to the role of remand prisons in New Zealand's imprisonment regime more generally. It is not known by many that a notable proportion of people in prison in New Zealand and around the world have not yet been convicted of a crime. In New Zealand, as of 2014, 21.6 per cent of the entire prison population is on remand, arguably violating the principle that a person should not have their liberty significantly restricted until convicted through a fair trial.[35]

What I've just said assumes some degree of political will for changes in the criminal justice system, which is not inconceivable given certain moves by the National-led government and global trends away from imprisonment (including in the US, where there has been bipartisan support for attempts to phase out mass incarceration). But what if there is no political appetite for these changes?

The public campaign in favour of decarceration, already strongly initiated by groups such as the Howard League for Penal Reform, Rethinking Crime and Punishment, and JustSpeak, should continue. More thought could be directed towards building creative alliances of partners supportive of transforming New Zealand's criminal justice system. Some attempt was made to do this in Wellington through a formation of a Justice Coalition in 2010–11; such efforts could be redoubled. Groups that could be engaged include activists coming from a religious perspective (who currently contribute large numbers of prison volunteers), mental health advocates, those interested in fiscal responsibility in government, retired judges (who have been influential in various campaigns in the UK, including the campaign for the government to take more refugees in 2015), campaigners for just treatment of Māori in Aotearoa, and others. Lessons can be learned from environmental campaigners, who have shown that positive messaging is a more effective way to mobilise people into action on the environment;[36] it might be noted that New Zealand will be on the right side of history if it chooses to think beyond the prison.[37]

While the campaign should focus on policy and political action, language matters in shaping how we see people within our community – and part of the campaign might involve seeing prisoners as human beings who have committed crime, rather than as 'criminals' (a label that defines a person by the worst thing they have done). This reshaping of the debate could be done in part by focusing on the impact of prison on prisoners' families. The New Zealand television series *Prison Families*; the New Zealand charity PILLARS, which concentrates on prisoners' children; and JustSpeak have all begun to highlight this harmful effect of prisons.

Some will dismiss this as unrealistic. But we all – the public, the media, politicians – define what is politically realistic in New Zealand. We decide how wide or narrow our Overton window of political possibility can be. These suggestions for our prison system require debate, further consideration and action; it is those people who reject the suggestions outright who need to be fought against, to ensure that our politics can be less cramped and more visionary.

addressing child sexual abuse and other forms of sexual and family violence

When I worked as a judge's clerk, a friend – also working as a judge's clerk in the High Court, primarily on criminal cases – observed that what surprised her most about working for judges was the number of sex offending and child sex offending cases in the New Zealand courts.[38] Sexual violence, especially involving children – and the inability of families and communities to address such violence – is a strong theme across New Zealand television and movies, including the late Brad McGann's film *In My Father's Den* (based on Maurice Gee's novel), and Jane Campion's series *Top of the Lake*.

New Zealand has a serious sexual violence problem that remains under-discussed in the media, schools and other forums. Family violence, which includes some sexual violence, is now an increasing focus of political attention. In late 2015, the Ministry of Justice released a discussion document reviewing family violence laws, which noted that New Zealand has the highest reported rate of intimate-partner violence in the world and the fifth-highest rate of child abuse.[39] New Zealand's rates of sexual violence, including child sexual violence, are similarly horrific. A 2011 United Nations report on the status of women ranked New Zealand as the worst of all OECD countries measured in terms of rates of sexual assault.[40] The New Zealand Crime and Safety Survey in 2006, which could have under-reported rates of sexual violence, showed that 29 per cent of women – almost one in three women in New Zealand – experienced sexual violence over their lifetime. In the Health and Wellbeing of Secondary School Students in New Zealand survey in 2007 and 2012, 20 per cent of young women – one in five – said they had been touched in a sexual way or made to do unwanted sexual things in the previous 12 months. In the World Health Organization's 2003 Multi-country Study on Violence Against Women, 20 per cent of New Zealand women said they had experienced child sexual abuse. To corroborate these statistics, the much-lauded Dunedin Multidisciplinary Health and Development Research Study found that of its 465 female participants, 30 per cent had experienced childhood sexual abuse.[41]

It hardly needs to be said that these are shocking figures. Child sexual abuse, other forms of sexual violence, and family violence, can have a deep, damaging effect on individual wellbeing, future relationships, and physical health. Child sexual abuse can be an underlying factor in the patterns of many offenders discussed in this chapter (though of course it does not follow from this that all who are abused are at high risk of abusing others). What the statistics cited above show is that victims or survivors of sexual and family violence are not alone – and that New Zealand has a problem.

But we are not talking about it – or at any rate not talking about it enough. Sexual violence and family violence are different issues, with some distinct causes, features and patterns. What they share, however, is that they are both matters of justice where New Zealand has high rates of offending, and as a society – in families, in communities, in media, in law enforcement and in politics – those high rates of offending have been ignored for too long. They are not easy issues to discuss, and they should be discussed on the terms of people who have survived and experienced sexual and family violence. Yet the space has not been created to welcome those discussions.

What can be done? I sat down with Fiona McNamara from the Sexual Abuse Prevention Network and Eleanor Butterworth of Wellington Rape Crisis to discuss this; Butterworth has also worked with Women's Refuge on family violence issues and was able to share some experiences of working in this field. We sat in a boardroom in Willis Street, with the two women seated in front of a wall that displayed a 'herstory' – a set of photographs and articles – of different organisations that have fought sexism of various forms in New Zealand society. The Sexual Abuse Prevention Network aims to stop sexual violence before it happens, and carries out trainings with schools, bar staff, the defence force and others; it aims to change the culture and the discussion of sexual abuse. Rape Crisis works on awareness-raising and provides support to survivors of sexual violence, especially in building life skills and managing symptoms of trauma.

McNamara and Butterworth told me that the causes of sexual violence in New Zealand are complex, and suggested that more work needed to be done on thinking through why the country has such high rates. What is known is that rape culture 'is really prevalent in New Zealand society', said McNamara – 'widespread attitudes and behaviours' that encourage sexual violence (including through film and television depiction of sex) and that are 'just considered normal'. Legislation matters, Butterworth observed: the fact that marital rape remained legal in New Zealand until 1985 created a mindset about violence within the family. The effects of colonisation for Māori are relevant, Butterworth noted. They have contributed to a loss of faith in the law, which has been caused by other factors too – and which has also limited the ability for people facing oppression to address other injustices through the legal system. McNamara said that technology and the digital world should not be given too much blame for sexual violence. 'It's behaviours that are the issue, and not the technology,' she observed, saying that technology can be a part of healthy sex lives. Butterworth agreed: 'Technology multiplies and magnifies what we see, but it's just a reflection of our offline selves.'

They went on to say that in some ways family violence and sexual violence have overlapping causes: they cited research by Janet Fanslow of the New Zealand Family Violence Clearinghouse indicating that 50 per cent of people suffering sexual violence go on to face family (domestic) violence. But interventions need to be carefully tailored. Women's Refuge has designed responses for those facing family violence, and there are service providers (including Rape Crisis and the Sexual Abuse Prevention Network) addressing sexual violence specifically. WellStop is a New Zealand provider of treatment for individuals who have committed sexual abuse; and McNamara noted that UK service providers, such as Stop it Now!, have made good use of phone helplines to allow people at risk of committing sexual abuse to discuss their concerns.

Research is being developed on family violence and sexual violence issues, and in some ways sexual violence is in the spotlight in New Zealand and globally, they noted. But big holes remain in the discussion, Butterworth said: university complaints processes for sexual violence aren't functional, and there is little consent education or education about healthy relationships in schools or among parents (although healthy relationships education improved over the course of the writing of this book between 2015 and 2017, as Butterworth told me).

Even more worryingly, while awareness is slowly growing, practical sources of support for sexual violence and family violence have been undercut in recent years. Butterworth drew on her eighteen months at Rape Crisis and five years of work at Women's Refuge to explain what had happened. 'I've watched a really serious erosion of people's rights,' she said, in 'access to legal aid, their access to benefits – and those are effectively the tools that let you leave a violent relationship or recover from sexual violence.' She glanced at me. 'Despite all of this noise, in terms of actual protections, those have been eroded more in the last seven years [2008–15] than I've seen in my previous seven years doing this sort of work. We keep talking about it, but no one is talking about the fact that now it is very difficult to access legal aid if you have any sort of employment or assets, regardless [of whether] you are too low-earning to be able to afford $150–300 per hour for legal representation, which is what you need to defend a protection order … They have to pay $800 if they want to lodge with the Family Court. … We've lost the lawyers for children. The list goes on and on.'

Why have those protections been eroded? 'I think it's about money,' Butterworth told me. 'And it's about ideology: we think people use the Family Court to sort out petty differences rather than to seek protection as a last resort.' Her final comment on this topic was perhaps the bluntest: 'I was talking to a lawyer who was involved in the original DVA [Domestic Violence Act] 1995 drafting and they said to me: "The people who are making these choices know the impact this is going to have on victims and don't give a shit".'

What can be drawn out from these comments is that the rise in victims' rights advocacy from groups such as the Sensible Sentencing Trust has supported some victims but not others. Victims' rights advocacy has not been consistent. From that realisation it's not a stretch to conclude that it hasn't been sincere or wholehearted.

There are some obvious practical steps that might be taken to begin to address the scandal of sexual and family violence in the New Zealand community, alongside the need to tackle aspects of New Zealand masculinity discussed in Chapter 10. First, there needs to be more of a society-wide conversation about sexual and family violence (while of course respecting the privacy and autonomy of victims or survivors), and greater efforts to reduce stigma for those coming forward as victims or survivors.

Second, support services need to be properly funded. As Eleanor Butterworth has said, 'It's about money'. Without sufficient funding, organisations are not able to provide the support needed for victims or survivors, which can result in further social or health problems. Some $700,000 of funding was cut by the government in 2011; it should be accepted that a re-investment of this amount will be necessary to restore an appropriate level of funding. The government should also consider boosting funding to services such as WellStop and helpline providers, which can prevent sexual and family violence offending, and identify at-risk behaviour. It may be that money can be redirected from current public spending in prisons.

Third, researchers should be encouraged to continue to investigate the New Zealand-specific causes of sexual and family violence, in order to highlight to policy-makers the levers that should be pulled to address this violence. Work should continue to go into considering the recommendations of the Law Commission's 2015 report on sexual violence and the justice system, relating to changes in courtroom procedure, alternatives to trial, and support for victims or survivors of sexual and family violence.[42] It must be hoped that these steps will reduce the number of horrific sexual and family violence cases coming through our courts, and make it less likely that these stories will continue to run like a thread through New Zealand film and television.

removing financial barriers to justice

Eleanor Butterworth spoke about cuts to legal aid, and their devastating impact on victims of family and sexual violence. Legal aid is the system of state funding for those who cannot afford a lawyer. Between 2010 and 2014, the Key-led government cut $55 million in funding for legal aid, and passed the Legal Services Act 2011. That prohibited legal aid from being granted in certain immigration cases (a seemingly controversial move that was little discussed at the time), and set out a repayment system for legal aid, managed by the Legal Services Commissioner, which requires interest to be paid on legal aid debt. The Legal Services Regulations 2011 set out eligibility for legal aid in noncriminal matters. They note, for instance, that any single person earning more than $22,366 is not eligible for legal aid. The eligibility cap increases in light of family size, so that, for example, a person with a spouse and two dependent children or a person with three dependent children will be eligible for legal aid if they earn under $57,880. The regulations also specify a maximum level of disposable capital for those receiving legal aid and note that a person's capital will be evaluated before legal aid is granted. The interest rate for repayment of legal aid debt is set at 8 per cent. For criminal matters, the Legal Services Act requires that the Legal Services Commissioner considers various factors, but a prerequisite under section 8 is that a person 'does not have sufficient means to enable him or her to obtain legal assistance'.

Restrictions on legal aid create numerous problems, which have been relayed in three particularly powerful articles, by lawyer Frances Joychild QC; then Chief High Court Judge (now Court of Appeal Judge) Helen Winkelmann, and Chief High Court Judge Geoffrey Venning. Lawyers and judges are very much on the front line in the law; they see the impacts of policy and legal changes every day, and their view should be given significant weight.

Joychild has noted that the legal aid rules are particularly complicated. This deters individuals from seeking legal aid. Nineteen matters have to be explained to individuals considering legal aid. Then the person has to be told that they might have to repay some of the legal aid granted to them, that interest will be charged on all outstanding debt after the conclusion of the case (with seemingly no time for a person to collect the money to pay for it), that debt collectors could be sent and that debt collection fees may have to be paid, that debts can be deducted from income or bank accounts, and that legal professional privilege (the legal protection of confidentiality between lawyer and client) has to be waived.[43] Apart from being bureaucratic, the problem with this regime of rules is that if it discourages people from seeking legal aid, they may not take, say, a civil case. They might decide to take an injustice 'on the chin', resulting in it being left to fester.

The limitations of legal aid cuts go beyond bureaucracy and deterrence. The cuts are also inefficient and lead to stress. Justice Venning and Justice Winkelmann, in their speeches on access to justice, both speak about how legal aid cuts have increased the number of people choosing to represent themselves rather than to hire a lawyer. They note that this can lengthen trials, thereby increasing legal costs for the other side, and they cause difficulties for judges and court staff, resulting in heightened workplace stress. They both hint that such cuts could be a violation of the Magna Carta, which says, 'To no one will we see, to no one deny or delay right or justice' – and that they might imperil access to justice principles. Magna Carta is not binding in New Zealand but it is an important source of legal principle. Justice Venning notes that cuts have resulted in a 'limited number' of litigants being publicly funded, and points out that the income caps for legal aid provision are 'relatively low'. Justice Winkelmann is even more strident:

> The court system is for many a foreign land and the notion of bringing proceedings without legal representation can be compared to the fearful prospect of being stranded in a foreign land unable to speak the language, and without the money needed to find your way home. We should be very concerned to assess the extent of this unmet need for justice. If courts dispense justice for only the few, what does this mean for our concept that we are a nation that exists under the rule of law?[44]

The upshot of all of this is that cutting funding for legal aid might make the justice system more expensive for all. The other side in a dispute may have to pay more for their lawyers, since trials might be lengthened through the presence of self-represented litigants. The government may have to pay more, as court staff work overtime and around the clock. Government lawyers may also have to work more to deal with appeals from self-represented matters. Restrictions on legal aid are therefore inefficient as well as unprincipled. The broader principles of any justice system – that it be effective, legitimate and accessible (among others) – cannot be maintained while legal aid is approached in this way.

But we cannot just throw up our hands in despair. We should try to be practical in recommending a way forward for lawyers, policy-makers and politicians. First, it is incumbent upon future New Zealand governments to reassert the centrality of legal aid to a progressive state. New Zealanders value public education and public health. Public funding for justice – through legal representation – should be valued in a similar way.[45] Lawyers and judges can support this cause by drawing attention to success stories, where injustices have been addressed through the public funding of legal advocacy. Second, the legal aid cuts of the early 2010s should be reversed. But policy-makers and politicians could go further still. A broader review should be undertaken into the various ways (including financial) in which our system of justice is accessible. Do the rituals and ceremonies of our justice system (the language of courts, the clothing and the design of courtrooms in particular) make justice seem less welcoming to some in the New Zealand population? Investing in this review, and in legal aid, is a reasonable price to pay to ensure that justice is done and seen to be done in Aotearoa New Zealand.

making the judiciary legitimate

The discussion of legal aid highlights that it is not just issues of justice we must consider (such as prisons, and family and sexual justice) but how institutions of justice are designed. Politicians, policy-makers and committed citizens must constantly ask whether our institutions of justice – the courts, for instance – are discouraging people from resolving injustices. Do courts appear hostile towards Māori litigants, for example, and should courts and the justice system be transformed so that Māori approaches to justice are better reflected in the New Zealand justice system? This question has begun to be addressed in a limited way, with the introduction of rangatahi (marae-based) courts for some offending and the increased use of te reo Māori in courtroom greetings by judges and lawyers from the mid-2010s.[46] As with the Roper Review, there is a report from the 1980s that is worth revisiting on this issue: Moana Jackson's *He Whaipaanga Hou: Māori and the Criminal Justice System – A New Perspective*.[47] Some of Jackson's proposals – such as the creation of a public defence service and the establishment of a Māori centre for cultural research – have been taken up since they were offered in 1988, but a number (including the proposal for a creation of a Māori law commission and greater restriction of police discretion) remain relevant and have not been implemented.[48]

In this final section of the chapter, I want to touch on one discrete justice-related institutional change: the need to increase the diversity of judges. As of 2017, while three out of six of New Zealand's Supreme Court judges were women (none identifying as Māori), just two out of ten Court of Appeal judges were women; one identified as Māori. In 2015, there were 38 High Court judges; eleven were women and two were Māori. Of 158 District Court judges, 46 High Court judges were women and figures were not readily available on Māori identification among those judges. At every level except the Supreme Court, women make up less than 33 per cent of New Zealand judges; and at every level except the District Court (where figures are unknown), 10 per cent or fewer judges are Māori. This does not even consider socio-economic background, sexual orientation or legal background. Information about these issues is not easily accessible, though there is likely to be under-representation of judges from a low socio-economic background or who are Pasifika, or lesbian, bisexual, gay or transgender. There is only one openly gay judge, for example, on the High Court, Court of Appeal or Supreme Court. It is also well known that the majority of judges appointed to the High Court and above have been commercial barristers; there are fewer judges with significant experience in criminal, public or community law. These numbers reveal a problem in the New Zealand justice system: judges, who wield significant power, do not reflect the population.

To some this might not seem a problem: judges are different from politicians, after all; they are not voted in by the general public, and for good reason – so that they can make independent judgments about what is right in a particular case. I will return to this claim below. But for now it is important to explain why these figures are worrying. As Chief Justice Elias has said of the under-representation of women in the judiciary, the figures are a denial of equality under international law for women, Māori and others. They also undermine the legitimacy of the judiciary. Further, having women judges – and perhaps Māori judges – may lead to different and better outcomes, not only because of the different life experiences of women and Māori, but also because the appointment of women and Māori judges results in 'shifts in the attitudes of judges, which can be attributed to working contact with people of the other sex, of different sexual orientation or of different race or culture'.[49] Judges are not mechanical discoverers of the law; judges make law (as part of the development of the common law), and draw on life experiences in making decisions about competing interests and values. Justice Susan Glazebrook, a Supreme Court judge, has added an additional reason in favour of greater diversity among judges: she has said that a judiciary that is not diverse is unlikely to be making the best use of 'available human resources'.[50]

Explanations for the lack of diversity in the judiciary are many. Stereotypical assumptions about leadership, traditional networks, role modelling and mentoring, and (for women) family responsibilities have been given as reasons for the under-representation of certain groups.[51] It is a common response to this problem that there are fewer women and Māori in the senior levels of the legal profession, and that therefore there are not enough qualified candidates to improve diversity in the judiciary. This may be partly true, but it is not a benign development in itself, and politicians and policy-makers have a role in changing the profile of the legal profession, in decisions about who to appoint as QCs (Queen's Counsel – that is, senior barristers) and in monitoring discrimination. Another claim is that things are getting better – that it is just a matter of time. Justice Susan Glazebrook has demolished this myth, showing that in the area of appointments of women to the judiciary, recent stagnation in the progress of women within the legal profession is concerning and we should not be complacent.[52]

The current process for appointments cannot continue without a shift in approach. At present, the attorney-general (also a politician, who is part of the government) recommends judicial appointments to the governor-general. The process is a little opaque. Advice is taken from the solicitor-general and chief justice for Supreme Court appointments, and from the secretary of justice and the chief District Court judge for District Court appointments. A unit within the Ministry of Justice also supports the attorney-general in making appointments.

The Courts of New Zealand website notes that:[53]

Successive Attorneys-General have announced new systems designed to widen the search for potential candidates and increase the opportunity for input. Within the past 10 years the systems adopted by Attorneys-General have resulted in a more diversified judiciary.

However, there is room for disagreement with this claim – and more importantly, it seems that not enough is being done. Two practical changes could be implemented. First, aspirational targets could be adopted by the attorney-general and Ministry of Justice support unit, aiming to boost significantly the appointment of judges from under-represented groups, such as women, Māori, Pasifika and those from lower socio-economic backgrounds. Second, consideration could be given to establishing a judicial appointments commission of the kind established in the UK in 2006.[54] This would build more independence into judicial appointments (although the attorney-general would still be involved, and notwithstanding the fact that judicial appointments are allegedly not currently influenced by politics). The existence of a judicial appointments commission would also ensure that explicit attention is being paid to diversity in the judiciary. Funding for the new commission would be necessary, but would require a relatively small amount of funds. Not all aspects of the UK model, such as the written test for new judges that its commission has used, need to be adopted. Moreover, such a commission would not be a panacea to diversity problems. In the UK, there remains just one female judge on the Supreme Court, out of the eleven judges that sit on that Court, though a Judicial Appointments Commission has been in operation for almost a decade. But the commission has been said to have increased the proportion of female judges in the UK from 18 per cent to 25 per cent (admittedly, mostly at the lower levels), and to have moved away from a system that was 'pure establishment – a tap on the shoulder, a cup of tea and Bob was your uncle'.[55] A similar change might need to be considered in New Zealand.

conclusion

Debate on justice in this country has become skewed in recent years. Justice is not only about victims' rights, or safety through imprisonment, or revenge. Justice is a complex concept that requires a holistic approach, an accessible system, legitimacy, effective policy and humanity. I have tried here, sensitively, to apply these principles to topics that have been ignored for too long.

If all of the recommendations of this chapter were implemented, injustices would still remain in New Zealand – the analysis here isn't a complete blueprint for achieving justice. However, what can be hoped is that a more just Aotearoa would be achieved if debate and action were to be kick-started on issues of imprisonment, family and sexual violence, legal aid and diversity in the judiciary.

If we all worked together to address these issues, we would be resisting the temptation to play down to our fears and to the base parts of humanity in the formulation of justice policy. We would instead be choosing courageously to live up to the legacy of the thinking done already by people like Clinton Roper, Moana Jackson and Kim Workman – and the work done every day, on the front line, by people like Fiona McNamara and Eleanor Butterworth.

Chapter 8 shifts tack, and turns attention to the future of work in New Zealand. It asks: how should the changing world of work be addressed in this country? And can a politics of love be applied to this sphere?

8 the politics of love: and the changing world of work

So far in this book, the values of care, community and creativity have been explained and applied to different policy contexts. In certain policy spheres, one particular value has loomed large. The approach taken to foreign policy in Chapter 4 drew on creativity, since I believe that the best understanding of 'independent foreign policy' is a foreign policy that is ethically justified, relatively non-aligned and pursued creatively. The discussion of social infrastructure – health, housing and education – in Chapter 6 placed emphasis on community: the need to engage the community in order to build responses to rheumatic fever, and the importance of seeing us all as a part of one broader community when considering homelessness and educational inequality. Care was central in Chapter 7, in the analysis of justice policy and moving New Zealand away from its reliance on imprisonment.

A love-based politics is an extension, not just an application, of values of care, community and creativity. Love is a stronger value than care. Whereas care is interest in, and concern for, the position of others, love is a deep warmth directed towards another. Love is more visceral and more active than care. But it emerges from the same root: the 'extremely difficult realisation', in Iris Murdoch's words, 'that something other than oneself is real'.[1] It's about looking outside of ourselves.[2] A politics of love is also connected to community and creativity. As in the Māori concept of aroha, love is associated with relationships: it is a relational sentiment, which requires at least two actors to be expressed. (The only exception is self-love, though even self-love can be understood relationally: as the passing of warmth from one part of our self to another.) Community, too, is grounded in the idea that we are all related and that we should all seek to build relationships with each other. A politics of love is creative in the sense that it aims to be imaginative in finding fresh ways of thinking about politics, and in the sense that it aims to *create* and build new approaches to policy, rhetoric and the interactions between people and politicians.

This chapter presents the politics of love as a possible resource that goes beyond the cornerstone progressive values and can be used by those engaged in politics – activists, politicians and all who have opinions about how power should be organised and used. I attempt to apply a politics of love to a cluster of challenges relating to the changing world of work, in order to show that a politics of love is not some distant fantasy, but rather a framework that can be practically useful. I explore the position of people who can face work-related challenges in Aotearoa New Zealand: beneficiaries, those receiving accident compensation, the elderly, and people with disabilities. Attention then turns to those in paid employment but in an insecure position, or what has come to be known as 'the precariat'.[3] I address the position of those in more secure work, discussing the future of unions. I close with some reflections on a world beyond work.

Before love is connected to these various public policy puzzles, a little more should be said about the politics of love.[4] What would it mean for love – a deep warmth directed towards another – to be more broadly incorporated into politics? A politics of love can mean at least four things. It can mean that political action is *motivated* by love: that activists, politicians and others ensure that everything they do is driven by a desire to direct warmth towards others, as opposed to being motivated by power or prestige or self-interest. It can mean that political action ought to *express* love: that the language of politics, and the substance of policy, should radiate love. It can mean that love is the *end-goal* of politics: that all political action is focused on achieving love. It can mean that love is a *virtue* that we appreciate in those participating in politics – a quality that we seek and acknowledge in those doing political work. Those interested in a politics of love can select which version is most attractive to them. But the most fully realised, thoroughgoing politics of love integrates all four forms of love into politics: love as motivation, love as expressed through politics, love as end-goal, and love as virtue.

It is important to distinguish the registers in which a politics of love can be presented as well as its forms. A politics of love can be superficial (articulated to get votes), minimalist (thinly defined, with different people drawing on love to reach different conclusions about policy) or substantive (defined 'thickly', in a way that requires the preconditions of love to be secured and people's need for love to be recognised). My preference is for a substantive politics of love. It fulfils the promise of love most fully, by not merely nodding to love rhetorically or minimally but ensuring that love is genuinely translated into policy and political action.

On all views of a politics of love, the group of people that receive love – the recipients of love – should be defined as widely as possible, to include all people within a political community. It is in the essence of love itself that attention is given to another, and that the circle of our concern is widened,[5] so it would be inconsistent with love to artificially restrict the scope of a politics of love.

Love is not the same as compassion or empathy – both of these are less active sentiments – and cannot be reduced to these other values. A politics of love is compatible with anger and conflict, since anger can be expressed out of love. Finally, love is not a value easily translatable into policy trade-offs. But nor is freedom or equality. That is not the point of values. Rather, values lie outside or above the judgments about particular trade-offs (made, say, within the public sector), as principled benchmarks against which we should judge the outcome of trade-offs.

In the time of Trump, when political values seem to be so easily flipped towards hate, it might be wondered whether introducing love into the political realm is a dangerous move – a move that makes a politics of hate more likely. But to avoid this we need a clear articulation of values – as well as people willing to stand up for those values. This chapter and this book are contributions to that enterprise of more clearly articulating what values require, and creating a constituency that can defend those values when they are under attack.

All the people described in this chapter engage with the world of work in different ways. Society can be inhospitable towards those receiving some form of state benefit, those on ACC, people with disabilities and the elderly; this is an insight that can be drawn from the social model of disability, which sees disability not as an immutable medical impairment, but rather as an impairment that affects everyday functioning because of an inhospitable social (and political) environment. This chapter asks whether a politics of love might shift the social barriers that some people in these groups face, including in the world of work. It then explores how policies addressing insecure work and unions might also be advanced by a politics of love.

the treatment of beneficiaries

'Unfortunately the way that we're going is to continuously treat beneficiaries as "the other". *They* are separate from *us*. *They* need to be policed and controlled, and if they don't conform they will be punished, they will be sanctioned, some of them will be sent to jail. *We'll* make sure that those people out there are forced to behave in a particular way ... It's extremely damaging. And we didn't use to do that.'

So says Susan St John, an associate professor in economics at the University of Auckland, whom we first met in Chapter 4, and who has also been a tireless advocate for beneficiaries' rights through the Child Poverty Action Group and other projects. We met at her office at the University of Auckland Business School in 2015. She spoke passionately about the position of people on benefits – in the courts, in homes around the country, in the community. When I refer in this section to people on benefits, or beneficiaries, I mean those receiving a benefit through the welfare system, including Jobseeker Support for the unemployed, the Domestic Purposes Benefit (now Sole Parent Support) and various health entitlements.

This is an area where love is conspicuously lacking in our politics: the treatment of beneficiaries by certain media commentators, politicians, public sector officials and laws. Beneficiaries are not a homogenous group – but they also may represent some of the people in the community most in need of support. As well, many in New Zealand receive some form of government assistance in their lifetime, especially if a government benefit is defined broadly to include public education, student loans, public transport, public health care, a home-ownership subsidy or a pension. Yet beneficiary-bashing, where beneficiaries are maligned with targeted comments, is a prominent feature of New Zealand public debate. Louise Humpage has recorded, drawing on research by Paul Perry and Alan Webster, that the 'number of people regarding "laziness" as the main reason "why people who live in need are poor" ... grew from 38 per cent to 60 per cent over the period 1989–2004'.[6] That this figure increased by such a margin from 1989–2004 suggests that it is a product of political messaging, and it is reasonable to assume that some of the neoliberal maxims discussed in Chapter 4 contributed to this shift – towards harsher and more hard-hearted attitudes.

Beneficiary-bashing since the late 1980s can be split into five strands, though these strands often come together in different ways in public debate. Beneficiaries are often portrayed, first, as irresponsible or, worse, lazy. John Key said on 23 March 2010 that he believed in 'a welfare system that supports people when they are most in need, encourages them to get back to work, and occasionally gives them a kick in the pants when they are not taking responsibility for themselves, their family and other taxpayers'.[7] This line sends a message that those on welfare need 'a kick in the pants' and (at least on occasion) 'are not taking responsibility for themselves, their family and other taxpayers'. That perspective doesn't square with my contact with needy individuals, nor with the evidence of economist Sendhil Mullainathan and psychologist Eldar Shafir, which is that individuals who are under pressure to fulfil their basic needs may lack cognitive 'bandwidth' and may be more likely to engage in 'tunneling' – a single-minded focus on important activities (such as fulfilling basic needs) at the expense of others.[8] In other words, it is rarely accurate to describe those on welfare benefits as irresponsible; rather, those on welfare are generally making good-faith attempts to manage a large number of responsibilities. Yet beneficiaries themselves have reported internalising this stigma. In the words of the Alternative Welfare Working Group report produced in 2010, '[the] sense of being an outsider, of being under attack from politicians, many media commentators and from a number of elements in the general public, and the stigma of being a "beneficiary" was a strong theme at both the regional meetings around the country and in the written submissions we received and has been an important element in the attacks on beneficiaries over recent decades.'[9]

Second, this suggestion that beneficiaries are irresponsible or lazy has a racial, and racist, dimension in many instances, with laziness being associated with Māori or Pasifika individuals. Take Al Nisbet's 2014 cartoon in the *Marlborough Express*, not explicitly about welfare benefits, but about Māori or Pasifika (the cartoon does not make it clear who is represented) as beneficiaries of government transfers.[10] The cartoon depicts a group of overweight Māori or Pasifika adults, walking, carrying bowls. A few kids walk in front of them, in school uniforms; a 'free school meals' sign points to the left of the cartoon. One of the adults says: 'Psst! … If we can get away with this, the more cash left for booze, smokes and pokies!'

The cartoon suggests that Māori or Pasifika are keen to 'get away with' free school meals – which is to say, that they have a fraudulent mentality. It also signals that they are overweight, and primarily concerned with 'booze, smokes and pokies'. This portrayal harms the general image of Māori and Pasifika in the minds of all New Zealanders, stokes racial prejudice, and shows no real effort to engage with longer-term causes of economic vulnerability (such as the structural racism that particularly affects Māori and Pasifika).

The cartoon image is related to a third strand of beneficiary-bashing: the false view that all beneficiaries 'cheat' or exploit the welfare system. Benefit fraud costs the country far less than tax evasion each year: in 2010, benefit fraud cost New Zealand $22 million, while in 2011 (according to the Tax Justice Network) tax evasion resulted in $7.4 billion in lost revenue.[11] But benefit fraud is the subject of more extensive legislation and media coverage. The heightened scrutiny faced by benefit recipients – it was announced in 2016 that the Ministry of Social Development was monitoring the social media of beneficiaries[12] – creates a climate of suspicion and distrust that does nothing to improve their self-esteem. As Gareth Morgan has explained, this may undermine the chances that a beneficiary returns to the workforce:[13]

> When you feel bad about yourself and your life circumstances, it makes it pretty hard for most people to get motivated to upskill, to take risks, to look for and take employment on when the opportunity arises. When someone else behaves in a way that confirms those feelings of stigma it makes the problem even worse. On the other hand, there is good evidence that a positive experience when receiving welfare, a supportive and encouraging attitude from case workers and agencies is key to successfully moving off welfare – especially for those on it long term.

A fourth, more subtle, form of marginalising beneficiaries has been the rhetorical emphasis on the importance of paid work since the late 1980s. Of course, paid work can be a source of social cohesion, income and self-esteem. But 'paid work' has been linked to wellbeing in a way that undermines the position of those who cannot carry out full-time work. To take just one example: the Social Security Legislation Rewrite Bill contained as one of its principles in clause 4 the line that 'work in paid employment offers the best opportunity for people to achieve social and economic wellbeing'. This is just not accurate for all people, and it undermines the social contribution made by those people with disabilities who are unable to work, people in unpaid work (including doing domestic work), and others.[14]

Fifth, beneficiaries have been undermined in how they are treated when applying for, receiving or appealing benefit payments. Many Work and Income employees do their best to treat people with dignity and respect. But a rigorous report from the Canterbury Community Law Centre on beneficiaries' experiences confirms anecdotal evidence that beneficiaries face a tough time wading through the bureaucratic processes. '[W]e're treated as non-human,' one interviewee said. Another observed that 'WINZ premises are colourless, impersonal open plan environments that have no semblance of privacy. Reinforcing the notion of alienation is the ubiquitous presence of security guards and the banks of security cameras.' Another: 'I don't like having to explain my situation every time I go ... I'm embarrassed by it. Constantly going over your situation and providing proof of everything every single time.'[15]

The report notes that there is a lack of general awareness about available benefits, and that the gathering of information to apply for benefits can also be difficult. Some of these experiences might be thought to be inherent in a welfare system. But it is clear that efforts could be made to improve privacy, retain data (to reduce the need for repetition), and ensure that beneficiaries feel respected. The Canterbury report represents a small sample size. But these are the experiences of vulnerable New Zealanders, whose voices should contribute to shifts in policy.

How would a 'politics of love' make a difference to this beneficiary-bashing? Beneficiary-bashing is one area where political debate has not been lacking in references to morality or principles. But the principles in question, such as discipline and responsibility, have been used in a harsh and mean-spirited way. Replacing them with the value of love should result in greater warmth being directed towards beneficiaries accused of being irresponsible or lazy. The politics of love involves a recognition that we are all interdependent. It leads to the conclusion that relying on the state for some support is not a source of shame, but a part of being human, which involves accepting that we are often dependent on others over the course of our lives.[16] The politics of love also underscores that we all need love, which should help individuals to see the justification for welfare benefits: to provide warmth and support, through income transfers, to vulnerable individuals. In short, the politics of love should shift the language and substance of debates about welfare beneficiaries, so that a greater effort is made to understand and empathise with them.

In the end, though, changes in rhetoric do not go far enough. The politics of love also involves expressing love through policy. This requires adequacy of benefit levels (sometimes called income adequacy) to prevent beneficiaries from experiencing financial insecurity. As Mike O'Brien has said, pithily, in the context of welfare, 'money matters'.[17] Benefit levels should be constantly reviewed to ensure that they provide for a *reasonable* standard of living compared to that enjoyed by the rest of the community', in the words of the Alternative Welfare Working Group.[18]

In recent years, a National-led government appeared more willing than its opposite number to increase benefit levels, perhaps because the Labour Party has been more concerned about the perception of being a profligate spender in government.[19] Both parties must ensure that adequate transfers are made when they are in government, especially since both Labour and National share some responsibility for the beneficiary-bashing of the 1990s and 2000s, as Sue Bradford has pointed out.[20] Such an increase may effect a gradual shift in public mindset, by highlighting that beneficiaries are deserving of higher income transfers. It would also help satisfy New Zealand's obligations under international law, since under Article 25 of the Universal Declaration of Human Rights and Article 11 of the International Covenant on Economic, Social, and Cultural Rights – both ratified by New Zealand – all citizens have a right to an adequate standard of living.

Internationally, we are known for our shining record in providing social security: I was reminded of this, when in his modest house in north Oxford, the economist Tony Atkinson spoke glowingly about New Zealand's historical achievements in providing social security, beginning with the Social Security Act 1938. We need to live up to the highest ideals of our history, including the ideal of love, to end beneficiary-bashing and ensure that benefit levels are sufficient for those who have to face some of life's greatest challenges.

acc

Imagine two people, one a construction worker, the other a house painter. The construction worker falls from scaffolding one day, permanently injuring his spine, causing deep pain, stress and trauma, and an inability to work. The house painter also wakes up to discover a serious spinal injury, but cannot trace it to any work condition. It is then discovered that the painter's spinal injury, which involves daily pain and mental distress, and prevents work, is the result of a genetic condition. Under New Zealand's current system of accident compensation, the construction worker is entitled to 80 per cent of weekly earnings for the spinal injury, on top of the health care support available through the public health care system. The painter can receive no weekly earnings through accident compensation for the spinal injury that is the result of a genetic condition. They may get help through the public health care and welfare system, but will be left on their own to find alternative sources of income.

New Zealand has a unique system of accident compensation. ACC (the Accident Compensation Corporation) boasts many advantages, including the fact that it creates a sense of communal responsibility and reduces adversarial tort litigation. But one problem with the ACC system as it is currently designed is the significant arbitrariness shown in my example. The arbitrariness comes from a decision made through the original ACC legislation in 1972 to provide cover for work-related injuries, and other accidents, but not for injuries arising from long-term illness.

In 1988, the Royal Commission on Social Policy recommended a change to the legislation so that ACC would henceforth cover injuries from long-term illness or sickness. In 1990, Labour MP Michael Cullen introduced a bill to give effect to this proposal.[21] It did not pass. The Royal Commission's recommendation has never been implemented.

This fork in the compensation road is unfair, especially as the person suffering a long-term illness might even be more deserving of government support, since no argument can be constructed to claim that this person has 'chosen' the activity resulting in the injury (though that argument is, at any rate, weak).

In 1967, judge Owen Woodhouse drafted (with the help of others) the Woodhouse Report, which proposed an ACC-like system. Injuries and accidents are a 'social problem which cries out for co-ordinated and comprehensive treatment', Woodhouse wrote.[22] The current system is neither coordinated nor comprehensive in the way that it excludes those who suffer from a long-term illness. Woodhouse even acknowledged the point specifically, noting: 'In logic there is no [way]' that 'incapacity arising from sickness and disease can be left aside'. 'A man [or woman] overcome by ill health,' said Woodhouse, 'is no more able to work and no less afflicted than his [or her] neighbor hit by a car.'[23] Woodhouse only held back from recommending cover for long-term illness because he thought this was best viewed as a political decision: '[T]he proposals now put forward for injury leave the way entirely open for sickness to follow whenever the relevant decision is taken.'[24]

The main objection to the extension of ACC coverage to include long-term illness has been cost. Some costs of long-term illness are already borne by the welfare and health system, which indicates that we accept that long-term illness should be the subject of government support. The cost of the coverage must also be weighed against the cost savings made by government once greater security is provided to those with long-term illnesses. It may well be that there are reduced costs in the areas of mental health and housing as a result, since people might be less likely to require mental health or housing support if they have secure ACC funding to deal with long-term illness.

A government need not extend ACC immediately, without further evidence becoming available. The cost of extending ACC to long-term illness, using a reasonable definition of 'long-term illness' and estimating likely cost savings, should be calculated. Different methods of paying for this extension could be canvassed, including levies, increases in general taxation, and perhaps other creative forms of revenue mobilisation such as an insurance duty. Indeed, this is what Woodhouse himself wanted in 1967. He spoke of a 'virtual absence of the statistical signposting which alone can demonstrate the feasibility of the further move'.[25] It can then be left to a future government to decide, in light of this statistical signposting, whether my construction worker and house painter should be placed on the same compensatory footing. But there is at least an available argument that a government does not express much deep warmth – or love – for individuals who are struck down by long-term illness and are not given ACC cover, when ACC cover is given to other individuals who acquire long-term conditions.

disability policy

Extension of ACC coverage to those with long-term illness will also be valuable for some New Zealanders with disabilities. The Ministry of Health provides some support for individuals with disabilities, but it is capped and involves far greater scrutiny than ACC funding. People with disabilities have highlighted how ACC generally provides hearing aids to individuals who lose their hearing because of accidents, for example, whereas for other deaf individuals it only subsidises hearing aids.[26]

But much more needs to be done in relation to disability policy. Twenty-four per cent of New Zealanders, or more than one million people, identify as having a disability – a long-term impairment that affects their ability to carry out everyday activities.[27] Sign language has been an official language of New Zealand since 2006. And we were one of the leading countries behind the drafting of the UN Convention on the Rights of Persons with Disabilities, effective from 2008. Yet despite New Zealand's past policy steps and the numbers of people affected, and notwithstanding the existence of the New Zealand Disability Strategy, disability policy is relatively marginalised in public policy debate. In discussions of disability policy, it is important to remember that there is much diversity within the category of 'people with a disability', including young and old, people in work and out of work, and those with very different life circumstances.

Two disability policy priorities could now be given particular attention, based on what has been said by those identifying as having a disability in New Zealand. First, further work could go into ensuring that people with disabilities are properly engaged in policy-making and the various branches of government. 'Nothing about us without us,' has been the refrain of disability rights activists for decades. This means that people with disabilities could be more fully consulted on policy change, consistent with New Zealand's obligations under Article 4(3) of the UN Convention on the Rights of Persons with Disabilities. The Disabled Persons Assembly has identified insufficient consultation as a major problem: '[M]ost decisions continue to be made with little or no regard to the voice and perspectives of disabled people,' it has written, 'or the expertise of disabled advocates and Disabled Person's Organisations'.[28] Further consultation could throw light on policy solutions in spheres away from disability policy, too, given the intersections between people with disabilities, people in relative poverty and Māori. Also, efforts could be made to ensure that disability advocacy groups (including, and especially, self-advocacy groups such as the Disabled Persons Assembly) are properly funded.

The courts, and not only the government (or executive) and Parliament, should ensure they are open and accessible to all people with disabilities, too. The UN Committee on the Rights of Persons with Disabilities, in its concluding observations on New Zealand, expressed concern that 'no specific training of judges by the Institute of Judicial Studies has been given either on the Convention or on the requirement that justice be accessible to all persons with disabilities'.[29] The government's response noted, rightly, that the Institute of Judicial Studies is independent from government, but meekly noted that it would draw the institute's attention to the recommendation.[30]

As far as I am aware, it does not appear that the Institute of Judicial Studies has held a dedicated seminar on justice for persons with disabilities since this episode. Ensuring that the government is doing enough to engage people with disabilities is consistent with the social model of disability I have discussed.

Second, governments could commit to ensuring decent treatment of carers for those people with disabilities that need and want care – in other words, governments could commit to treating carers with love. The history of disability law in New Zealand is generally shameful, with past laws banning people with disabilities from travelling, and sanctioning sterilisation, as Hilary Stace has described.[31] However, recent years have seen successful attempts to use litigation in order to claw back legal rights for carers. The late Susan Atkinson worked full-time as caregiver for her daughter, Imogen, who had cerebral palsy. Because Imogen was part of her family, Susan was not paid. Her husband, Peter, took a case, along with a number of family caregivers of children with disabilities, which led to a finding that family caregivers should be fairly compensated for up to 40 hours a week.[32] Phil Dickson, an overnight disability support worker working for IDEA Services, a branch of the IHC, at a residential house for people with disabilities in Horowhenua, also won a case claiming he should be paid minimum wage for each hour of a sleepover shift. The Court of Appeal upheld decisions of the lower courts finding that Dickson's sleepovers were 'work', and that he was therefore entitled to the minimum wage.[33]

These cases have secured hard-won gains for disability carers, but they reveal an underlying problem: that disability carers, like Phil Dickson and Susan Atkinson, have not had their work fully appreciated, financially and socially. This has flow-on harms for people with disabilities. Given that 414,000 people relied on disability support as of 2006 (a figure that has likely increased since then), the number of people affected by insufficient support for carers is likely to be significant.[34]

A 2008 report by Parliament's Social Services Committee into the quality of care and service provision for those people with disabilities in need of care offers some useful suggestions (albeit from a slightly technocratic, parliamentary perspective). It notes that there is a lack of coordination across the patchwork of contractors and service providers that offer care. This is partly the fault of government. The report also observes that there may be shortcomings in the audits done by government of contractors. Some of the general problems may relate to the weaknesses with contracting out, discussed in Chapter 6. A campaign run by the Service and Food Workers Union, the Public Services Association and the Council of Trade Unions on raising the status of disability carers outlines further valuable proposals.[35] A paper on the campaign, 'Up Where We Belong', suggests a code of ethics for disability workers, and points out that the three unions have established a tripartite forum bringing together employers of disability support workers, the workers and the Ministry of Health.

There is a need for greater centralised supervision of the quality of disability carer work, conditions and contracts. (The position of carers in general is returned to in Chapter 10.) Contracting out has resulted in some competition for services, but it has also resulted in inconsistent service delivery, complexity in the Needs Assessment and Service Coordination (NASC) services, and a lack of accountability. The risk of centralised supervision is that it creates a paternalistic approach to people with disabilities, and too much distance between service providers and people with disabilities themselves. To square this circle it is important that the first step I have recommended is adopted, and that people with disabilities are brought into the leadership of a supervisory body. The second proposal is in line with what the Disabled Persons Assembly has called for.[36] The assembly has suggested that a disability commission is set up – a proposal first made by the parliamentary Social Services Committee, which said that a commission would be needed in the absence of significant policy progress by 2014. Political parties should do further work, in conjunction with people with disabilities, to outline the responsibilities and structure of a disability commission. They should also recognise and encourage, where appropriate, work being done by unions to lift the status and conditions of care workers.

These steps – engaging people with disabilities in governance, and adopting more centralised supervision of carers – would make the politics of love a reality. Both steps recognise the webs of loving interdependence that run through all our lives, and that are important in the lives of people with disabilities. People with disabilities may require the support of government, and the support of carers. The government, to govern well, needs the expertise of people with disabilities. Carers need support and oversight. These policies manifest a politics of love, too, by expressing a deep warmth for people with disabilities, and those people that care for them: a warmth that is not patronising or condescending but that offers the respect and attention to which all people are entitled.

the elderly

Constraints of space mean that I cannot address all policy challenges involving elderly people in New Zealand, such as whether the retirement age should be raised. Instead, this section makes one brief point: that we need a national conversation about how we treat older people in Aotearoa New Zealand. Since 1980, the number of people over the age of 65 has doubled, so that there are over 600,000 senior citizens.[37] But there has not been the same rise in critical debate about elderly care and integration into broader society.

'[T]he value we place on older people in New Zealand society is linked to the value we place on those who care for them,' the Human Rights Commission points out.[38] One major challenge, just as with carers for people with disabilities, is ensuring that those caring for seniors (these carers are overwhelmingly women) are paid enough and are working in good conditions – in order to ensure that elderly people get the love that they deserve.

After the release of the Human Rights Commission's landmark report on elderly care, *Caring Counts*, a Coalition for Caring Counts has been formed and litigation has been advanced to improve the pay and conditions of the elderly care workforce. Furthermore, former National MP Jackie Blue has proven to be an effective Equal Employment Opportunities Commissioner on these issues. But more work needs to be done to consider the underlying structural reasons for low-pay and low-status elderly caring, which include the fragmented and largely for-profit nature of elderly care, and the disconnection between elderly people and the rest of society.

Loneliness – a gap between desired and actual social contact – is a social reality in New Zealand, about which more data need to be gathered. It may be that, in an age of social media and increased individualism, there is more loneliness than ever before. (A key question that requires further inquiry is whether increased virtual contact via social media is an adequate substitute for face-to-face interaction.) And though loneliness among young people is a cause of concern,[39] loneliness among the elderly deserves greater attention than it is currently getting in policy debates. Loneliness among the elderly represents a society-wide failure to realise and uphold the value of community (as is the case with loneliness among the young), but elder loneliness is also concerning because of the other challenges (for example, health issues) that the elderly are likely to face, with which they might require social assistance.

In the UK, elderly loneliness has been the subject of a documentary, *The Age of Loneliness*.[40] Age Concern New Zealand suggests that about half of older people feel lonely at least some of the time. In some communities in New Zealand, loneliness is well addressed through local voluntary or befriending initiatives. But the availability of these initiatives is inconsistent across communities. It may be that there are cultural differences in levels of elderly loneliness: it is not inconceivable, for example, that older Pākehā New Zealanders might be more lonely because of the relative weakness (on average) of communal ties in Pākehā communities compared to Māori or Pasifika communities.

To ensure a nationwide response to the social integration of older people and the conditions of carers, it might be that political leaders need to start a high-profile dialogue on the place of the elderly in the New Zealand community. As Nicky Hager told me, in a wide-ranging interview that I return to in Chapter 11: 'Leaders ... set the tone or character of the country.' Political leadership, he says, 'has a powerful demonstration effect'. This is one lesson that can be drawn from President Obama's leadership in the United States: for all his flaws (and he is open to criticism on several grounds), he was willing to initiate moral debates on subjects like religion, race and gun ownership.

New Zealand is not the United States. But why couldn't a New Zealand prime minister give a prominent speech on the place of older people, the risk of rising loneliness, and the importance of putting value on the people who have given their lives to our communities? And, if one definition of loneliness is simply an absence of love where love is desired, why couldn't such a speech take as its theme a politics of love, which might provide policies to address loneliness, among older people and the wider community? Speeches on their own are not enough. The status of older people also needs to be fortified by public resources, and decent treatment by communities and businesses. But an address of this kind might be a high-profile way of starting a much-needed public conversation.[41]

insecure work

In 2011, the economist Guy Standing developed the concept of 'the precariat', a precarious socio-economic group that has 'truncated status' and lacks various forms of security, including the certainty that their voice will be represented at work or security of income.[42] Standing argued that globalisation and a focus on flexibility at work has fragmented traditional class structures, creating a new set of structures to replace the idea of a working class, middle class, and upper class. Among the new classes are a very wealthy elite, a salariat (salaried white-collar workers), proficians (professional technicians), manual employees and the precariat, in addition to the unemployed. People in the precariat may experience anger, anomie, anxiety and alienation – and they lack time and leisure. Standing estimated that at least a quarter of the adult population in most countries is in the precariat, in for example part-time work, call-centre work or 'temp' work.

Standing may have been a little quick to set aside traditional class structures. His new proposed classes are a little rigid themselves, and he also perhaps downplayed the extent to which all people are facing some level of increased anger, anomie, anxiety and alienation – and a squeeze on their time and leisure. To some extent, too, precarious work is nothing new.

Yet the concept of 'the precariat' captures the reality of an insecure existence for many workers. (Some of the people discussed in the previous sections, including people with disabilities and the elderly, will also be in insecure work.) Employing a slightly broader definition of insecure workers – which takes in the unemployed, those temporarily employed or those expecting job losses – the New Zealand Council of Trade Unions (CTU) noted that as of December 2012 there were 635,000 insecure workers in New Zealand. This comprises over a quarter (28.6 per cent) of the New Zealand workforce.[43] You probably know some of them. The friend who is juggling being a waiter and studying, and can't guarantee how many hours they will get in their catering job per week. The sibling with a job as a film-maker or builder, who can guarantee their next period of employment but cannot be sure that they will have work beyond the period in front of them. The family member who has seasonal work, perhaps in fruit-picking, but no prospects of a future career. A rough definition of 'an insecure worker' that covers all of these individuals is: a person whose work gives no guarantee of income sufficient to maintain a reasonable standard of living, or for whom there is a reasonable likelihood of facing an imminent drop in income beneath what is needed to have a reasonable standard of living (because of, say, the threat of redundancy).

Some people want multiple jobs, or temporary employment – and still others are unable to work. But in most cases insecure work is a pressing problem in modern Aotearoa New Zealand. Many insecure workers are unable to gain the stable employment they need in order to acquire a decent income, and perhaps some level of self-worth and solidarity (depending on the nature of the work and the industry). Insecure workers often do not have the benefits provided to others in paid employment, such as the ability to join a union or to take sick days.[44] Insecurity itself may create mental health challenges – a subject on which there should be more New Zealand research. Insecure employment could well be economically inefficient in the long term, in that it hinders the build-up of skills and creates transition costs in between periods of employment. And the burden of insecure work falls disproportionately on women, young people, Māori and Pasifika, recent migrants and the disabled, groups that already tend to deal with heightened disadvantage.[45] In short: insecure work is unfair, on top of being personally damaging and economically counter-productive.

Some steps have been taken to address insecure work. In 2016, New Zealand became one of the first countries in the world to ban 'zero-hours contracts': contracts that demand that workers be on-call, but do not guarantee any hours of work in a week. The Labour Party's Future of Work Commission has been investigating solutions to the changing nature of work since 2015. The sections that follow offer two distinct solutions to address insecure work. The second, the idea of a universal basic income, has been the subject of some discussion in New Zealand and overseas. To provide a little more depth, I travelled to Finland to discuss their tentative moves in the direction of a universal basic income. The first, the idea of an insecure work benefit and index, has been discussed less in New Zealand and carries risks as well as considerable promise. The aim within this chapter, consistent with the aim of this book, is to widen the frame of debate, and to provide a broader collection of ideas for people and politicians looking to take action (constructively, not necessarily just incrementally) on emerging political challenges.

measuring those in insecure work — and a benefit for insecure workers

A person in insecure work may fall between the cracks of reliable sources of income – not getting enough money from either a job or a benefit. They may have some prospects of an income from a job, but that job may not provide enough hours in a week for the person to make ends meet. On the other hand, the fact of some employment may mean that the person cannot apply for a benefit. Radio New Zealand (RNZ) has reported on people in this position, and interviewed Hayley (not her real name), who said she did not apply for a benefit while in insecure work because it would be a complete 'stuff-around' to 'declare' the hours each week when the hours would vary due to the nature of her work.[46]

One proposal to address this would be to create an insecure work benefit.[47] A person would register with Work and Income New Zealand (WINZ) as being in insecure work. This category would cover those who have at least the prospect of some work, but whose work cannot guarantee a minimum weekly standard of living, which could be worked out by reference to the amount generally received by a single beneficiary ($234.78 a week at the time of writing in 2016).[48] The benefit would top up weekly work to ensure that the insecure worker gains enough to make ends meet. At the same time, the beneficiary would be allowed to do some work, which may have the advantage of providing affirmation or social contact, at least in some cases. This would involve an additional outlay from government, though some money might be saved. It is likely that this would reduce stress and anxiety, possibly thereby lowering public health care costs; it may also be that other categories of benefit, such as the Seasonal Work Assistance benefit, can be reduced or eliminated with the introduction of an insecure work benefit.

The measure has the appeal of enhancing people's security and ability to live well from week to week. However, it carries some risks. Tony Atkinson, whom we first encountered in Chapter 4, was no fan of the proposal. He told me that an insecure work benefit would give employers an incentive to hold down wages, and to reduce working hours offered to employees. When I mentioned that legal safeguards would be necessary to ensure that employers did not abuse their powers, he said that this left the 'wrong people' in charge of enforcing their 'legal rights'. The beneficiaries drawing on an insecure work benefit would already be vulnerable, and should not then be asked to bear the burden of taking abusive employers to court.

It is true, too, that an insecure work benefit would involve some administrative costs, since WINZ would need to be able to vary amounts paid each week in response to information about hours worked. But a variable benefit system is already operated for the Minimum Family Tax Credit (albeit in a slightly different way) to ensure families with dependent children receive a minimum weekly income.

It would be important, in designing the benefit, to minimise the responsibilities on beneficiaries to enter the number of hours worked; otherwise the danger would be that the kind of bureaucratic 'stuff-around' mentioned by Hayley above would arise again. One idea is that employers could be given the responsibility to enter the number of hours paid to employees each week. This employer acknowledgment that they are providing insecure work, along with the logistical responsibility of entering the hours provided weekly, might subtly disincentivise the provision of insecure work by employers.

With our existing benefits, we can sometimes forget that the system has not always been this way. In relation to benefits, deliberate political choices were made to create benefits for categories of people in need of support; such as unemployed people, sole parents or young parents. Norman Kirk's government, for example, created the Domestic Purposes Benefit (DPB) in 1973 in response to a perception that single parents with dependent children were in need of additional support. It is therefore imperative that governments continually review whether the benefit system correctly identifies groups of people in need of support – and are willing to extend benefits to new groups of people such as those I have described (and, perhaps, other groups like recently released prisoners).

The creation of an insecure work benefit would help the government to gather more authoritative information on the number of people in insecure work. But a more limited move to recognise the problem of insecure work, which would incur less expenditure, would be the development of an insecure work index. The Treasury or another appropriate agency would be charged with defining 'insecure work'. Should it include, as with the CTU measure, the unemployed, as well as those in seasonal employment and temporary employment? How could the likelihood of a future job loss be captured? These are practical questions involving value judgments that would have to be settled. But an insecure employment rate could be calculated, alongside the unemployment rate. It may even be that the insecure employment rate should be referred to more frequently by governments, since it indicates those for whom work is associated with insecurity and uncertainty – those in need of some kind of attention, support, or even love. Such a rate would be easier to introduce than the insecure work benefit, but might be a step in the direction of creating an insecure work benefit, since it would involve preliminary conceptual work to determine who is in 'insecure work'.

universal basic income

A more radical response to the problem of insecure work is to establish a universal or unconditional basic income. (I'll use 'universal basic income'.) This is a guaranteed income paid by the government to every person within a political community, regardless of whether they are working. Instead of getting their wages 'topped-up', as with the insecure work benefit, a person would know that they were getting (every week, month or year) a stable income.

I have been interested in the idea of a universal basic income for some time, and co-wrote a discussion paper for the Labour Party's Future of Work Commission that was released in early 2016.[49] It has many benefits. In addition to the obvious additional security it would provide to those in insecure work, it could reduce the stigma faced by those in receipt of benefits. In one sense, everyone would become a beneficiary, and those in great need of a basic income would face less bureaucracy. It would, ideally, free up time for individuals to pursue projects they are passionate about – whether in the field of the arts, business, community work or household labour. It could reduce administrative costs for government. Household labour would receive some form of recognition or remuneration (though it would not be specifically acknowledged).

Versions of a universal basic income have been tried in the state of Alaska, in Canada and India – but evidence about its success is either thin or difficult to generalise about. Thus, a number of lingering questions remain. Would a universal basic income be available to all people resident in New Zealand, all New Zealand citizens, or anyone in New Zealand? Would it be affordable, and what tax increases would be required to make it so? Would the amount given as part of a universal basic income have to be so low, to make it affordable, as to deprive people of a minimum standard of living? Would existing benefits be abolished, to remove stigma entirely, or would some benefits be retained, increasing the cost of a universal basic income? Would a universal basic income make people more individualistic or lonely (because people might lose the social connections that exist in some workplaces, and be encouraged to spend time on their own in a society that under-appreciates the value of community), or would it free people up to develop deeper friendships and stronger communal bonds?[50] Would a universal basic income depress economic activity, leaving people idle, or make people more willing to find work they are truly passionate about?

These questions aside, there are more direct objections that people might raise. A universal basic income might undermine support for traditional social welfare supports, such as public health care and public education; this is a particular worry, given that a theme of this book is the need for the state (and state institutions) to be seen as playing important, strong functions in social and economic policy. Thomas Piketty, the economist discussed in Chapter 4, has raised this concern.[51] Some might also claim that a universal basic income is unfair, since it provides direct transfers to individuals who do not really need the income, including millionaires.

There are tentative responses that can be given here. On the unfairness objection, a universal basic income could be taxed, so that individuals on higher incomes would not in effect receive the same benefit as others; it might also be pointed out that the same objection applies to public health care and public education, both of which provide services to people who might be able afford their own health care and education.

To investigate some of these concerns, I travelled to Finland. Many local governments and central governments have recently announced that they are considering piloting a universal basic income policy, including those in the Netherlands and in Ontario, Canada. Finland is the country most prominently developing a plan, which its centre-right government announced in 2015 it was considering.

In late March 2016, I made a trip to the easternmost Scandinavian country, which shares a border with Russia. I started out by speaking to people informally about the policy. I was told about Finland's economic woes – unemployment was 10 per cent when I visited Helsinki – and I saw some of it with my own eyes, too, outside the welfare benefits office where lines snaked far down the street. The only thing I had seen like this in New Zealand was people queueing for tickets to a gig or to get into a stadium, but the looks on people's faces in that Helsinki line made me realise that this was no queue for music or sports.

The universal basic income was a creative way to address these economic difficulties, young people told me.

I was fortunate enough to arrange a meeting with Olli Kangas, the public servant and academic in charge of writing the report on the Finnish universal basic income pilot. Kangas worked for Kela, the Finnish Social Insurance Institution, and people told me that the universal basic income was his 'legacy' project before he retired. I met him at the Ateneum Café, in the downtown Helsinki Art Museum. I was late to our interview, thanks to Helsinki's winding streets, and rushed in to find a serene, urbane man sitting at a table waiting for me. Kangas, in his late 60s and wearing round glasses, spoke carefully and with caution at times – he had just completed his report, but it had not yet been released – though he also showed a clear commitment to addressing long-standing problems with the Finnish welfare system.

Kangas told me that some unions were opposed to a universal basic income in Finland, because unions provided welfare benefits and were concerned that the introduction of a universal basic income would remove a key attraction of union membership. Nevertheless he had pressed ahead with proposing several models for a pilot in his report. A universal basic income could create 'a streamlined benefit [system] where people don't fall through cracks', he told me. There were a lot of freelancers, contractors and journalists who needed 'money for a rainy day', he said, and these individuals would appreciate a kind of 'basic benefit'. I asked Kangas whether a universal basic income might make people lonelier, and he said that it was possible that a pilot would measure mental health prescriptions to test this. As for whether it should be paid to recent migrants, Kangas had an answer that might not apply to New Zealand: Finland is not that attractive as a country in the best of times, he told me, and so was unlikely to attract people in droves. There are 'five reasons' not to come to Finland, Kangas told me drolly: 'September, October, November, December and January.' The long winter months.

Would a universal basic income make people less likely to work? This, Kangas said, depends partly on one's view of human nature. If you believe that human beings tend to be hedonistic and in pursuit of pleasure, perhaps you'll worry about people wasting their time and money with a universal basic income. If you believe that human beings are inherently active and creative, then you will be less concerned about people's capacity to find things to do. Five months later, as I was writing these words in first draft in August

2016, the Finland government announced it was moving ahead with a pilot, involving the payment of €560 a month (about NZ$860) to 2,000 randomly selected people.[52]

Kangas's words, along with the other informal conversations I conducted, persuaded me that a pilot universal basic income would be a desirable policy move. A pilot would allow further information to be gathered about its possible effects. It would incur a reduced cost, even if it was run while existing benefits were maintained (which would be my preference). And it could help to raise awareness and debate about how a universal basic income might operate.

A pilot would not be without its difficulties. Tony Atkinson told me, 'You won't learn much from a pilot.' Important reactions to policies such as a universal basic income are society-wide, and might not be captured by a pilot. The media coverage of a pilot is likely to be different from the coverage of a nationwide policy, Atkinson pointed out. These worries are not fatal to the success of a universal basic income pilot. They should be borne in mind – and care should be taken not to be too confident in generalising based on a pilot – but they should not scupper the possibility.

My view is that a universal basic income pilot could be more significant and useful to people than an insecure work benefit, if there was a need to choose between these policy options. A universal basic income best gives effect to a politics of love. It expresses confidence in people's ability to determine their own life courses, rather than demeaning or belittling them. This is equivalent to showing deep warmth towards people – showing love to people, to use another formulation. It also advances the cause of love in a less cerebral way. It could free people up within relationships, allowing people to leave abusive situations (if they are no longer financially dependent), and making it possible that people can realise love more fully in their own lives. A pilot universal basic income should, therefore, form part of the New Zealand project.

making the case for unions (again)

What about those in work who remain unhappy, badly treated or in need of solidarity and support? There are many good workplaces in New Zealand. There are also a variety of policy challenges relating to workplaces across the country, including health and safety legislation, the pace of automation, and the way mental health is treated in work. But the role of unions is fundamental to the status of many people at work in New Zealand, and deserves some discussion. Defending and bolstering unions is a part of a politics of love, since it involves recognising individuals in need of love and support, and acknowledging the interdependence of us all and the power that comes from turning that interdependence into a collective organising force.

Union membership (or 'union density') has dropped significantly since 1991, when the Employment Contracts Act was passed. In 1991, 514,325 people – 42.5 per cent of the workforce – were part of a union. By December 2014, that number had dropped to 361,419 people: 18.5 per cent of the workforce.[53] (Membership had been declining before 1991, but fell at a quicker rate after 1991.)[54] This trend has many causes, and union membership has declined over time in other countries, including Australia and the UK. But changes specific to New Zealand have made a big difference. The Employment Contracts Act 1991 made joining a union voluntary, restricted the circumstances under which strikes were lawful, and reduced the default powers of unions as agents for employees. That political action can shift the size of union membership is confirmed by the fact that union membership increased from 2000 to 2006 (from 318,519 to 382,538 people) after the passing of Employment Relations Act 2000, which repealed the Employment Contracts Act and returned some powers to unions.

New Zealand unions have shown that they continue to provide significant services and benefits to the wider community. In 2016, Unite and FIRST unions led the campaign against zero-hours contracts, which resulted in a unanimous vote in Parliament to ban these contracts. (FIRST represents workers in finance, industrial, retail, stores and transport sectors; Unite represents workers in hotels, restaurants, cinemas, call centres, security, casinos, hospitals and other areas.) The New Zealand Council of Trade Unions has continued to produce important research, including the report on insecure work that I quoted earlier. And union representatives offer regular public comment on policy issues, in addition to the important everyday work done by unions in representing workers and negotiating to secure their rights.

But the case needs to be continually made for unions – including by other groups in the community. There are two reasons why unions are more relevant than ever. First, unions provide the opportunity for genuine relationships to be built among people of different economic, social and ethnic backgrounds. As I have discussed throughout this book, one of the most pernicious consequences of persistent inequality in New Zealand is the social distance it has created between people from different backgrounds. Spatial segregation and segmentation of schooling and services have meant it is harder for friendships to develop among people with differences in incomes or wealth. This in turn makes it more difficult for people to empathise with others who have different life prospects from their own. Along with sport, unions are one of the only channels available where people can build relationships that transcend these differences (albeit with people who are in the same industry). This community-building function of unions deserves to be better appreciated.

Second, unions offer an outlet for democratic voice at a time when many people feel disengaged from electoral politics (as I discuss further in Chapter 11), and disempowered in employment, for example through the rise of insecure work. Work plays a big part in many people's lives. Unions create an opportunity for people to speak up about conditions, relationships and treatment at work. Of course, some unions are better than others at representing workers effectively, and without proper resources, unions' job in this regard is made difficult. But this commitment to voice, democracy and people power also deserves to be lifted up as one major appeal of unions in our time.

It is not enough for the benefits of unions to be publicly articulated. For there to be real change in the capacity of unions to realise genuine relationships and democratic voice, resources have to be put behind unions and legal change has to attempt to support the work they do. One possibility, which requires further debate, is whether employment agreements should as a default rule include membership in a relevant union, with prospective employees being allowed to 'opt out' of union membership rather than 'opting in'. It is not clear that this would violate section 8 of the Employment Relations Act 2000, which requires that membership of a union be voluntary.[55] An opt-out union membership system would simply involve a 'nudge' towards union membership,[56] from which an employee can voluntarily withdraw. The financial implications of union membership could be made clear in the employment agreement, too.

With greater resourcing and legal support, unions in New Zealand will be better positioned to expand their work and improve the lives of workers. Future steps might include the unionising of new industries, as is occurring overseas. In recent years, halting steps have been made to unionise lawyers (in the UK, among other places) and graduate students or teaching assistants (in the US). As well, unions might do more to offer critical adult education to willing learners, and to promote worker ownership as a more thoroughgoing way to democratise workplaces. New Zealand unions have been undertaking these activities. But they will find it easier to move further in these directions with better resourcing and legal support.

conclusion

Some of the discussion in this chapter could have gone even further. In particular, I have not talked about the bold idea of moving beyond work altogether. Disability rights advocates have talked in similar terms for some time. Sunny Taylor, for example, has written about 'the right not to work', 'an ideal worthy of the impaired and able-bodied alike', which highlights that '[p]eople can be useful to society' in ways that go beyond formal employment.[57] Maurizio Lazzarato, the Italian political economist, has said we need a mass refusal of work, a move that 'specifically and above all means not wanting to be assigned a function, a role, and an identity predetermined in and by the social division of labor'.[58] And in their book, *Inventing the Future: Postcapitalism and a World Without Work*, Nick Srnicek and Alex Williams propose 'the establishment of a three-day weekend' as part of a post-work world, in which we would need to overcome 'the pervasive pressure to submit to the work ethic'.[59] A six-hour working day is said to have been piloted in Sweden – a related policy proposal that clears more space for time away from formal employment.[60]

A less radical idea is that we should simply reclaim our time and redefine our approach to it. One shift in work patterns is that, on top of being preoccupied by work once people have left their place of employment, the rise of email has meant that people have had to continue to work – at least in some jobs – in the mornings, evenings and weekends. People who are employed have lost chances that they might otherwise have had to enjoy time with their families, leisure or personal projects. One response in France has been a labour agreement signed by unions and employers in some fields that obliges people to disconnect from email in the evenings once a certain number of hours have been worked in the week (incorrectly reported by some media as a ban on emails after 6 p.m.).[61] Another weaker policy response is to preserve and defend public holidays, which at least safeguard a small amount of free time in the course of a frenzied working year. Both policy proposals allow some increased space for people to do what matters to them, whether that involves gaming or sport or love.

That brings us back to the politics of love. What this chapter has discussed is a variety of new political ideas that address people in and out of work. And it has attempted to show that what might be a theoretical fantasy to some is not only practically workable but also helpful in highlighting fresh directions for political action.

9 'clean and green'?: environmental politics and policy

'We should go wild-swimming sometime,' a friend in the UK said.

'Wild-swimming?' I asked. 'What's that?'

'Y'know, like going for a swim in the river ...'

'Ah!'

We're lucky in New Zealand. Unlike people in the UK, we do not think about swimming in rivers or lakes as 'wild'. We don't call it 'wild-swimming'. It's just swimming. It's part of what many kids do growing up: on holidays, on camping trips, maybe even after school. Like many others, I assumed I was swimming in clean water.

No more. Aotearoa New Zealand may claim to be 'clean and green', or '100% Pure', as the overseas branding puts it. However, '[w]ater quality has significantly worsened over the last twenty-five years (1985 to 2013) at the vast majority of sites'.[1] And our environmental problems don't end with water. We have the highest proportion of threatened or at-risk species in the world.[2] As of 2015, our gross greenhouse gas emissions were trending upwards.[3] In short, the country's record on environmental protection, particularly in recent years, is more 'murky' than 'clean and green'. The word 'murky' sums up New Zealand's water quality, the country's emissions profile and the direction of policy and politics on the environment. This trajectory carries significant risks for New Zealand's reputation in trade and tourism, as economist Ralph Chapman has pointed out,[4] as well as being problematic in its own right.

Do we want that future, where we are no longer clean and green, where we are seen as shirking our climate responsibilities globally, where we are 100 per cent murky? This chapter makes the argument for a different kind of future, focusing on action that can be taken on climate change and resource management.

the themes of this book and environmental politics

Maintaining a good environment is central to everything else that I have written about. Without a climate human beings can live in, we cannot pursue an independent foreign policy or a principled approach to justice; without clean water, we cannot live from day to day, let alone reconceptualise the future of work. The environment is also fundamental to New Zealand history and identity. Why else would an anthology of our best songs be called *Nature's Best*, inspired by Wayne Mason's memorable refrain, 'Nature/enter me'? We are associated internationally with the breathtaking landscapes that appeared in *The Lord of the Rings* movies. Some of our best-known art captures the natural world: Colin McCahon's stark paintings of dimpled hills, or Lisa Reihana's 2015 panoramic video work *In Pursuit of Venus*, depicting encounters between Europeans and Polynesians against an almost cartoonishly beautiful backdrop (drawing on an early-nineteenth-century wallpaper).

So why are we talking about the environment only now rather than at the outset?

Part of the answer is that addressing the challenges of environmental politics and policy requires an integrated approach: an approach that understands our politics as a kind of ecosystem in which various challenges are interconnected. It requires rethinking of, and redoubled action on, economic policy, indigenous issues and the design of our political institutions. It is easier to discuss the environment in this book, therefore, once these other areas of policy have been analysed.

Here's an example of what I'm saying: the writer and anthropologist Jason Hickel has pointed out that climate change is partially caused by an excessive focus in many economies on GDP growth as a primary political goal. A shift away from GDP as a measure of progress (and an accompanying questioning of the ideal of aggressive growth) – which we have already touched on in Chapter 4 – might be helpful in developing the mindset that is needed to address climate change.[5]

The interconnectedness of policy challenges is one theme of this book; indeed, that is why this book has aimed to range across policy areas as diverse as foreign policy, the economy, justice and the environment. But the other core themes of this book – the need for a renewal of values-based politics, the importance of decolonisation and the centrality of Māori world views to New Zealand policy solutions, the significance of the state in economic and social policy, and the imperative to boost people power – are also especially important in the sphere of environmental policy and politics.

We know that tapping into people's values is crucial for mobilising political action on the environment. The campaign for New Zealand to be nuclear-free demonstrates this, but empirical evidence backs up New Zealand history. As the WWF has said, 'simply "re-stating the science", or underscoring the "common sense" of taking mitigating action is unlikely to help much in stimulating involvement of a wider constituency of people in debate about responses to anthropogenic climate change'.[6] According to research done by the Cultural Cognition Project, moves 'to flood the public with as much sound data as possible' are misguided, because if 'the truth carries implications that threaten people's cultural values', the data 'is likely to harden their resistance and increase their willingness to support alternative arguments, no matter how lacking in evidence'.[7] What is needed instead is an appeal to values (grounded in factual accuracy), which 'can have a profound influence on people's motivation to engage with bigger-than-self problems'.[8]

Thus, the approach in this book – to aim to make the values of care, community and creativity central in New Zealand politics – chimes with what research says is important for action on environmental issues. The specific values of care, community and creativity are useful in this context, since action on the environment requires deep care for nature, an interest in the long-term survival of the human community, and creative policy solutions.

Throughout this book, much has been made of the need for a decolonisation process to be initiated, as a part of which there is an imperative to integrate Māori world views into policy solutions – because Māori world views hold much that is relevant to the unique needs of Aotearoa New Zealand, because to integrate Māori world views into politics is to give full effect to biculturalism, and because these world views mark out what is distinctive about this country. Adopting a values-based approach to politics is itself influenced by te ao Māori, since Māori dispute resolution is centred around values.[9]

Guaranteeing that Māori world views are given prominence within environmental policy and politics – best achieved by ensuring that Māori are in positions of leadership and decision-making – is particularly valuable for this sphere of policy and politics. As Andrea Tunks has explained, the Māori focus on the interconnectedness of all things provides a useful reminder of the need to be sensitive about humanity's impact on its environment. Other Māori values – such as mauri, wairua, kaitiakitanga and utu – offer a powerful way to ensure there is balance, collective custodianship or guardianship and respect for the spirit or force of the natural world.[10] Care must be taken not to lift Māori values unthinkingly out of their context as part of an integrated Māori view of the world. It is also important not to co-opt Māori values strategically for particular purposes. But if done with sensitivity, integrating Māori world views into environmental politics and policy is a promising part of developing solutions to the crises facing us in the field of climate change, water, and resource management (discussed further below). Protecting the environment for Māori, and drawing upon the Māori spiritual relationship with the land, is also a legal requirement under the United Nations Declaration on the Rights of Indigenous Peoples, which New Zealand endorsed in 2010.[11]

A more powerful role for the state, discussed at length in Chapters 4 and 6 (and elsewhere), is also necessary, given the specific environmental challenges facing Aotearoa New Zealand. Long-term challenges in regard to water, resource management and climate change cannot be addressed in an ad hoc fashion. What is needed is planning, measuring, regulating and enforcing. While the private sector and the community can also engage in planning (and measuring, regulating and enforcing), the state is best placed to plan for the long term for the community as a whole, and to use its law-making powers and information-gathering tools to monitor and ensure compliance with environmental standards.

Naomi Klein has argued that Germany's (incomplete) transition to being a low-carbon economy involves a new vision of government, entailing a reassertion of the value of planning, steering and regulating. It's 'a departure from neoliberal orthodoxy [in Germany],' Klein writes. '[T]he government is engaging in long-term national planning: it is deliberately picking winners in the market (renewables over nuclear power, which it is simultaneously closing down); it is fixing prices (a clear market interference); and creating a fair playing field for any potential renewable energy producer – big or small – to enter the market.'[12] The New Zealand Productivity Commission, which comes from a different perspective compared to Klein, has – in what is only, admittedly, a draft report – made similar noises about the significance of some state functions in the future of resource management. 'Making progress on environmental priorities will require more robust monitoring and enforcement,' the commission notes. 'Performance by regional councils on this front has been disappointing. Monitoring efforts are often under-resourced …'[13] Diverse commentators are therefore highlighting the need for a relatively muscular state to drive environmental protection.

This state cannot become detached from the people, however, and environmental progress will only be made through a thoroughgoing bottom-up movement that supports and pushes top-down change. Klein again: '[O]nly mass social movements can save us now.'[14] She adds:[15]

> Winning will certainly take the convergence of diverse constituencies on a scale previously unknown. Because, although there is no perfect historical analogy for the challenge of climate change, there are certainly lessons to learn from the transformative movements of the past. One such lesson is that when major shifts in the economic balance of power take place, they are invariably the result of extraordinary levels of social mobilisation.

Klein is talking about climate change, as opposed to the environment as a whole; she is referring to global action, not just action in one country. But it is nevertheless true that for New Zealand to retain its 'clean and green' image – for that phrase to become a powerful statement of what we continue to stand for, and not just a mendacious myth – there will need to be a movement of people from diverse constituencies. There will need to be genuine, informed people power, which I return to in the next chapter.

These, then, are the guiderails for environmental politics and policy. We need a values-based politics, which integrates Māori world views and is accompanied by decolonisation. We need a strong role for the state, disciplined and driven by people power. What specifically can be done to realise this?

commitment to addressing climate change

Climate change is *the* moral and political issue of our time. If the world warms by more than two degrees by 2100, it does not matter what else we dream of for our politics. Our world may not be capable of containing the people that drive it. Sea level rise, ocean acidification, desertification, extreme weather events and damaged ecosystems may create catastrophic effects. In some ways, this realisation relegates all other political concerns to secondary importance. But it also highlights the importance of collective global action on climate change.

At present global action on this front is inadequate: the pledges undertaken by countries at the 2015 Paris talks 'will fall far short of cuts needed to have a reasonable chance of avoiding global warming of more than 2C', in the words of Lord Nicholas Stern, a leading climate expert and economist – though the Paris Agreement included an aim to keep temperatures 'well below' two degrees of warming by 2100.[16] Continued efforts are therefore needed to ramp up the ambition to cut human emissions of carbon dioxide, methane, nitrous oxide and other gases, which almost all scientists now agree contribute significantly to the greenhouse gas effect and global warming.

Why should New Zealand, whose contribution to global greenhouse gas emissions is so small, play a part? This is a common argument. It was even alluded to by one New Zealand judge, now on the Supreme Court, in a recent decision on climate change and the Resource Management Act 1991.[17]

But how we act as a country is not only determined by the size of the consequences of that action. That has never been the only factor we've considered when weighing up policy steps. Had it been the case, New Zealand may never have become nuclear-free. We make policy decisions sometimes because of the consequences of those decisions, and sometimes out of principle: because we believe that a decision conforms to the kind of nation we want to be. We decided to become a nuclear-free nation as a stand against nuclear weapons and nuclear energy worldwide, and to show that we were willing to take a stand even if it carried foreign relations consequences, with the United States. It was a values-based decision. In the climate change realm, we might act to reduce our climate change emissions because we believe that it would be irresponsible ethically not to contribute to global reductions.

However, there might also be consequence-based reasons – what philosophers call 'consequentialist' reasons – for New Zealand to act to reduce its emissions. Our contribution to global emissions – 0.3 per cent, according to the court decision discussed on the previous page (probably in fact closer to 0.2 per cent) – is not insignificant. Moreover, New Zealand risks reputational harm if it continues to brand itself as environmentally friendly while at the same time failing to reduce carbon emissions. This could have real effects for tourism revenue, trade positioning and perceptions of New Zealand's integrity in global negotiations. As well, there is an available argument that with a greater number of countries committing to act on climate change, it may become harder for other countries to shirk responsibilities: these countries might be more obviously marginalised. We can therefore make genuinely global action more likely by contributing to global reductions in emissions.

So there is a case for acting to reduce greenhouse gas emissions. Our size should not hold us back. But what can be done, concretely, beyond what is happening already?

a carbon tax

In 2008, the Labour-led government launched an Emissions Trading Scheme (ETS), a trading scheme for carbon emissions. Here's how it roughly worked: tonnes of carbon emissions were converted into 'units'. Units were initially allocated to companies that reduced carbon emissions: in forestry, for example, since forests absorb carbon dioxide rather than emitting it. It was then required that other companies, in industry and waste, 'surrendered' units if they emitted carbon dioxide: one unit was equivalent to two tonnes of carbon dioxide. Alternatively, these companies would have to buy units from the government at $25 per unit. So emitting companies paid for their emissions, while companies that reduced overall emissions got paid for offsetting activities. Different private sector areas had phased entries into the emissions trading scheme – forestry entered in 2008, waste in 2013 – with agriculture (contributing almost half of New Zealand's emissions) being exempted from the scheme. It also allowed the purchase of international units, and created New Zealand Units (NZUs) that were allocated for free to certain sectors at the outset.

There are at least four problems with the current scheme. First, it is highly opaque and difficult to understand (something your glazed eyes might have picked up from navigating the fine print of the last paragraph). I have taken an active interest in climate change policy, have studied climate change at a master's level, and gave a presentation on the Emissions Trading Scheme with a friend in Wellington in 2012. Yet I still find aspects of the scheme hard to grasp. And there is a widespread lack of understanding about how free allocations were initially determined. This complexity means it is hard to develop public support for the scheme. But it also means that the scheme may not have all of the behavioural change effects that it promises.

Nevertheless the scheme's complexity can be overstated, and those companies most affected by it are likely to have taken the time to clarify its logic. It has yet more serious shortcomings. In particular, as a second point, there is evidence that a significant number of overseas credits used in the New Zealand scheme are fraudulent. The Morgan Foundation has in recent years produced important policy work on subjects such as a universal basic income and climate change – and one of its reports showcases the problem of phony carbon credits within the New Zealand scheme. The report, *Climate Cheats*, shows that the New Zealand government holds 97 million Emissions Reduction Units (ERUs), a form of international carbon credit, 11 per cent of the total number of these units that exist worldwide. Ninety-nine per cent of these units held by the New Zealand government come from Ukraine and Russia, and the report says that it is highly likely that these credits do not reflect emissions-reducing projects. Why is this a problem? It means that not only is the ETS, in its use of these credits, dishonest about reducing carbon emissions – it may also be subsidising and encouraging polluting behaviour. New Zealand may be complicit in fraudulent behaviour overseas.[18] The problem highlights a lack of regulation within the ETS, and insufficient regulation in the global market for carbon credits.

On top of the ETS's excessive complexity and the fraud made possible by the scheme, the ETS may have allowed manipulative pricing by electricity and fuel companies – as the Morgan Foundation points out.[19] When the ETS was first introduced, electricity and fuel prices were lifted on the grounds that companies needed to pass on the cost of the ETS to their consumers. But the evidence suggests that the price of electricity and fuel has not dropped and varied with fluctuations in the carbon price. In other words, the ETS may have justified unfair pricing practices, at the expense in particular of the most disadvantaged in Aotearoa. Perhaps electricity and fuel companies are primarily to blame for such pricing practices, and it is true that the companies could be pursued through competition law (though it is difficult to prove price gouging of this kind, and indeed the Commerce Commission has refused to look into the nexus between the ETS and electricity or fuel pricing). But the fact that the ETS may have resulted in this manipulative pricing – and the fact it is difficult to corroborate or deny – reflects a further flaw in the ETS model.

Finally, but perhaps most crucially, the ETS does not appear to have had a significant impact on reducing emissions. Partly as a result of a low carbon price and the 'two-for-one' discount for energy, transport and industrial sectors, New Zealand's emissions were increasing as of 2015.[20] So could New Zealand's emissions be increasing at an even higher rate without the ETS? Fair question. What *is* clear is that the ETS is not succeeding in significantly lowering New Zealand's emissions, which is the accepted aim of the scheme.

What can be done about all this? The Morgan Foundation's report suggests some changes. It proposes that problematic Emissions Reduction Units are dumped, that the 'two-for-one' discount (which weakens the incentive to reduce emissions for certain sectors) is dropped, and that foreign carbon credits are banned, at least for now.[21]

These are constructive suggestions. However, they do not go far enough. Some of the weaknesses in the ETS can be regulated away. But its opacity and the fact that it has not lowered New Zealand's emissions raise serious doubts about whether it is the effective tool that is needed to fight climate change.

Perhaps it is time for an alternative mechanism: a carbon tax. A carbon tax, supported by the ACT Party at the time of this book's writing in late 2016 and by the Green Party at the 2014 election, would be based on similar logic to the emissions trading scheme. It would impose a levy on carbon-emitting activities, to ensure that the price of products fully takes into account the environmental cost of producing those products. It would make large polluters pay for the emissions. The tax would do less to reward emissions-reducing activities: it wouldn't pay individuals or groups directly to take steps to reduce emissions. But those activities would be implicitly rewarded, since they would not have to pay the tax. Moreover, the government could take other actions to encourage emissions-reducing activities, through steering of the economy (discussed in Chapter 4) or forestry-supporting policy steps discussed in the next section of this chapter. A carbon tax would be far simpler to understand for industry and the general public. It would not be without value judgments and some complexity: the size of the tax would need to be carefully calibrated. But a carbon tax would be just as capable as the ETS of shifting behaviour towards emissions-reducing activities. And the impact on consumers would lessen over time as behavioural shifts reduced reliance on emissions-reducing activities.

The carbon tax used in the Canadian province of British Columbia provides one model for a carbon tax in New Zealand. Introduced in 2008 by a centre-right government, it was phased in and increased over time. It was revenue-neutral, meaning that it was accompanied by reductions in other taxes, such as income tax (especially for low-income people who might have been affected by the tax). The British Columbia action has resulted in fuel use dropping between 2008 and 2013 at a rate quicker than other provinces in Canada, and overall emissions dropping by between 5 and 15 per cent. GDP growth in British Columbia was higher than other provinces in this period, suggesting that the economy was not harmed by the introduction of this tax (notwithstanding the limitations of GDP discussed earlier in the book).[22]

Progress on emissions reductions stalled when the British Columbia provincial government stopped raising the tax incrementally as planned in 2012 – but this, if anything, highlights the effectiveness of the tax in shifting behaviour.[23] *The Economist*, hardly radical in its views on climate change action, has written in support of the British Columbia carbon tax model.[24] Over time, as well, the people of British Columbia have become more supportive of the tax, showing that as its effects become clear, a carbon tax is likely to become popular. In 2009, 47 per cent of people in British Columbia opposed it. By 2015, that number had dropped to 32 per cent, according to the *New York Times*.[25] Other countries have adopted a carbon tax, too – from Finland to Japan – but the British Columbia model is a particularly promising one, especially since (despite some obvious differences between British Columbia and New Zealand) the population is similar to New Zealand's, at 4.6 million as of 2016.

If we are serious about tackling climate change, major reforms need to be made to the Emissions Trading Scheme at the very least. I think there are good arguments to replace a trading scheme with a carbon tax, possibly starting at the level of $100 per tonne.[26] A government should flag in advance an intention to adapt the Emissions Trading Scheme to a carbon tax, if that policy option is pursued, in order to give businesses and individuals time to plan for the change.

For a carbon tax to be effective in the long term, there will need to be a public movement for change. Although the choice between an emissions trading scheme and a carbon tax may appear wonkish or complicated, only through bottom-up and local pressure will political change occur – and be sustainable. Groups like Generation Zero – the youth-based climate activist group that has pushed effectively for public transport reforms in Auckland and other changes – would need to work alongside local leaders, commentators and affected groups to create the space for political change. As Naomi Klein says, there is 'no way to confront the climate crisis as a technocratic problem'.[27] Climate change policy requires not just a change in the global climate, but also a change in the political climate: towards increased ambition, heightened care for future generations, more hard thinking about creative solutions. Groups such as Generation Zero can and should spearhead that change. But young people need the help of elders, politicians, farmers, businesses and others within a broader movement. A carbon tax might be at its centre.

agriculture and forestry

The sheep in the room in discussions of climate change policy in New Zealand is agriculture. How should ambitious climate change policy interact with New Zealand's significant agriculture economy?

Agriculture is the sector that contributes the highest proportion of emissions of any sector in the New Zealand economy: around 46 per cent of our emissions. (The OECD average for the agricultural contribution to national emissions is 12 per cent.)[28] Agriculture does not produce carbon emissions, but instead generally produces methane and nitrous oxide. Agricultural emissions are made up primarily of enteric fermentation (causing belching of methane by livestock); manure and manure management, which in turn produces nitrous oxide and methane; and other fossil fuel use in agriculture.[29] For the last twenty years, New Zealand farmers have made major efficiency gains. But agricultural greenhouse gas emissions are projected to rise steadily at their current rate through to 2030.[30]

An important decision will have to be made about whether New Zealand 'prices in' the greenhouse gas emission effects of agriculture, either through including it in the Emissions Trading Scheme or through extending a carbon tax to agriculture alongside other industries. In late 2015, public servants recommended to the National-led government that agriculture be included in the scheme. There are strong reasons of fairness, effectiveness and reputation for a government to ensure this happens. While farmers will face some burden through incurring the full cost of their greenhouse gas emissions, other industries are already facing that burden. If those other industries are willing to accept their responsibility to pay for their emissions, it seems unfair for farmers not to face the same responsibility. With agriculture feeding so significantly into New Zealand's overall emissions, if New Zealand is genuinely committed to reducing its emissions it should ensure that the sector responsible for 46 per cent of the country's emissions is included in these reduction efforts.

Finally, as has been noted by the research work of New Zealand's own Andrew Reisinger and the New Zealand Agricultural Greenhouse Gas Research Centre (of which Reisinger was deputy director as of 2016), the world is moving towards greater commitments to reduce agricultural emissions. One hundred and nineteen countries pledged, in late 2015, to reduce agricultural greenhouse gas emissions as part of statements of Intended Nationally Determined Contributions, and scholars are pushing for a global target for reducing agriculture emissions.[31] If this target is adopted, either without New Zealand support or without New Zealand follow-through, the country could continue to damage its 'clean and green' image – with accompanying harm to tourism revenue and trade negotiating positioning.

Leaving aside the point about pricing in the greenhouse gas emissions of agriculture, there are further steps the government could take to encourage climate-friendly agriculture that do not penalise farmers. The New Zealand Agricultural Greenhouse Gas Research Centre is already doing impressive work, in addition to farmers' own initiatives to improve efficiency, to develop and test climate-friendly technologies. The Centre is discussing and beginning to experiment with low nitrogen feed, reducing nitrogen fertiliser use and improving manure management. It has discovered some weaknesses in nitrification inhibitors, which can leave residues in milk.[32] New Zealand is also the site of the Secretariat for the Global Research Alliance on Greenhouse Gases. However, technological development and ongoing research, while important, cannot be the only path towards climate-friendly agriculture, and the government can play a greater leadership role – without interfering excessively with farmer practices – to encourage sound practice.

As part of my master's research at Oxford, I investigated various policy options for climate-friendly agriculture in Aotearoa. At least one merits further attention.[33] The government could set up a system of sustainable certification and labelling for climate-friendly agricultural practices. This would be voluntary. Farmers would not have to join the certification system. But the system would provide the possibility for New Zealand farmers (and overseas farmers using climate-friendly practices) to be rewarded in the market for emissions-reducing activities. The move could be justified as a measure to enhance the information available to consumers when considering purchases. An Origin Green certification and labelling system was adopted, and met with positive feedback, in Ireland. The system measured farms' greenhouse gas emissions, waste management and biodiversity, among other factors. As part of this certification and labelling system, the New Zealand government (perhaps through New Zealand Trade and Enterprise) might construct a scale of farmer performance that – with farmers' permission – could be used to promote New Zealand agriculture overseas. The scale would encourage farmers to adopt climate-friendly technology, and might improve export performance.

One area of climate change action that is related to agriculture, and not discussed enough, is forestry. Forests form carbon sinks, absorbing carbon dioxide and directly offsetting emissions, while also providing quality-of-life benefits to individuals and families. A report by Pure Advantage, the environmental advocacy group founded by New Zealand business leaders, shows that New Zealand has removed more forests than it has planted since 2008 (despite the existence of 'walls of wood' – major wood harvests – in parts of the country).[34] The report, *Our Forest Future*, points out that the Emissions Trading Scheme has not adequately incentivised the planting of forests – a further flaw with the scheme. The report proposes the establishment of a national forest strategy, and a possible target of 1.3 million hectares of new forest by 2050. If 1.3 million hectares of *Pinus radiata* were planted, while other existing climate change actions were pursued, New Zealand would have net-zero emissions by 2050. *Our Forest Future* also nominates tools that could be used to fund or value afforestation, including climate bonds (which involve private investors stumping up capital for forests and gaining a return where afforestation targets are met) or putting a price on the benefits of forests.[35] A major tree-planting scheme has also been advocated by Generation Zero.[36]

This discussion needs to continue. The Pure Advantage report cannot be expected to traverse all the details of a national forest strategy. It is commendably specific in its constructive proposals, but more thought needs to go into who would do the planting, how the government (or others) might fund a massive forestry planting, and how the land for planting would be procured or secured, without disadvantaging those in need of land.

Some connections could be drawn between a national forestry strategy and other proposals in this book. Chapter 11, 'People Power', mentions briefly the idea of government funding of a 'civic year' for students out of school: one possibility is that young people get involved in tree planting as part of this paid year of national civic service. The government might fund a massive tree-planting project through increased revenue gains from the reorganisation of income tax outlined in Chapter 4, consistent with the 'steering' role in the economy discussed in that chapter. Land for planting could draw, at least in part, on council land and a more coherent relationship between local and central government, which I have discussed elsewhere. But it would be important for the government to proceed cautiously around land belonging to farmers, and Māori land. I make no particular proposals here. However, forestry must be included as part of a redoubled effort to tackle climate change in Aotearoa New Zealand.

This section has not covered all policy moves that might be considered. Instead, here as elsewhere, a few select topics have been highlighted – areas of action that could make a real difference to the future of the country and that have been relatively little discussed by politicians. This is not to say, however, that other actions should not be taken. In particular, there must be continued commitment to public transport, which reduces emissions through weaning off reliance on cars, and may boost community. At a global level, difficult conversations around air travel and meat consumption – both activities that contribute significantly to greenhouse gas emissions – are only slowly emerging. New Zealand should prepare itself for demand shifts and changing practices in such areas. A whole-of-government, and whole-of-community, effort will be needed to ensure New Zealand contributes to reducing its greenhouse-gas emissions and taking its share of responsibility to tackle climate change globally.

resource management

Resource management raises knotty questions about the appropriate extent of regulation, the importance of the environment and its interaction with development, public participation, the role of courts, the relationship between central government and local government, and the relative significance of cities and the provinces. No one would pretend that it is an easy job to draft legislation to oversee resource management. But the Resource Management Act (RMA) has been the subject of significant criticism since it was passed in 1991, by people from vastly different backgrounds and people right across the political spectrum. It is not a sexy topic. It is central, though, to the future of the environment in this country.

Some of the most incisive commentary on the RMA has been written by Chief Justice Sian Elias, Ralph Chapman and the Productivity Commission. These three sources span legal, environmental and economic perspectives. Chief Justice Elias gave the Salmon Lecture on the Resource Management Act in 2013. Ralph Chapman wrote a book touching on the subject, published in 2015; I interviewed him in Wellington in December 2015. The Productivity Commission has written an extensive draft report on improvements to urban planning, released in 2016.

Elias, Chapman and the Productivity Commission differ in the extent of their criticism of the RMA. However, interestingly, some common observations emerge. These form a useful starting point for considering how the RMA might be reformed in a bipartisan fashion.

Elias and the Productivity Commission agree that the RMA is overly complex. There have been attempts to simplify and streamline it in recent years. But, in the words of the Productivity Commission, '[r]epeated amendment to the planning statutes have [*sic*] increased their complexity and reduced their coherence'.[37] Chief Justice Elias has said that, whereas the Income Tax Act is understandably complex, the Resource Management Act is 'meant to engage communities, not alienate them', making 'impenetrability and complexity ... not a good thing'.[38]

These expert commentators also suggest that the RMA is insufficiently strategic in its approach to resources. '[The RMA] doesn't have a strategic bone in its body,' Ralph Chapman told me at his Wellington home. 'The private sector takes the action and the government stands back and waits for the problems to appear, and then remedies them.' It's an 'essentially reactive' piece of legislation, he said. 'It may articulate certain values and matters of importance,' he added, 'but that is different from being strategic.' The Productivity Commission's report nicely sums up this ethos: 'predict-and-control'. The commission is critical of this: 'The existing ... approach struggles to cope with the complexity and uncertainty of natural systems,' it writes.[39] Chief Justice Elias is not directly critical of the RMA's ad hoc philosophy, but notes that opinions may have shifted towards thinking that more centralised planning is preferable. She says that 'the pendulum may have moved back from "effects-based management" to a preference for more government and local authority control over activities and outcomes'.[40]

All three say that a clearer statement of the values underlying the RMA – going beyond the principles in sections 6–8 of the Act – would be desirable. Elias notes that rather than leaving the courts the task of making sense of the Act, 'the better course may be to make more political effort to identify and prioritise the values the courts are to apply'.[41] The Productivity Commission's draft report recommends that '[a] future system should be clearer about its priorities, especially at a national level and regarding land use regulation and infrastructure provision'.[42] Chapman contrasts the RMA with the Local Government Act, or at least the version of the Act that was in place prior to its being amended to remove references to the different types of wellbeing to be pursued by local government. Chapman says that the Local Government Act 'started from the presumption that we had goals, something we wanted to get to, and therefore we could deduce the path we want to follow'. There is less clarity in the RMA, through which 'people can do what they want, [and] we just tidy up the mess'.

So the Resource Management Act is overly complex and insufficiently strategic, and lacks a statement of values. Can or should anything be done about it?

The Productivity Commission was in the early stages of its review of planning legislation in 2016, but there are some worries about the direction in which its draft report was moving. The report's title, *Better Urban Planning*, is telling – since the report involves a review of the RMA, and other legislation more generally. It seems that the commission views much of the RMA as being concerned with urban planning, or at least wants to move the Act in that direction. This is corroborated by the fact that the commission favourably cites Ed Glaeser's book *The Triumph of the Cities*, quoting Glaeser's line that 'cities are humanity's greatest invention'.[43] It is true that major controversies can arise over resource use in cities, whose development needs are great. It is also true that city-level planning will be crucial to progress on climate change and other social justice causes. Nevertheless there is a risk that, if the commission pursues this urban-centric approach, unique issues relating to regional and rural planning will be ignored. There is already a danger in New Zealand of regional welfare being marginalised, as I have discussed elsewhere. There is also, in some circles, a belittling of the regions and provinces by those in major cities.[44] Against that backdrop, it is important that future reform of the RMA addresses the needs of regions as well as cities. If what emerges is a proposal for distinct legislation to address urban planning, there are separate risks of incoherence and uncertainty.

The Productivity Commission's document puts great weight on economic development as a goal in urban planning. It proposes that there should be a presumption in favour of development in urban areas. In some ways, it is unsurprising that the Productivity Commission is making this proposal: the commission's priority is productivity, not the environment. But it is potentially quite a radical change to the current approach to planning. Development concerns are given significant weight in legislation. But the Resource Management Act contains environmental bottom-lines, and is primarily concerned with sustainable management of resources, as reflected in section 5. In 2013, the Parliamentary Commissioner for the Environment, Jan Wright, said that the RMA 'is not, and should not become, an Economic Development Act'. That comment remains valid.[45]

Another worry is that the Productivity Commission is using its review of urban planning to advance a privatisation agenda. The early pages of the report hint at this. The commission says there should be a resistance of 'rules and other command and control methods'. This bundling together of 'rules' and 'command and control' methods seems a slanted way to present how centralised planning might operate: 'command and control' implies Soviet-style directives, when – as Ralph Chapman pointed out – a central government role in resource management can involve more flexible instruments, too. It then goes further, arguing that councils should be 'encouraged to adopt more sophisticated approaches to procuring infrastructure, and central government could provide greater advisory support to local authorities wishing to use such tools (e.g., public-private partnerships)'. This suggestion that public–private partnerships or involvement of the private sector is necessarily 'more sophisticated' is misleading, given that the state can be innovative and is responsible for major technological development historically (see Chapter 4). The Productivity Commission should also do more to accept the past failings of privatisation in related fields, such as the building sector under the Building Act 1991. For-profit private providers are not always more sophisticated planning actors – or they might be sophisticated in ways that are not desirable, given the values we seek to uphold through planning.

The Productivity Commission, to be fair, does offer some more helpful pointers in the report about the state of resource management in New Zealand. It says that better regulation of resources is needed because 'there are insufficient checks on regulatory quality'. It highlights the need for more upskilling and 'stronger professional capabilities', including among government.[46] It notes that there is some concern over whether the Environment Court is playing the right role in resource management and in ensuring public participation. Elias also raises concerns over whether the RMA has created too much litigation. This comment that the Act has made resource management overly legalistic echoes a common public perception.

These remarks and reservations provide some steer as to the appropriate future direction of the Resource Management Act. The fact that amendments and attempts to simplify the Act have only made it more complicated suggest that it is time to start afresh: to scrap the Act in its current form, and to draft new legislation.

It is not possible or desirable to set out in detail what might replace it. A future government could, through a working group or its own ministers, hold a series of consultations about how communities themselves would like their resources managed. Because of the importance of resource management legislation, it would be ideal for this process to be initiated and managed in a bipartisan way. The consultations could ask broad questions. When there is a possibility of a new commercial development on a site, what factors should be considered? Who should make a final decision? What weight should be given to environmental protection, as opposed to development interests? It could also address specific controversies within resource management, such as the approach to resource consents for water use and whether it is legitimate for a territorial authority to weigh the effects on climate change when considering a resource consent application.[47] These consultations could be underpinned by certain principles, which I have attempted to clarify:

- As far as possible, resource management legislation should strive for simplicity and should be understandable.
- Resource management legislation should be strategic – perhaps by setting goals or targets – and should avoid being overly reactive or ad hoc.
- Legislation should set out clearly the values at stake in resource management, including relevant Māori values.
- Resource management legislation must take into account the unique needs of regional, rural, and urban communities, and must avoid turning resource management into an exercise only in one-size-fits-all urban planning.[48]
- As long as New Zealand retains its 'clean and green' identity and prioritises environmental protection, resource management legislation must not become economic development legislation.
- Lessons should be learned from past experiences with privatisation in planning and building.
- The roles of central and local government need to be spelled out in legislation, and governments must be properly resourced and equipped with sound training.
- Public participation in resource management must be prized, with consideration given to the benefits and harms of involving courts in the process.

Are these principles too vague? It might also be said that they contradict each other: is it even possible to guarantee public participation while avoiding an overly reactive or ad hoc resource management process? A nationwide, preferably bipartisan, process can work through these tensions from a place of principle, allowing more specific rules and guidelines to be drafted that ensure a resource management system that better suits the needs of people and the imperative of environmental protection.

conclusion

In primary school – that same year I was first introduced to the concept of 'values' – the class I was in at Clyde Quay School did a project on erosion. As part of the research, we travelled to the Kapiti Coast. We wandered along the windswept beach on a murky day, noticing areas where the sea was eating into the shore and identifying where banks and other barriers had been built to tackle the erosion. It was difficult to imagine, looking at the coast at age 10 or 11, that the water was slowly beating back the shore: that gradual natural processes were taking away the land under our feet. But we could tell that it was happening, and a longer-term view of measurement and assessment confirmed the slow-moving trend.

Erosion itself is worsened by rising sea levels and extreme weather hazards caused by climate change. But the erosion we noticed that day also symbolised how New Zealand's political commitment to environmental protection has been scraped back in recent years. Like the erosion on the Kapiti Coast, it isn't easy to see the whittling away of political commitment on a day-to-day basis. But taking the long view – with reference to indicators such as water quality, greenhouse gas emissions and biodiversity – it becomes clear that foundational commitments to environmental action have become weaker, even as environmental challenges have become greater.

It doesn't have to be this way. Te ao Māori offers ways of thinking that help to see human beings as intertwined with the environment historically. In the Māori world view, human beings are at once dependent on the environment and exceeded by it. 'Kaua hei riri mō te whenua, whenua i waho', goes the proverb: do not fight over the land, the land remains. In some ways, in light of this, it is even wrong to speak of 'the environment' or 'resource management' – terms that imply that human beings are at the centre, with the natural world being only our surroundings. Pope Francis, seemingly for similar reasons, has preferred to use the word 'nature' over 'the environment' in his recent writings: a word that better captures the independent beauty and worth of the world away from human beings.[49] These views help us to understand how fundamental nature is for our ability to survive and thrive.

Policy and political action are tools to ensure that these ways of thinking are applied in everyday life. This chapter has canvassed several policy and political options, including a carbon tax, action on agricultural emissions, support for forestry, and reform of the Resource Management Act. More could have been said on environmental rights being enshrined in law, ending fossil fuel subsidies, the need to support cycling, or the emphasis that ought to be placed on the safeguarding (and expansion) of national parks. But what is clear is that if New Zealand seeks to maintain its 'clean and green' reputation, if we want to continue to be a place where the outdoors and swimming are a core part of lifestyle and identity, where we do not speak of 'wild-swimming' and where we do not have to be overly concerned about water quality, we need to match rhetoric with action. We can spot the erosion of our values. And we can stop it.

10 genders, masculinities and sexualities

This chapter discusses genders and sexualities, and how some contemporary thinking about justice for women, masculinity and other forms of sexuality is inconsistent with core values of care, community and creativity.

In this chapter, more than any other, I feel apprehensive about setting out a topic-specific snapshot of the present and future of New Zealand politics. My perspective on genders and sexualities is bordered and blinkered by my own life experience. I have benefited from the privilege of being a member of the male sex, and being gendered as male.[1] I cannot understand in full what it is like to be a woman in modern New Zealand, or to have another gender identity. I cannot completely appreciate the pain of prejudice or the complexity of certain identities, and what I notice – and fail to notice – will be different because of who I am and where I come from. Nevertheless, especially after consulting people who have been involved with political work on gender and sexuality, I felt that to leave an analysis of gender and sexuality out of a book that tries to apply a values-based approach to major political challenges in New Zealand would be a problematic omission.

This is not an authoritative account of the history of gender and sexuality in New Zealand, nor does it pretend to capture all of the rhythms of contemporary activism and campaigning in these spheres. It is one window into the realm of gender, sex and sexuality. I draw on interview material – in this chapter, an interview with Eleanor Bishop – and other sources to supplement my own knowledge and views, though I accept (as with other interviews in this book) that an interview offers only a singular perspective. I cleave to subjects where I have some background or limited expertise: I write below, for example, about pay equity (an issue I've explored using my legal training in the past) and about masculinity. Throughout, but especially where I touch on subjects on which I have less background education or experience, I offer observations and proposals tentatively – in the hope that they will start further debate about genders, masculinities and sexualities in Aotearoa New Zealand today.

beyond top-floor triumphalism

When I was finishing high school in 2005, many leadership roles in New Zealand were filled by women. In this period, in the mid-2000s, New Zealand had a woman prime minister (Helen Clark, from 1999), chief justice (Sian Elias, also from 1999), governor-general (Silvia Cartwright, 2001–6), speaker of the House (Margaret Wilson, 2005–2008), and CEO of Telecom (Theresa Gattung, 1993–2007). These were major individual achievements, which involved overcoming discrimination, and each achievement was a product of past campaigning work – and had significant role-modelling and symbolic effects.

New Zealand was rightly lauded for this. We slapped ourselves on the back. Many of my male friends, in particular, expressed pride in our achievements – noting, of course, that we were also the first country to give women the vote in 1893. A glance at some of the headlines of the time is revealing. A BBC headline from 2000 reads: 'New Zealand Glass Ceiling Shattered.'[2] The *Guardian* published a piece (admittedly critical in parts) entitled 'As Good As It Gets'.[3] The *New Statesman* headed its profile, 'New Zealand – A Woman's Land'.[4]

But New Zealand was not a land where these individual achievements were matched by equality for women as a group. And the impressive achievements of women leaders, despite the best efforts of Helen Clark and others, ushered in some collective complacency about the position of women in New Zealand society. There was a kind of 'top-floor triumphalism' on women's rights that obscured other challenges facing women, and allowed people to paper over the fact that all five women leaders in the mid-2000s were Pākehā.

There is perhaps greater critical consciousness on gender issues a decade or so on compared to when I finished high school. Some of the backslapping may now be in abeyance as women no longer occupy the high-profile leadership positions they held in the mid-2000s. But a certain amount of top-floor triumphalism lingers – and there is little reason for it As of 2016, there was not one woman CEO among New Zealand's top 50 businesses.[5] New Zealand has dropped down the World Economic Forum's aggregate gender gap rankings since 2006.[6] Just 38 out of 121 members of Parliament were women in 2014. In 2013, 84.2 per cent of single-parent families were headed by a woman, with 6 in 10 of those families being defined as poor (or having under 60 per cent of the median income after taking into account housing costs).[7] As discussed in Chapter 7, sexual and family violence against women and girls is endemic.

Patriarchal practices – practices that uphold the power of men in society – seep through politics, the media and universities. In Aotearoa New Zealand, as elsewhere, prejudices based on ethnicity, disability, beauty or body size can also intersect with sexism to amplify the effect of gender-based oppression. New Zealand is still a sexist society, with widespread biases and blind spots, and power imbalances that disadvantage women and those who do not identify as men.

The lingering top-floor triumphalism, which obscures more entrenched sexism, is a product of multiple factors. I talked about it over lunch with Eleanor Bishop, a New Zealand artist, theatre writer and director. Bishop identifies as a feminist artist, and makes artistic and social work about (among other things) gender oppression.

'Women at the top is the sexy issue,' she told me. It's a product of a kind of 'trickle-down logic' – the same faulty logic that has pervaded neoliberal economic thinking (as discussed in Chapter 4), which holds that support for the wealthy in society will 'trickle down' to benefit the rest of society. It's also a 'flaw in liberal white feminism', Bishop noted, which has failed to consider sufficiently the structural barriers existing in society, and the way that ethnicity and colonisation have combined with patriarchal prejudices.

In some ways, then, this reinforces two broader points touched on earlier in the book: the need for an alternative economic framework, and a renovated role for the state; and the need for thoroughgoing, society-wide decolonisation. Top-floor triumphalism on issues of sex and gender may also exist because it suits the interests of men in positions of power and influence below or on the top floor, who can bask in some supposed egalitarian glory without the need for any loss of power or questioning of their (our) positioning. It may be the result of a cultural reflex to prove that Aotearoa New Zealand punches above its weight in the world – a nationalistic reflex that can lead to the neglect of serious domestic social challenges.

Ensuring that women are strongly represented in leadership positions – so that leadership is not just 'equalised' in terms of gender representation, but is transformed as a concept – remains important. Debates should continue about the necessity of quotas or targets in some sectors, and decision-makers (including those in politics and business) who have some influence over appointments should ensure that women are appointed to high-level positions. If women are left out of such appointments, it is likely that injustices have been perpetrated or that opportunities have been missed: the appointment of women has important symbolic effects, and there is growing evidence, especially in the private sector, that women's leadership can improve the performance of teams and workplaces.[8]

But it is clear that success at the top for women is not enough. So how can real gains be made to secure liberation and emancipation for women, in a manner that does not privilege Pākehā or women at the top?

Sexism is a product of many economic, social and cultural (including colonial) forces. To tackle sexism, and to create the conditions for more transformative positive possibilities, a whole-of-society commitment is needed: among other things, to decolonisation (in order to undo the effects of colonisation on sexism, especially for Māori women); and to addressing rape culture, the culture that contributes to the view of women as sexual objects (discussed a little in Chapter 7). Campaigns should continue to address everyday sexism and to advance the cause of reproductive rights, amongst other things. There are two interventions, however, that could have an outsized impact on sexism and patriarchal practices. I explain what these two interventions, or clusters of interventions, are below. I also explain why these interventions could have larger knock-on consequences for the achievement of sexual equality.

achieving genuine pay equity

Inequitable levels of pay between men and women in work are both a cause and a consequence of entrenched sexism in New Zealand society. Inequitable pay contradicts basic standards of fairness. It undermines the principle of the same pay being given for the same work. (It is worth remembering that the term 'pay equity' refers to fairness, too: 'equality' refers to the same treatment in comparable circumstances, whereas 'equity' is about basic fairness.) Different levels of pay are based on internalised stereotypes and prejudices about women's economic worth and abilities. Inequitable pay gives women materially fewer resources than similarly situated men, which can in some circumstances make women more financially vulnerable and reliant on others. It also sends a message to society that women are of lesser value.

New Zealand passed equal pay legislation that seemed ahead of its time: the Equal Pay Act 1972. This prohibited employers from offering different benefits, terms, conditions or opportunities in work 'by reason of the sex of that person' to people 'of the same or substantially similar qualifications' where those people are 'employed in the same or substantially similar circumstances'.[9] It set out standards for evaluating equal pay, as well as a process for determining equal pay, with modifications for different types of work (such as apprenticeships and in agriculture). One might assume that equal pay has since been largely secured in New Zealand – but the failure of this legislation to realise genuine pay equity highlights the limits of law.

As of 2016, there remained a 14 per cent national gender pay gap. Confirming the claims of activists and theorists who speak of 'intersectionality' – the idea that prejudices based on race, sex, disability and other grounds intersect to amplify oppression – there are greater gaps in pay for Māori, Pasifika and disabled women: Māori women, for example, are paid on average 76 per cent of what all men are paid.[10] What these enduring differences show is that legal changes do not guarantee changes in social attitudes. They also gesture at the problems with New Zealand's legislation, which is aimed primarily at equal pay rather than a broader notion of 'pay equity' grounded in fairness.

A landmark case in 2013, brought by care worker Kristine Bartlett, clarified how the Equal Pay Act 1972 should apply and raised broader issues with the legislation. The legislation is designed so that employers compare the pay of men and women in a sector to determine whether there is unequal pay. But what happens if, as in the care sector, there are very few men working in a sector? (The judgment recorded that 92 per cent of those employed in the sector are women.)[11] How can women argue that they might be systematically underpaid, in the absence of a male comparator? What happens if an entire sector, dominated by women, appears to be underpaid?

The Employment Court, in a strong judgment by Judge Christina Inglis, said it was not enough for women and men's pay to be compared within the care sector in such circumstances. The court noted that the care sector involved unusually low levels of pay, despite the 'physically, mentally and emotionally demanding work', with the fact that women predominated in this sector being no coincidence.[12] There appeared to be occupational segregation by gender, the court said, and perhaps an 'artificially depressed' rate of pay as a result. Given that the legislation is aimed at removing and preventing discrimination on the ground of sex, the court decided that comparisons of male and female pay must not in this case be limited to the care sector. It concluded that employers should consider what levels of pay might be if they were 'uninfected by current or historical or structural gender discrimination', and if no comparator could be found to make this judgment, 'it may be necessary to look more broadly, to jobs to which a similar value can be attributed using gender neutral criteria'.[13] Employers should consider 'what men would be paid to do the same work abstracting from skills, responsibility, conditions and degrees of effort as well as from any systemic undervaluation of the work derived from current or historical or structural gender discrimination'.[14]

Business New Zealand had intervened in the case and had, along with others, raised the concern that the approach adopted by the court would be unworkable and would lead to higher costs. The court was forthright in its response:

> ... the expressed concerns relating to cost overlook one important point, namely the unquantifiable cost (including societal cost) of adopting an approach which may have the effect of perpetuating discrimination against a significant and vulnerable group in the community simply because they are women, doing what has been described as undervalued women's work.
>
> History is redolent with examples of strongly voiced concerns about the implementation of anti-discrimination initiatives on the basis that they will spell financial and social ruin, but which prove to be misplaced or have been acceptable as the short term price of the longer term social good. The abolition of slavery is an old example ...

The Court of Appeal upheld the decision of the Employment Court, after the decision was challenged on appeal.[15] The Court of Appeal, in a comprehensive judgment by Justice Christine French, reiterated that the Equal Pay Act 1972 had been largely mute and that the case sought 'to reactivate it'.[16] The Court of Appeal recorded the view of a 1987 report that the Equal Pay Act 'had failed to reduce the gender pay gap significantly and had failed to deliver equal pay for work of equal value to working women in New Zealand'.[17] It also said that 'the Act is very poorly worded', 'the syntax ... cumbersome' and 'the drafting elliptical'.[18]

These decisions underscored the inadequacy of the Act – and a need for a full legislative review. The National-led government – also in response to advocacy work by the Pay Equity Challenge and Equal Pay Equal Value, and others –

established a joint working group on pay equity in 2015, facilitated by Dame Patsy Reddy (later to become governor-general). In 2016, it recommended a set of principles that could guide how pay equity is applied in practice. It accepted that in areas dominated by women, work might be systemically undervalued, in the phrase used by the Employment Court. It then called for parties to bargain to resolve claims drawing on an assessment of 'the skills, responsibilities, conditions and degrees of effort' required; this assessment must be 'objective, free of assumptions based on gender', and comparators can be used as long as comparators are not distorted by systematic undervaluation. The working group accepted that some amendments would be needed to the Equal Pay Act.[19]

It is valuable that these principles were teased out. But the suggested changes did not go far enough. The decisions in the Bartlett case about pay for aged care workers made it clear, albeit in the usual guarded language that judges use, that the Equal Pay Act is past its use-by date. It needs to be thoroughly overhauled, for reasons of substance and for style or clarity.

A new Act might redraft the key provisions of the Equal Pay Act, and make clear that legislation aims at a broader notion of pay equity and not just equal pay. A key question is: what more can be done to ensure that pay equity is realised, between and not just within sectors? Two strong suggestions have been put forward by Catriona MacLennan, Vicky Mee and Judy McGregor, all individuals with significant expertise in this area. Catriona MacLennan is a lawyer who has made important policy interventions in relation to family violence and other issues, Vicky Mee is a past president of the Federation of Business and Professional Women, and Judy McGregor is a renowned academic and former Equal Employment Opportunities commissioner with the Human Rights Commission. They propose, first, that a positive duty be imposed on employers to remedy wage differentials, taking the onus off individuals (often women) to make complaints. They cite the UK Equality Act 2010 as a model for such positive duties. Second, they call for more transparency around the gender pay gap, and indicate that individuals should have a right to ask what their colleagues earn, in order for information to be more widely disseminated about pay rates.[20]

Those are important starting points. Imposing a positive duty on employers is a workable move. Many employers will already be taking active steps to investigate differences in pay. Principles can be developed to determine what employers must do to discharge this positive duty; there is guidance from the UK around how positive duties operate, and it is likely that the duty will require different behaviour depending on context and sector. One example: where employers are made aware of evidence of differential pay, or ought to be aware of that evidence, they might be required to review the reasons for that pay gap, and to propose and implement actions to reduce that pay gap. For a positive duty to have proper effect (unlike the UK's Equality Act, which applies only to the public sector), it should be applied to the private and public sectors in Aotearoa New Zealand.

Being aware of the pay gap is a first step towards action being taken to address it. In this sense, a right to inquire into other employees' pay would be a positive development. It is not an unreasonable intrusion into the privacy of others. There is a risk, however, that in situations of employment insecurity (discussed in Chapter 8), individuals might not take up this right out of a fear of backlash from their employers. It would be important, then, for legislation to spell out that it would be unlawful for employers to penalise employees for requesting information about the pay of others. Legislation could also empower the Human Rights Commission (perhaps with the support of Business New Zealand) to undertake annual reviews of the gender pay gap in different sectors. This would remove the burden from individuals and would make information about the gender pay gap publicly known.

Finally, these legislative changes must be undertaken alongside ongoing efforts to extinguish the underlying sexism that gives rise to inequitable pay. Legislative overhauls can only go so far. Even with positive duties on employers and improved transparency, if certain areas of work remain socially under-valued, pressures towards unequal and inequitable pay will remain. Politicians, using their ability to steer public debate, can speak up about the value of care work and other sectors dominated by women – responding to the important ongoing work done by activists and campaigners. One other way to change the perception of work predominantly done by women in the market is to alter perceptions of work in the home, and it is to this subject that we turn next.

care in the home

It is plausible, and it has been suggested by many activists and philosophers, that one of the reasons care work is undervalued in the aged care sector and elsewhere is that care work is undervalued in the home, where it is done overwhelmingly by women.[21] In New Zealand homes where people live in hetero-sexual relationships (and I will return below to homes where this is not the case), cleaning, cooking, emotional labour, care for children, elderly and the sick, and other forms of nurturing still tend to be done more by women.[22] There is a persistent perception in many parts of New Zealand culture that this is 'women's work'.[23] In my own life, when I went through heart surgery in 2014, much of my care – the work of supportive conversation, checking in, reassur-ance and organising – was provided by my then girlfriend and my mother.

What evidence exists on this subject suggests there are much broader trends at work, and the results are not surprising. Statistics New Zealand's 2009/10 Time Use Survey showed that 65 per cent of female work was unpaid, compared to 63 per cent of male work being paid – a statistic that hints at the amount of unpaid domestic labour done by women, but is not conclusive. The same survey noted that women in New Zealand, on average, spent 'about an hour more on household work than males' every day, and 'women still spent more than twice as much time on child care as men'.[24] (Statistics are not easily available on how household work differs based on class or income levels. It is possible that men growing up in lower-income backgrounds are more likely to have developed skills in household labour, because of the greater need to help out within families with lower incomes; it would be useful for further research to be done on this point.) Some women make active choices to pursue domestic labour, and those choices should not be criticised. But it is not inconsistent with that to say that the structure of our society imposes greater expectations on women to carry out that labour. Those heightened pressures faced by women may undermine the value placed on care in broader society, and they certainly make it more difficult for women to secure economic equality.

The American academic Nancy Fraser has argued, persuasively, that the contemporary economic system has depended on domestic labour – mostly carried out by women – to survive in its different forms. In Fraser's words, 'the capitalist economy relies on – one might say, free rides on – activities of provisioning, care-giving and interaction that produce and maintain social bonds, although it accords them no monetised value and treats them as if they were free'.[25] Fraser writes that the separation of unpaid domestic work from paid work in the market 'created an institutional basis for new, modern forms of women's subordination'; 'those who do this work', she observes, 'are structurally subordinate to those who earn cash wages, even as their work supplies a necessary precondition for wage labour.'[26] In other words: the unpaid nature of domestic work places domestic work on a lower tier and standing than paid work, even though it is that domestic work that makes paid work possible. Fraser sees a contradiction in capitalism, though, which threatens the stability of the system: the drive for profit in the market undermines the ability for care to be given. For this reason, she diagnoses a 'crisis in care' in contemporary societies, a diagnosis relevant to this book's call for a renewed focus on values of care, community and creativity.

You do not need to agree with all of Fraser's analysis to accept that the New Zealand economy relies on care and labour in the home (so that those who work can rest, be nurtured, and be rejuvenated), or to accept that the failure to pay for that work signals a reduced public appreciation for the contribution of those in the home. There are two possible ways to address this problem, at least in the short term: make sure that work is paid, or make sure that individuals are equally capable of doing that work, regardless of gender, so that pressure is not unduly channelled towards women to carry out that work.

A universal basic income, which I put forward in Chapter 8, should be piloted. It might pay for domestic labour in one sense, though it does not mark out domestic labour for specific recognition. It would be interesting to monitor how a pilot affects who does domestic work.

In the absence of a universal basic income or other payment for domestic labour, men can also be encouraged to take more responsibility for labour in the home. It is not clear that men and women are equally willing and able to do this work at present, though some men play a role as stay-at-home dads or equal participants in domestic labour. To speak from my own experience – an experience I am not especially proud of – I entered into romantic relationships committed to doing a fair and equal share of domestic labour (without needing to look after children), but found myself slipping from my responsibilities over time. I should take my share of blame for this.

However, it is also possible for relevant parties to do more, and for policy settings to be shifted, to ensure that men are willing and able to do this work. Parents can ensure they are raising young men who are confident and competent in all forms of domestic labour. Public schools could do their part to guarantee that both men and women have necessary domestic skills. If necessary, male role models – for example, in sports – could also encourage men to carry out their fair share of domestic work.

The provision of substantial paid parental leave by government, and the encouragement to men to take this leave as well as women, is another policy that supports the same objectives. It might seem in some ways remarkable that I am writing this in 2017. But we should be honest about the state of the division of domestic labour in Aotearoa New Zealand today, even if there are many households that are happy and fair in how they split domestic work. A bigger nationwide conversation about this, and an ongoing shift in male practices (something I myself am working on), could help to place more weight on care throughout society. This is beneficial for workers in the care sector, and for the standing of the value of 'care' generally. It will also avoid unfair burdens being placed on women (in the spheres of childcare and housework), so that men and women are equally free to take up paid work if they want to pursue that route – or free to pursue the essential work of domestic labour if that is what they want to do.

The two policy areas I have discussed – pay equity, and care and work in the home – focus on work as a tool to address sexism and patriarchal practices. I have also outlined these interventions in a way that could be said to assume heterosexual relationships and particular household structures. But work is not the only route for women's emancipation, and a large number of New Zealanders are not living in heterosexual relationships – or in a relationship at all. I explain later in this chapter how more can be done to secure society-wide care for those who identify as lesbian, gay, bisexual, trans, intersex or queer. And Hannah August's recent book, *No Country for Old Maids? Talking About the 'Man Drought'*, addresses the position of single women, an often-forgotten group in discussions of gender, sex and sexuality in Aotearoa New Zealand.[27] I have concentrated on pay equity and policy relating to care in the home only because these are areas where, with some additional political pressure and activism, particularly significant gains can be made – to address sexism in different forms, and avoiding the kind of top-floor triumphalism that has lingered in this country in the past decade.

masculinities

I returned to the subject of masculinity in my conversation with Eleanor Bishop. Seated in a café, she talked about a theatre project she was working on that addressed masculinity in Aotearoa New Zealand. Bishop explained that masculinity, especially Pākehā masculinity, was shaped by colonisation and farming, and was tied up with 'the taming of the land' and ideas of 'domination'. New Zealand cultural products have had a role in shaping expectations on New Zealand men, she continued, including John Mulgan's *Man Alone*, and the work of Barry Crump and Bruno Lawrence. She said that the actions of public figures – such as former prime minister John Key evaluating the attractiveness of women (as he did in 2011 when discussing Liz Hurley), or the way broadcaster Tony Veitch minimised his perpetration of domestic and family violence – contribute to norms around New Zealand male behaviour. Finally, while 'you can't pin everything' on rugby, 'it's undeniable' that the centrality of rugby in New Zealand life creates a culture that 'foster[s]' certain kinds of attitudes towards women, Bishop added.

It's in public discussions of domestic or family violence that the most troubling aspects of modern masculinity seep into mainstream New Zealand culture, she said. 'We ... sort of accept [family violence] as a given,' Bishop observed. 'We understand it through the framework of a mistake ... not something that is culturally conditioned.' There is an unwillingness to call sexual harassment out, too. She noted her surprise at the very few people who had described John Key's behaviour – when it was revealed in 2015 that he'd repeatedly pulled the ponytail of an Auckland waitress despite her objections – as sexual harassment. One additional possible effect of dominant masculine thinking, according to Bishop, might be the crowding out of progressive values such as care and community – since 'to be in community' is sometimes seen as 'feminine'.

In an interview with RNZ's Kathryn Ryan, Brendan Hokowhitu – dean of Māori and indigenous studies at the University of Waikato – outlined a perspective on Māori masculinity in particular that shares some parallels and some differences with Eleanor Bishop's general account. Hokowhitu noted that early travel writers to New Zealand, though seeing Māori through a particular lens, described Māori men as people who 'talked a lot', who were 'emotional' and 'passionate', and who toyed with gender, even sometimes wearing 'women's clothing'. In other words, there were diverse conceptions of masculinity within Māoridom prior to contact with Europeans. But as British settlement expanded, elite Māori 'imbibed ... Victorian masculinity', Hokowhitu said. All-boys schools that replicated elite boarding schools in Britain shifted how some Māori viewed being a man. The limitations of education within a system that discriminated against Māori 'forced' others 'into the manual labour force', producing a stereotype that associated Māori men with physical activities, 'whether at the end of the shovel or in the engine-room of a scrum.' The cumulative effect of this has been a 'narrowing' in perceptions and expectations of Māori men, which can hamper their own sense of ambition, according to Hokowhitu.[28] Of course, different stories can also be told of the experiences of Pasifika and Asian men – and Bishop's and Hokowhitu's accounts represent only two perspectives on New Zealand masculinities.

There is much in Bishop's and Hokowhitu's insights that chime with my own experience of growing up as a man in Aotearoa New Zealand. I was lucky that I didn't have a dad who talked much about what it means to be a 'man', or to be 'manly'. Lucky, because I had no real desire to fit the dominant stereotype of a New Zealand man – muscular, well-built, sporty. I loved rugby and cricket, but I had little natural talent for them. (I'll always remember one prize-giving for my Pōneke rugby team, when I was 10 or 11. Everyone got a prize, befitting New Zealand's egalitarianism. My prize? 'Most Tactical Player.') Parental pressure to fit some masculine mould would have created even more anxiety and confusion than that which I already carried.

It is hard to isolate cause-and-effect in relation to New Zealand masculinities in my own life, partly because I also spent stints overseas – in China as a young child, and in Indonesia from age 12 to 16. But my period at the all-boys Wellington College, albeit a short one, was instructive. There was a legitimate space for someone like me, who wanted to explore creative pursuits like music and theatre, and who was ultimately a bit of a geek, as much as I resisted that label. That school deserves credit for endorsing different paths for young men, and it was an enormously supportive place for my own learning and personal development. But there were also pressures and prejudices, many of which were a product of broader culture as opposed to the school's own teaching. There was a strain of homophobia – as in the throwaway use of terms like 'fag' and 'gay' (the latter often interchangeable with 'uncool'). There was, in some circles, a sexist set of attitudes towards women, such as those who studied at neighbouring girls' schools. There wasn't a great deal of discussion of emotions or personal challenges, partly, of course, because we were young, despite the best efforts of some empathetic teachers. School chants and songs were a way to build community, as were particular words and phrases that were known primarily to students at the school. From my conversations with other young men in New Zealand, I would suggest that my experiences are also true of a much wider sample of all-boys schools around the country.

Some of these pressures and prejudices lingered at university after the end of school. I went to a hostel, O'Rorke Hall, for students at the University of Auckland, where guys clustered together ('the lads' was the far-from-unusual name of the subgroup around me). Prospective relationships with women were a buzzing topic; I'm not proud to say that I also was part of a group of relatively progressive people that used the language of conquest ('the summit' was one term I remember) to describe interactions with women. That language can feed into attitudes justifying violence towards women. Because I was not much of a drinker, I noticed, too, how central alcohol was to these gatherings, as was watching sport. In such settings, it was not easy to talk about feelings, or insecurities, or vulnerabilities, much less sex; this at a time when we could have all used companions to work through various personal challenges. (These gatherings became a normal part of student life, and continued as many of us in the hostel went flatting and beyond.) These activities were all regarded as a way to build bonds and to develop self-confidence, and there were also many good experiences with men and women that did not involve misogyny. But in hindsight it is clear that norms of masculinity were entrenched through being at an all-boys school, through life at a hostel and flatting.

This is a description of my personal experience, and I do not mean to single out any of these institutions, since they are all reflections of a broader culture. There are many varieties of masculinity in Aotearoa New Zealand today. I think the dominant strand emphasises sport, physique, and a certain type of light (but perhaps unemotional) interaction between guys: a 'bros and brawn' masculinity. This has a social power: it is possible for pressure to be exerted for men to come into line with this strand of masculinity, and for alternative strands to be marginalised. But a 'metrosexual' maleness is increasingly accepted, which involves a more feminine fashion sense and a different set of interests, as an example of just one other strand of masculinity. The strengthening of the identity of the LGBTIQ (lesbian, gay, bisexual, transgender, intersex and queer) community has created further diverse strands of acceptable masculinity. Jock Phillips, in his groundbreaking book on Pākehā masculinity, notes the ongoing need to investigate the many 'male sub-cultures' that exist.[29] Masculinities have also changed over time, influenced by broader social changes and global developments. As an example of this, Brendan Hokowhitu in his interview with

Kathryn Ryan cites the differences in how the All Blacks tend to celebrate tries today compared to yesteryear: whereas once there was a quiet trudging back to the mark, there is now much more hugging and open celebration.

The question that is raised in my mind, as I write this against the backdrop of thinking about politics grounded in progressive values, is whether it is possible to retain the sense of community that comes from some aspects of male bonding and masculinity in a way that is more caring, towards ourselves, others and in particular those who do not identify as men. And are there creative ways that this sense of caring community can be fostered?

It is clear to me that there could be a greater openness to talk about masculinity in all of the spaces that norms of masculinity are reproduced: in the home, in schools, in workplaces, in university hostels, in universities, in sports clubs and in flats. We could have a conversation about the types of masculinities produced by all-boys schools and rugby culture, and whether it is possible to lop off the more problematic parts of those masculinities from the rest.[30] We could ask whether there is too much time spent within exclusively male groups, and if we need to find ways to make more mixed-gender interactions a normal part of contemporary social life.

British artist Grayson Perry, in his book on masculinity, offers a 'manifesto for men', which lists 'the right to be vulnerable, the right to be weak, the right to be wrong, the right to be intuitive, the right not to know, the right to be uncertain, the right to be flexible' and 'the right not to be ashamed of any of the above'.[31] Perhaps partly because of the influence of Britain on our culture (at least Pākehā culture), many of these appear to me to be relevant to Aotearoa New Zealand, too. In 2015, New Zealand had the second-highest suicide rate in the OECD, with young Māori men disproportionately represented in these figures.[32] Though the causes of suicide are complex (and include the ongoing effects of colonisation), there can be little doubt that a greater willingness by men to talk about vulnerabilities and insecurities might support those men struggling with mental health issues or considering suicide.

It is not unrealistic for men to lead conversations about a reshaped masculinity, to take responsibility for the toxic masculinity that contributes to some of the worst social problems in New Zealand – such as the sexual violence (and indifference to sexual violence by police and others) that was so horrifically exemplified by the Roast Busters scandal that came to light in 2013. Overseas, projects have been initiated involving men talking to primarily male audiences about gender, sex and masculinity; in Oxford, this has taken the form of the Good Lads Project, which involves men (especially current or former sports players) facilitating discussion sessions at schools, sports clubs and other male-dominated environments. There are risks with these initiatives – they cement some idea of 'lads' or what it means to be a man, and they do not encourage greater levels of mature contact with women – but they are promising steps forward for reflecting on what it means to be a man in a thoughtful way. The Sexual Abuse Prevention Network, discussed in Chapter 7, recognises men's involvement as key to violence prevention; and Celia Lashlie's work provides a basis for addressing masculinity in a New Zealand context.[33] New Zealand celebrities and the media can play a part, too, by highlighting different ways to model being a man. Brendan Hokowhitu points to rugby player and coach John Kirwan as an example of someone who has legitimised discussions of mental illness. Certainly, I have seen the effect of Kirwan's openness about mental illness on friends of mine who have felt more comfortable talking about mental health due to his courage. Hokowhitu adds that the media can play a good role in highlighting men doing 'different things' within the Māori community, too.[34] Values – such as the values of care, community and creativity – might not be a bad starting point for some of these discussions.

Given that family violence is primarily perpetrated by men, male solidarity with activists campaigning on family violence or related gender-based issues is important. Men are also capable of having different kinds of conversations, in different spaces, from others. They can use their privileges to try to shift norms. That said, it is important that in harnessing their privileges, men (and I include myself) do not perpetuate the structures that they are trying to undo: it is important that they (we) do not dominate conversations where the voices of others need to be heard, and that they (we) listen to women's and others' views on how to undo problematic patterns of sexual and social behaviour. Achieving progress on masculinities in Aotearoa New Zealand requires not just a taking of responsibility by men in an effort to realise values of care, community and creativity, but also an exercise of those values in practice in interactions with others.

sexuality, homophobia and gender minorities in new zealand

I have discussed the position of women in New Zealand, and masculinities associated with men. But this does not exhaust the priorities for political action in the space of sex and gender relations, since there has been little analysis thus far of sexual orientation and trans issues.

There was much collective pride and justified joy in the passage of MP Louisa Wall's Marriage (Definition of Marriage) Amendment Act 2013, which secured marriage equality for same-sex couples in New Zealand. That was one moment in my life when I saw, through social media and my wider circle of friends, relatively apolitical people feeling like politics can make a positive difference. And that legislative change will have gone some way in shifting the views of people opposed to same-sex marriage, in both direct and indirect ways.

However, as activists and campaigners noted at the time, the introduction of the marriage equality law did not abolish homophobia or hostility towards the LGBTIQ community. There is a danger that law change is once again given too much prominence, over social and attitudinal change – and continued collective self-congratulation in Aotearoa New Zealand around marriage equality obscures the virulent, violent prejudices that remain towards people identifying as lesbian, gay, bisexual, trans, intersex or queer.

There is no doubt such prejudices are prevalent. I've mentioned the casual homophobia I saw around me growing up, which made it even more difficult for friends of mine to come out. In a survey on homophobia, 80 per cent of New Zealanders surveyed said they had experienced homophobia in sport.[35] John Key's use of 'gay' in a radio interview to describe an item of clothing in a pejorative way in 2012 cemented an association between 'gay' and uncool, undesirable, or abnormal; it may seem like an isolated, unimportant example, but language use by prominent political figures can have far-reaching consequences on how others use or regard language, like the word 'gay'.

Despite the widespread evidence of homophobia, political leaders do not seem to accept that homophobia is a major social challenge in Aotearoa New Zealand. After the Orlando, Florida, shooting in 2016, when 49 people were killed inside the Pulse gay club (a shooting that then prime minister John Key resisted calling a homophobic attack), Key and Opposition leader Andrew Little were reluctant to say that homophobia was a problem in New Zealand – with both falling back on marriage equality legislation as a sign of evidence to the contrary. Key said: 'I think New Zealand's a lot more tolerant; I mean if you think about when I passed the marriage equality bill in New Zealand you didn't see a particular backlash.' Andrew Little used similar words: 'I think we're pretty tolerant actually,' he said; 'that's why we have marriage equality legislation and people are accepted for who they are'.[36]

Homophobia can undermine the standing, security and sense of belonging of those who identify as LGBTIQ. When homophobia is so widespread, especially in schools and other spaces that people are exposed to growing up, it can be internalised by those who identify as LGBTIQ. These are the primary reasons why the community as a whole should be concerned about homophobia. But homophobia also affects everyone. To take just one example: when men discussing feelings, vulnerabilities or insecurities is described as 'gay' or associated with being feminine, and frowned upon as a result – in a judgment that represents a skewed mixture of sexism and homophobia – it's harder for all men to deal with difficult personal challenges that require reflection, sensitivity and conversation. As long as entrenched sexism and homophobia exist, everybody is worse off.

For homophobia to be combated, it would be a useful start for those involved in parliamentary politics to recognise it as a problem. But to say that this is a sufficient response is to make the same mistake made by those who point to marriage equality legislation and claim that enough is being done on LGBTIQ issues: it is to place too much confidence in the ability of parliamentary politics to extinguish social problems.

Role-modelling, including by sports stars, can serve a significant function. Rower Robbie Manson courageously came out in 2014, but in 2017 New Zealand still did not have an All Black who had come out as gay or bisexual. Coming out cannot be coerced by others.[37] But it is clear that this step, or even simply the step of an All Black taking a strong stand against homophobia (as Australian rugby player David Pocock has done), could have powerful effects. Yet there is still a strain of top-down logic in this reliance on role-modelling. At the community level, individuals and groups need to continue to call out homophobia where it exists. One major benefit of social media, in my view, is that it has led to a heightened scrutiny on the words and phrases people use in casual conversation, which forces everyone to consider the embedded prejudices in how we speak and carry ourselves. Sometimes 'calling out' on social media can appear harsh. But it may be that such strong stands need to be taken, for example against homophobia, as norms shift.

Transsexual or transgender people (hereafter, trans people) – people who identify with a gender that is different from their biological or sexual characteristics – are a subset of the LGBTIQ community that have faced particular oppression in Aotearoa New Zealand. There are many empowered and active trans activists, artists and writers, and organisations such as Gender Minorities Aotearoa and No Pride in Prisons have done important advocacy work (led by trans people) for trans and other gender-minority or gender non-binary people in recent years. But everyday hostility and structural barriers remain in place for people who identify as members of this community. An inquiry by the Human Rights Commission in 2008 noted that transgender people were historically accepted in many Māori and Pasifika communities. In contemporary New Zealand society, however, it reported difficulties for young trans people, 'constant harassment and vicious assault' for some, and 'significant gaps and inconsistencies in the provision of health services'.[38]

Events since 2008 suggest that these problems have not disappeared. There are regular reports of violence against trans people, even though these are not well covered in the mainstream media. The excellent blog *The Hand Mirror* reported for example that a Māori trans woman had her arm broken by police in the Auckland Pride parade in 2015.[39] Prejudice at a street level and on social media remains worrying. Some have even taken to questioning trans women's experiences, partly on the ground that transitioning cements patriarchal gender norms (following the views of Germaine Greer, Sheila Jeffreys and others), or sometimes on the flippant ground that changing sex is a lifestyle choice.[40] In 2014, the sole surgeon capable of carrying out male-to-female sex reassignment surgery in New Zealand retired (there being no surgeon in New Zealand able to do female–male sex reassignment surgery), leaving trans people seeking sex reassignment surgery to attempt to fund this surgery themselves overseas. There was also limited funding and long waiting times for those seeking genital reconstruction or transition or affirmation surgery; surgery that is considered imperative by some trans people wanting to lead a healthy life. To secure funding for such surgery, an application must be made to the Ministry of Health's Special High-Cost Treatment Pool; case-by-case decisions are made by the ministry, which accepts only 20 or 30 applications a year for a variety of treatments (including cancer and other treatments, in addition to reconstruction, transition or affirmation surgery).[41]

There are actions at the level of parliamentary politics that could make a difference, and paying attention to what has been called for by groups such as Gender Minorities Aotearoa is instructive here. There remains no explicit reference to 'gender identity' as a ground of prohibited discrimination under the Human Rights Act 1993, despite efforts by the former MP Georgina Beyer in the mid-2000s. While complaints are generally dealt with under the 'sex' provision, the addition of 'gender identity' as a prohibited ground would clarify the legal position, show a strong stand against transphobia, and ensure that service provision is trans-friendly.

Governments could also do more to build partnerships with countries like Australia that do perform transitioning surgery. New Zealand has a small health care system, and agreements with other countries like Australia to supplement New Zealand's health care expertise could be valuable for a number of rare conditions and treatments. Increased funding for transitioning surgery would also prevent the painful wait that now exists for those trans people that seek such surgery (not necessarily all members of the trans community). Above all else, as Eleanor Bishop told me, there is a need for those who do not identify as trans – especially for those who will deny the reality of trans people's lives – just to 'listen to a trans person', and their account of their experiences and their needs. Trans experiences are likely to be diverse, and will not reflect one political or cultural or economic perspective. Beyond being heard, too, trans people need to participate in and lead policy-making that affects their own lives. Ensuring that current decision-makers create opportunities for such participation and leadership by trans people may be the best way to realise the value of care in this sphere of policy.

conclusion

Lurking near the discussion of each of the major topics of this chapter – top-floor triumphalism in relation to women's emancipation, masculinities and sexualities – is the question of the politics of voice. Who gets to speak on what contemporary problems are in these spaces, and who should speak?

The advantages of social media – in particular, the importance of 'calling-out culture' – have already been mentioned in this chapter. Another feature of social media is related to the politics of voice, and concerns what might be called 'the online politics of privilege': the discussion of the privileges that people bring to discussions, the authority that people have (or do not have) to speak on topics, the question of how much space people take up in discussions. Anyone who is active on social media, especially Twitter and Facebook, will be familiar with the norms and language of the online politics of privilege.

It is associated with the concept of 'checking your privilege' (being aware of your privilege, and acting appropriately in light of that); and it has resulted in especial attention being paid to the experiences and voices of, among others, indigenous peoples, people of colour, survivors of sexual violence, trans people and people with disabilities – all groups relatively lacking in certain types of privilege and groups that have been too long marginalised in offline political debates. In one sense, 'privilege' here is a reframing of the concept of the 'capital' that people might have, though where 'capital' generally refers to stocks of social and economic advantages ('social capital', for example), 'privilege' has tended to concentrate on racial, gendered and other advantages. The online politics of privilege has in some ways supplemented the gaps in political analysis based on 'capital'.[42]

It may seem surprising or paradoxical at first that discussions online, where people can be anonymous or discreet, have led to so much attention being paid to people's identities, backgrounds and privileges. The internet might be thought to be a place where someone's past is most easily obscured. Considered from another perspective, though, the rise of this kind of politics is not surprising at all. In social media platforms with relatively low barriers to entry,[43] the person who is heard in a discussion is not the person who is loudest or brashest, or the person who is favoured because of society's majoritarian prejudices. This is an atmosphere where those who are quiet offline, or those who are not given opportunities to speak offline, can be heard. It makes sense, therefore, that some trans people or people of colour are able to have strong profiles online, and to build communities of solidarity. Of course, we should not romanticise social media or the online world: it is also a space of trolling, where misogynistic and homophobic abuse is easily communicated; where stalking and revenge porn are possible; and where the lack of strong regulation results in arbitrary self-regulation by social media conglomerates like Twitter or Facebook.[44] But we can nevertheless acknowledge that social media offers some opportunities for power for particular groups that tend to be more marginalised offline. This helps explain the rise of the online politics of privilege.

It is common to see criticism of this online politics of privilege, by people on social media and elsewhere (and especially by older commentators less engaged in online discussions). The centring of certain voices is seen as 'politically correct', as being excessively concerned with feelings or offence, or as too focused on people's background. These counter-arguments may have some force in some contexts, but in my view they are generally reductive and simplistic. In discussions of indigenous issues, or race issues, or trans issues (to take just three examples), those who are not indigenous or not of a minority ethnic group or not trans have a responsibility to hear indigenous, minority and trans voices. They have a responsibility because of the need to redress the ignorance of these groups in political forums historically. It should also be accepted that indigenous, minority or trans people are likely to be best placed to speak to the experience of discrimination or what it is like to live with these particular identities. This is not to shut down critical discussion or free speech (as some hyperbolic interveners tend to claim online). It is merely to give particular weight to certain voices with expertise, since lived experience is a form of expertise. This is hardly a groundbreaking norm of public discourse.

This digression is relevant to the preceding chapter because the lessons of the online politics of privilege need to be learned and applied offline, to the way that the politics of feminism, masculinity and LGBTIQ issues are practised in contemporary New Zealand society. In conversations about these issues, straight white men (who have for too long dominated discussions) need to learn to listen. That is as true in activist and campaigning spaces as in parliamentary or electoral politics. We can call this practice good 'allyship'; we could also say it follows from acknowledging who is likely to have expertise and who should fairly be given the opportunity to speak. There is, of course, a role for solidarity and support. Those who face oppression should not face the double burden of experiencing that oppression, and being solely responsible for advocacy to end it. But solidarity and support should be offered on the terms – and with the permission – of women, LGBTIQ people and others.

I have wondered whether in writing this chapter I have fallen into the trap of taking up too much space, and detracting from the voices of those most affected by patriarchy, sexism, homophobia, transphobia or other related forms of oppression. I'm open to being criticised along these lines.

But I hope in the preceding pages to redirect the attention of you, as the reader, to individuals and groups who are directly affected by these prejudices, and who are struggling to fight those prejudices: people like Eleanor Bishop, Brendan Hokowhitu, Nancy Fraser, Catriona MacLennan, Vicky Mee, Judy McGregor, Grayson Perry or Gender Minorities Aotearoa. *Who speaks* in this conversation going forward may be just as important as *what* is said – since being able to speak authoritatively in a political context is a form of power itself. Put differently, power can be redistributed not only through legislative and policy change of the kind called for in this chapter (to address pay equity, or establish gender identity as a ground of prohibited discrimination), but also through care and thought going into who is participating in and speaking about these changes.

11   people power

'Who's got the power? We've got the power! What kind of power? People power!!'

This was the powerful message of a 10,000-strong crowd that moved down Queen Street, Auckland, on 15 August 2015, in a protest about the Trans-Pacific Partnership Agreement (TPP). I joined the rolling maul of protesters in Aotea Square, and felt a genuine sense of passion and optimism – along with anger and frustration – among the crowd as it made its way towards the waterfront. I bumped into old friends on the march, and was commended by people I'd never met for vocally leading several chants. There was a belief that change was possible. We could make change happen.

In some ways this change was not achieved: the trade deal was signed in February 2016. Eleven months on, though, the new US President Donald Trump withdrew the US from the deal.

However one views the impact of activism on the TPP, it is clear that genuine people power is still a work in progress in contemporary Aotearoa New Zealand.

For all of the strengths of our political system, and for all the sporadic moments of perceived people power, we do not live in a society where any individual is empowered enough to try to create political change on an issue that they care about. Most people in New Zealand have opinions on political matters, but for a variety of reasons we do not all feel able to engage with political processes to try to translate those opinions into social change. As Jane Kelsey told me: 'People aren't complacent and they're not sedated and they want to have a voice. They just have to have the spaces in which they can have a voice.'

Those spaces do not exist in sufficient quantities at the moment in New Zealand. There is a widespread disenchantment with politicians and politics. There has been a general downward trend in voter turnout since 1984, when 93.4 per cent of registered voters cast their ballots; in 2014 that number had dropped to 77.9 per cent.[1] Away from the ballot box, public perception of political processes is often negative, with politicians ranked the second-least trusted profession in one recent survey, ahead only of journalists.[2]

Maybe not every person in New Zealand will be politically engaged, although I am not sure we should be so resigned to some 'natural' level of disengagement. And maybe this decline in voting, which is global, has at least occurred at the same time as the rise in other forms of political engagement, such as social media. Maybe. But my argument in this chapter is that, when it comes to widening the group of individuals engaged in politics and realising people power, we could do so much better.

Transforming the structures of political participation and social activity in New Zealand society will help to achieve some of the changes suggested in this book. Addressing New Zealand's homelessness problem, tackling rheumatic fever, bolstering ACC, building a movement to challenge mass incarceration – all of these things can only happen if there is a shift in patterns of political engagement which means people believe that change is possible, and have the tools to enact that change. This chapter therefore gives a partial answer to the question of *how* we move from the society in which we find ourselves in to a society underpinned by care, community and creativity.

Quite apart from its role in facilitating the realisation of the proposals in this book, securing genuine people power is an achievement in its own right. Improving our country is not just about tinkering with policy, or replacing one set of specific solutions with another. Put another way, the New Zealand project is not simply about getting better ideas into our communities and into our politics. It is also about power, and changing who has it in this country. If we can continually expand the circle of those who feel they can contribute to New Zealand politics – and in doing so, alter who holds power – we will not only be in a position where good ideas can be implemented. We will also have a groundswell of individuals, groups and organisations willing to continue to channel evidence-based, values-driven solutions into our politics in the years to come. And we will help people to feel empowered, to be more in control of their own lives and livelihoods.

To get to this point we need to understand the forces impeding genuine people power in Aotearoa New Zealand today. These forces are numerous, but can be roughly divided into two categories: desensitisation and demoralisation. With this analysis in place, I sketch out how the structures of people power can be rebuilt – through civics education, NGOs and civil society, the public service, Parliament, the media and work.

what stands in the way of people power?

The twin interlocking forces of desensitisation and demoralisation are key to the curtailment of people power.

By 'desensitisation', I mean a loss of collective sensitivity to injustice and political challenges. There are several causes of it.

First, we are now overwhelmed with information. Multiple stories are thrown together on one web page. Multiple tabs are open on our browsers (if we have internet access). In the offline world, we are surrounded by advertising and marketing. We have become numb to suffering, wrongs and causes for concern. We can still be moved to fight injustice by images or stories. But it may be that the deluge of data that fills our everyday lives makes it harder for us to feel impelled to act; our emotional reactions are blunted by the sheer quantity of daily information.

Second, as a result of ethnic and income inequality in New Zealand, embedded over time, it is becoming harder for people to empathise with those whose struggles seem very different from their own. Inequality creates a gap between people's lives and experiences, an empathy gap, that is difficult for even well-intentioned individuals to overcome. Former Green MP Holly Walker expressed this to me in a conversation at her home in Petone. She talked of 'increasing atomisation' of individuals in Aotearoa New Zealand, an 'increasing separateness' that means 'we're not as close to one another as we need to be to understand what it's like for others'. A prerequisite of being sensitised to injustice – that we can imagine ourselves in others' shoes – cannot be experienced because of inequality.

Third, the loss of political power experienced by people has left some indifferent to political developments. It is now accepted by many New Zealanders that politics does not govern some aspects of their life: food prices were once the subject of protest and debate, but seem to be beyond the reach of politicians, except to the extent that they can change GST levels or inquire into anti-competitive supermarket practices. Meanwhile, inflation targeting by the Reserve Bank, and other Reserve Bank powers, appear to have narrowed the scope of meaningful economic debate. Whatever the merits of taking these issues off the political agenda (and it may be that there are good reasons for some subjects to be out of the reach of politicians), it is plausible that this process has resulted in people caring less about politics. It may also have resulted in a narrowing of the issues discussed by the media. Saul Alinsky explains how restricted political power can exacerbate disengagement in his book *Rules for Radicals*, arguing that 'if people feel they don't have the power to change a bad situation, then they do not think about it'.[3]

'Demoralisation' overlaps with 'desensitisation' to some extent, but offers further explanations for this disengagement. Nicky Hager first used the term to describe the state of democratic debate in New Zealand when I interviewed him in January 2016. I understand it to refer to a loss of collective faith and confidence in traditional political processes. While it is hard to pinpoint precise causes, demoralisation is a phenomenon that arises from long-standing, slow-burning pressures. But three dimensions – three proximate causes – can be identified.

First, there has been a hollowing-out of principles and values in New Zealand political debate. While my conversations with friends and other New Zealanders may not be representative, I have noticed an informal perception that politicians lack authenticity: they may refer to principles and values, but they do not live them out. This perception has resulted in a dismissiveness towards politicians, especially among young people. Politicians are seen by many as petty squabblers who fight boring battles with each other rather than tackling big challenges.

Chelsea Robinson, a young campaigner who has worked as a facilitator with the social entrepreneurship hub Enspiral, expressed this to me in September 2015, saying that 'competitive adversarial politics' has 'so many aspects … that don't create the outcomes that we need'. Alternatively, politicians are seen as self-interested. Ben Knight, the co-founder of collective decision-making software Loomio, told me in the same conversation that he viewed politicians as 'experts in self-promotion, experts in cutting other people down, more than [experts in] putting forward practical ideas that are in the interests of the people they supposedly represent'. Nicky Hager echoed this, noting that our political system 'tends to [produce] people who are tricky, non-transparent, who manage by secrecy, and who [exercise] non-democratic control'.

Second, there is among many New Zealanders a stifled sense of community that leaves them feeling removed from the political sphere – without any of the collective morale that is needed to sustain political engagement. Young people are lonelier, on average, than older people in New Zealand (see Chapter 8), with 2010 data showing that 18 per cent of young people are lonely all, most or some of the time, compared to 11 per cent of older people. The same data demonstrates that higher levels of loneliness are associated with lower standards of living.[4] It is not inconceivable that these levels of loneliness for young people, and those from lower socio-economic brackets, contribute to the fact that these groups tend to turn out to vote in lower numbers. A dented sense of community or social connectedness may result in people feeling less keen to make an effort to engage in politics. That sensibility has many causes, including the rise in individualism and competitiveness since the 1980s.

Third, groups that have experienced repeated political injustices in New Zealand may feel resigned to the fact that politics will not be a vehicle for positive change – and this might sap their faith and confidence in political processes. Māori and Pasifika, for example, have had to deal with recurrent episodes of politicians undercutting their rights (the Foreshore and Seabed Act 2004, say, or the dawn raids of the 1970s), and some Māori and Pasifika campaigners may therefore, with justification, feel no hope that mainstream politics can advance their interests. It might be argued that such groups should be even more mobilised, in order to defend their rights when they are under threat; but it seems overly demanding to expect members of these groups to continue to mobilise if there is a perception that political resistance is only ignored. It is at least plausible that this aspect of demoralisation helps to explain relatively low levels of voter turnout among Māori and Pasifika communities,[5] though a variety of factors are relevant to this.

The data for all of this is inconclusive. But it is intuitively convincing that the twin forces of desensitisation and demoralisation help to explain why New Zealand has seen fading levels of formal political engagement in recent years.

These trends need to be reversed. With an increasing sector of the population disengaged from politics, it could become easy for politicians to give even less attention to the interests of the disengaged. Political disengagement could also narrow the political debate, with some perspectives not represented. Re-engaging those who feel uninspired by politics may have collateral benefits, such as improving the strength of community ties in Aotearoa New Zealand, or reducing income inequality. The following sections suggest practical steps that could be taken to ensure that New Zealanders are re-sensitised to political developments, and have greater faith and confidence in the political process. (Some other steps, such as moves to address historical injustices, have been proposed in earlier chapters.) The aim is to build a political system where individuals who want to intervene politically are empowered. The focus is on traditional forms of political engagement, especially voting – but I would hope that a rejuvenated sense of people power in formal political processes will ripple out to create more energetic activism and richer community participation in general.

civics education

People power can be revitalised at an early stage in people's lives, through the education system – and the introduction of a programme of civics education in New Zealand schools.

Successive inquiries into New Zealand's constitution have proposed the introduction of civics education. The 2005 inquiry into New Zealand's constitutional arrangements recommended that 'increased effort should be made to improve civics and citizenship education in schools to provide young people with the knowledge needed to become responsible and engaged citizens'.[6] The Constitutional Review Panel's report of 2013 also recommended that the government 'develops a national strategy for civics and citizenship education in schools and in the community, including the unique role of the Treaty of Waitangi, te Tiriti o Waitangi, and assign responsibility for the implementation of the strategy'. The report observed that 'the implementation of the strategy could include the co-ordination of education activities; resource development, including resources for Māori medium schools; and professional development for teachers and the media'.[7] This was one of the firmer recommendations of the panel, which otherwise was relatively tentative and called merely for the continuation of a constitutional conversation. But neither the 2005 nor the 2013 recommendations have been taken up by the various governments.

It is worth outlining what currently exists by way of civics or citizenship education in New Zealand, before turning to the benefits of this form of education, the challenges of introducing it and the key strategic choices open for those interested in seeing more of it in New Zealand schools.

The current New Zealand curriculum contains no explicit reference to civics education – education about politics, the institutions of government and the practices of civic life. One of the principles of the curriculum is the slightly strangely named 'Future Focus', which observes that the curriculum 'encourages students to look to the future by exploring such significant future-focused issues as sustainability, citizenship, enterprise and globalisation.'[8] The mention of 'citizenship' possibly allows teachers to justify some teaching about the rights and responsibilities of citizens in New Zealand, but the phrase is fuzzy. One of the values in the New Zealand curriculum is 'community and participation for the common good', and one of the key competencies is 'participating and contributing'.[9] These references might also be a hook used by teachers to talk about social life and political institutions in New Zealand – but again the link to civics education is a little thin. Social studies, taught from Year 1 to Year 10, often allows teachers to encourage students to think about local community issues, or social questions such as immigration. There is certainly the opportunity for teachers to deliver content akin to civics education here, and the social sciences component of the curriculum refers to some concepts that echo notions of civics education. But no formal civics education is mandated. Overall, the position in 2017 was that civics education is not formally a part of primary and secondary school education in Aotearoa New Zealand.

There are multiple benefits to civics education. Students can currently get a form of political education at school, but it depends on where they study and who their teachers are. At Clyde Quay Primary School, I participated in two class elections styled on political elections, learned about 'values', and took part in other political projects. Years later, when I was working at the Supreme Court as a clerk, I arranged a tour for the classes of an energetic former teacher of mine from Wellington College. The approach to civics education under the curriculum at the moment creates major inequalities of experience, with some individuals gaining valuable insights if they have particularly committed or confident teachers – but others learning nothing at all about social and political institutions. Making civics education a formal part of the curriculum would ensure that everyone gets a basic minimum of political education.

Civics education would be valuable for other reasons. With additional learning about politics, institutions of government and civic practices, it's likely that individuals would improve their general knowledge of government and be more informed in their participation in civic activities such as jury service and voting. It is not inconceivable that civics education would slightly increase voter turnout, especially among 18–24-year-olds, only 63 per cent of whom voted in the 2014 election (of those who were enrolled).[10] It might improve civic-mindedness and social capital, as journalist Lee Suckling has suggested, even if community participation is already a part of the New Zealand curriculum.[11]

International researchers comparing civics education worldwide found the greatest gap between New Zealand students and their counterpart overseas in levels of campaigning, including on human rights and environmental issues. Further political education might heighten student concern for these issues, and encourage practical community action.[12] It could help students to live out values when they leave for the world outside.

An attempt could be made to assess these outcomes five and ten years after the introduction of civics education (including through interviews with students as well as reviews of statistical changes), though of course no control group would exist and causation would be difficult to infer with any degree of confidence. Civics education is no silver bullet, as writer Di White has said, but it is one promising tool to address political disengagement.[13]

There are challenges involved with introducing civics education. There is a possible risk that classes become politicised, and that teachers find it difficult to set aside their own political views when delivering content about, say, institutions of government or civic life. But this is also possible within social studies classes, and the risk can be managed through existing accountability mechanisms – such as the reports of the Education Review Office (ERO) – as well as through giving teachers sound guidance and content that has to be taught. Moreover, politicisation does not seem to have been a major problem in Australia's teaching of civics education – or in other countries with similar programmes. An additional challenge is that if civics education is dull or boring, students could be further put off voting or engaging in politics.[14] Some civics education classes in some schools could be less interesting to some students. This is a risk of any subject. However, with the right guidelines in place – use of local examples that are relevant to students, a mixture of activities and learning of facts and a willingness to inquire into how students have perceived the classes when civics education is reviewed after introduction – this risk can be managed.

I propose the introduction of civics education, or something akin to civics education, as a learning area in the New Zealand Curriculum. But should civics be taught throughout primary and secondary school, or be confined to secondary school, at a stage where students have slightly heightened political consciousness? Should it be examined as an NCEA subject, in Years 11–13? And should the subject be taught as 'civics' or as a broader form of 'citizenship education'?

As with other learning areas in the curriculum, the default position would be that civics would be woven throughout primary and secondary education – with schools being relatively free to decide how they teach the subject and apply it locally. Creating an examination for the subject could render it far more formulaic. It would seem most promising to leave civics education as a subject that runs throughout primary and secondary school, but not to offer it as an examinable NCEA subject.

The question of whether the subject should be 'civics education' or 'citizenship education' is slightly trickier. Bronwyn Hayward, an academic at the University of Canterbury and author of the book *Children, Citizenship and Environment*, argues that we should 'move away from the narrow term civics'. '[T]here is so much about citizenship that is active and engaged,' Hayward told me, 'and when kids and children do engage with others in real communities then they do learn.' She added: 'We need the ability to understand power … but civics, as facts alone, I am less convinced by.' Hayward raises a good point: teachers may find it easier to make 'citizenship education' relevant and interesting (as opposed to 'civics as facts'), and such a subject would build on the existing references to community and participation in the New Zealand Curriculum. On the other hand, 'citizenship education' has its own difficulties. What is 'citizenship' in New Zealand? If taught in a particular way, could 'citizenship education' exclude recent immigrants? In the UK, 'citizenship education' is a subject (for those aged 11–16), and includes material about democracy, Parliament, laws, rights and liberties, volunteering, electoral systems, ethnic diversity and budgeting and money.[15] The teaching of the subject has not been met with opposition or arguments that it has been exclusionary. Perhaps the context in New Zealand may be more complex, and it's possible that it would be less easy – among other things – to integrate Māori and non-Māori approaches to citizenship.

I do not want to press any conclusion on the 'civics' versus 'citizenship' debate too far. There are researchers and policy-makers with far more expertise on this than me. But a cautious course would be to begin by introducing 'civics education' as a learning area, with the possibility of supplementing or replacing civics with a more fully fledged 'citizenship education' after some initial years of experience with civics. It is civics education that has been proposed by multiple constitutional inquiries, and civics education may be capable of including material from citizenship education. It would start to help to sensitise young people to political developments, addressing the trends I have discussed towards desensitisation and demoralisation.

A more moderate alternative path would be to beef up the social studies curriculum to ensure that it has an even stronger civics education component. What is important, regardless of what form the subject takes, is that students are given a role within classes to inquire and apply abstract political ideas to their own communities and their own lives. With some level of student ownership and participation, this may yet play an important role as a tool of political empowerment.

Different political parties have proposed civics education, alongside constitutional inquiries. Sue Bradford, formerly of the Green Party, proposed it in her Civics Education and Voting Age Bill. Adoption of civics education has long been the policy of the United Future Party under Peter Dunne. There are several ways these nascent efforts could be supported to press civics education forward. A youth-led campaign, perhaps co-sponsored by leading youth activist groups and an umbrella organisation (like ActionStation), could create greater urgency for political action. An effort might be made in Parliament to build bipartisan support. It is not for me to set out the detail: the movement should be bottom-up. But interlocking groups of supporters exist: academics with data, young people who care about political engagement, educators passionate about the subject, and some policy-makers. What is needed is for these groups, along with politicians, to make civics education a priority and to continue to build public support for the idea in whatever way they think is most effective and appropriate.

ngos, charities and civil society

New Zealand has a relatively active NGO, charity and civil society landscape – all set apart from government and not driven by profit. Many in the sector work hard to draw attention to social challenges in New Zealand or to deliver services. But two features of this sector could be changed in order to arrest desensitisation and demoralisation.

In Chapter 6, I mentioned the problems created by the increasing use of contracting out of social services. (Among these problems is the fact that NGOs, charities and other civil society organisations, anecdotally, are forced to spend more and more of their time applying for grants rather than doing core service delivery or advocacy work.) One particular harmful development for the state of public debate in New Zealand, which was also discussed in Chapters 6 and 7, is the caution shown by NGOs in speaking out on policy and politics when they are delivering services by contract to government. Some might contest the extent to which NGOs have been muzzled by governments; there are disputes, for example, over whether the Problem Gambling Foundation's loss of funding in 2014 was a result of its criticism of government policy. Prohibitions on non-discrimination, and freedom of speech provisions, arguably protect these NGOs. But the legal position is unclear,[16] and what is important is that there is a perception by many within the NGO community that vocal criticism of government policy will lead to an impact on contract provision and NGOs' survival. That this perception has some grounding in reality is supported by Grey and Sedgwick's research, cited in Chapter 6.[17] Nicky Hager confirmed this, a trend he has been observing for some time, in our conversation. '"Relaxed" New Zealand has this culture of fear around any groups that get government funding,' he said, 'because it's shamelessly used to put pressure on them and to punish them. ... And this is all so avoidable.'

Is it wrong for NGOs to voice criticism of government when they are in receipt of government funding? As with public servants, it could be said that if the government needs to cooperate and liaise with NGOs, that relationship will be strained where the NGOs have openly criticised the government. But the comparison with public servants is inapt. NGO service providers are not giving advice to ministers, in the same way as some members of the public service. They are delivering a service. And their work with individuals in the community gives them an important base of expertise that they ought to be entitled to share with the general public, including through criticism of government policy. Their highlighting of weaknesses in government policy or implementation can help to sensitise citizens to political problems they should be aware of. And such speaking out can result in a livelier public debate.

Governments should be secure enough to accept NGO criticism as an attempt to improve public policy. They should recognise that a high-energy democracy, involving experimentation and a vibrant public sphere, requires criticism and constructive comment.[18] Repeated public announcements to this effect by government ministers could open the way for healthy criticism by NGOs, charities and civil society. A stronger protection for NGOs and others, however – if there is a continuation of contracting out – would be for a legal change underscoring NGOs' ability to speak out even while they are under contract with government.[19] One option is for a provision to be inserted into the principles of government procurement; another is for a standard term to be inserted into government contracts.[20] A risk is that this term is then used to cut down the ability of NGO service providers to speak out. It is important that it is drafted broadly, perhaps in the following terms: 'The contractor retains a right to express, through any form, a view on all aspects of government policy and practice.' Such a firm statement should ensure that NGOs, charities and civil society feel able to express views, thereby contributing to a more vibrant public sphere, and perhaps a less desensitised general public.

A second feature of the NGO, charity and civil society sector that could be changed relates to the existence of think tanks to kickstart discussion on politics and public policy. It is a widely commented on feature of New Zealand public life that we lack the culture of think tanks that can be found in the UK and even Australia. There are a number of single-issue groups in New Zealand that produce focused research, through more or less formal structures: the Child Poverty Action Group and JustSpeak among others. Yet there are far fewer umbrella groups capable of offering in-depth research on a range of topics. In fact, it seems possible to list all of the groups that do exist in this category: the New Zealand Initiative, the Maxim Institute (which is open about its conservative starting points), Motu Economic and Public Policy Research (which has a focus on environmental and economic issues), the Morgan Foundation, the McGuinness Institute, and Economic and Social Research Aotearoa (launched in September 2016 with an explicit left-wing orientation).

There is a variety of reasons for this paucity of multi-issue think tanks, including the limited tradition and culture of philanthropy in New Zealand (which blocks one source of funding that is available in most other countries), our small population, and the relative accessibility of politicians in the past (which has perhaps suggested that there is less of a need for an intermediate layer of political commentary). This thin layer of think tanks is one reason for a lack of depth in political debate. The absence of think tanks providing reasoned analysis of new ideas and thoughtful proposals has contributed to demoralisation and desensitisation. Publications from think tanks can help to create shared principled benchmarks for politics (to reverse demoralisation) and alert the public to neglected policy areas (to reverse desensitisation).

What can be done to produce more think tanks in New Zealand? There needs to be, at the very least, a continued appreciation of the value of research, ideas and depth of thinking in politics. Politicians can underscore this by being open to new ideas and giving credit to new narratives or approaches developed by think tanks. (I return to the theme of New Zealand as a 'smart country' in Chapter 12.) This will encourage individuals to pursue careers in think tanks, and show potential donors that these bodies can play a central role in public life. And individual and corporate donors could be more willing to support this nascent work. The risk is that contributions will be regarded by companies and high net-worth individuals less as donations and more as investments, with the expectation that they also receive some benefit from the contribution. As far as possible, no-strings-attached donations should be made to ensure that the research direction of think tanks is not driven by companies' or individuals' self-interest. This can be achieved if donors acknowledge that think-tank work is a public good that deepens the evidence base of all political activity, and view it as part of their civic duty to contribute to that public good where they have achieved some measure of personal or economic success.

The question of whether governments should fund think tank activity is more tricky. Germany has a strong tradition of this, as do several Scandinavian countries. Governments can provide much-needed funding for think tanks in an early stage of development, reinforcing the view that politically relevant research is a public good. Government funding could also address the possible unfairness of some individuals securing think tank funding simply because they are more proximate to private sources of wealth. On the other hand, there is a danger that governments only fund bodies that reflect their own ideological position. They might then use them to entrench public support for their policies, and to skew rather than facilitate thoughtful public debate. Additionally, government funding might mean that think tanks do not feel genuinely independent from government in the ideas they advocate and criticise. They might, however subconsciously, feel a need to hold back from criticising government if they are reliant on it for future funding.

Steps could be taken to minimise these risks: roughly equal amounts of funding could be earmarked for think tanks from different parts of the political spectrum, and think tanks could be assured of their independence, with this assurance possibly being written into legislation. But these steps are imperfect solutions: it might be difficult (and undesirable) to categorise think tanks in terms of their ideological orientation, and even legislative guidance about their independence would bring them within a government remit in awkward way.

A further alternative is setting up a contestable fund for think tank funding – a proposal suggested to me by Jonathan Boston in an interview in January 2016. However, even Boston was circumspect about this idea (though it might merit further consideration), noting that it would be difficult to develop an objective and broadly acceptable criterion of 'quality' as a basis for allocating funding. Overall, on balance, it might be preferable for governments not to fund think tanks in the contemporary political climate, although politicians and donors can be encouraged to change their behaviour to make it easier for new and existing think tanks.

A brief comment is needed here about academia and the arts. Academics (inside and outside of institutions of higher learning) and artists arguably, form part of the civil society world, though some would say that certain artists fall outside of this world on this definition because they are motivated by profit. These individuals contribute significantly to sensitising people to political problems and opportunities. We have already seen examples of this: Moana Jackson draws attention to problems of incarceration, institutional racism and constitutional change; Tono, through his music, provides a hook for people to grasp the importance of housing issues, among other political matters; and films like *In My Father's Den* underscore problems of family and sexual violence. Academia and the arts should not be reduced to what they can offer to political debates and political participation; to focus only on this dimension of academic and artistic work is to under-appreciate the rich, creative contributions of people working in these spheres. But scholars and artists can raise the profile of social challenges in unique ways; artists, in particular, have the power to ignite thinking about political issues among individuals who might not otherwise be excited by conventional politics. This public contribution should be borne in mind when decisions are made about public funding of academia and the arts – though, of course, such funding should never be made crudely contingent on the extent to which academics and artists can enhance political participation.

the public service

This is not the place to offer a full review of the operation and design of New Zealand's public service, and I make no attempt to be comprehensive in my criticism and assessment of the public service. What is possible and relevant here is to pinpoint two developments in the public service that have a bearing on people power, and to offer some suggestions about how these developments might be arrested.

The first development is the shift in public service culture towards offering advice that aligns with what ministers would like to hear. There is much anecdotal evidence that I have gathered, through off-the-record conversations with policy advisors, that some public servants are now increasingly willing to tailor advice to fit a minister's preferences or ideological orientation. That anecdotal evidence is supported by the comments of informed observers, such as Chris Eichbaum, who has said: 'Over time, and indeed over successive governments, there has been an increasing tendency for the public service to tell the government of the day what it wants to hear, sometimes at the expense of what it needs to hear.'[21]

This is not to diminish the work of public servants, many of whom are committed to non-partisan advice. Some might on occasion offer advice that ministers want to hear as part of trying to build a trusting relationship that allows better advice in the long term.[22] It should also be noted that some ministers have a good reputation for encouraging critical advice; I repeatedly heard that Bill English as minister of finance was one such minister. Undoubtedly some commentators and observers would also query the claim that public servants are pandering to ministers' interests with more frequency than ever before; the aforementioned Jonathan Boston, of Victoria University of Wellington, who has deep experience in both public policy scholarship and policy advocacy, was sceptical of the claim when I spoke to him. Nevertheless, despite the absence of a strong counterfactual, I think there is a firm basis for arguing that public servants in recent years have found it harder to communicate advice that ministers do not want to hear. Some might say this is no big deal, since public servants are meant to serve the government of the day. But it seems obvious that pandering like this might inhibit public servants' independence, and their ability to provide frank advice as a basis for government action.

In Richard Mulgan's eloquent words, 'Public servants should not compromise their respect for truth and evidence in order to accommodate the views of their political masters.'[23] Compromised respect for the truth in public servant–minister interactions – which really seems more to have been the fault of ministers than public servants – contributes to demoralisation of public debate, since it means that the public service is less capable of confronting politicians with difficult political challenges that need to be addressed.

The position cannot be remedied merely through rule changes. After all, references to independence and 'free and frank advice' are already written down in numerous places: in the Cabinet Manual (where the need for impartial advice is underscored), and in section 32(1)(f) of the State Sector Act 1988 (where departmental chief executives are said to be responsible for ensuring that 'free and frank' advice is tendered). What is needed is a correction in culture, and for that change to be genuine we also have to understand the causes of the shift in advice-giving practices in the public services. There are several ways that understanding can be achieved: perhaps through an inquiry led by the Office of the Auditor-General, as Chris Eichbaum has proposed,[24] or through a royal commission into the public service, as Geoffrey Palmer has recommended.[25] Following this inquiry, if evidence of the trend described above were to be substantiated, clear leadership should be shown by departmental heads and ministers to ensure that advice can be given in a genuinely free and frank manner.

In seeking a return to that kind of advice, two models might be consulted. The first is from a New Zealand public service of an earlier generation. From the 1940s to the 1960s, there were numerous examples of independent public service research and writing that pioneered new ideas in public policy. In the field of criminal justice, John Robson as Secretary of Justice from 1960 developed alternatives to imprisonment (such as periodic detention) and a humane approach to punishment, working independently from Minister of Justice Ralph Hanan, but in harmony with Hanan. Their relationship has been celebrated through the naming of the Robson Hanan Trust, which oversaw the work of Kim Workman (interviewed in Chapter 7) in the late 2000s and early 2010s. In the field of education, meanwhile, Clarence Beeby as Secretary for Education (1940–60) applied educational psychology insights in order to develop policy. The primary school curriculum was revised under his leadership, special education was developed for children with disabilities, rural schooling was supported and class sizes were reduced in post-primary education. Like Robson, Beeby built a strong relationship with politicians, and in particular worked closely with Labour Prime Minister Peter Fraser.[26] Of course, in some ways Robson and Beeby were far from typical public servants. And it is important not to romanticise the public service of the past. But Robson and Beeby do demonstrate the value of independent public policy work through the public service – and they provide an example to follow for a modern public service seeking to return to the ideal of free and frank advice.

The second model that might guide a public service recommitting to free and frank advice is the idea of New Public Passion. Articulated by New Zealand public servant Ryan Orange, New Public Passion is an alternative to or extension of New Public Management, the approach to public service pioneered in New Zealand in the 1980s, which borrowed techniques from the private sector – in particular, targets and heightened accountability – in order to change public sector practice. New Public Passion suggests that there needs to be a renewed focus on the intrinsic motivation of public servants (in addition to extrinsic motivators such as discipline or pay) in order to improve the morale of the public service and to unlock the ideas and independent thinking of public servants.[27] While New Public Passion is an embryonic framework and is not explicitly directed at the problem of public servants pandering to ministers, it is conceivable that encouraging passion and independent thinking from public servants will help to safeguard the ideal of free, frank and independent advice.

Another development in the public service with an even more direct impact on desensitisation is the increasing restriction on public servants' political activities outside of work. The theoretical link to desensitisation is clear: if there are around 45,000 full-time-equivalent public servants in New Zealand (about 1 per cent of the population), and all of these people are inhibited from taking part in political activities, there is an overall loss of people who can engage in politics and a flow-on decrease in the information that could be supplied to the public about New Zealand's political problems.[28] In short: when a large segment of people are unable to be active politically, fewer matters can be brought to the attention of the public – or the same number of matters can be brought to the attention of the public, but with less vigour and volume. People power is also directly undercut if a portion of the people have their political power limited.

But is it true that public servants are more muzzled in their political activities than they have been previously? Nicky Hager, a seasoned investigative journalist, has been observing trends in the public service closely for many years. In his 2012 Bruce Jesson lecture, he said: 'Today many public servants believe they are not allowed or that somehow it may hurt their job to be involved in politics. The public service code guarantees their rights as citizens, but other more or less subtle messages have discouraged or frightened most of them.' And when I met Hager in early 2016 in his Wellington home, he did not resile from these claims. A review of the relevant public sector rules would appear to confirm his observations. In 2010, tighter guidance (described by the *New Zealand Herald* as 'more prescriptive') was released by the State Services Commission on the political activities of public servants.[29] The guidance emphasises, in somewhat vague terms, the need for public servants to be aware of 'perceptions'. It notes, 'We must maintain in our non-working lives the level of political neutrality that is appropriate for the responsibilities we have.' Thus, the problem is not just that public servants perceive their political participation rights to be restricted – a problem that should not be dismissed, since perception has an effect on actual levels of political participation. The restriction of political participation is real, as demonstrated by the release of this guidance.

But if there are greater restrictions on public servants today, are these restrictions justified? Is it not necessary, as the guidance says, for ministers to be trusting of the advice that they receive, especially if policy advisors (and public servants more broadly) are encouraged to develop independent thinking? And can ministers only trust the advice if they are sure that public servants do not have any political conflicts of interest? I accept that it would be inappropriate for public servants to try to advance a partisan agenda through work in the public service. However, rather than public servants needing to change their practices (or their guidance being changed), maybe it is ministers who need to change. Public-service advice can be relatively technical and descriptive, but it is difficult for such advice to be value-free. In advising ministers on the likely costs and benefits of particular policy options, for example, public servants make value judgments in selecting particular costs and benefits to highlight; their description and assessment of these will also be informed by their education and world view. Ministers should accept that. Once accepted, it seems harder to maintain that politicians would distrust public servants if they discovered that they were involved with political activity outside of work. Ministers might instead see these public servants as part of a broader group that inevitably brings values, background and world view to their work – but that aspires to serve the government of the day, and undertakes not to advance a partisan agenda through that work.

Building a new model of the relationship between ministers and public servants requires further discussion. But there is no doubt that the new view that

I have begun to sketch above, which would allow greater latitude for public servants to participate in politics away from work and would lead politicians to understand advice slightly differently, requires adjustments to the State Services Commission's guidance for these employees. More importantly, though, this approach would require a shift in the norms of public service practice – and clear assurances from those in leadership positions in the public service.

Hager offered some suggestions for how this change could be implemented. He reminded me that, only a generation ago, public servants were allowed to be more involved politically: most of the people he met in campaign groups as a young person were civil servants. What would be needed is 'serious top-down direction', Hager said. A minister of state services would have to appeal to everyone 'to get out there and participate in your society' – to say, 'I promise: you will only be rewarded for doing this'. Of course, 'there'd be a fight and there'd have to be a culture change,' he acknowledged. But this modification to public service guidance, accompanied by a change in understanding, would help to dent the development of desensitisation and restore political rights to public servants, all the while maintaining independent, high-quality public service advice.

select committees and a politics of listening

Parliament, like many of the institutions and actors discussed in this chapter, could be revitalised in multiple ways to support people power.[30] I suggest here that two changes are considered. One – the reform of select committees – is more of a practical change; the other – a focus on genuine, thoroughgoing listening in politics – is more theoretical. Both could contribute to a more sensitised public.

Holly Walker, the former Green Party MP, has been honest and outspoken about the challenges she faced in Parliament: she has written about how inhospitable it was for her as a mother, and how hard it could be to keep up with parliamentary paperwork and meetings as a new MP.[31] Many of her proposals – including allowing MPs to take an unpaid year off from Parliament, and rethinking parliamentary sitting hours (more days of sitting in a week, but for fewer hours, and fewer weeks overall in a year) – deserve more consideration.[32] I spoke with her about the concept of 'people power', and how among other things Parliament might be transformed to give greater effect to people power.

Walker told me that parliamentary processes were not being properly used as a 'vehicle for public debate and discussion' – and noted, in particular, that she 'went in [to Parliament] with a lot of hope' for select committees, but was disappointed with how formulaic they turned out to be. The processes of select committees are a prime area where some change might be relatively easily implemented, with the result that people could more readily participate in parliamentary politics.

Two possible changes should be considered in more detail, alongside the introduction of civics education, which might improve general awareness of what select committees are and do. First, while it is now less complex than it once was to submit to a select committee – submissions are possible using an online form – the process remains daunting. The guide to select committee submissions alone is twenty pages long. The parliamentary web page describing bills before select committees could be made to appear less austere and dry (including through digestible but accurate summaries of bills) and serious thought should go into allowing select committee submissions via social media, especially Facebook. Could this lead to messy and ill-informed submissions? Not necessarily. Submissions can be unstructured in their current form, and politicians should do all they can to encourage political engagement, including by engaging people through media like Facebook that they currently use.

Second, select committees could be reconstituted so that they are closer to people making submissions. Today, select committees sit in Parliament, in relatively drab rooms that require individuals outside Wellington to travel to give their views. Select committees could consider relocating to community centres for more bills and inquiries: they might sit on marae (with the permission of local iwi), or in town halls, or sites relevant to the bills they are reviewing. This is not without precedent. Inquiries and committees have travelled around the country on occasion. Judges are able to visit sites as part of evidence-gathering in trials. Other countries have trialled 'community cabinets' where the Cabinet sits in a community, in part to engage with people outside of a capital city.[33] The changing of the surrounds for select committees might allow more informal discussion, make submissions easier and help reduce the extent to which Parliament is perceived as Wellington-centric. Along with physical relocation, a technological upgrade of select committee practices could also be undertaken to allow, for example, submissions by Skype.

Both the streamlining of select committee submission processes and greater flexibility in how and where select committees sit might incur additional costs.

It should be ensured that the physical relocation of select committees does not impose excessive burdens on MPs, of the type highlighted by Holly Walker. If these costs and complications are managed, however, it would appear that these changes might be a painless and productive way of bringing Parliament to people – thereby boosting people power.

Beyond select committees, more emphasis could be placed on the need for politicians to listen. I have written about a 'politics of listening' in the context of the UK with Marek Sullivan,[34] but the concept is equally relevant in New Zealand.

Politicians often speak rhetorically about 'listening' to the public. But political listening could be much improved, at both an interpersonal and a collective level. Active listening involves a single-minded focus on what another person is saying – not only through words, but also body language, mood and emotion. It avoids interruption, digression or judgment as far as possible. It requires meaning to be teased out and carefully understood.[35] Politicians could begin by redoubling their commitment to the ideal of active listening in their everyday practice. Not all New Zealand politicians are good active listeners in my experience – and this is not always their fault: multiple claims on their time and the stresses of their work can prevent it. Certainly, most politicians do not model good listening in the raucous, theatrical exchanges during parliamentary questions and parliamentary debate.

A stronger commitment to active listening – which might be supported by training courses in listening for politicians, or active listening being emphasised in politicians' first few months on the job – might improve how politicians are perceived. It could help politicians to represent constituents' concerns (whether they have a local constituency or represent a broader group by virtue of being a list MP), and might encourage individuals to approach MPs in their offices or via select committees. A useful side-effect of emphasising the value of listening by politicians is that we might shift our understanding of what a good politician is, and appreciate a broader sum of skills in politicians (and prospective politicians) beyond good public speaking. In sum, public indication that listening is taken seriously by politicians might encourage political engagement by the public in various ways, thereby beginning to alleviate the trend towards desensitisation.

But if a 'politics of listening' is to be more than just a nice-sounding phrase, it requires structural changes to political practice, as well as improvements in interpersonal contact. Listening does not mean placing weight on every demand made by a member of the public. It requires discerning the agendas and interests that can lie behind demands. A good collective politics of listening also requires an awareness of who has traditionally been listened to in New Zealand politics, and who has *not* been listened to – and a special effort to address these past patterns of ignorance and silencing. An acknowledgment that there has been insufficient listening to, say, Māori voices in New Zealand politics may be a first step towards helping Māori feel more welcome within parliamentary politics (though it is by no means all that must be done, as discussed in Chapter 5).

In my earlier article on the politics of listening, I added that a politics of listening ultimately should lead us to a sea-change in politicians' attentiveness to the people around them; a heightened sensitivity to the problems that might lie behind what is said by a constituent in hurried, nervous exchanges; and a much greater generosity and curiosity towards the concerns of the public, in place of the cynicism and dismissiveness that have crept into politicians' attitudes toward constituents.[36] We may, I wrote, need more experimentation in tools used by politicians (such as through social media), as well as institutional change: more time set aside to allow politicians to listen, more encouragement given to the public to speak to politicians, more bodies charged with seeking out public views. All of these points remain relevant today, and highlight that a 'politics of listening' might be a useful theoretical frame, which – alongside specific changes to select committees – could help to rebuild parliamentary levers of political participation.

the media

It is a cliché, especially in left-wing circles, to criticise the quality of media in New Zealand. Such criticism ignores a number of positive media developments: such as the rise of outlets like *The Spinoff* and *The Wireless* (Radio New Zealand's portal for youth-focused digital content), and the excellent quality of much journalism on Māori Television (including stories produced on *Native Affairs*, especially when it was hosted by Mihingarangi Forbes before her move to RNZ). Despite these welcome developments, New Zealand appears to have a relative paucity of long-form, investigative public-interest journalism – partly because of our size, but for other reasons, too. Worryingly, recent years have also seen threats to the independence of media. RNZ's funding was frozen from 2008 and remained so in 2017, and political appointments have been made to various media boards.[37] At the same time, the 'celebritisation' of content (described in Chapter 2) has continued, especially through privately owned outlets. The cumulative effect of these trends has been the erosion of a shared base of reliable information for political debate; that erosion is arguably being seen in other places around the world, too, including in the United States. As Nicky Hager told me, there has been a loss of the 'unifying power of mass media' (even if town- and city-specific newspaper mastheads give people some unifying base of information).[38] This worsens both desensitisation and demoralisation. People cannot be sufficiently sensitised to threats to the public good in the absence of high-quality, in-depth journalism. The media, after all, in Hager's words, are 'the mediators between the "what happens" or "what is" and what people hear about'. As for demoralisation, it is much more difficult for common political principles to be strengthened when there is no foundation of information for analysis and debate.

The Civics and Media Project (coordinated by the McGuinness Institute), the Coalition for Better Broadcasting and independent commentators and academics have converged in proposing how public media might be revitalised in New Zealand. All have suggested some version of a merger of RNZ and TVNZ 1, backed with strong funding and a commitment to media independence. The idea, which could involve the creation of one service known as Public Broadcasting New Zealand (PBNZ) has considerable appeal. Public broadcasting now is segmented across RNZ and TVNZ 1. While each has some ability to invest and commission and coordinate content, economies of scale for major projects are not as great as they might be. A sizeable, secure pool of funding for one public broadcaster would allow creative decisions to be made, including to develop diverse content and investigative journalism. That single large pool of funding might also allow major sporting events to be free-to-air once again, a move that could support the value of community, though this is by no means guaranteed.[39]

Some might claim that this could diminish the range of public broadcasting voices, but there is no reason why multiple voices and perspectives could not be maintained within an expanded single public broadcaster. The move would require increased funding for public broadcasting (possibly funded, as some have suggested, by a small levy on private media providers). But as Hager told me, '[t]he main ingredient isn't the extra money; it's the extra independence' –

and there would also need to be a commitment by successive governments not to interfere in public broadcasting decisions. Māori Television should remain distinct, in order to safeguard Māori content; how NZ On Air is connected to the new enlarged broadcaster should be the subject of further debate.[40] In some ways the move would involve a return to the position prior to the splitting of the old New Zealand Broadcasting Corporation, TV One and TV Two in 1975. In addition to the supporters already mentioned, the idea has been backed by an unlikely coalition of commentators, including the former MediaWorks head of news and current affairs (and one-time TV3 news chief) Mark Jennings,[41] right-wing blogger David Farrar[42] and Winston Peters's New Zealand First Party.[43]

As with all of the topics in this chapter, unanswered questions remain. Should there be more concern about media ownership patterns in New Zealand and the state of media regulation? What, if anything, is to be done about declining newspaper turnover? Is it worrying that many New Zealanders, including young New Zealanders, now get their news through social media, especially Facebook? Can policy or politics address the especial difficulties faced by Māori media in a still Pākehā-dominated media establishment, as recently outlined by Mihingarangi Forbes?[44] Can action be taken to ensure journalists are less pressed for time in preparing stories, so that they are able to exercise more critical judgment about press releases or PR-influenced content? These are all important matters that need to be explored.

For now, I suggest that the main way that the media can be transformed to address desensitisation and demoralisation is through investing in public broadcasting, and building RNZ and TVNZ 1 into a high-quality single-banner public broadcaster. Public spaces, in the form of parks and squares, are important for allowing us to come together as a community, and to rub shoulders with others within inclusive surrounds. And the media is a virtual public space: an open forum to which we are all welcome and where we can 'bang into each other', in Hager's words. Working towards an expanded and revitalised public broadcaster strengthens and broadens that virtual public space.

public service careers, volunteering and public interest law

The last section in this chapter is the most speculative, but it remains necessary: it concerns the connections between careers and reduced people power. New Zealand tertiary education has become more expensive in recent years, as the shift has been made from publicly funded tertiary education to part-public, part-private funding, where students have had to pay an increasing proportion of their fees. The impact of this financial burden on students has been mitigated to some extent by the introduction of interest-free student loans, and some might say that given the private benefit of tertiary education to individuals, the funding regime is justified. But what is clear is that those who can afford to attend university (which continues to be a minority of the general population) face a bigger debt burden now than in the past.

The number of people who are indebted is significant: as of 2014, there were over 720,000 people with student loan debt.[45] And the sense of stress and emotional weight associated with debt is considerable: in Andrew Dean's book *Ruth, Roger and Me: Debts and Legacies*, he quotes one ex-student as saying that his loan was 'just one of those things that is so monstrous I don't even think about it'.[46] Such stress has been exacerbated by the National-led government's aggressive pursuit of individuals who have not paid off their student loans.

This debt burden on university graduates is having an impact on desensitisation and demoralisation. One link between the debt burden and desensitisation is that, with a significant debt burden, it is likely that more students feel pressured to enter jobs that will pay well, rather than 'public interest' jobs – and this choice of career results in less political engagement.

The field of law is a good example, though it is an area where graduates have the relative privilege of a legal education and are often beneficiaries of other forms of privilege. I helped to set up Law For Change with Louis Chambers and Matt Smith in 2012. It was an organisation to encourage students to pursue public interest law jobs: in human rights law or community law centres or with NGOs, for example. Law students responded positively to the initiative when we visited campuses in Auckland, Wellington and Otago, but there was a strong response to our cries about the benefits of public interest law: we were told, rightly, by countless students that with high student loans, or families to provide for or support, public interest law was simply less attractive than more highly paid corporate law jobs.

More evidence is required to substantiate this link, especially given that I am claiming that it also exists in fields other than law. But there are some studies from overseas that suggest that, at least in law, debt has hindered the pursuit of public interest jobs. The social theorist Henry A. Giroux, writing from the US (where debt burdens are more significant), quotes a study showing that two-thirds of law graduates view debt as the main reason they do not pursue public interest law careers, and noting that 'half of the students who begin law school with stated public interest law commitments go into private practice law upon graduation in large part because of their debt burden'.[47]

Taking the argument one step further and applying it to New Zealand, it is plausible that individuals pursuing higher-paying careers over public interest careers are less sensitised to political developments and priorities, including the concerns of those most marginalised. Individuals in these careers – say, in accountancy firms, or large law firms, or consulting firms – can still be politically active. But they are likely to have less time to engage with politics because of the long hours that they work. They will have fewer opportunities to engage broadly with the community than individuals working in public-interest jobs. Again, there is a need for further investigation of this hypothesis, but there is certainly anecdotal evidence available (from individuals I know in corporate law firms, consulting jobs and accountancy practices) that career pressures towards high-paying jobs – motivated by the debt burden, as well as other factors such as rising house prices – contribute to the broader pattern of desensitisation.

Is it the government's role to intervene so that career choices do not decrease political engagement? One of the roots of this problem is student debt. The most direct way of reducing the impact of the debt burden is therefore to make tertiary education free. But other steps are possible. Governments can consider funding public interest projects that might induce individuals away from more corporate employment. In the field of law, for instance, there have been various proposals for a public interest law clearinghouse, which would support lawyers working on public interest projects. That might require (at least initial) government support, which could be justified on its own terms, but also as an indirect contribution to arresting the trend towards desensitisation.

Government funding for community law centres, mentioned in Chapter 7, serves a similar purpose. A more radical proposal would be for the government to fund a 'civic year' for individuals after the completion of secondary school. Quite apart from being a useful way to provide additional practical skills, such a programme might help to engage young people with local communities and society-wide priorities: for example, in elderly care, work with iwi (especially for iwi members less engaged with their Māori heritage) or disability work. US President Bill Clinton set up an analogous programme, AmeriCorps, in 1993, and Germany (among other countries) has long had a Zivildienst (civil service) scheme as an alternative to military service, though Zivildienst has been suspended since the abolition of conscription in 2011. It has been suggested that Germany's Zivildienst scheme contributes to high general levels of social responsibility and volunteering in Germany, where 36 per cent of people over the age of 14 are engaged in some kind of pro bono work.[48] The idea should be fully reviewed by a think tank or future government. What is important to recognise, generally, is that – while this last section relates to a relatively privileged sector of the population – careers, and the work that people do (if they are lucky enough to be employed), are relevant to levels of political desensitisation and demoralisation. Also, governments can take steps to support career choices in the public interest, which might boost people power in the long term.

conclusion

People power in New Zealand has been in decline for some time and for many reasons. But it is helpful to see this decline as a product of desensitisation and demoralisation. And there are actions that can be taken to address the loss of people power, in areas as diverse as education policy, the NGO sector, the structure of Parliament and the public service, the news media and the world of work. This chapter has focused on actions that are useful for the general population, but people power will only be fully harnessed if some of the actions proposed in other chapters of this book are implemented, such as economic transformation in the interests of the most marginalised and a shift in Aotearoa New Zealand's approach to 'race relations'.

Ultimately, if the ideas in this book are to be advanced – and if other ideas are to be considered and acted on – there is a need for a shift in the structures of political power. The public cannot be dismissed as not worth listening to. A change in culture is required. But rules, policies and laws also matter. Allowing NGOs to speak up when they are contracted to government, giving children the opportunity to learn about politics from an early age, or reorganising public broadcasting (to take just three examples from this chapter) can have a far-reaching effect on how people relate to politics and society.

We need a movement of people, rallying around the values of care, community and care – with solutions and proposals at their fingertips. We need that movement because, as I have assumed elsewhere, politicians do not create change on their own. They respond to latent moods that develop in the broader population, groundswells of interest that create room or impulse for political change. Nicky Hager expressed this idea to me better than I could ever have expressed it. 'Politicians follow ... in nearly all cases. What do they follow? If the rest of the machine's not working, they don't follow anything.' This chapter has explained why the machine isn't working, and what can be done to repair it.

The final chapter of this book sketches a vision of politics, beyond 'the machine', which might meet the needs of modern New Zealand and the changing conditions of our time.

12   taking the new zealand project forward

So, stepping back from the minutiae of policy arguments – from the details of reform of the Resource Management Act, or specific explanations about how civics education might be introduced or how school zoning might be changed – how could *The New Zealand Project* feed into global debates? How do the proposals of the preceding pages respond to the weaknesses of Third Way politics, represented by Tony Blair in the UK and Bill Clinton in the US in particular? If we are in-between political paradigms – in an 'interregnum', as one recent New Zealand book put it – is there material in our discussions that could give rise to a new paradigm?[1] What about claims globally that the welfare state and social democracy are dead? Does this book show a way to rejuvenate the welfare state and social democracy, or does it offer something beyond these institutions?

Within a less global and more national frame, is this book – guided by 'progressive values' – only really useful for progressive political parties such as the Labour Party and the Green Party? Or are there lessons for so-called left and right? And what are the general frames that can be drawn from this book and used by activists, politicians and concerned New Zealanders to take the New Zealand project forward? Finally, what can we all do to continue these conversations?

This final chapter is split broadly into a discussion of how the New Zealand project could shape global debates, and then a discussion of how it can be taken forward nationally. I touch briefly on conversations I had with people during the research phase for this book – in New Zealand, Norway and the UK – about the meaning of social democracy. I hope that what follows, while perhaps abstract and sweeping, makes more sense because it draws together what has been said in previous sections of this book.

We live in simultaneously troubling and exciting times. Change is in the air. There is increasing discontent with our current economic and political system, and aspects of our way of life. But New Zealand is also a place where change is possible: where problems are rarely so gigantic that they are unmanageable, where people generally are not completely defeatist or resigned, and where it is possible to gather together the people needed to create change. To make change happen, we need to get our thinking straight about what is wrong and why change is necessary, we need to plumb our imaginations to find ways to address what is wrong, and we need then to reach outwards (to other individuals and groups) and upwards (towards our highest ideals) to achieve the change that is needed. We need to commit to taking action, even where it is hard and where it is met with opposition. This is what the book has been about. This is the New Zealand project.

'the third way' — and the fourth way ahead

This book has called for a values-based politics, a strong role for a decolonised state (in economic and social policy in particular), and genuine and informed people power. I hope I have made the case for why these are all important achievements in their own right. But a further reason is that these themes address specific weaknesses or gaps in Third Way politics: in pursuing a new politics and bolder political leadership, New Zealand might be able to contribute to thinking around the world about the best political system for our time. Before we elaborate on this point in more detail, we need to say a bit more about 'the Third Way'.

The Third Way congealed into a coherent political position during Bill Clinton's presidency in the US (1993–2001) and Tony Blair's leadership of the UK Labour Party (1994–2007). Inspired by the work of sociologist Anthony Giddens, it had forerunners before the early 1990s and has had other political adherents after Clinton and Blair (notably Matteo Renzi in Italy). But it was in the two-decade period between the end of the Cold War around 1990 and the Global Financial Crisis in 2008 that it gathered support and locked in particular approaches to politics.

The Third Way claimed to be a middle-ground position between capitalism and socialism. But in practice it was nested within the neoliberalism, described in Chapter 4, which had come to reign as the dominant system of ideas since at least the 1980s. Thus, Nancy Fraser has recently described Third Way politics as 'progressive neoliberalism'.[2]

Third Way politicians such as Blair and Clinton argued that centrist or centre-left parties should be more comfortable about the role of markets. Blair said in Labour's 1997 election manifesto that 'what counts is what works', not whether the state or the market delivered policy outcomes.[3] This resulted in greater use of public-private partnerships in the UK, including the use of private providers in the National Health Service (NHS). It was a logical accompaniment to this position that Blair, Clinton and other Third Way politicians were broadly well-disposed towards to business and the private sector. There was also an indifference, in Third Way times, to the growth of private wealth: Lord Mandelson, an advisor to Blair, famously said in 1998 that he was 'intensely relaxed about people getting filthy rich'.[4] Clinton and Blair were also less supportive of unions than previous left-of-centre politicians, with Clinton signing the North American Free Trade Agreement despite major union opposition and Blair repeatedly referring to the goal of a 'flexible' labour market, which was sometimes code for weakened unions. Both proffered punitive approaches to welfare and crime policy, too. Clinton signed the Personal Responsibility and Work Opportunity Act in 1996, restricting the availability of welfare. Tony Blair, building on the 'tough-on-crime' policies of Conservative Prime Minister John Major, introduced policies that increased the UK's prison population by 85 per cent from 1993 to 2006.[5] In foreign policy, Blair and Clinton were relatively aggressive and interventionist: Blair, of course, led the move – contrary to vast swathes of public opinion – for the UK to join the US in the war in Iraq in 2003.

The Third Way has had a complex relationship to New Zealand. Helen Clark's Labour-led government distinguished itself from Tony Blair's administration, by refusing to support the Iraq war in 2003, being relatively supportive of unions (through, among other things, the Employment Relations Act 2000) and pursuing its own social and cultural agenda. But the prison population rose sharply between 1999 and 2008, and some of the Clark government's policies echoed Third Way priorities: the Working for Families package resembled in broad terms the thrust of Bill Clinton's Earned Income Tax Credit.

The Clark government aside, the Third Way has had a lingering effect on political debate in New Zealand and on the current National government. In particular, its influence has been seen in John Key's centrist, compassionate brand of conservatism, to some extent taken up by his successor, Bill English; in the continued influence of private providers of social services; and in the ongoing dominance of the language of 'flexibility' in discussions of the labour market.[6] Overall, while New Zealand politics has been influenced by a number of forces (and not just US and UK leadership), the Third Way has cast a long shadow over the rhetoric, policies and directions of New Zealand politics – even if the Third Way in New Zealand has taken on its own particular shape.

To some, the Third Way continues to represent an attractive compromise position – and it should be said that it has resulted in progress in certain areas of policy. Should we, therefore, stick to the Third Way? My view is that the Third Way, pursued against a neoliberal backdrop, has contributed to broader failings in politics in the past twenty years. I elaborate on this below, and explain how a values-based politics, a robust role for a decolonised state (serving a decolonised society) and genuine and informed people power can directly address the failings of the Third Way. Out of these criticisms, we can start to see, if only in outline, what a different political paradigm might look like.

the limitations of 'what works' politics – and the need for coherent values

Clinton and Blair both claimed they were driven by values. Blair, for example, said: 'My kind of socialism is a set of values based around social justice ...'[7] However, the Third Way drifted away from being values-based in practice. Its 'what works' mentality implied that governments could avoid making value judgments and could simply look at 'the evidence' behind different policies. But this assumption ignores the fact that value judgments must be made in picking policy priority areas (in which the evidence is considered) and in extrapolating from evidence. It evades the fundamental question of what it means for something to *work* – which requires values to be supplied.

Third Way politicians also failed to recognise that the policies they pursued brought their supposed values into conflict. The core strategy document *Europe: The Third Way/Die Neue Mitte*, authored by Tony Blair and German chancellor Gerhard Schroeder, talks of 'solidarity and responsibility to others' as key values.[8] But Third Way policies, such as the welfare-to-work programmes discussed in the same document, in practice undermined solidarity and weakened social bonds, apparently in the pursuit of responsibility. This contradiction suggests that either the commitment to values by Third Way politicians was not wholehearted – or not fully thought through.

What is needed is an end to the myth that governments can do 'what works' without thinking about values. Values are needed to define what it means for something to 'work'. The end results of government programmes need to be tested against values. And governments must ensure, as far as possible, that their values are not inherently contradictory. Evidence is fundamental to policy-making, and there continues to be a need for academic research and other forms of evidence to be integrated into policy in New Zealand.[9] In one sense, being careful with evidence in politics is an outgrowth of the value of care. But there should be an acknowledgment that value judgments need to be made, even when evidence is used in policy-making; and a values-based and evidence-based politics can be pursued simultaneously.

I have suggested that the values of care, community and creativity – and, perhaps, love (as an extension of care, in particular) – offer particular promise for the future of progressive politics. I have tried in this book to propose ways they might be applied in harmony. But, thinking globally, other values might work better in different communities. What is important is that we are transparent about the place of values in politics, and committed to striving to ensure that our cornerstone values are applied in practice and do not contradict each other.

In his beautiful book *Ill Fares the Land*, Tony Judt writes, 'What we lack is a moral narrative: an internally coherent account that ascribes purpose to our actions in a way that transcends them.'[10] We 'need a language in which to express our moral instincts', along with 'a sense of moral direction'.[11] Values may provide the narrative, language and sense of moral direction that we are struggling to find. Less tainted than morality, and more visceral than ethics, values can give 'purpose to our actions'. New Zealand is a small country, and some things that are possible in New Zealand might not be possible elsewhere.[12] But a values-based politics is a form of politics that other countries can also pursue; this form of politics might be especially necessary in other countries at a time when xenophobia is on the rise, and political decisions appear to be based on fear or scaremongering, rather than principle.[13] Values can provide benchmarks for our politics and a common end for us all to unite around.

sloppy thinking about institutions – and bringing back the state

A related problem of Third Way politics is its approach to the institutions of the market and the state. Sometimes Third Way politicians have claimed they are indifferent to whether the state or the market are the key actors in delivering policies: this has been expressed in the 'what works' ethos. But at other times, Third Wayers have aimed actively to rehabilitate the market's role in social services and economic strategy. The Blair/Schroeder document says, for example, 'the weaknesses of markets have been overstated and their strengths underestimated'.[14] Simultaneously, Third Way politicians have caricatured the state as a top-down, rigid, inflexible institution. Blair and Schroeder said in 1998, 'Rigidity and over-regulation hamper our success.'[15]

The Third Way, nested as it has been within neoliberalism, has been overly sanguine about the flaws of the market and excessively negative about the state. Most of all, it has ignored that opting for the state or the market to be in charge of particular policy functions is a value judgment that reflects a commitment to certain ideals. Allowing the state to deliver, say, health care services necessarily expresses a commitment to solidarity and universal provision. Deciding on market provision of health care services, meanwhile, expresses faith in principles of competition and individualism. Opting for one institution or another is not value-neutral.

Clarifying the role of the state – articulating what the state is uniquely capable of doing, and what it should do – is imperative in New Zealand and elsewhere, in light of these problems of the Third Way. It is also necessary to be realistic about the shortcomings of the market, as I discussed in Chapter 4. A strong state addresses the shortcomings of the market and puts an end to the view that markets and the state are interchangeable. It is, in my view, a key part of the new paradigm that has to emerge all around the world in the wake of the Third Way's demise. There are risks associated with a strong state, including increased xenophobic nationalism, abuse of power, and the fact that the state in New Zealand remains in the eyes of many an illegitimate colonial institution. But this is why a strong state must be accompanied by a wholehearted values-based politics, people power and an ongoing process of decolonisation: values, social movements, and Māori perspectives can help to discipline the state, as can judicially enforced constitutional protections of the kind I described in Chapter 5.

neglect of the people

It is unlikely, again, that Tony Blair or Bill Clinton would admit to being anti-democratic or ignorant of the interests of their people. Both were charismatic politicians who carefully cultivated their public images. Nevertheless the brand of politics that they practised was in several key respects undemocratic.

Blair and Clinton tried to get a lot of things done through executive power, rather than legislative support; such dependence on advisors and a small number of executive politicians undermined accountability. (Jeremy Corbyn's push, in

2015–16, to restore power to members of the Labour Party for developing policy received strong support partly because Blair had deprived party members of power and had developed a top-down decision-making style. That decision-making style was criticised, and commented on most prominently in the 2016 Chilcot report on the Iraq war.) Blair and Clinton also shifted public service provision to private providers, which are subject to fewer legal and political forms of democratic accountability. Finally, Blair's conduct in the lead-up to the Iraq war was emblematic of his neglect of social movements. More than one million people marched against the war, possibly the biggest ever protest in the UK's history. He went ahead with the war nonetheless, leaving many with a sense of disenfranchisement and alienation.

A restoration of genuine people power can help fill this gap in Third Way politics. As discussed in the previous chapter, there must be a redoubled effort to address deep-seated demoralisation and desensitisation, which exist not only in New Zealand but also in other countries where the Third Way has prevailed. But people power must go beyond this, too. Marginalised groups, including indigenous peoples, must be brought back into the democratic fold. Members of those groups must be given decision-making power and leadership roles. Ideas emerging out of the struggles of those groups should be given significant weight.

In this book, within a New Zealand context, emphasis has been placed in Chapter 5 and other sections on listening to, and giving effect to, Māori world views and ideas. Young people, referred to particularly in Chapter 10's discussion of climate change, also need to be empowered to take part in public debates. As Tony Judt writes, 'Dissent and dissidence are overwhelmingly the work of the young. … Rather than resign themselves, young people are more likely to look at a problem and demand that it be solved.'[16] And as mentioned in Chapter 11, artists and academics have to be given time, space, and power to develop their ideas. The value of democracy must be taken into many spheres, including the sphere of economic policy, as we discussed in Chapter 4. Through this widespread empowerment of people, the aim should be a society of democratic experimentation where diverse, dissenting ideas are tried out and tested. These ideas might be expressed in different ways, sometimes with calm and sometimes with anger, and through different media (art, music, writing, activism and other forms). But all of these ideas should encouraged as part of a fully fledged, flourishing, people-powered democratic conversation.

The ultimate end is that the strong state discussed in the last section is driven by, and subservient to, people power.

A values-based politics, a strong decolonised state and genuine people power – these might be some of the planks, but not necessarily the only planks, of a new political paradigm. The quarter-century experiment with the Third Way should now be ended. The global financial crisis, endemic public alienation from politics and other emerging social problems (such as inequality and loneliness) confirm that the Third Way has failed. I have attempted to suggest in this book how New Zealand might pioneer a different approach: a Fourth Way.

beyond social democracy

What does all this mean for the welfare state or social democracy? Does a Fourth Way involve leaving 'social democracy' behind?

'Social democracy' refers to the model of government first developed in Germany in the late nineteenth century and consolidated particularly in Western Europe in the early to mid-twentieth century. Despite being a term frequently used in public debates, its contours are a little fuzzy.

I asked Jan Egeland, whom we encountered in Chapter 3, what social democracy is today. 'Perhaps too many things,' he replied. That insight was confirmed in the many interviews I conducted for this book, and by the visit I made to Norway to investigate the Nordic model of social democracy, which many say represents its most successful version. Different people had different definitions of social democracy. Mads Andenas, a well-known Norwegian lawyer who was the United Nations Special Rapporteur on Arbitrary Detention, said that social democracy involves a particular concern for 'the weakest twenty per cent' of society. For Thomas Mathiesen, a Norwegian criminologist, social democracy is about 'care for others'. Holly Walker, the former Green MP whom we have already encountered in this book, said social democracy involves everyone getting 'what they need to thrive'. Avner Offer, an economic historian and emeritus fellow of All Souls College in Oxford, told me that social democracy was about achieving 'economic security over the life cycle'.

Out of these interviews and the existing scholarship on social democracy, we can describe some of its key pillars as a model of government. First, social democracy involves the pooling of resources through taxation in order to provide public services. These public services have been conceived of in different ways, as entitlements or on other occasions as a form of social insurance.[17] Some public services have tended to be provided universally, such as health care and education. Others, such as legal services or housing, have tended to be provided only to those most in need. Despite various attempts to rationalise which services warrant universal provision, there does not appear to be a persuasive distinction explaining how services should fall into one of these two camps. Second, and relatedly, social democracy has always involved particular concern for those most in need. It led to the creation of the welfare state: the provision of benefits to those unable to find employment. It has also entailed the regulation of markets to blunt the harshest edges of capitalism. The ethos underpinning this concern for the neediest is well expressed by Bill Sutch in his description of the New Zealand Social Security Act: the Act would, as with the welfare state as a whole, 'provide a minimum below which living standards will not fall'.[18] The 'Nordic model' of social democracy – pursued in Scandinavia (Sweden, Norway, Finland, Iceland and Denmark) – has driven towards these goals with great vigour, through the use of highly progressive tax systems and strong unions.

In sweeping, crude and somewhat reductive terms, social democracy has had at least four weaknesses in all the places it has been implemented over time.

First, beyond its concern for those most in need, social democracy has failed to produce secure bonds of community. The leader of the Norwegian Labour Party, Jonas Gahr Støre, told me that 'loneliness is one of the modern diseases', even in Norway (though Støre at the same time respected the choices of people to live alone) – and there is arguably a link between the rise of loneliness and the failure of social democracy. While I was only in Norway for a week during winter, I could almost feel the absence of tight-knit connections between people there, despite the country probably embodying the most successful version of social democracy. People welcomed me into their homes and were extremely warm in private, but public squares were deserted (not only because it was winter), strangers seemed somewhat distant (as if they were avoiding each other), and there appeared to be a lack of cohesion. In short, social democracy has failed to realise fully its promise to be 'social'. The focus on minimum social standards has not been enough. In Judt's words: '[W]e have to decide what the state must do in order for men and women to pursue decent lives. Merely providing a welfare floor below which people need not sink does not suffice.'[19]

Second, and this helps to explain social democracy's first weakness, social democracy has permitted levels of inequality that appear increasingly intolerable to people. An ardent Norwegian unionist, Vegard Holm, a long-time member of the Transport Workers' Union, who welcomed me into his home by serving me traditional Norwegian porridge, risgrøt, with lashings of butter, told me there was widespread concern with inequality, even in Norway. 'Norwegian people believe that ... [there should be a] short gap from bottom to top,' and they see that gap getting bigger, Vegard said. Avner Offer explained why he thought this was the case: neoliberalism and social democracy, he said, are 'adversaries in a marriage of convenience'. In other words, social democracy should be opposed to neoliberalism – its endorsement of wealth, its push towards deregulation and its call to reduce redistribution – but social democracy has not proven muscular enough to withstand neoliberalism's pressures. A marriage of convenience has been borne, and that has allowed the gradual escalation of inequality, or at the very least – as in New Zealand – the persistence of inequality over time.

Third, social democracy has never had a stable or clear position on immigration. Social democracy may claim to be committed to 'the social', or 'power of the people' (democracy), but how is the society to be defined – and who are 'the people' served by social democracy? These questions have rarely been given a clear answer. The result has been fluctuating positions on immigration, and lingering xenophobia in many social democratic countries, including, perhaps especially, in Scandinavia. It is possible that the concern about immigration, especially in Europe and the US (where it is also combined with Islamophobia, racism and other forms of prejudice) at the time of this book's completion is partly a product of the theoretically shaky foundations of social democracy.

Fourth, social democracy has been inadequate in giving power to all people. In most social democratic countries, political participation is declining, as discussed in Chapter 11. This is not entirely the fault of social democracy, but the underlying political system is part of the reason for this decline. Public services have too often appeared distant from people, and governed in a top-down manner. Minority groups – African Americans in the United States, black people in the UK, Roma in Scandinavia, Māori in Aotearoa New Zealand – have been marginalised over time, including because of the ongoing effects of colonial attitudes. Social democracy has provided only incremental gains at best for these groups. Genuine democracy, including in the economic sphere, remains unrealised.

Some of these problems can be remedied through tweaks to social democratic structures. Perhaps public services can be made less top-down, or inequality can be ameliorated through greater redistribution. But many of these problems are general, deep-seated and incapable of quick resolution.

What all this suggests is that our task is not to revitalise social democracy – it is to go beyond social democracy, to trace the outlines of a new political system that addresses its weaknesses. This book has offered some sketches of the elements of that new political system, with reference to New Zealand. That new system requires a strong but decolonised state, which is disciplined by values and democratised by people power. On top of these elements, to overcome the shortcomings of social democracy, the post-social democracy model will have to take seriously the need to forge bonds of community and solidarity.

The new political model beyond social democracy might be called 'public democracy': a model where all people are appreciated, where public services are properly protected, and where – away from the state – public spaces and interaction are prized. Public democracy could draw here on emerging notions of 'the commons' and 'the under-commons'.[20] Street art, a prominent form of public art, might be one emblem of this new model: it involves a public activity, designed by and for diverse members of the public. Public democracy has to address inequality and other harms of neoliberalism that tug away at what that holds us together as a 'public', including by engaging with debates about 'postcapitalism'.[21] It should, I think, take an unashamedly welcoming approach to immigration, discussed briefly in Chapter 5.

Sue Goss's notion of an 'open tribe', in which community is treasured and at the same time we find 'ways to continue to feel open, curious, confident, hospitable, generous', may be a helpful concept.[22] The model must empower minorities and indigenous groups, encourage political participation and embed democratic practices throughout society – in education, the workplace, activism, and elsewhere. The model needs to be fleshed out in more detail; in particular, more work needs to go into defining 'the public'. But the ideal of 'public democracy' could be one label for the Fourth Way that comes after the Third Way, and there is no reason why New Zealand could not set the first example for what public democracy might look like.

for left and right?

Turning from the future of social democracy globally to Aotearoa New Zealand, is this a project for the left of New Zealand politics only, or for particular political constituencies?

This book has largely avoided interviews with politicians, since it's premised on there being problems with our politics – an overly narrow political debate and a neglect of persistent social challenges, among other things – that are best addressed by people outside of politics. It has also attempted to speak not just to one political party or a set of political parties (say, on the 'right' or 'left') but to people, both politicians and non-politicians, across Aotearoa New Zealand. The proposals in this book are designed to appeal people across the political spectrum, and to people who do not identify as political at all: this should be true of ideas like the reassertion of an independent foreign policy, developing alternatives to GDP, a review of school zoning, a push for alternatives to incarceration, a written constitution, a universal basic income pilot, reform of the Resource Management Act, a franker discussion of the effects of New Zealand masculinity, and civics education in schools.

The proposals in this book chime with policies from almost every political party in Parliament in 2017: for example, the National Party has adopted the generally pro-immigration stance discussed in Chapter 5, the Labour Party has stressed the need to address homelessness (Chapter 6), the Green Party has pushed for awareness of climate change refugees (Chapter 3), New Zealand First has supported investment in public broadcasting (Chapter 11), the Māori Party has called for compulsory te reo Māori in schools (Chapter 5), the Act Party has suggested a carbon tax (Chapter 9), and United Future has pressed for civics education (Chapter 11). Other proposals discussed here have not been mooted by any of them.

Ultimately this book has attempted to show that holding certain values – in particular, the values of care, community and creativity – should take us, logically, in the direction of some big new ideas for the future of our country. Some might disagree with the reasoning that moves from these starting point values to certain policy conclusions. This is not a problem: this book will not persuade everyone. But it has assumed that we do all cherish these values, and has aimed merely to tell one story about what might follow from those values. It should be a book for left and right, and people in between.

how new zealand can take the project forward

What frames, narratives and tools – alongside the measures argued for in Chapter 11 – could citizens, politicians and others use to advance the New Zealand project? This final section expands on two key themes that have run throughout the previous chapters, partly as a way of drawing together the disparate threads of this book.

a smart country

When writing about the future of the UK, writer David Marquand has said one of the key questions that must be answered is: 'Who are we?'[23] The same is true of New Zealand. When talking about the future of the country, we need to ask who we have been, who we are and who we want to be. There are no easy answers. There are lots of New Zealands, and some might even ask whether it is possible to talk about 'we' and 'us' given our differences. Nevertheless, amid our variety and our multiple identities, one thing I think it is possible to say – and that may be practically useful for the New Zealand project – is that we are a smart country.

It is a common claim that New Zealand is anti-intellectual. This might be an initial reason to think we are not a smart country: we do not appreciate intellectuals or ideas. But I think this notion is, at the very least, overstated, and possibly wrong altogether.

It is, first, unclear that New Zealand is any more anti-intellectual than other countries, since anti-intellectualism is also a charge levelled (especially by academics) at other countries, such as Australia or the UK. One might ask, in fact, whether the claim that we do not appreciate intellectuals or ideas is one we have inherited, somewhat uncritically, from the UK.

Second, the accusation that New Zealand is anti-intellectual – hostile to intellectuals, insufficiently appreciative of intellectuals' contributions – ignores the long tradition of respect for intellectual thought within te ao Māori. Numerous examples could be drawn upon from te ao Māori to substantiate this point: the whakataukī 'Ko te kai a te rangatira, he kōrero' ('Talk is the food of chiefs'), or the even more directly relevant 'Whāia te mātauranga hei oranga mō koutou' ('Seek after learning for the sake of your wellbeing') demonstrate the points. Writer Scott Hamilton expands on this idea: 'Nineteenth and early twentieth-century Māori society was … a place of intellectual ferment,' he writes, adding that '[i]n the early twentieth century university-educated Māori like Te Rangi Hīroa and Āpirana Ngata began to reinvent disciplines like anthropology, so that they served indigenous rather than colonial ends'.[24] The rich body of work on kaupapa Māori is further evidence of this indigenous intellectual tradition.[25]

The accusation also overlooks the number of world-leading academics that New Zealand has produced, a disproportionately large group for our size (though this requires further empirical work). Such academics include Jeremy Waldron (in legal and political philosophy), Linda Tuhiwai Smith (postcolonial studies), Robert Wade (economics and political economy), the late Susan Moller Okin (philosophy), James Belich (history) and Chris Kraus (gender studies); this is not to mention academics of past generations, including Ernest Rutherford (physics) and Bill Phillips (economics). Ernest Rutherford once said of growing up in New Zealand, 'We haven't the money, so we've got to think.'[26] New Zealand might have more money now than when Rutherford was living. But we still have to think – and we *have* done that thinking consistently over the years.

Third, it seems that often 'anti-intellectual' is a word grasped when people really want to criticise something else – perhaps the fact that insufficient resources have been allocated to academics in universities in recent years, or the fact that our policy framework has not been bold or imaginative. It may often be a slightly imprecise way of demanding more tentativeness or humility from academics engaging in public debate. (In a similar vein, my view is that 'tall poppy syndrome' does not really exist in New Zealand: success *is* celebrated, and 'tall poppies' are only cut down when individuals show off or arrogantly claim exclusive credit for their own success and do not acknowledge those to whom they owe that success.)

With the anti-intellectualism myth swept off the table, we are in a better position to realise that we are a smart country: a country that has a history of ideas driving politics, policy and society, and a country with the capacity to draw on ideas in the future. We should also be clear when saying that we are a 'smart country' that we are not talking just about a narrow form of academic intelligence. Intelligence comes in many forms – not only in the scholarly ability to cite theory or grasp concepts (analytical intelligence), but also in the ability to be sharp and thoughtful in how we deal with situations emotionally and socially (emotional and social intelligence), in the practical ability to be quick-thinking in identifying problems and finding solutions to those problems (practical intelligence), in the ability to understand cultural traditions and to apply them sensitively in context (cultural intelligence), and other forms. We are a country that contains all of these forms of intelligence, and a country that can embrace that smartness moving forward. Jonas Gahr Støre, the Norwegian politician, spoke to me about 'reinvigorating the smart state'. But New Zealand could celebrate both the smart state and the smart society, welcoming a vision of us as peoples that carry practical intelligence in our bones, and ideas within our soul.

One implication of seeing ourselves as a smart country is that we should be secure in debating bold proposals and big ideas. I have attempted to put forward some ideas of this kind. The most detailed practical proposals can be condensed into fifteen bullet points (drawing between one and three proposals from each chapter):

- New Zealand needs to rejuvenate its 'independent foreign policy', including through pushing for a global legal framework on climate change refugees, a different approach to aid, a strategy for engaging with Asia, and building capacity in peace and mediation.
- Strong consideration should be given to restoring a more progressive system of income taxation.
- The move towards a single written constitution for Aotearoa New Zealand should continue to be debated.
- Te reo Māori should be a learning area in the New Zealand curriculum. Inequalities between Māori and Pasifika, and non-Māori and non-Pasifika, must be reduced.
- Future governments must redouble efforts to treat and eliminate rheumatic fever.
- A review of school zoning, enrolment schemes, and school inequality should be undertaken.
- The number of homeless people in New Zealand needs to be authoritatively measured, a Housing First model should be adopted, and political and public indifference to homelessness must end.
- 'Decarceration' should guide criminal justice policy, with progress made towards alternatives to incarceration and a moratorium on building new prisons.

- There should be an end to beneficiary-bashing, people with disabilities should be engaged to a greater extent in policy-making, and a national conversation should be started on the place of the elderly in the community (including on the related subject of loneliness).
- Insecure work should be addressed through an insecure work index, insecure work benefit or the piloting of a universal basic income.
- A carbon tax should replace the emissions trading scheme (unless far-reaching reforms to the scheme are adopted).
- The Resource Management Act should be replaced with new legislation, in conjunction with the introduction of a national forestry strategy.
- The Equal Pay Act should be overhauled, with particular changes including a positive duty on employers to review pay equity and increased transparency for pay levels.
- Civics education should be introduced in New Zealand schools.

As I have noted at many points throughout the book, the aim of these fifteen proposals has been to stir up debate. No doubt other suggestions could be added to this list, and with further debate, it is possible that some of these proposals should be discarded. What is important is that we avoid any knee-jerk dismissal of such ideas. We should be secure enough that we can have patient, thoughtful, respectful conversations about the future of our country. If we can achieve that, we will widen the Overton window – the window of what seems politically possible in a country.[27] An overly narrow political debate was one of the problems that this book identified with contemporary culture in New Zealand, and one of the problems that I set out to address.

Though we are a smart country, we should not pretend that we have a monopoly on knowledge about solutions to our own problems. This book has looked elsewhere for guidance, to Australia (with its strategy on Asia), Norway (on climate change and prisons), Finland (on a universal basic income), and Canada (on a carbon tax). We should continue to attempt to build partnerships with other countries, as citizens, yes, but also in spheres of activism, policy-making and politics. We will build a broader degree of knowledge about political approaches and solutions if we go beyond our usual political 'partners' such as Australia and the UK. We should be careful, of course, in understanding policies in context. But that does not mean we should not at least consider what is being done, say, in Scandinavia on criminal justice; in parts of South America on indigenous rights; or in South Africa in student activism. Perhaps New Zealanders should cement stronger relationships with individuals in these countries as we continue to move out of the shadow of the UK and forge our own identity as a Pacific, immigrant-rich nation, differentiated from others by particular indigenous traditions. Cementing these relationships is important as the world retreats back behind national borders in the aftermath of the UK's Brexit vote in 2016 and the election of Donald Trump.

The final implication of being a smart country is that we should allow ourselves the space to dream – as an extension of the value of creativity discussed earlier in this book. Thinking big has had a bad name since Muldoon. But for New Zealand to address its problems, we need not only people power, a transformation of the economic framework and a values-based politics, but also a willingness to be bold in our individual and collective thinking, and a desire to push the boundaries of what is acceptable or normal or realistic. This is the path towards developing singular solutions to our singular problems. The point has not been put better than by Robin Kelley in his inspiring account of the history of the black radical imagination in the US. A movement of dreamers requires struggle, Kelley notes – and courage and toughness and persistence. But 'unless we have the space to imagine and a vision of what it means fully to realise our humanity, all the protests and demonstrations in the world won't bring about our liberation'.[28]

Ani Mikaere has written in the New Zealand context about the power of dreaming, with specific reference to the value of dreaming for decolonisation. Mikaere notes that the legacy of 'messages about the inferiority of tikanga Māori' is, for many Māori, 'a lack of imagination and an unwillingness to dream'.[29] Mikaere has noted that dreaming is a key part of decolonisation: bold, broad thinking allows the ongoing impact of colonisation to be realised and for new ways of thinking to be constructed. '[C]linging to narrowly constructed notions of what is realistic and showing a reluctance to dream' are a product of fear, Mikaere argues. That fear has to be left behind to build a smart, decolonised vision for Aotearoa.[30]

recovering the best from our past

This book has not been a history of politics in New Zealand. In order to illuminate the present and the future of New Zealand politics, reference has been made to historical episodes, and for certain chapters – for example, in

Chapter 5 – there have been more extended diversions into history. Perhaps some readers will be disappointed that there has not been more historical analysis.

In closing, and in partial response to that concern, it is worth noting that we must not ignore our history. In our internet age, it is easy to neglect historical events, since the internet gives more prominence to recent news and commentary of the moment. But we must be willing to engage with, and recover the best from, our past as we look to take the New Zealand project forward.

When we speak of New Zealand history, it is important to recognise that this country's history did not begin in 1645 (when Abel Tasman sighted New Zealand), 1769 (when James Cook came ashore) or 1840 (when the Treaty of Waitangi was signed). New Zealand history can be traced at least as far back as Māori arrival, if not earlier – and 'recovering the best of our past' must mean, first and foremost, Māori political actors deciding how to apply Māori values and ways of thinking to emerging challenges. Ani Mikaere, again, is right in pointing out that non-Māori, such as me, should be cautious in using Māori concepts. 'Is it not inevitable,' Mikaere asks, 'that [outsiders'] interpretations of the subject culture will be distorted through the lens of their own cultural understandings and beliefs?' I have aimed to suggest, with humility and tentativeness (and as far as possible drawing on Māori voices such as those of Mikaere, Moana Jackson, Kim Workman, and others), that Māori values have much to offer New Zealand politics and society. Te ao Māori and tikanga Māori provide us with a model of the very idea of a values-based politics, which has been at the heart of this book. Specific Māori values like whanaungatanga, manaakitanga and auahatanga can enrich our understandings of the progressive values underpinning this book: community, care and creativity. Aroha underpins and deepens the notion of a politics of love, discussed in Chapter 8. And Māori notions of kaitiakitanga can change how we understand human beings' interaction with their environment, as outlined in Chapter 10. New Zealand history should not be romanticised, and as was discussed in Chapter 5, lessons of history should not be forgotten. Tikanga Māori – the first law of Aotearoa – remains an important foundation and model for how politics should be done in the present.[31]

This book has also thrown light on ideas, policy proposals and examples buried in New Zealand history that deserve to be excavated. In foreign policy, Te Whiti's example at Parihaka in 1881 provides inspiration for the notion that New Zealand might build capacity in peace-building and mediation. More recently, in the twentieth century, we find a reservoir of policy reports and public interventions that were not given particular attention in their own time but that retain relevance today. To be sure, these contributions need to be treated with care where they emerge out of a slightly different historical context. Nevertheless, there is much in these documents that can be applied to present.

Resources mentioned have included Gareth Morgan and Susan Guthrie's work on alternative forms of taxation beyond income tax (Chapter 4), the Moana Jackson- and Margaret Mutu-chaired research project on Matike Mai Aotearoa (Chapter 5), the 2014 JustSpeak report on the New Zealand prison system (Chapter 7), the 2010 Alternative Welfare Working Group report and the 1967 Woodhouse Report (Chapter 8), and the 2016 work of Geoff Simmonds and Paul Young on fraudulent carbon credits (Chapter 9). Of course, it is important not to privilege wonkish policy analysis exclusively over other valuable forms of knowledge: for that reason, this book has attempted also to draw upon stories (such as rugby player Buxton Popoali'i's experiences with rheumatic fever, recounted in Chapter 6), music (like Tono's track on housing, also discussed in Chapter 6), and oral histories as recorded through interviews. Expertise comes from many sources, including through experience (as discussed in Chapter 10), and is not limited to intellectual or analytical expertise. The general point is that we can sometimes forget, when addressing major policy problems, that we are not the first generation to notice or confront these problems – and we can often learn from work done in the past, and solutions that were suggested but never taken up.

There's no need for nostalgia. This book doesn't advocate for a return to an earlier era. As well, it is true that we do face some trends and phenomena that appear to be genuinely novel: demographic change, insecure work, worsening climate change, and the like. Those new challenges or opportunities require a new politics. But at the same time, we need to remember our history. We need to remember what happened; what was suggested; what was done and not done. We need to recognise the visible and sometimes more imperceptible ways in which New Zealand history has left its imprint on society today. Revisiting the past, by giving us a stock of values and ideas and experiences, gives us more power as we face a difficult and intimidating present.

conclusion

The New Zealand project, at its core, is not only about politics or policy. It is about the future of the country.[32] We have lost sight, I've argued, of the big-picture direction for our country as a whole. We have forgotten or neglected some of the key principles that can guide that journey. William Pember Reeves, the great social reformer of the nineteenth century, said in 1898, in *The Long White Cloud: Ao Tea Roa*, that reforms in New Zealand 'were the outcome of a belief that a young democratic country, still almost free from extremes of wealth and poverty, from class hatreds and fears and the barriers these create, supplies an unequalled field for safe and rational experiment in the hope of preventing and shutting out some of the worst social evils and miseries which afflict great nations alike in the old world and new'.[33] New Zealand is not such a young country any more. And it is no longer clear that the land beneath our long white cloud is free (if it ever was) from those 'extremes of wealth and poverty', of 'class hatreds and fears and the barriers these create', of 'the worst social evils and miseries' that Pember Reeves referred to.

In order to address the major social, economic, cultural and political challenges that face us, I've argued that we need to build a values-based approach to power and society. We cannot do this without constructing an alternative economic model, decolonising the state and society and restoring genuine people power. Along the way, in securing a values-based politics and an alternative economic model and genuine people power, we may also need a new vision of the Kiwi dream – one that is not about individual home-ownership, but that involves realising a life that places care, community and creativity at the centre.

This project needs all of us to play a part: to roll up our sleeves and to work out how we might contribute.

If the New Zealand project is a mural that stretches into the distance, rolling on because of the contributions of people continuing the work of others, what will you paint on the wall?

If the New Zealand project is a waka on which we all have a place, the 'spirit vessel' or va'a which Courtney Sina Meredith speaks of in *The Interregnum*,[34] what will your role be in this waka?

If the New Zealand project is a crackling campfire, which can flame outwards to create the heat and energy and light that will sustain us, what's your offering that you'll throw into the fire?

This book was completed on Waitangi Day 2017. Almost two-and-a-half years earlier I lay in a hospital bed readying myself for open heart surgery. It was successful.

Today, perhaps projecting a little based on my own experience, I think a different kind of heart needs repairing: the heart of our country. This repair is about all of us. We've stumbled and fallen. Our heart's connective tissue has been weakened. And we need the pulse of our social conscience to start beating harder again.

So … what are we waiting for?

endnotes

chapter 1

1 I expect that we will come to see evidence that supports these claims, including through the New Zealand Attitudes and Values Survey, based at the University of Auckland and launched in 2009.

2 I am thinking especially of the work of Frankfurt School philosophers, such as Theodor Adorno and Max Horkheimer, who made versions of this argument.

3 See, for example, George Lakoff, *Don't Think of an Elephant! Know Your Values and Frame the Debate – The Essential Guide for Progressives*, Chelsea Green Publishing, 2004.

4 This point is discussed in: Clare Land, *Decolonizing Solidarity: Dilemmas and Directions for Supporters of Indigenous Struggles*, Zed Books, 2015.

5 For an account of some of my background thinking on this subject, see: Max Harris, 'What Are Progressive Values?', *The Aotearoa Project*, 5 January 2014, https://theaotearoaproject.wordpress.com/2014/01/05/what-are-progressive-values (accessed 7 December 2016). For further background about the health scare discussed at the start of the chapter, see: Max Harris, 'A Second Chance: Of Hearts and Hospitals', *The Pantograph Punch*, 25 March 2015, www.pantograph-punch.com/post/of-hearts-and-hospitals (accessed 19 March 2017); and Max Harris, 'This Could Be It', *The Pantograph Punch*, 24 June 2015, www.pantograph-punch.com/post/this-could-be-it (accessed 19 March 2017).

6 My thanks to Tai Ahu for a very helpful exchange on this point.

7 For some more introductory discussion of this strand of thinking, see: Stanford Encyclopedia of Philosophy, 'Feminist Ethics', revised 2009, https://plato.stanford.edu/entries/feminism-ethics/#CarEthTheDifVoi (accessed 7 December 2016).

8 My thanks to Tai Ahu for discussions about this.

9 I am inspired here by Ronald Dworkin's approach to legal and political principles: his approach, to summarise very crudely, is to find principles that are both consonant with past practice and attractive on their own terms.

chapter 2

1 Francis Fukuyama, 'The End of History?', *The National Interest* (Summer 1989).

2 Paul Mason, *PostCapitalism: A Guide to our Future*, Allen Lane, 2015, and Wolfgang Streeck, *How Will Capitalism End?: Essays on a Failing System*, Verso, 2016.

3 David Goodhart, 'A Postliberal Future?', *Demos Quarterly*, (January 2014), http://quarterly.demos.co.uk/article/issue-1/a-postliberal-future (accessed 18 January 2017).

4 Brian Eno, 'What's Happening Here, on Earth', *openDemocracy*, 9 November 2016, www.opendemocracy.net/brian-eno/whats-happening-here-on-earth (accessed 18 January 2017).

5 Jameson actually wrote that '[s]omeone once said' this: Frederic Jameson, 'Future City', *New Left Review*, 23 (2003), https://newleftreview.org/II/21/fredric-jameson-future-city (accessed 18 January 2017).

6 David Hall, 'Liberals Got Walloped in 2016. Can "Post-Liberalism" Rise from the Ashes?', *The Spinoff*, 16 January 2017, http://thespinoff.co.nz/society/16-01-2017/liberals-got-walloped-in-2016-can-post-liberalism-rise-from-the-ashes (accessed 18 January 2017).

7 As discussed in: Alina Siegfried, 'From Occupy to Online Democracy: The Loomio Story', *openDemocracy*, 3 April 2014, www.opendemocracy.net/participation-now/alina-siegfried/from-occupy-to-online-democracy-loomio-story (accessed 18 January 2017). It is worth noting that there might have been less questioning of democracy in New Zealand because of our relatively recent adoption of a mixed-member proportional (MMP) voting system from 1996 onwards. That reform showed a willingness to address defects in the structure of our representative democracy.

8   Committee of Economic Development for Australia, *Australia's Future Workforce?*, CEDA, 2015, p.8, http://adminpanel.ceda.com.au/FOLDERS/Service/Files/Documents/26792-Futureworkforce_June2015.pdf (accessed 19 January 2017).

9   Tae Yoo, 'Is the World-Changing Impact of Mobile Phones a Myth?', World Economic Forum, 24 January 2015, www.weforum.org/agenda/2015/01/is-the-world-changing-impact-of-mobile-phones-a-myth (accessed 19 January 2017).

10   I helped to write a paper on the universal basic income for that Commission. I discuss this more in Chapter 8.

11   Statistics New Zealand/Tatauranga Aotearoa, 'Household Use of Information and Communication Technology: 2012', 22 April 2013, www.stats.govt.nz/browse_for_stats/industry_sectors/information_technology_and_communications/HouseholdUseofICT_HOTP2012/Commentary.aspx (accessed 14 March 2017).

12   Morgan Tait, 'How Many Kiwis Use Facebook?', *The New Zealand Herald*, 22 April 2015, www.nzherald.co.nz/business/news/article.cfm?c_id=3&objectid=11436706 (accessed 14 March 2017).

13   See Robert J. Gordon, 'Off Its Pinnacle', International Monetary Fund – Finance & Development, 53, 2 (June 2016), www.imf.org/external/pubs/ft/fandd/2016/06/gordon.htm (accessed 4 October 2016).

14   See Difficult Lemon, 'The Uselessness of Civility – Guest Post by Difficult Lemon', *The Aotearoa Project*, 26 March 2015, https://theaotearoaproject.wordpress.com/2015/03/26/the-uselessness-of-civility-guest-post-by-difficult-lemon (accessed 14 March 2017). Difficult Lemon is obviously a pseudonym.

15   As claimed by Thomas Friedman in *The World is Flat*, Farrar, Strauss, and Giroux, 2005.

16   Kevin H. O'Rourke and Jeffrey G. Williamson, 'When Did Globalization Begin?', NBER Working Paper Series, Working Paper 7632, 2000, www.nber.org/papers/w7632.pdf (accessed 14 March 2017).

17   Wendy Brown, 'The End of the World As We Know It', *Artforum*, December 2016, www.artforum.com/inprint/issue=201610&id=64809 (accessed 20 January 2016).

18   Nations are also constructions, as Benedict Anderson explains in *Imagined Communities: Reflections on the Origin and Spread of Nationalism*, Verso, 2006.

19   I had some involvement with this campaign, as I mention in Chapter 5.

20   Tariana Turia, 'Time to Tackle Institutional Racism', *New Zealand Herald*, 4 October 2016, http://m.nzherald.co.nz/nz/news/article.cfm?c_id=1&objectid=11721558 (accessed 21 January 2017).

21   Statistics New Zealand/Tatauranga Aotearoa, 'Demographic Trends: 2012', www.stats.govt.nz/browse_for_stats/population/estimates_and_projections/demographic-trends-2012.aspx (accessed 14 March 2017).

22   Guy Debord, *The Society of the Spectacle*, Rebel Press, 1967.

23   George Monbiot, 'Celebrity Culture Isn't Just Harmless Fun – It's the Smiling Face of the Corporate Machine', *The Guardian*, 20 December 2016, www.theguardian.com/commentisfree/2016/dec/20/celebrity-corporate-machine-fame-big-business-donald-trump-kim-kardashian (accessed 22 January 2017).

24   Yalda T. Uhls and Patricia M. Greenfield, 'The Rise of Fame: An Historical Content Analysis', *Cyberpsychology: Journal of Cybersocial Research on Cyberspace*, 5, 1 (2011), www.cyberpsychology.eu/view.php?cisloclanku=2011061601 (accessed 22 January 2017).

25   My thanks to Louis Chambers for a conversation on this point.

26   Xiaoming Huang and Jason Young, 'China and the World Economy: Challenges and Opportunities for New Zealand', New Zealand Contemporary China Research Centre (Victoria University of Wellington), China Research Centre Discussion Paper 13/01, August 2013, p.36, www.victoria.ac.nz/chinaresearchcentre/publications/papers/China_and_the_World_Economy.pdf (accessed 22 January 2017).

27 Elena Holodny, 'The 13 Fastest-Growing Economies in the World', World Economic Forum, 13 June 2015, www.weforum.org/agenda/2015/06/the-13-fastest-growing-economies-in-the-world (accessed 22 January 2017).

28 United Nations Development Programme, *The Rise of the South: Human Progress in a Diverse World*, 2013 Human Development Report, http://hdr.undp.org/en/2013-report (accessed 22 January 2017).

29 McKinsey Global Institute, *Urban World: Cities and the Rise of the Consuming Class*, June 2012, www.mckinsey.com/global-themes/urbanization/urban-world-cities-and-the-rise-of-the-consuming-class (accessed 22 January 2017).

30 The trends described in this chapter mostly originated in the US and Europe. I am aware that this appears narrow. But it is a reflection of New Zealand's existing networks, partnerships, linguistic competencies, and where New Zealand tends to look for news, ideas, and relationships. Should New Zealand pursue a different set of partnerships, it might be that a book like this one written in twenty or thirty years' time would document a set of trends that do not just come from the US or Europe.

chapter 3

1   Terence O'Brien, 'Paremata Probus: Some Ingredients of New Zealand Foreign Policy', Centre for Strategic Studies Working Paper, 2013, www.victoria.ac.nz/hppi/centres/strategic-studies/documents/Terence-OBrien-Paremata-Probus.pdf (accessed 8 September 2015).

2   Peter Greener, *Timing is Everything: The Politics and Processes of New Zealand Defence Acquisition Decision Making*, Australian National University Press, 2009, pp.2–5.

3   See Chapter 6 in Malcolm McKinnon, *Independence and Foreign Policy: New Zealand in the World Since 1935*, Auckland University Press, 1992.

4   'Q+A: PM John Key – "NZ at more risk from doing nothing"', *Q+A*, TVNZ, 1 March 2015, www.scoop.co.nz/stories/PO1503/S00004/qa-pm-john-key-nz-more-at-risk-from-doing-nothing.htm (accessed 9 September 2015).

5   Helen Clark, 'New Zealand Foreign Policy', Oxford Union Debating Chamber, 1 October 2007, www.scoop.co.nz/stories/PA0710/S00026.htm (accessed 9 September 2015).

6   This distinction maps roughly on to two schools of thinking in international relations: realism (which says, in outline, that countries tend to pursue their self-interest at an international level) and liberalism (which claims, roughly, that countries tend to pursue ethical values).

7   Juliet Lodge, 'In Pursuit of Regionalism: New Zealand's Foreign Policy under Mr. Kirk', *Cooperation and Conflict*, 10, 3 (1975), p.108.

8   Rt. Hon. David Lange, 'Nuclear Weapons are Morally Indefensible', Oxford Union, 1 March 1985, http://publicaddress.net/great-new-zealand-argument/nuclear-weapons-are-morally-indefensible (accessed 8 September 2015).

9   'Interview with the Rt. Hon. Jim Bolger', Commonwealth Oral Histories, www.commonwealthoralhistories.org/2015/interview-with-the-rt-hon-jim-bolger (accessed 27 January 2017).

10 Ibid.

11 See Greener, *Timing is Everything*, p.5.

12 Bruce Robert Vaughn, 'The United States and New Zealand: Perspectives on a Pacific Partnership', Ian Axford (New Zealand) Fellowships in Public Policy Report, 2012, www.fulbright.org.nz/wp-content/

uploads/2012/08/axford2012_vaughn.pdf (accessed 8 September 2015).

13 The factual background draws heavily on Catalinac's account in: Amy L. Catalinac, 'Why New Zealand Took Itself out of ANZUS: Observing "Opposition for Autonomy" in Assymetric Alliances', *Foreign Policy Analysis*, 6 (2010), pp.318–19. The quotation is taken from p.319 of the same article.

14 Lodge, 'In Pursuit of Regionalism', p.107.

15 These words were prominent in the brochure used in New Zealand's pitch for a seat on the UN Security Council: see www.nzunsc.govt.nz/docs/NZUNSC-Brochure.pdf (accessed 10 September 2015).

16 Some of these details are drawn from: New Zealand History, 'HMNZS *Otago* Sails for Mururoa Test Zone (28 June 1973)', Ministry for Culture and Heritage, https://nzhistory.govt.nz/hmnzs-otago-sails-for-mururoa-test-zone (accessed 14 March 2017).

17 Geoffrey Palmer, *Reform: A Memoir*, Victoria University Press, 2013, p.462.

18 Ibid., p.464.

19 Rt. Hon. Jim Bolger, 'Foreword' in New Zealand Ministry of Foreign Affairs and Trade, *New Zealand at the International Court of Justice – French Nuclear Testing in the Pacific – Nuclear Tests Case New Zealand v France*, 1995, cited in: Palmer, *Reform*, p.464.

20 See Joseph Nye, *The Future of Power*, Public Affairs, 2011.

21 John Key, 'The Price of Being Part of Five Eyes is Joining ISIS Fight', *One News*, TVNZ, 20 January 2015, www.tvnz.co.nz/one-news/new-zealand/john-key-the-price-of-being-part-five-eyes-is-joining-isis-fight-6221595 (accessed 10 September 2015).

22 Paul G. Buchanan, 'Assessment: Partners But Not Allies – New Zealand and the US Sign the Washington Declaration', *36th Parallel*, 27 June 2012, http://36th-parallel.com/2012/06/27/assessment-brief-partners-allies-new-zealand-us-sign-the-washington-declaration (accessed 10 September 2015).

23 See, for example, the work of Norman Myers at the University of Oxford.

24 ABC News, 'Tuvalu Prime Minister Enele Sopoaga Says Climate Change "Like a Weapon of Mass Destruction"', 15 August 2014, www.abc.net.au/news/2014-08-15/an-tuvalu-president-is-climate-change-27like-a-weapon-of-mass-/5672696 (accessed 10 September 2015).

25 *Teitiota v Chief Executive of the Ministry of Business, Innovation, and Employment* [2015] NZSC 107 at [13].

26 See 'The Nansen Initiative – About Us', www.nanseninitiative.org/secretariat (accessed 14 September 2015).

27 Not all lawyers and academics agree on the value of a global legal framework of this kind. Some prefer a focus on regional approaches or bilateral agreements.

28 Jonas Gahr Støre, 'Why We Must Talk', *New York Review of Books*, 7 April 2011, www.nybooks.com/articles/archives/2011/apr/07/why-we-must-talk (accessed 14 September 2015).

29 Jonas Gahr Støre, 'In Defense of Dialogue', TED, November 2011, www.ted.com/talks/jonas_gahr_store_in_defense_of_dialogue?language=en (accessed 23 September 2015).

30 See New Zealand Cabinet Paper, 'New Zealand Agency for International Development (NZAID): Mandate and Policy Settings', www.beehive.govt.nz/sites/all/files/CAB%20paper%203.doc.pdf (accessed 21 September 2015).

31 For a discussion of these different types of aid, see: Roger C. Riddell, 'Does Foreign Aid Really Work?', Keynote Address to the Australasian Aid and International Development Workshop, Canberra, 13 February 2014, http://devpolicy.org/2014-Australasian-Aid-and-International-Development-Policy-Workshop/Roger-Riddell-Keynote-Address.pdf (accessed 21 September 2015).

32 OECD, 'The 0.7% ODA/GNI Target – A History', www.oecd.org/dac/stats/the07odagnitarget-ahistory.htm (accessed 21 September 2015).

33 OECD, 'Charts, Tables, and Databases: The Global Picture of Official Development Assistance (ODA)', www.oecd.org/development/stats/data.htm (accessed 21 September 2015). See also OECD, 'Compare Your Country', www.compareyourcountry.org/oda?page=0&cr=oecd&lg=en (accessed 21 September 2015).

34 The Treasury, 'Revenue', www.treasury.govt.nz/government/revenue (accessed 21 September 2015).

35 United Nations, 'World Population Prospects – The 2015 Revision: Key Findings and Advance Tables', United Nations, New York, p.1, http://esa.un.org/unpd/wpp/Publications/Files/Key_Findings_WPP_2015.pdf (accessed 22 September 2015).

36 Ministry of Foreign Affairs and Trade, *Statement of Intent: 2011–2014*, www.mfat.govt.nz/downloads/media-and-publications/soi-mfat-2011-14.pdf (accessed 22 September 2015).

37 Ministry of Foreign Affairs and Trade, *New Zealand's ASEAN Partnership: One Pathway to Ten Nations*, www.mfat.govt.nz/downloads/NZinc/NZ-Strategy-ASEAN-2013.pdf (accessed 22 September 2015).

38 Ministry of Foreign Affairs and Trade, *Opening Doors to India: New Zealand's 2015 Vision*, http://mfat.govt.nz/downloads/NZinc/NZInc-%20Strategy%20-%20India.pdf (accessed 22 September 2015).

39 Ministry of Foreign Affairs and Trade, *Our Future with Asia*, Printlink, 2007, pp.6–7, http://mfat.govt.nz/downloads/foreign-relations/asia/asiawhitepaper.pdf (accessed 22 September 2015).

40 Australian Government, *Australia in the Asian Century*, 2012, www.murdoch.edu.au/ALTC-Fellowship/_document/Resources/australia-in-the-asian-century-white-paper.pdf (accessed 22 September 2015). Certainly Australia's commitment on paper to embracing Asia has been partially undermined in practice by its inhumane detention of asylum seekers coming from Asia and elsewhere.

41 See p.160 onwards.

42 For further discussion of this, see Henry Kissinger, *On China*, Penguin, 2012.

43 I learned Indonesian after spending four years in Jakarta as a child. It is widely regarded as one of the easiest languages to learn. However, knowledge of Indonesia is very limited in New Zealand (many New Zealanders know of Bali, but might not know it is in Indonesia), though Indonesia is New Zealand's closest Asian country, and Indonesian is offered in very few schools and universities. A push to offer it might be one part of this emphasis on learning Asian languages in schools.

44 See New Zealand History, 'Read the Treaty: Page 1 – Introduction', www.nzhistory.net.nz/politics/treaty/read-the-treaty/english-text (accessed 23 September 2015).

45 Thanks to Tai Ahu for this insightful qualification.

46 The Waitangi Tribunal, *The Taranaki Report – Kaupapa Tuatahi* (Chapter 8: Parihaka), www.justice.govt.nz/tribunals/waitangi-tribunal/Reports/wai0143/chapt08 (accessed 23 September 2015). The phrase 'author of peace' originally appeared in the Bible, in 1 Corinthians 14:33.

47 Ibid.

48 'Preamble to the Charter of the United Nations', www.un.org/en/documents/charter/preamble.shtml (accessed on 23 September 2015).

49 My thanks to Jaakko Kuosmanen for an informal conversation that deepened my knowledge of the Finnish situation and pointed me in the direction of further resources.

50 Ministry of Foreign Affairs for Finland, 'Peace Mediation – Finnish Guidelines', 2010, http://formin.fi/public/default.aspx?contentid=324339&contentlan=2&culture=en-US (accessed 23 September 2015).

51 Ibid., p.13.

52 Ibid., p.14.

53 Kinley Salmon has suggested that New Zealand might play a role in mediating the South China Sea dispute. See: Kinley Salmon, 'Time NZ Took a Leadership Role in Global Affairs', *Nelson Mail*, 25 July 2014, www. stuff.co.nz/nelson-mail/opinion/10309892/Time-NZ-took-a-leadership-role-in-global-affairs (accessed 23 September 2015).

54 The book is Jan Egeland, *Impotent Superpower – Potent Small State: Potentials and Limitations of the Human Rights Objectives in the Foreign Policies of the United States and Norway*, International Peace Institute, 1985.

chapter 4

1 I have been influenced in my thinking of neoliberalism as a set of maxims by Mauricio Lazzarato's notion that capitalism reflects a set of 'axiomatics': see Mauricio Lazzarato, *Governing by Debt*, Semiotext(e), 2015.

2 It was, of course, Margaret Thatcher who first said 'There is no such thing as society' in 1987.

3 Philip Mirowski, 'Postface: Defining Neoliberalism', in Philip Mirowski and Dieter Plehwe, *The Road from Mont Pelerin: The Making of the Neoliberal Thought Collective*, Verso, 2009, p.419. Philip Mirowski is among the best exponents of the history and structure of neoliberalism. For other good accounts, see: David Harvey, *A Brief History of Neoliberalism,* Oxford University Press, 2005; Wendy Brown, *Undoing the Demos: Neoliberalism's Stealth Revolution*, ZONE Books, 2015; Jane Kelsey, *The New Zealand Experiment: A World Model for Structural Adjustment?*, Auckland University Press, 1995; and Michel Foucault, *The Birth of Biopolitics: Lectures at the College de France*, Picador, 2004.

4 David Harvey, 'Neoliberalism is a Political Project', *Jacobin*, 23 July 2016, www.jacobinmag.com/2016/07/david-harvey-neoliberalism-capitalism-labor-crisis-resistance (accessed 1 August 2016).

5 See Harvey, *A Brief History of Neoliberalism.*

6 I also think it has failed elsewhere – but that is another matter.

7 This data is taken from the World Bank: 'GDP Growth (Annual %) – New Zealand, 1978–2015', http://data.worldbank.org/indicator/NY.GDP.MKTP.KD.ZG?end=2015&locations=NZ&start=1978&view=chart (accessed 5 August 2016).

8 Rick Boven, Dan Bidois, and Catherine Harland, *A Goal is not a Strategy*, New Zealand Institute Discussion Paper, 2010, p.8.

9 Ibid., p.12.

10 Brian Easton, 'Economic history – Government and market liberalization – Unemployment 1896–2006', Te Ara – the Encyclopedia of New Zealand, www.teara.govt.nz/en/graph/24362/unemployment-1896-2006 (accessed 5 August 2016).

11 Brian Easton, *The Commercialisation of New Zealand*, Auckland University Press, 1997, p.44.

12 Statistics New Zealand/Tatauranga Aotearoa, 'NZ Progress Indicators/Tupuranga Aotearoa: Unemployment Rate', www.stats.govt.nz/browse_for_stats/snapshots-of-nz/nz-progress-indicators/home/economic/unemployment-rate.aspx (accessed 5 August 2016).

13 4 per cent of the working-age population as of June 2016 was 148,640 people. Figures calculated by author based on 'Statistics New Zealand/Tatauranga Aotearoa: Labour Market Statistics – June 2016 Quarter', www.stats.govt.nz/browse_for_stats/income-and-work/employment_and_unemployment/LabourMarketStatistics_HOTPJun16qtr-incl-HLFS.aspx (accessed 9 January 2017) and 'Statistics New Zealand/Tatauranga Aotearoa: A Guide to Unemployment Statistics (Second Edition)', www.stats.govt.nz/browse_for_stats/income-and-work/

employment_and_unemployment/a-guide-to-unemployment-stats.aspx (accessed 5 August 2016).

14 New Zealand Treasury, 'New Zealand's Productivity Performance – International Comparisons', 2008, www. treasury.govt.nz/publications/research-policy/tprp/08-02/05.htm (accessed 5 August 2016).

15 New Zealand Productivity Commission, 'An International Perspective on the New Zealand Productivity Paradox', Working Paper 2014/01, 2014, www.productivity.govt.nz/sites/default/files/international-perspective-working-paper.pdf (accessed 5 August 2016).

16 Reserve Bank of New Zealand/Te Pūtea Matua, 'Household Debt', 2016, www.rbnz.govt.nz/statistics/key-graphs/key-graph-household-debt (accessed 5 August 2016).

17 Trading Economics, 'New Zealand Households Debt to Income', www.tradingeconomics.com/new-zealand/households-debt-to-income (accessed 9 January 2017).

18 Bryan Perry, 'Household Incomes in New Zealand: Trends in Indicators of Inequality and Hardship 1982 to 2014', Ministry of Social Development/Te Manatū Whakahiato Ora, 2015, pp.5–6, www.msd.govt.nz/about-msd-and-our-work/publications-resources/monitoring/household-incomes (accessed 5 August 2016).

19 See, for example, Evan Te Ahu Poata Smith, 'Inequality and Māori', in Max Rashbrooke (ed.), *Inequality: A New Zealand Crisis*, Bridget Williams Books, 2013, pp.148–58.

20 Statistics New Zealand/Te Tari Tatau, 'Impacts of Unemployment', www2.stats.govt.nz/domino/external/web/nzstories.nsf/3d7ba81fd31d11adcc256b16006bfcf3/4ec3eca00597817fcc256b1800046afc?OpenDocument (accessed 5 August 2016).

21 For example, the work of Max Rashbrooke: Rashbrooke (ed.), *Inequality*.

22 Jonathan D. Ostry, Prakash Loungani, and Davide Fuceri, 'Neoliberalism: Oversold?', *Finance and Development*, June 2016, www.imf.org/external/pubs/ft/fandd/2016/06/pdf/ostry.pdf (accessed 5 August 2016).

23 I am indebted to Ronan Harrington for this term.

24 I have drawn this term from two Australian authors: Tom Bentley and Jonathan West, 'Time for a New Consensus', *Griffith Review*, May 2016, https://griffithreview.com/time-for-a-new-consensus-e-book (accessed 5 August 2016).

25 There is discussion on this in Paul Mason, *Postcapitalism: A Guide to Our Future*, Allen Lane, 2015. The argument about power imbalances in a communal setting is an echo of the critique made by Jo Freeman of anarchist, 'leaderless' groups in: 'The Tyranny of Structurelessness', Southern Female Rights Union, 1970, www.jofreeman.com/joreen/tyranny.htm (accessed 8 August 2016).

26 My particular thanks to Stephen Parry for his comment on this section and the chapter as a whole.

27 Kevin O'Rourke, 'Brexit: This Backlash Has Been a Long Time Coming', *VoxEU*, 7 August 2016, http://voxeu.org/article/brexit-backlash-has-been-long-time-coming (accessed 13 August 2016).

28 Jonathan D. Ostry, Andrew Berg, and Charalambos G. Tsangarides, 'Redistribution, Inequality, and Growth', IMF Staff Discussion Note, April 2014, p.4, www.imf.org/external/pubs/ft/sdn/2014/sdn1402.pdf (accessed 9 August 2016).

29 As far as I know, the term 'social distance' was first used by German philosopher Theodor Adorno in *Minima Moralia: Reflections on Damaged Life*, Verso, 1951, p.176.

30 Zadie Smith, 'Fences: A Brexit Diary', *New York Review of Books*, 18 August 2016.

31 There is some evidence from US states that tax flight from increases in top tax rates has occurred, but only at the margins. See Young et al., 'Millionaire Migration and Taxation of the Elite: Evidence from Administrative Data', *American Sociological Review*, 81, 3 (2016), pp.421–46.

32 My thanks to an anonymous Bridget Williams Books reviewer for highlighting that the number of people paying this top tax rate would be small. I have drawn figures for people paying more than $150,000 from www.budget.govt.nz/budget/2016/economic-fiscal-outlook/facts-taxpayers.htm (accessed 9 January 2017).

33 Anthony B. Atkinson, *Inequality: What Can Be Done?*, Harvard University Press, 2015, p.185.

34 Ibid., p.187.

35 Thomas Piketty, *Capital in the Twenty-First Century*, Harvard University Press, 2014, p.513.

36 Atkinson, *Inequality*, p.179.

37 Piketty, *Capital in the Twenty-First Century*. Piketty's famous idea is that r > g, or that the rate of expansion of capital has exceeded the rate of growth in countries, highlighting the disproportionate expansion of housing and finance wealth.

38 Gareth Morgan and Susan Guthrie, *The Big Kahuna: Turning Tax and Welfare in New Zealand on its Head*, Public Interest Publishing Company, 2011, Chapter 7.

39 Oxfam New Zealand, 'The Robin Hood Tax: Tax on Bankers Could Raise Billions of Dollars to Tackle Poverty', www.oxfam.org.nz/what-we-do/issues/the-robin-hood-tax (accessed 10 August 2016). See also Mike Dinsdale, 'Hone Harawira's Plan for a "Hone Heke" Tax Supported', *Northern Advocate*, 3 May 2011, www.nzherald.co.nz/northern-advocate/news/article.cfm?c_id=1503450&objectid=11027080 (accessed 14 February 2017).

40 Chapple talks of the 'higher marginal utility' of income for beneficiaries in the course of the discussion of an earlier iteration of the social investment approach: the forward liability investment model. See Simon Chapple, 'Forward Liability and Welfare Reform in New Zealand', *Policy Quarterly*, (May 2013), p.58.

41 Colin James, 'Social Investment: Chance for a Mentality Shift: Revisiting a 2015 Working Paper', Treasury Seminar, 7 March 2016, www.colinjames.co.nz/2016/03/07/investment-chance-for-a-mentality-shift (accessed 10 August 2016).

42 Bill Rosenberg, 'The "Investment Approach" is Not an Investment Approach', New Zealand Council of Trade Unions/Te Kauae Kaimahi, http://union.org.nz/sites/union.org.nz/files/Investment%20Approach%20is%20not%20an%20investment%20approach%20-%20Rosenberg_0.pdf (accessed 10 August 2016).

43 Keith Ng, 'I'm a Data Nerd and a Data Cheerleader, But Still I Fear Bill English's Datatopia', *The Spinoff*, 13 January 2017, http://thespinoff.co.nz/society/13-01-2017/im-a-data-nerd-and-a-data-cheerleader-but-still-i-fear-bill-englishs-datatopia (accessed 14 January 2017).

44 Simon Wilson, 'Social Investment: The Two Uninspiring Words upon which the Entire Election Could Hang', *The Spinoff*, 12 January 2017, http://thespinoff.co.nz/politics/12-01-2017/social-investment-the-two-uninspiring-words-upon-which-the-entire-election-could-hang (accessed 13 January 2017).

45 James, 'Social Investment'.

46 [2010] NZSC 146, [2011] 2 NZLR 131.

47 A compelling critique of the judgment is made by Sir Edmund Thomas in: E. W. Thomas, 'A Critique of the Reasoning of the Supreme Court in GE Custodians v Bartle', (2011) 17 NZBLQ 97.

48 [2012] NZSC 72, [2013] 1 NZLR 741, at [149].

49 See Trading Economics, 'New Zealand Households Debt to Income', www.tradingeconomics.com/new-zealand/households-debt-to-income (accessed 9 January 2017).

50 Chris Hunt, 'Household Debt: A Cross-Country Perspective', *Reserve Bank of New Zealand/Te Pūtea Matua Bulletin*, 77, 4 (October 2014), http://rbnz.govt.nz/~/media/ReserveBank/Files/Publications/Bulletins/2014/2014oct77-4.pdf (accessed 10 August 2016).

51 Mariana Mazzucato, *The Entrepreneurial State: Debunking Public vs. Private Sector Myths*, Anthem Other Canon Books, 2013. The general gist of her argument, described here, can also be found in: Mariana Mazzucato, *The Entrepreneurial State*, Demos, 2011, www.demos.co.uk/files/Entrepreneurial_State_-_web.pdf (accessed 11 August 2016).

52 Mazzucato, *The Entrepreneurial State*, 2011, p.53.

53 Bloomberg, 'Who Created the iPhone, Apple or the Government?', 19 June 2013, www.bloomberg.com/view/articles/2013-06-19/who-created-the-iphone-apple-or-the-government- (accessed 11 August 2016).

54 Mazzucato, *The Entrepreneurial State*, 2011, p.112.

55 See, for example, Dani Rodrik, 'Normalizing Industrial Policy', The International Bank for Reconstruction and Development, 2008, http://siteresources.worldbank.org/EXTPREMNET/Resources/489960-1338997241035/Growth_Commission_Working_Paper_3_Normalizing_Industrial_Policy.pdf (accessed 11 August 2016).

56 I am here indebted to the word play of Keeanga-Yamahtta Taylor in her writing on Black Lives Matter. Taylor notes that historically, in the Soviet context, it was not only state ownership but also 'who owned the state' that mattered: Keeanga-Yamahtta Taylor, 'Extract from *From #BlackLivesMatter to Black Liberation*', *Salvage #3: Or What's a Hell For?*', Salvage Publications, 2016, pp.147–64 p.152.

57 See, for example, discussion of this in the British context in Ken Loach (dir.), *The Spirit of '45*, 2013.

58 Many of these criticisms are outlined in the report commissioned by French President Nicholas Sarkozy in 2008: 'Report by the Commission on the Measurement of Economic Progress and Social Performance', www.insee.fr/fr/publications-et-services/dossiers_web/stiglitz/doc-commission/RAPPORT_anglais.pdf (accessed 12 August 2016).

59 Max Harris, 'Alternative Measures of Progress – and Making Our Metrics Meaningful', *The Aotearoa Project*, 24 May 2015, https://theaotearoaproject.wordpress.com/2015/05/24/alternative-measures-of-progress-and-making-our-measures-meaningful (accessed 12 August 2016).

60 Girol Karacaoglu, 'Improving the Living Standards of New Zealanders: Moving from a Framework to Implementation – Conference Paper', Treasury/Kaitohutohu Kaupapa Rawa, June 2012, p.21, www.treasury.govt.nz/publications/media-speeches/speeches/livingstandards/sp-livingstandards-paper.pdf (accessed 13 August 2016).

61 Piketty, *Capital in the Twenty-First Century*, p.574.

62 Ibid., p.575.

63 I am indebted to New Zealand academic Ngaire Woods for this point, which she has made in many public lectures.

64 Piketty, *Capital in the Twenty-First Century*, p.513.

chapter 5

1 See, in particular, Aimé Césaire, *Discourse on Colonialism*, Monthly Review Press, 1972; Franz Fanon, *The Wretched of the Earth*, Grove Press, 1961; Linda Tuhiwai Smith, *Decolonising Methodologies: Research and Indigenous Peoples*, Zed Books/University of Otago Press, 1999. For a good reading list, see: 'Decolonization: Indigeneity, Education and Society', https://decolonization.wordpress.com/decolonization-readings (accessed 10 January 2017).

2 Ani Mikaere, *He Rukuruku Whakaaro: Colonising Myths, Māori Realities*, Huia Publishers and Te Tākupu, Te Wānanga o Raukawa, 2011.

3 Harsha Walia, 'Decolonising Together', *Briarpatch Magazine*, 1 January 2012, https://briarpatchmagazine.com/

articles/view/decolonizing-together (accessed 10 January 2017).

4   'I, Too, Am Auckland Experiences', 18 March 2015, *YouTube*, www.youtube.com/watch?v=4iKLJTbN7uc (accessed 10 January 2017).

5   Mikaere, *He Rukuruku Whakaaro*, p.91.

6   See, for example: Samantha Vice, 'How Do I Live in this Strange Place?', *Journal of Social Philosophy*, 41, 3 (2010), pp.323–42; and Tim Wise, 'On White Privilege', *YouTube*, 19 February 2008, www.youtube.com/watch?v=J3Xe1kX7Wsc (accessed 10 January 2017).

7   Mikaere, *He Rukuruku Whakaaro*, p.91.

8   Ibid., p.117.

9   Walia, 'Decolonising Together'.

10 See Clare Land, *Decolonizing Solidarity: Dilemmas and Directions for Supporters of Indigenous Struggles*, Zed Books, 2015.

11 As Fanon argued in *The Wretched of the Earth*.

12 Mikaere, *He Rukuruku Whakaaro*, p.74.

13 See Atholl Anderson, Judith Binney and Aroha Harris, *Tangata Whenua: A History*, Bridget Williams Books, 2015, p.261. There is also a persuasive argument that the Māori seats represented an attempt to cap, not boost, Māori political power.

14 Ibid., p.289.

15 Ibid., p.282.

16 Ibid., pp.369–70.

17 For the 1840s reference, see the work of David Williams: for example, David V. Williams, 'The Treaty of Waitangi – The Maori Magna Carta', Public Address, 13 September 2015, Wellington. For the 1930s reference, see: Radio New Zealand, 'The Māori Magna Carta' (original 1991 broadcast), rebroadcast on 25 June 2013, www.radionz.co.nz/collections/treatyofwaitangi/audio/2533042/the-m-ori-magna-carta (accessed 26 January 2016).

18 Anderson, Binney and Harris, *Tangata Whenua*, pp.254, 281 and 287.

19 David Lange, '2000 Bruce Jesson Memorial Lecture', Bruce Jesson Foundation, 18 November 2000, www.brucejesson.com/david-lange-2000 (accessed 26 January 2016).

20 Don Brash, 'Nationhood', Orewa Rotary Club, 27 January 2004, www.scoop.co.nz/stories/PA0401/S00220.htm (accessed 26 January 2016).

21 Anderson, Binney and Harris, *Tangata Whenua*, pp.292–93.

22 This point is brilliantly made by Lindsey Te Ata o Tu MacDonald in 'Decolonisation Starts in a Name', *Political Science*, 68, 2 (2016), pp.105–23.

23 Roberto Unger, 'What is Structural Change and What Kind of Structural Change Do We Need?', The RSA London, 14 November 2013, www.youtube.com/watch?v=A1MthzjqeWE&feature=c4-overview-vl&list=PLNdEBvVYMvsBWULxWoqvoqQQVuMylDhRa (accessed 2 February 2016).

24 I am grateful to an anonymous Bridget Williams Books reader for helping me with the framing of this point.

25 The term 'entrenched' means that the constitutional law cannot be overturned by a simple majority in Parliament. It would require a special process to be overturned, usually at least requiring a much larger majority than is usually required.

26 Under s 7 of the New Zealand Bill of Rights Act 1990, the Attorney-General 'vets' legislation and has to write a report on whether the legislation violates rights. The Attorney-General brings this report to the attention of Parliament before the Bill becomes law. One example of a Bill being passed after an Attorney-General report has said that the Bill violates rights is National MP Paul Quinn's Electoral (Disqualification of Sentenced Prisoners) Amendment Bill, which banned all prisoners from voting in 2010.

27 Again, my great thanks to a Bridget Williams Books reader for highlighting this point.

28 Chief Justice Sian Elias, 'Mapping the Constitutional', Legal Research Foundation Conference, 29 June 2012.

29 Max Harris, 'Is New Zealand Law Ready for a *Marbury v Madison* Moment?', *New Zealand Universities Law Review*, 25, 2 (2012), p.210.

30 This was in a case called *Taylor v Attorney-General* [2015] NZHC 1706.

31 The report of Matike Mai Aotearoa is www.converge.org.nz/pma/MatikeMaiAotearoaReport.pdf (accessed 15 February 2016). The report of the government-led Constitutional Review Panel, 'New Zealand's Constitution: A Report on a Conversation – He Kōtuinga Kōrero mō Te Kaupapa Ture o Aotearoa', is at www.ourconstitution.org.nz/store/doc/FR_Full_Report.pdf (accessed 15 February 2016).

32 See Constitutional Review Panel, 'New Zealand's Constitution', pp.10–11.

33 Lots of colonial constitutions were not just unjust, but also sloppily or lazily drafted – often copied from template constitutions.

34 Max Harris, '*Are We There Yet? The Future of the Treaty of Waitangi:* A Review', Māori Law Review, (April 2015), http://maorilawreview.co.nz/2015/04/are-we-there-yet-the-future-of-the-treaty-of-waitangi-a-review (accessed 15 February 2016).

35 See report of Matike Mai Aotearoa, p.69.

36 See Constitutional Review Panel, 'New Zealand's Constitution', p.17.

37 Geoffrey Palmer and Andrew Butler, *A Constitution for Aotearoa New Zealand*, Victoria University Press, 2016, p.70.

38 This was an idea first suggested to me by Billy Matheson.

39 My thanks to discussions with Kingi Snelgar on this topic.

40 Ibid., p.18.

41 My thanks to Tai Ahu for underscoring this point.

42 This is according to 2012 statistics: Statistics New Zealand/Tatauranga Aotearoa, 'New Zealand's prison population', vwww.stats.govt.nz/browse_for_stats/snapshots-of-nz/yearbook/society/crime/corrections.aspx (accessed 14 March 2017).

43 Lisa Marriott and Dalice Sim, 'Indicators of Inequality for Māori and Pacific People', Victoria University of Wellington Working Papers in Public Finance, Working Paper 09/2014, p.12, www.victoria.ac.nz/sacl/about/cpf/publications/pdfs/2015/WP09_2014_Indicators-of-Inequality.pdf (accessed 16 February 2016).

44 Ibid., p.15.

45 Ibid., p.18. Oliver Hartwich, the executive director of the New Zealand Institute, told me that socio-economic inequality in general had not increased over the last 20 years – but inequality between Māori and non-Māori was a 'genuine concern'.

46 Statistics New Zealand/Tatauranga Aotearoa, 'Statistics NZ: Māori', www.stats.govt.nz/maori (accessed 16

February 2016).

47 Marriott and Sim, 'Indicators of Inequality', p.23.

48 Ibid.

49 This was said in *R v Gladue* [1999] 1 SCR 688 at para 64.

50 The English version of Article Two remains strong in its wording – it talks of 'full exclusive and undisturbed possession' of all properties – though it does not refer to rangatiratanga.

51 This statistic can be found from Statistics New Zealand's '2013 QuickStats about Māori', www.stats.govt. nz/Census/2013-census/profile-and-summary-reports/quickstats-about-maori-english.aspx (accessed 19 February 2016).

52 Riki Mihaere, 'A Kaupapa Māori Analysis of the Use of Māori Cultural Identity in the Prison System', thesis submitted for Doctor of Philosophy in Criminology, Victoria University of Wellington, 2015, http://researcharchive.vuw.ac.nz/xmlui/bitstream/handle/10063/4185/thesis.pdf?sequence=2 (accessed 19 February 2016).

53 See the helpful discussion by Rawinia Higgins, 'Those that Trespass Will Be Relish for My Food', PostTreatySettlements.Org.NZ, http://posttreatysettlements.org.nz/those-that-trespass-will-be-relish-for-my-food (accessed 19 February 2016).

54 I do not have the space in this chapter to discuss Treaty settlements in full. But there should be real concern about whether the rash negotiation of some Treaty settlements, and clumsy grouping together of iwi and hapū, may make inevitable a further round of Treaty settlements in future.

55 Aroha Harris, 'Theorize This: We Are What We Write', *Te Pouhere Korero – Maori History, Maori People*, 3 (2009), cited in Rachel Buchanan, 'Telling the Truth in Our Streets: Story-Telling and Treaty Settlements', PostTreatySettlements.Org.NZ, http://posttreatysettlements.org.nz/telling-the-truth-in-our-streets (accessed 19 February 2016).

56 Ibid.

57 Waitangi Tribunal, 'Report of the Waitangi Tribunal on the Te Reo Maori Claim', Department of Justice, 1986, p.17, https://forms.justice.govt.nz/search/Documents/WT/wt_DOC_68482156/Report%20on%20the%20 Te%20Reo%20Maori%20Claim%20W.pdf (accessed 23 February 2016).

58 Jennifer Humphreys, 'Groser's Support for Te Reo Impractical, Says Peters', *Newshub*, 28 April 2012, www. newshub.co.nz/politics/grosers-support-for-te-reo-impractical-says-peters-2012042819#axzz40zMxG4fR (accessed 23 February 2016).

59 *New Zealand Herald*, 'Should Te Reo Maori Be Compulsory in Schools?', 21 March 2015, www.nzherald.co.nz/nz/news/article.cfm?c_id=1&objectid=11421013 (accessed 23 February 2016).

60 Waitangi Tribunal, 'Te Reo Maori Claim', p.17.

61 Waitangi Tribunal, 'Ko Aotearoa Tenei – Report on the Wai 262 Claim (Volume 2)', 2011, p.477, https://forms. justice.govt.nz/search/Documents/WT/wt_DOC_68356606/KoAotearoaTeneiTT2Vol2W.pdf (accessed 23 February 2016).

62 Ibid., p.468.

63 Ibid., p.440.

64 Ibid., p.394.

65 Credit for this point goes entirely to a Bridget Williams Books reader, who suggested it.

66 Ibid., p.407.

67 Ibid., pp.468–69.

68 Stephens' piece of writing on this topic is available on her excellent blog: 'In Praise of ... Pākehā Learning and Teaching Te Reo Māori', Sparrowhawk/Kārearea, 24 July 2014, https://sparrowhawkkarearea. com/2014/07/24/in-praise-ofpakeha-learning-and-teaching-te-reo-maori (accessed 10 January 2017).

69 Ibid., p.411.

70 Ibid., p.470.

71 Mercator-Education, 'Welsh: The Welsh Language in Education in the UK', 2001, www.linguae-celticae.org/ dateien/Welsh_in_Education.pdf (accessed 23 February 2016).

72 Tom Sheldrick, 'Exclusive Poll: 64% Oppose Compulsory Welsh to Age 16', ITV, 10 July 2015, www.itv.com/ news/wales/2015-07-10/exclusive-poll-64-oppose-compulsory-welsh-to-age-16 (accessed 23 February 2016). The headline is misleading and does not examine the more fine-grained statistics showing support for compulsory Welsh at different levels.

73 BBC UK, 'Census 2011: Number of Welsh Speakers Falling', 11 December 2012, www.bbc.co.uk/news/uk-wales-20677528 (accessed 23 February 2016). Again, the headline focuses on the negative statistics, but the story reveals more positives.

74 I am very grateful to Gregor Fountain for this point and for an extended discussion of this issue.

75 Willie Jackson, 'Compulsory Te Reo', Auckland Now, 27 July 2012, www.stuff.co.nz/auckland/local-news/ local-blogs/willie-jackson/7360371/Compulsory-te-reo (accessed 14 February 2017).

76 Waitangi Tribunal, 'Ko Aotearoa Tenei – Report on the Wai 262 Claim', p.462.

77 Ibid., pp.438–39.

78 Jodie Ranford, 'Pakeha, Its Origin and Meaning', Maori News, http://maorinews.com/writings/papers/other/ pakeha.htm (accessed 23 February 2016).

79 Ibid.

80 See the extended discussion in Philippe Legrain, Immigrants: Your Country Needs Them, Abacus, 2009.

81 Gregor Fountain alerted me to this point.

82 The film was, at the time of publication, available online on NZ On Screen: see www.nzonscreen.com/title/ dawn-raids-2005 (accessed 23 February 2016).

chapter 6

1 Ben Heather, 'Buxton Popoali'i: I'm Just Grateful to Be Alive', The Press, 5 May 2014, www.stuff.co.nz/the-press/news/10008087/Buxton-Popoali-i-I-m-just-grateful-to-be-alive (accessed 22 March 2016).

2 Ben Heather, 'Living with a Broken Heart: Rheumatic Fever Put an End to Career', The Dominion Post, 5 May 2014, www.stuff.co.nz/dominion-post/news/wellington/10007915/Living-with-a-broken-heart (accessed 22 March 2016).

3 Mayo Clinic Staff, 'Diseases and Conditions – Rheumatic Fever: Definition', www.mayoclinic.org/diseases-conditions/rheumatic-fever/basics/definition/con-20031399 (accessed 22 March 2016). The Mayo Clinic is one of the best-regarded medical practice and research groups in the United States.

4 Health Navigator New Zealand, 'Rheumatic Fever: Overview', www.healthnavigator.org.nz/health-a-z/r/ rheumatic-fever (accessed 22 March 2016).

5 Health Promotion Agency, 'Rheumatic Fever', www.hpa.org.nz/what-we-do/rheumatic-fever (accessed 23

March 2016).

6   J. M. Neutze and P. M. Clarkson, 'Rheumatic Fever: An Unsolved Problem in New Zealand', *New Zealand Medical Journal*, 97, 763 (1984).

7   This comparison combines Ministry of Health figures for 0- to 30-year-olds (kept up until 1994–95) with figures from the New Zealand Child and Youth Epidemiology Service for 0- to 24-year-olds (kept from 1990–91) onwards. The admission rates appear to have worsened since 1992–93, when admissions reached a low of around 7–8 acute rheumatic fever admissions per 100,000. Source: Slides provided by Diana Lennon (internal Starship update, 2014).

8   State Services Commission, 'Better Public Services: Supporting Vulnerable Children', www.ssc.govt.nz/bps-supporting-vulnerable-children#rheumatic (accessed 23 March 2016).

9   See questions from Barbara Stewart to Jonathan Coleman: 'Questions for Oral Answer: Rheumatic Fever – Prevention Initiatives', New Zealand Parliament, 27 August 2015, www.parliament.nz/en-nz/pb/business/qoa/51HansQ_20150827_00000007/7-rheumatic-fever%E2%80%94prevention-initiatives (accessed 23 March 2016).

10 Jason Gurney, Diana Sarfati, James Stanley, Nigel Wilson, Rachel Webb, 'The Incidence of Acute Rheumatic Fever in New Zealand, 2010–2013', *New Zealand Medical Journal*, 128, 1417 (2015).

11 Allen+Clarke, 'Evaluation of the 2015 Rheumatic Fever Awareness Campaign', 3 December 2015, p.42, www.health.govt.nz/system/files/documents/publications/evaluation-2015-rheumatic-fever-awareness-campaign-december15.pdf (accessed 23 March 2016).

12 Jo Moir, 'Education Funding Review: What Will Replace School Deciles?', *Stuff*, 15 March 2016, www.stuff.co.nz/national/education/77882570/education-funding-review-school-decile-system-to-be-scrapped.html (accessed 25 March 2016).

13 All of these details are laid out in s 11 of the Education Act 1989.

14 Post-Primary Teachers' Association (Waikato), 'Zoning, Enrolment Schemes, and School Choice – Educational Apartheid?', PPTA Annual Conference Papers 2014, pp.4–7, www.ppta.org.nz/events-info-forms/doc_view/1779-zoning-enrolment-schemes-and-school-choice-educational-apartheid (accessed 25 March 2016).

15 Liz McDonald, 'School Zones Cripple Buyers', *Stuff National*, 29 September 2014, www.stuff.co.nz/national/10555157/School-zones-cripple-buyers (accessed 25 March 2016).

16 Radio New Zealand, 'Minister Seeks Advice over Skewed School Zones', 26 June 2012, www.radionz.co.nz/news/national/109202/minister-seeks-advice-over-skewed-school-zones (accessed 25 March 2016).

17 Post-Primary Teachers' Association (Waikato), 'Zoning', p.11.

18 Steve Thomas, 'School Zones and Social Exclusion', Maxim Institute, 5 July 2012, www.maxim.org.nz/Blog/School_zones_and_social_exclusion (accessed 25 March 2016).

19 Valmoana Tapaleao, 'Zone-Fixing Claim Stirs Call for Change', *New Zealand Herald*, 26 June 2012, www.nzherald.co.nz/nz/news/article.cfm?c_id=1&objectid=10815517 (accessed 25 March 2016).

20 Ibid.

21 Thomas, 'School Zones and Social Exclusion'.

22 You can get it online on Tono's website, at http://anthonietonnon.com/track/marion-bates-realty (accessed 14 March 2017). My thanks to Alaister Moughan for drawing my attention to the track.

23 McKinsey Global Institute, 'Tackling the World's Affordable Housing Challenge', October 2014, www.mckinsey.com/global-themes/urbanization/tackling-the-worlds-affordable-housing-challenge (accessed 28

March 2016).

24 For the New Zealand Initiative perspective, see, for example, Michael Bassett, Luke Malpass, and Jason Krupp, 'Free to Build: Restoring New Zealand's Housing Affordability', 18 November 2013, http://nzinitiative.org.nz/shop/Library+by+type/Books+and+reports/Free+to+Build+Restoring+New+Zealands+Housing+Affordability/x_show_article/1.html (accessed 27 March 2016); and Michael Bassett and Luke Malpass, 'Different Places, Different Means: Why Some Countries Build More than Others', 12 September 2013, http://nzinitiative.org.nz/shop/Library+by+type/Books+and+reports/Different+places+different+means+Why+some+countries+build+more+than+others/x_show_article/1.html (accessed 27 March 2016).

25 Shamubeel Eaqub and Selena Eaqub, *Generation Rent: Rethinking New Zealand's Priorities*, Bridget Williams Books, 2015, pp.33–65.

26 Philippa Howden-Chapman, *Home Truths: Confronting New Zealand's Housing Crisis*, Bridget Williams Books, 2015, pp.86–89.

27 Amore's definition of severe housing deprivation is 'people living in severely inadequate housing due to a lack of access to minimally adequate housing'; it is based on the Statistics New Zealand definition. See Kate Amore, 'Severe Housing Deprivation in Aotearoa/New Zealand, 2001–2013', *He Kainga Oranga*/Housing & Health Research Programme, Department of Public Health, University of Otago, pp.3–4, www.healthyhousing.org.nz/wp-content/uploads/2016/08/Severe-housing-deprivation-in-Aotearoa-2001-2013-1.pdf (accessed 11 January 2017). My thanks to a Bridget Williams Books reader for drawing my attention to this research.

28 Michael Sergel, 'Big Increase in Homeless People in Auckland', *Newstalk ZB*, 2 June 2015, www.newstalkzb.co.nz/news/auckland/big-increase-in-homeless-people-in-auckland (accessed 4 April 2016).

29 Human Rights Commission/Te Kāhui Tika Tangata, 'Homelessness Part and Parcel of Christchurch's Social Crisis', 30 April 2015, www.hrc.co.nz/news/homelessness-part-and-parcel-christchurch-social-crisis (accessed 4 April 2016).

30 Elena McPhee, 'Marlborough Charity Concerned about Increasing Homeless Numbers', 29 March 2016, www.stuff.co.nz/business/farming/agribusiness/78333646/marlborough-charity-concerned-about-increasing-homeless-numbers (accessed 4 April 2016).

31 Statistics New Zealand/Tatauranga Aotearoa, 'New Zealand Definition of Homelessness: Update', 23 October 2015, www.stats.govt.nz/browse_for_stats/people_and_communities/housing/homelessness-defn-update-2015.aspx (accessed 4 April 2016).

32 These concerns are discussed in a brilliant report produced by the Auckland City Mission, *Speaking for Ourselves*, which documents the stories of 100 long-term food bank users, as part of the Family 100 Research Project. The report is www.aucklandcitymission.org.nz/uploads/file/Family%20100/City%20Mission%20Family100%20Speaking%20for%20Ourselves_website.pdf (accessed 4 April 2016).

33 I am very grateful to a Bridget Williams Books reader of this chapter, who nudged me towards this point.

34 I am indebted to Jane Kelsey, since it was only after my interview with her that I felt the need to address the challenge of contracting out in New Zealand policy-making.

35 See clause 17.6 of the contract, www.corrections.govt.nz/__data/assets/pdf_file/0010/674380/CMOP.pdf (accessed 8 April 2016).

36 See Atif Ansar, Bent Flyvbjerg, Alexander Budzier and Daniel Lunn, 'Big is Fragile: An Attempt at Theorizing Scale', forthcoming in Bent Flyvbjerg (ed.), *The Oxford Handbook of Megaproject Management*, Oxford University Press, 2017.

37 *Lab Tests Auckland Ltd v Auckland District Health Board* [2008] NZCA 835, [2009] 1 NZLR 776 at [22]. The

Supreme Court declined to hear the case on appeal.

38 Ibid., at [59].

39 Sandra Grey and Charles Sedgwick, 'The Contract State and Constrained Democracy: The Community and Voluntary Sector Under Threat', *Policy Quarterly*, 9, 3 (2013), p.7. My thanks, again to a Bridget Williams Books reviewer for pointing me to this resource.

40 Department of Corrections, 'Service Providers – Serco', www.corrections.govt.nz/about_us/working_with_us/partners/service_providers-Serco.html (accessed 8 April 2016).

41 House of Commons Committee of Public Accounts, 'Contracting Out Public Services to the Private Sector', Forty-Seventh Report of Session 2013–2014, 26 February 2014, www.publications.parliament.uk/pa/cm201314/cmselect/cmpubacc/777/777.pdf (accessed 8 April 2016).

42 See, for example, Jonathan Boston, *The State Under Contract*, Paul & Co Pub Consortium, 1995.

43 Jenesa Jeram and Bryce Wilkinson, 'Investing for Success: Social Impact Bonds and the Future of Public Services', The New Zealand Initiative, 2015, http://nzinitiative.org.nz/site/nzinitiative/files/Social%20Bonds%20-%20web.pdf (accessed 8 April 2016).

44 Robbie Nicol, 'Social Bonds', White Man Behind a Desk, 11 June 2015, www.youtube.com/watch?v=naqdZWjgak0 (accessed 8 April 2016).

45 Jeram and Wilkinson, 'Investing for Success', p.x.

chapter 7

1 See John Pratt and Marie Clark, 'Penal Populism in New Zealand', *Punishment and Society*, 7, 3 (2005), pp.303–22. Pratt and Clark focus on the 1985–99 period, but penal populism in New Zealand arguably continued through the Labour-led government of 1999–2008, and the National-led government from 2008 onwards.

2 Ibid. Pratt and Clark refer to the first and the third of these forces.

3 Generally tortious acts causing personal injury cannot be the subject of litigation, and are covered by ACC in New Zealand, but very severe cases (where what are known as 'exemplary damages' are awarded) can still result in compensation through the courts, despite the ACC bar. Prison rape would likely be such a case, where exemplary damages could be awarded.

4 All figures are taken from the World Prison Brief produced by the Institute for Criminal Policy Research, www.prisonstudies.org (accessed 15 March 2017).

5 See JustSpeak, *Unlocking Prisons: How We Can Improve New Zealand's Prison System*, Rimutaka Prison Printing Press, 2014, p.7. 2014 police crime statistics only show trends from 1996 onwards, but there is a steady decline in the total crime rate since then. There has been a slight increase in sexual assaults, but the murder rate has also trended downwards: 'New Zealand Crime Statistics 2014', Police National Headquarters, April 2014, pp.13, 14 and 16, www.police.govt.nz/sites/default/files/publications/crime-stats-national-20141231.pdf (accessed 11 January 2017).

6 It should be noted, however, that there is much anecdotal evidence that Māori offenders are less able to benefit from home detention, since those Māori who offend tend to have less stable family ties on which they can rely for home detention. It has also been noted that home detention turns a home into a prison and places a major burden on the families of offenders, especially women: see David Bullock, 'Home Detention as a Standalone Sentence', *New Zealand Law Students' Journal*, 2, 603 (2011), www.nzlii.org/nz/journals/NZLawStuJl/2011/5.html (accessed 15 March 2017).

7 This was said at a Families Commission forum on 11 May 2011. See analysis in: Editorial, 'Prisons: "A Moral and

Fiscal Failure?"', *Otago Daily Times*, 24 May 2011, www.odt.co.nz/opinion/editorial/161773/prisons-moral-and-fiscal-failure (accessed 7 November 2015).

8   I am not comparing prisoners to animals – as some of the worst penal populists do – but rather pointing out the sad reality that prisoners in New Zealand today are often treated like animals.

9   K. Anthony Appiah, 'What Will Future Generations Condemn Us For?', *Washington Post*, 26 September 2010, www.washingtonpost.com/wp-dyn/content/article/2010/09/24/AR2010092404113.html (accessed 1 November 2015).

10 See Angela Y. Davis, *Are Prisons Obsolete?*, Seven Stories Press, 2003.

11 See JustSpeak, *Unlocking Prisons*, p.63.

12 Michel Foucault, *Discipline and Punish*, Vintage Books, 1975, p.110.

13 Nicola Lacey and Hanna Pickard, 'To Blame or To Forgive? Reconciling Punishment and Forgiveness in Criminal Justice', *Oxford Journal of Legal Studies*, 2015, p.23.

14 See JustSpeak, *Unlocking Prisons*, p.60; Andrew Becroft used the phrase 'universities of crime' at several public talks from 2009 to 2011, and the phrase appears in Judge Andrew Becroft, 'How to Turn a Child Offender into an Adult Criminal: Ten Easy Steps', Children and the Law International Conference, 7 September 2009.

15 See Shadd Maruna, *Making Good: How Ex-Convicts Reform and Rebuild their Lives*, American Psychological Association, 2001.

16 JustSpeak, *Unlocking Prisons*, p.65. For more information about the harmful nature of at-risk units, see the Master's dissertation written by Alexis Harris on the use of at-risk units in New Zealand prisons: Alexis Harris, 'Care-Oriented Practice in At-Risk Units: Risks, Realities and Multi-Disciplinary Teams', Victoria University of Wellington Master's Thesis, 2015, http://researcharchive.vuw.ac.nz/xmlui/handle/10063/4997 (accessed 15 February 2017). Alexis is my sister.

17 Davis, *Are Prisons Obsolete?*, p.16.

18 JustSpeak, *Unlocking Prisons*, pp.63–64.

19 Ibid., p.67.

20 Ibid., p.64.

21 Synod Prison Task Group, 'Incarceration in New Zealand', 2011, p.2.

22 JustSpeak, *Unlocking Prisons*, p.55.

23 Harata Brown, 'Police Working on Unconscious Bias towards Māori', Māori Television, 29 November 2015, www.maoritelevision.com/news/national/police-working-on-unconscious-bias-towards-maori (accessed 11 January 2017). My thanks to a Bridget Williams Books reader for drawing this to my attention.

24 Ibid., p.7.

25 Ibid., pp.17–21.

26 On how what is 'fitting' and 'proportionate' can change over time and across context, see: Lacey and Pickard, 'To Blame or To Forgive?'.

27 JustSpeak, *Unlocking Prisons*, p.50.

28 There are, of course, some 'victimless crimes'. Some suggest that drug offences are of this kind, and that New Zealand should accordingly consider the decriminalisation of certain drugs. At the time of writing this book, the Canadian Liberal Party had just won the 2015 election and had promised to decriminalise marijuana.

29 Often this is described in terms of 'risk' or 'dangerousness'. These terms have little or no scientific basis.

30 There is useful analysis of this approach in: Allegra M. McLeod, 'Prison Abolition and Grounded Justice', *UCLA Law Review*, 62 (2015), pp.1156–239, at pp.1161–72.

31 Cited in Synod Prison Task Group, 'Incarceration in New Zealand', p.2.

32 Sentencing Act 2002, s 15A.

33 Sentencing Act 2002, s 24A.

34 For some small steps that can be taken in the direction of reducing Māori over-representation, see: JustSpeak, *Māori and the Criminal Justice System: A Youth Perspective*, Te Puni Kōkiri, 2012, www.rethinking.org.nz/assets/JustSpeak/JustSpeak%20-%20Maori%20and%20the%20Criminal%20Justice%20System%20-%20A%20Youth%20Perspective.pdf (accessed 1 November 2015).

35 International Centre for Prison Studies, 'World Prison Brief – New Zealand', www.prisonstudies.org/country/new-zealand (accessed 1 November 2015).

36 See discussion of this in, for example, Science for Environment Policy, 'Positive Environmental Messages Help Encourage Behavioural Change', European Commission, 2 December 2010, http://ec.europa.eu/environment/integration/research/newsalert/pdf/220na5_en.pdf (accessed 11 January 2017).

37 This phrase was originally used by Angela Davis: see University of Connecticut Advance, 'Political Activist Davis Critical of Prison System', http://advance.uconn.edu/1997/971027/10279702.htm (accessed 1 November 2015).

38 Thanks to Sarah Kuper, also involved with JustSpeak, for helpful conversations on this topic.

39 Ministry of Justice, *Strengthening New Zealand's Legislative Response to Family Violence: A Public Discussion Document*, Minister's Foreword, 2015.

40 Radio New Zealand, 'Feature: Tackling Rape Culture in New Zealand', 7 December 2014, www.radionz.co.nz/news/on-the-inside/261061/feature-tackling-rape-culture-in-nz (accessed 2 November 2015).

41 All of these statistics are taken from two documents by the New Zealand Family Violence Clearinghouse: New Zealand Family Violence Clearinghouse, 'Data Summary: Child Sexual Abuse', 4 June 2015, https://nzfvc.org.nz/sites/nzfvc.org.nz/files/DS4-Child-Sexual-Abuse-2015-0.pdf (accessed 2 November 2015); and New Zealand Family Violence Clearinghouse, 'Data Summary: Adult Sexual Violence', 5 June 2015, https://nzfvc.org.nz/sites/nzfvc.org.nz/files/DS5-Adult-Sexual-Violence-2015-0.pdf (accessed 2 November 2015).

42 Law Commission/Te Aka Matua o te Ture, *The Justice Response to Victims of Sexual Violence: Criminal Trials and Alternative Processes*, Report 136, December 2015, www.lawcom.govt.nz/sites/default/files/projectAvailableFormats/NZLC-R136-The-Justice-Response-to-Victims-of-Sexual-Violence.pdf (accessed 15 January 2017).

43 Frances Joychild, 'Continuing the Conversation ... The Fading Star of the Rule of Law', ADLSI, 5 February 2015, www.adls.org.nz/for-the-profession/news-and-opinion/2015/2/5/continuing-the-conversation-%E2%80%A6-the-fading-star-of-the-rule-of-law (accessed 3 November 2015).

44 See Justice Geoffrey Venning, 'Access to Justice – A Constant Quest?', Address to New Zealand Bar Association Conference, 7 August 2015; and Justice Helen Winkelmann, 'Access to Justice – Who Needs Lawyers?', Ethel Benjamin Address, 7 November 2014. Both are available through www.courtsofnz.govt.nz (accessed 3 November 2015).

45 I'm grateful for conversations on this subject with Fred Wilmot-Smith.

46 Justice Joe Williams, a High Court Judge, has been instrumental in advancing the use of te reo Māori in

courts and encouraging Māori language learning by judges. It should be noted that there is not unanimous support for rangatahi courts. Moana Jackson has in the past criticised rangatahi courts for bringing European notions of justice into marae, but expressed more support for the initiative in 2015: Toby Manhire, 'Unlocking Maori Identity: Keeping New Zealand's Indigenous People Out of Jail', *The Guardian*, 15 August 2015, www. theguardian.com/world/2015/aug/15/regaining-maori-identity-and-keeping-them-out-of-new-zealands-jails (accessed 8 November 2015).

47 Moana Jackson, *He Whaipaanga Hou: Māori and the Criminal Justice System – A New Perspective*, Ministry of Justice, 1988. The report is not widely available and was not posted online at the time of this book's writing. The Ministry of Justice should be encouraged to post this online, to further disseminate the Ministry's own past ideas.

48 A Māori Centre for Cultural Research was created in the form of Ngā Pae o te Māramatanga in 2002. However, its funding has been jeopardised, especially under the National-led government, and the Centre would benefit from more stable funding arrangements.

49 Sian Elias, 'Changing Our World', International Association of Women Judges' Conference, 4 May 2006.

50 Susan Glazebrook, 'Looking through the Glass: Gender Equality at the Senior Level of New Zealand's Legal Profession', Chapman Tripp – Women in Law, 16 September 2010.

51 See: Elias, 'Changing Our World'; and Glazebrook, 'Looking through the Glass'.

52 Susan Glazebrook, 'It is Just a Matter of Time and Other Myths', Get Up and Speak 2013, 15 August 2013.

53 See 'Courts of New Zealand: Judicial Appointments', http://courtsofnz.govt.nz/about/judges/appointments (accessed 8 November 2015).

54 This idea is also supported by Geoffrey Palmer and Andrew Butler in: Geoffrey Palmer and Andrew Butler, *A Constitution for Aotearoa New Zealand*, Victoria University Press, 2016, pp.137–41.

55 Jeremy Paxman, 'Who are the High Court Judges?', *Financial Times*, 30 October 2015, www.ft.com/cms/ s/2/49022de6-7d91-11e5-98fb-5a6d4728f74e.html (accessed 7 November 2015).

chapter 8

1 Iris Murdoch, 'The Sublime and the Good', *The Chicago Review*, 13, 3 (Autumn 1959), pp.42–55, at p.51. This is actually Murdoch's definition of love, but it captures well what 'care' and 'love' have in common.

2 My thanks go to David Cohen for this formulation.

3 The term was coined by Guy Standing, see, for example: *The Precariat: The New Dangerous Class*, Bloomsbury, 2014.

4 I first developed the idea in a blog co-written by Philip McKibbin: Max Harris and Philip McKibbin, 'The Politics of Love', *The Aotearoa Project*, 20 May 2015, https://theaotearoaproject.wordpress.com/2015/05/20/ the-politics-of-love-max-harris-and-philip-mckibbin (accessed 13 January 2017). I discuss a love-based politics in more depth in 'The Politics of Love' in Morgan Godfery (ed.), *The Interregnum: Rethinking New Zealand*, Bridget Williams Books, 2016. My thanks also go to Jordan Carter for an early conversation in 2012 about the place of love in politics, which helped to develop my thinking on the subject.

5 I draw the phrase 'circle of concern' from the work of Martha Nussbaum. Nussbaum uses this phrase in *Political Emotions: Why Love Matters for Justice*, Harvard University Press, 2015.

6 Louise Humpage, 'Towards Welfare Solutions: Public Attitudes and How We Should "Frame" the Debate', in M. Claire Dale et al. (eds), *Rethinking Welfare for the Twenty-First Century*, report from the forum held at University of Auckland Business School, 10 September 2010, p.62 (citing 'Perry unpublished 2004'), www.

cpag.org.nz/assets/PROCEEDINGS%20of%20the%20Forum%2010%20September%202010%20Final%20%282%29.pdf (accessed 16 August 2016).

7   Welfare Justice: The Alternative Welfare Working Group, 'Welfare for All – Reflections and Recommendations: A Contribution to the Welfare Reform Debate', Caritas Aotearoa, 2010, p.49, www.cpag.org.nz/assets/Welfare%20Reform/101201%20Welfare%20Justice%20for%20All%20AWWG.pdf (accessed 16 August 2016).

8   Sendhil Mullainathan and Eldar Shafir, *Scarcity: The New Science of Having Less and How it Defines Our Lives*, Picador, 2014.

9   Welfare Justice: The Alternative Welfare Working Group, 'Welfare for All – Reflections and Recommendations', p.36.

10 Al Nisbet, *The Marlborough Express*, 29 April 2014.

11 Victoria University of Wellington, 'Courts More Lenient on White Collar Criminals', www.victoria.ac.nz/research/expertise/business-commerce/fraud-sentencing (accessed 16 August 2016).

12 Kate Pereyra Garcia, 'Beneficiaries are Being Monitored by Social Media', *Radio New Zealand*, 10 February 2016, www.radionz.co.nz/news/national/296151/beneficiaries-being-monitored-online (accessed 16 August 2016).

13 Gareth Morgan, 'Why Do We Think Beneficiaries Are Nothing?', *The Morgan Foundation Blog*, 19 May 2015, http://morganfoundation.org.nz/why-do-we-think-beneficiaries-are-nothing (accessed 16 August 2016).

14 My thanks to a Bridget Williams Books reader for helping me to specify this point.

15 Kim Morton, Claire Gray, Anne Heins, Sue Carswell, 'Access to Justice for Beneficiaries: A Community Law Response', Community Law Canterbury, 2014, pp.31–32, www.bas.org.nz/wp-content/uploads/2015/03/Access-to-Justice-online-edition-11-Dec.pdf (accessed 16 August 2016).

16 This point has been made particularly strongly by Eliza Prestidge Oldfield in 'From the Cradle', *The Aotearoa Project*, 6 July 2015, https://theaotearoaproject.wordpress.com/2015/07/06/from-the-cradle (accessed 3 January 2017).

17 Mike O'Brien, 'Reflections: The Morning's Contributions and the Local Context', in Dale et al. (eds), *Rethinking Welfare for the Twenty-First Century*, p.35.

18 Ibid.

19 The Clark-led Labour Government did not increase benefit levels between 1999 and 2008. The Key-led National Government increased benefit levels in 2015.

20 Sue Bradford, 'Political Realities and Strategies: A Brief Reflection on Today's Forum', in Dale et al. (eds), *Rethinking Welfare for the Twenty-First Century*, p.67.

21 Grant Duncan, 'Expanding ACC to Cover Sickness', *Briefing Papers*, 13 June 2016, http://briefingpapers.co.nz/2016/06/expanding-acc-to-cover-sickness (accessed 18 August 2016).

22 Report of the Royal Commission of Inquiry, 'Compensation for Personal Injury in New Zealand', Government Printer, 1967, p.19. My views have been strengthened by many wonderful conversations on this topic, and others, with Ted Thomas.

23 Ibid., p.26.

24 Ibid.

25 Ibid., p.26.

26 Social Services Committee, 'Inquiry into the Quality of Care and Service Provision for People with

Disabilities', September 2008, p.20, www.parliament.nz/resource/en-NZ/48DBSCH_SCR4194_1/ cb220d2e3ba25dc33dec0b28b29b30578d110dd5 (accessed 19 August 2016).

27 Hilary Stace, 'Disability Policy in New Zealand', *Briefing Papers*, 15 February 2016, http://briefingpapers. co.nz/2015/02/disability-policy-in-new-zealand (accessed 19 August 2016). Disabilities can take many different forms, including invisible disabilities and mental disabilities, as Latifa Daud has pointed out. Daud has written excellently about disability and other issues, sometimes drawing on her own experience as a person with a disability. Her writing is available at http://thedailyblog.co.nz/author/latifa-daud (accessed 19 August 2016).

28 Disabled Persons Assembly NZ, 'Submission to "More Effective Social Services Inquiry"', 2 December 2014, p.6.

29 Committee on the Rights of Persons with Disabilities, 'Concluding Observations on the Initial Report of New Zealand', 31 October 2014, CRPD/C/NZL/CO/1, at [27], http://tbinternet.ohchr.org/_layouts/ treatybodyexternal/Download.aspx?symbolno=CRPD%2fC%2fNZL%2fCO%2f1&Lang=en (accessed 22 August 2016).

30 New Zealand Government, 'Government Response to the United Nations Committee on the Rights of Persons with Disabilities' Concluding Observations on New Zealand', June 2015, at [14].

31 Hilary Stace, 'Some Aspects of New Zealand's Disability History – Part One', *Public Address*, 3 November 2014, http://publicaddress.net/access/some-aspects-of-new-zealands-disability-history (accessed 22 August 2016).

32 The case is called *Ministry of Health v Atkinson* [2012] NZCA 184, [2012] 3 NZLR 456.

33 *Idea Services Ltd v Dickson* [2011] NZCA 14, [2011] 2 NZLR 522.

34 Social Services Committee, 'Inquiry into the Quality of Care', p.19.

35 Public Service Association and Service and Food Workers Union, 'Up Where We Belong: Raising the Status of Disability Support Work', November 2009, www.sfwu.org.nz/files/Up%20Where%20We%20Belong%20 Resource%20Aug09.pdf (accessed 23 August 2016).

36 Disabled Persons Assembly NZ, 'Submission', p.8.

37 Jackie Blue, 'Caring Counts and Beyond', SFWU Central Region Women's Conference, 5 November 2014, www. hrc.co.nz/news/dr-jackie-blue-caring-counts-and-beyond (accessed 22 August 2016).

38 The Human Rights Commission/Te Kāhui Tika Tangata, *Caring Counts/Tautiaki Tika*, 2012, www.hrc.co.nz/ files/1214/2360/8576/Caring_Counts_Report.pdf (accessed 22 August 2016).

39 The 2010 New Zealand General Social Survey showed young people are even more likely to feel lonely than older people: 18 per cent of young adults felt lonely all, most, or some of the time, compared to 11 per cent of older people. See Statistics New Zealand/Tatauranga Aotearoa, 'Loneliness in New Zealand: Findings from the New Zealand General Social Survey', www.stats.govt.nz/browse_for_stats/people_and_communities/ older_people/loneliness-in-nz-2010-NZGSS.aspx (accessed 22 August 2016).

40 Sue Bourne (director), *The Age of Loneliness*, BBC, released January 2016.

41 One good idea, worth more thought, is Owen Jones's proposal for a national government-supported scheme for young people to volunteer to spend time with the elderly. Owen Jones, 'The John Lewis Ad Trains a Telescope on the Scourge of Loneliness', *The Guardian*, 6 November 2015, www.theguardian.com/commentisfree/2015/ nov/06/john-lewis-advert-christmas-loneliness-ageing (accessed 19 March 2017).

42 Guy Standing, *The Precariat: The New Dangerous Class*, Bloomsbury, 2011. The term 'the precariat' combines 'precarious' and proletariat'. The reference to 'truncated status' is on p.8 of the book.

43 New Zealand Council of Trade Unions/Te Kauae Kaimahi, *Under Pressure: A Detailed Report into Insecure*

Work in New Zealand, October 2013, p.10, http://union.org.nz/sites/union.org.nz/files/Under-Pressure-Detailed-Report-Final.pdf (accessed 25 August 2016).

44 My thanks to an anonymous Bridget Williams Books reviewer for pressing me towards this point.

45 New Zealand Council of Trade Unions/Te Kauae Kaimahi, *Under Pressure*, pp.24–27.

46 Patrick O'Meara, 'Insecure Workers Forgoing Benefits', 17 November 2014, *Radio New Zealand*, www.radionz.co.nz/news/national/259483/insecure-workers-forgoing-benefits (accessed 25 August 2016).

47 My thanks to Max Rashbrooke for conversations on this topic.

48 There are some shortcomings of using this as a yardstick, since it may be that Jobseeker Support is not generous enough to ensure a minimum standard of living.

49 Max Harris and Sebastiaan Bierema, 'A Universal Basic Income for New Zealand', *The Future of Work*, 2016, https://d3n8a8pro7vhmx.cloudfront.net/nzlabour/pages/4208/attachments/original/1461211267/Background_Paper_-_A_Universal_Basic_Income_for_New_Zealand.pdf?1461211267 (accessed 26 August 2016). I have also spent time on the Labour Party's Jobs and Growth Committee exploring related issues.

50 I have explored this question in a blog written for *openDemocracy*: Max Harris, 'Will a Universal Basic Income Make us Lonely?', *openDemocracy*, 25 May 2016, www.opendemocracy.net/transformation/max-harris/will-universal-basic-income-make-us-lonely (accessed 26 August 2016).

51 Thomas Piketty, 'Basic Income or Fair Wage?', *Le Monde* Blog, 13 December 2016, http://piketty.blog.lemonde.fr/2016/12/13/basic-income-or-fair-wage (accessed 16 February 2017).

52 Raine Tiessalo, 'Finland Tests Giving Every Citizen a Basic Income', *The Independent*, 26 August 2016, www.independent.co.uk/news/business/news/universal-basic-income-finland-ubi-test-scheme-experiment-a7211241.html (accessed 26 August 2016).

53 Sue Ryall and Stephen Blumenfeld, 'The State of New Zealand Union Membership in 2014', Victoria University of Wellington Centre of Labour, Employment, and Work, 2014, p.3, www.victoria.ac.nz/som/clew/files/The-state-of-New-Zealand-Union-membership-in-2014-FINALwithtables.pdf (accessed 29 August 2016).

54 Andrew Morrison, 'The Employment Contracts Act and its Economic Impact', New Zealand Parliamentary Library, 1996, p.7, www.parliament.nz/resource/en-NZ/00PLSocRP96021/37b29473b64b0366d9217a27c32b48c7d35e22ca (accessed 29 August 2016).

55 It's not clear this would violate the New Zealand Bill of Rights Act 1990, either. It would arguably be a reasonable limit (under section 5) on the right to freedom of association.

56 This term is taken, of course, from Cass Sunstein, *Nudge: Improving Decisions about Health, Wealth, and Happiness*, Yale University Press, 2008.

57 Sunny Taylor, 'The Right Not to Work: Power and Disability', *Monthly Review*, 2004, http://monthlyreview.org/2004/03/01/the-right-not-to-work-power-and-disability (accessed 29 August 2016).

58 Maurizio Lazzarato, *Governing by Debt*, Semiotext(e), 2015, p.247.

59 Ibid., p.123.

60 Liz Alderman, 'In Sweden, An Experiment Turns Shorter Workdays into Bigger Gains', *New York Times*, 20 May 2016, www.nytimes.com/2016/05/21/business/international/in-sweden-an-experiment-turns-shorter-workdays-into-bigger-gains.html?_r=0 (accessed 29 August 2016).

61 *The Economist*, 'France's 6pm E-mail Ban: Not What it Seemed', 20 April 2014, www.economist.com/blogs/charlemagne/2014/04/frances-6pm-e-mail-ban (accessed 29 August 2016). A similar announcement was made in Western press in 2016 when no full ban on evening emails had been instituted.

chapter 9

1   Mike Joy, *Polluted Inheritance: New Zealand's Freshwater Crisis*, Bridget Williams Books, 2015, p.46.

2   Ibid., p.18.

3   Ralph Chapman, *Time of Useful Consciousness: Acting Urgently on Climate Change*, Bridget Williams Books, 2015, p.35.

4   Ibid., p.45.

5   See Jason Hickel, 'Clean Energy Can't Save Us – Only a New Economic System Can', 16 July 2016, *The Guardian*, www.theguardian.com/global-development-professionals-network/2016/jul/15/clean-energy-wont-save-us-economic-system-can (accessed 5 September 2016).

6   Tom Crompton, *Common Cause: The Case for Working with our Cultural Values*, WWF-UK, 2010, http://assets.wwf.org.uk/downloads/common_cause_report.pdf (accessed 5 September 2010). My thanks to Kirk Serpes for first telling me about the report at a Generation Zero hui in 2012.

7   Cited in ibid.

8   Ibid., p.40.

9   See, for example, the work of Moana Jackson or: Māori Law Review, 'Review of Te Ture Whenua Māori Act 1993 – Te Ture Whenua Māori Bill – Dispute Resolution', June 2016, http://maorilawreview.co.nz/2016/06/review-of-te-ture-whenua-maori-act-1993-te-ture-whenua-maori-bill-dispute-resolution (accessed 5 September 2016).

10 Andrea Tunks, 'Tangata Whenua Ethics and Climate Change', *New Zealand Journal of Environmental Law*, 1 (1997), pp.67–124.

11 See Articles 25 and 29, United Nations Declaration on the Rights of Indigenous Peoples.

12 Naomi Klein, *This Changes Everything: Capitalism vs the Climate*, Allen Lane, 2014, p.131.

13 Productivity Commission/Te Kōmihana Whai Hua o Aotearoa, *Better Urban Planning: Draft Report*, August 2016, p.11, www.productivity.govt.nz/sites/default/files/better-urban-planning-draft-report_2.pdf (accessed 5 September 2016).

14 Klein, *This Changes Everything*, p.450.

15 Ibid., p.459.

16 Robin McKie, 'Word Will Pass Crucial 2C Global Warming Limit, Experts Warn', *The Guardian*, 10 October 2015, www.theguardian.com/environment/2015/oct/10/climate-2c-global-warming-target-fail (accessed 6 September 2016).

17 The case was *Genesis Power Ltd v Greenpeace New Zealand Inc* [2007] NZCA 569, [2008] 1 NZLR 803; the judge was Justice William Young, then President of the Court of Appeal. He said at [16]: 'New Zealand's contribution to worldwide GHG emissions is comparatively low (less than 0.3 per cent). New Zealand's current policies, however, are based on the view that it is in the national interest to contribute to effective global action to reduce emissions.' The decision was later upheld in the Supreme Court.

18 This analysis is drawn from: Geoff Simmons and Paul Young, *Climate Cheats: How New Zealand is Cheating on our Climate Change Commitments, and What We Can Do to Set it Right*, Morgan Foundation, 2016, p.11, p.14 and p.29, http://morganfoundation.org.nz/wp-content/uploads/2016/04/ClimateCheat_Report9.pdf (accessed 7 September 2016).

19 Ibid., p.31.

20 Chapman, *Time of Useful Consciousness*, pp.33–35.

21 Simmonds and Young, *Climate Cheats*, pp.39–40.

22 Diane Toomey, 'Interview [with Stewart Elgie]: How British Columbia Gained by Putting a Price on Carbon', *Environment 360*, 30 April 2015, http://e360.yale.edu/feature/how_british_columbia_gained_by_putting_a_price_on_carbon/2870 (accessed 8 September 2016).

23 Carbon Tax Center, 'British Columbia/Canada', 2016, www.carbontax.org/where-carbon-is-taxed/british-columbia (accessed 8 September 2016). The Carbon Tax Center is a US-based advocacy group; I have therefore only used their data when they have been critical of British Columbia's record.

24 See *The Economist*, 'British Columbia's Carbon Tax: The Evidence Mounts', 31 July 2014, www.economist.com/blogs/americasview/2014/07/british-columbias-carbon-tax (accessed 8 September 2016).

25 Eduardo Porter, 'Does a Carbon Tax Work? Ask British Columbia?', *The New York Times*, 1 March 2016, www.nytimes.com/2016/03/02/business/does-a-carbon-tax-work-ask-british-columbia.html?_r=0 (accessed 8 September 2016).

26 This is Ralph Chapman's suggestion in his book: Chapman, *Time of Useful Consciousness*.

27 Naomi Klein, 'Let Them Drown: The Violence of Othering in a Drowning World', Edward Said London Lecture, 2 June 2016, *London Review of Books*, www.lrb.co.uk/v38/n11/naomi-klein/let-them-drown (accessed 8 September 2016).

28 New Zealand Agricultural Greenhouse Gas Research Centre and Pastoral Research Greenhouse Gas Consortium, *Reducing New Zealand's Agricultural Greenhouse Gases: What We Are Doing*, 2015, www.nzagrc.org.nz/home.html (accessed 8 September 2016).

29 New Zealand Agricultural Greenhouse Gas Research Centre, *The Impact of Livestock Agriculture on Climate Change*, NZAGRC Factsheet, 2012, p.2.

30 *Reducing New Zealand's Agricultural Greenhouse Gases*, p.3.

31 Eva Wollenberg et al. (including Andrew Reisinger), 'Reducing Emissions from Agriculture to Meet the 2°C Target', *Global Change Biology*, first published online 11 July 2016.

32 *Reducing New Zealand's Agricultural Greenhouse Gases*, pp.9–11.

33 This research was done as part of the 'Climate Change' elective on the Master of Public Policy at the Blavatnik School of Government in 2013. A condensed summary of my research, with other policy options mentioned in brief, can be found at: Max Harris, 'Unlikely Friendship Could See New Zealand Lead the Way on Climate Change Issues', *Blavatnik School of Government Blog*, 1 July 2014, http://blogs.bsg.ox.ac.uk/2014/07/01/unlikely-friendship-could-see-nz-lead-way-on-climate-issues (accessed 8 September 2016).

34 My thanks to Louis Chambers for discussion on this topic.

35 Pure Advantage, *Our Forest Future*, 2016, http://pureadvantage.org/news/2016/04/22/our-forest-future (accessed 9 September 2016).

36 Generation Zero, 'Ways to #CuttheGap: Carbon Forestry', Generation Zero, www.generationzero.org/ways_to_cutthegap_carbon_forestry (accessed 9 September 2016).

37 Productivity Commission, *Better Urban Planning*, p.5.

38 Sian Elias, 'Righting Environmental Justice', Address to the Resource Management Law Association: Salmon Lecture, 25 July 2013.

39 Productivity Commission, *Better Urban Planning*, p.8.

40 Elias, 'Righting Environmental Justice', p.11.

41 Ibid., p.13.

42 Productivity Commission, *Better Urban Planning*, p.6.

43 Ibid., p.12.

44 I have drawn this insight, in part, from helpful conversations with Andrew Dean.

45 Parliamentary Commissioner for the Environment/Te Kaitiaki Taiao a Te Whare Pāremata, 'News & Insights', 1 March 2013, www.pce.parliament.nz/our-work/news-insights/proposed-changes-unbalance-rma-environment-commissioner (accessed 12 September 2016).

46 Productivity Commission, *Better Urban Planning*, pp.5 (on regulation), 11 (on upskilling) and 9 (on the Environment Court).

47 These are the subject of contentious New Zealand court decisions: the High Court decision in *Aoraki Water Trust v Meridian Energy* [2005] 2 NZLR 268 (HC) and the Supreme Court decision in *West Coast ENT Inc v Buller Coal Ltd* [2013] NZSC 87, [2014] 1 NZLR 32. There are good arguments for both decisions to be overruled (though the *Aoraki* case has had its effect restricted already by later judgments).

48 Particular thanks to Ralph Chapman for his helpful comments and suggestions on this chapter, and on the phrasing of this point.

49 See Pope Francis, *Laudato Si: Encyclical Letter of our Father On Care for our Common Home*, 2015, http://w2.vatican.va/content/francesco/en/encyclicals/documents/papa-francesco_20150524_enciclica-laudato-si.html (accessed 13 September 2016).

chapter 10

1 This chapter generally follows the view that sex refers to the biology and anatomy associated with men and women, whereas gender concerns the social construction of what it means to be 'male', 'female' and other gender identities. However, as Judith Butler has pointed out in *Gender Trouble*, Routledge, 1990, and as trans activists have noted, this distinction is overly simplistic: even what is 'biological' is shaped by social conditions and constructions.

2 BBC News, 'New Zealand Glass Ceiling Shattered', 24 August 2000, http://news.bbc.co.uk/1/hi/world/asia-pacific/894292.stm (accessed 23 December 2016).

3 Patrick Barkham, 'As Good As It Gets', *The Guardian (Gender)*, 17 July 2001, www.theguardian.com/world/2001/jul/17/gender.uk (accessed 23 December 2016).

4 Jackie Ashley, 'The New Statesman Profile – New Zealand, A Woman's Land', *The New Statesman*, 2 April 2001, www.newstatesman.com/node/153156 (accessed 23 December 2016).

5 Rowan Quinn, 'CEO Gender Imbalance "Gobsmacking"', Radio New Zealand, 13 May 2016, www.radionz.co.nz/news/national/303777/ceo-gender-imbalance-'gobsmacking' (accessed 23 December 2016).

6 Eleanor Ramsay and Judy McGregor, 'Sex and Power in New Zealand: Stalled at the Crossroads?', *The Conversation*, 14 February 2014, https://theconversation.com/sex-and-power-in-new-zealand-stalled-at-the-crossroads-22233 (accessed 23 December 2016).

7 Maire Dwyer, 'Sole Parents in Poverty: It's Time to Update the Policy Paradigm', *Policy Quarterly*, 11, 1 (2015), pp.19–24, at p.19.

8 The IMF has found that firms with a larger share of women in senior positions have a significantly higher return on assets in Europe: Lone Christiansen et al., 'Gender Diversity in Senior Positions and Firm Performance: Evidence from Europe', IMF Working Paper, WP 16/50, 2016, www.imf.org/external/pubs/ft/wp/2016/wp1650.pdf (accessed 26 December 2016).

9 See s 2A, Equal Pay Act 1972.

10 Catriona MacLennan, Vicky Mee and Judy McGregor, 'New Zealand Should Legislate to Promote Pay Equity', *New Zealand Herald*, 10 June 2016, www.nzherald.co.nz/nz/news/article.cfm?c_id=1&objectid=11654046 (accessed 28 December 2016).

11 *Service and Food Workers Union Nga Ringa Tota Inc v Terranova Homes and Care Ltd* [2013] NZEmpC 157 at [2].

12 See ibid., at [21] and [41] of the judgment.

13 Ibid., at [46] of the judgment.

14 Ibid., at [118] of the judgment.

15 *Terranova Homes & Care Ltd v Service and Food Workers Union Nga Ringa Tota Inc* [2014] NZCA 516, [2015] 2 NZLR 437.

16 See ibid., at [1], citing the Employment Court decision.

17 Ibid., at [39] of the judgment.

18 Ibid., at [83] of the judgment.

19 Recommendations of the Joint Working Group on Pay Equity Principles, 24 May 2016, www.ssc.govt.nz/sites/all/files/pay-equity-jwg-recommendations.pdf (accessed 27 December 2016).

20 See MacLennan, Mee and McGregor, 'New Zealand Should Legislate to Promote Pay Equity'.

21 See, for example, Nancy Fraser, 'Contradictions of Capital and Care', *New Left Review*, 100 (2016), https://newleftreview.org/II/100/nancy-fraser-contradictions-of-capital-and-care (accessed 27 December 2016).

22 Part of this is because one dominant strand of masculinity in New Zealand culture, which I discuss in the next section of this chapter.

23 Thanks to Eleanor Bishop for this point – and for her comments on this chapter as a whole.

24 Statistics New Zealand/Tatauranga Aotearoa, 'Time Use Survey: 2009/10', p.6, www.stats.govt.nz/browse_for_stats/people_and_communities/time_use/TimeUseSurvey_HOTP2009-10.aspx (accessed 27 December 2016).

25 Fraser, 'Contradictions of Capital and Care'.

26 Ibid.

27 See Hannah August, *No Country for Old Maids?: Talking About the 'Man Drought'*, Bridget Williams Books, 2015.

28 This material is drawn from: 'Tackling Māori Masculinity and Re-thinking Stereotypes', Interview of Brendan Hokowhitu by Kathryn Ryan, *Nine to Noon*, 23 March 2016, www.radionz.co.nz/national/programmes/ninetonoon/audio/201794353/tackling-maori-masculinity-and-re-thinking-stereotypes (accessed 28 December 2016).

29 Jock Phillips, *A Man's Country: The Image of the Pākehā Male – A History*, revised edition, Penguin, 1996, p.vii (Preface).

30 The 2016 incident involving the Chiefs rugby team and the treatment of a stripper, along with New Zealand rugby institutions' response to the incident, occurred while I was writing this book. That incident cast the need for this conversation into stark relief.

31 Grayson Perry, *The Descent of Man*, Penguin, 2016, p.145.

32 Eleanor Ainge Roy, '"We Have to Start Talking About It": New Zealand Suicide Rates Reach Record High', *The Guardian*, 19 October 2015, www.theguardian.com/world/2015/oct/19/we-have-to-start-talking-about-it-new-zealand-suicide-rates-hit-record-high (accessed 3 January 2017).

33 See, for example, Celia Lashlie, *He'll Be Ok: Growing Gorgeous Boys into Good Men*, Harper Collins, 2005.

34 'Tackling Māori Masculinity', *Nine to Noon*.

35 Tom Furley, 'NZ Sports Wants to Combat "Casual Homophobia"', Radio New Zealand, 31 May 2016, www. radionz.co.nz/news/national/305240/nz-sports-want-to-combat-'casual-homophobia' (accessed 29 December 2016).

36 Lloyd Burr, 'Key Refuses to Say Orlando Attack "Homophobic"', Newshub, 14 June 2016, www.newshub.co.nz/ home/politics/2016/06/key-refuses-to-say-orlando-attack-homophobic.html (accessed 29 December 2016).

37 On this point, see: Owen Jones, 'George Michael Was a Defiant Gay Icon. His Life Must Not Be Sanitised', *The Guardian*, 26 December 2016, www.theguardian.com/commentisfree/2016/dec/26/george-michael-defiant-gay-icon-sex-life-lgbt-rights (accessed 29 December 2016). Jones writes: 'Coming out wildly differs from person to person: it is an experience imposed upon gay men – and all LGBT people – by a society still far from entirely accepting us.'

38 See Human Rights Commission/Te Kāhui Tika Tangata, *To Be Who I Am/Kia Noho ki Tōku Anō Ao*, 2008, pp.3–4, www.hrc.co.nz/files/5714/2378/7661/15-Jan-2008_14-56-48_HRC_Transgender_FINAL.pdf (accessed 29 December 2016).

39 LudditeJourno (author), 'It's Raining Racism and Transphobia on my Pride Parade', *The Hand Mirror*, 22 February 2015, http://thehandmirror.blogspot.co.uk/2015/02/its-raining-racism-and-transphobia-on.html (accessed 29 December 2016).

40 Judith Butler, a prominent writer, has criticised the way that individuals such as Sheila Jeffreys have used social constructionist arguments to deny the agency of trans women. Butler has said: 'One problem with that view of social construction is that it suggests that what trans people feel about what their gender is, and should be, is itself "constructed" and, therefore, not real. And then the feminist police comes along to expose the construction and dispute a trans person's sense of their lived reality. I oppose this use of social construction absolutely, and consider it to be a false, misleading, and oppressive use of the theory.' See 'Judith Butler Addresses TERFs and the Work of Sheila Jeffreys and Janice Raymond', The TERFs, 1 May 2014, http:// theterfs.com/2014/05/01/judith-butler-addresses-terfs-and-the-work-of-sheila-jeffreys-and-janice-raymond (accessed 29 December 2016).

41 Ministry of Health, 'High-Cost Treatment Pool', www.health.govt.nz/our-work/hospitals-and-specialist-care/ high-cost-treatment-pool (accessed 29 December 2016).

42 Thanks to Heather Anderson for a conversation that helped me to think through some of these points; this analysis is as much hers as mine.

43 Of course, there are still barriers to entry to these social media platforms, including access to the internet and knowledge of key terms in some spaces.

44 My thanks to an anonymous Bridget Williams Books reviewer for underscoring this point.

chapter 11

1 The 2014 turnout was a slight increase on 2011 voter turnout, which reached an all-time low of 74.2 per cent: Electoral Commission/Te Kaitiaki Take Kōwhiri, 'General Elections, 1853–2014: Dates and Turnout', www. elections.org.nz/events/past-events/general-elections-1853-2014-dates-and-turnout (accessed 6 May 2016).

2 A list of ten professions had been given to the public: 'Trust Survey Results Revealed: MPs, Journalists Least Trusted', *New Zealand Herald*, 9 June 2015, www.nzherald.co.nz/nz/news/article.cfm?c_id=1&objectid=11462191 (accessed 6 May 2016).

3 Saul Alinsky, *Rules for Radicals: A Pragmatic Primer for Realistic Radicals*, Knopf, 1971, p.105.

4 Statistics New Zealand/Tatauranga Aotearoa, 'Loneliness in New Zealand: Findings from the 2010 NZ General

Social Survey', www.stats.govt.nz/browse_for_stats/people_and_communities/older_people/loneliness-in-nz-2010-NZGSS.aspx (accessed 23 May 2016).

5   In every age bracket, Māori voter turnout in the 2014 election was lower than non-Māori voter turnout. The differences range between 4 per cent and just under 10 per cent: the greatest gap exists in the 18- to 24-year-old bracket, where only 55 per cent of enrolled Māori voters voted, compared to around 65 per cent of non-Māori 18- to 24-year-olds. See: Electoral Commission/Te Kaitiaki Take Kōwhiri, 'New Zealand Voter Turnout Statistics', www.elections.org.nz/events/2014-general-election/election-results-and-reporting/2014-general-election-voter-turnout?electorate_name=All+electorates&voter_descent=2 (accessed 20 May 2016).

6   Constitutional Arrangements Committee (New Zealand Parliament), 'Inquiry to Review New Zealand's Existing Constitutional Arrangements', Forty-seventh Parliament, August 2005, p.26, www.converge.org.nz/pma/cacrep05.pdf (accessed 24 May 2016).

7   Constitutional Advisory Panel/Ko Ranga Kaupapa Ture, *New Zealand's Constitution: A Report on a Conversation - He Kōtuinga Kōrero mō Te Kaupapa Ture o Aotearoa*, November 2013, p.16, www.ourconstitution.org.nz/store/doc/FR_Full_Report.pdf (accessed 24 May 2016).

8   Ministry of Education, *The New Zealand Curriculum*, 2007, p.9.

9   Ibid., pp.10 and 12, respectively.

10 Electoral Commission/Te Kaitiaki Take Kōwhiri, '2014 General Election Voter Turnout Statistics', www.elections.org.nz/events/2014-general-election/election-results-and-reporting/2014-general-election-voter-turnout (accessed 19 March 2017).

11 Lee Suckling, 'Should We Teach Civics in School?', *New Zealand Herald*, 3 September 2014, www.nzherald.co.nz/lifestyle/news/article.cfm?c_id=6&objectid=11318328 (accessed 24 May 2016).

12 Rachel Bolstad, 'Participating and Contributing?: The Role of School and Community in Supporting Civic and Citizenship Education – New Zealand Results from the International Civics and Citizenship Study', New Zealand Council for Educational Research, p.30, www.nzcer.org.nz/system/files/Participating-and-Contributing-The-Role-of-School-and-Community.pdf (accessed 31 May 2016). The report notes: 'We looked at New Zealand students' responses in relation to the other ICCS countries. The largest difference between New Zealand students and the ICCS average was students' involvement in groups of young people campaigning for an issue (Schulz et al., 2010, pp.132–133). The mean response for New Zealand students (14%) was 15 percentage points below the ICCS average (29%). New Zealand students scored slightly below the ICCS average for the following activities: participation/involvement with an environmental organisation, participation/involvement with human rights organisations.'

13 Di White, 'The State of Civics Education', *The Wireless*, 17 February 2014, http://thewireless.co.nz/themes/knowledge/the-state-of-civics-education (accessed 24 May 2016).

14 While this is not a new concern with civics education, I should credit then deputy prime minister Bill English with raising this possibility in a discussion in April 2016.

15 Department for Education, 'National Curriculum in England: Citizenship Programmes of Study for Key Stages 3 and 4 (Statutory Guidance)', 11 September 2013, www.gov.uk/government/publications/national-curriculum-in-england-citizenship-programmes-of-study/national-curriculum-in-england-citizenship-programmes-of-study-for-key-stages-3-and-4 (accessed 31 May 2016).

16 As far as I know, this legal point has not been settled in New Zealand. My thanks to Ralph Hall for drawing it to my attention.

17 See Sandra Grey and Charles Sedgwick, 'The Contract State and Constrained Democracy: The Community and Voluntary Sector Under Threat', *Policy Quarterly*, 9, 3 (2013).

18 The phrase 'high-energy democracy' comes from Roberto Unger's work. See, for example: Institute for Government, 'Big Thinkers: Roberto Mangabeira Unger on Empowered Democracy in the UK', 15 November 2013, www.instituteforgovernment.org.uk/events/big-thinkers-roberto-mangabeira-unger-empowered-democracy-uk (accessed 7 June 2016).

19 See discussion of this in Chapter 6.

20 It is somewhat surprising that principles for government procurement are not set down in legislation, and have only the status of 'principles'. A move to a more robust legislative footing for these principles is another long-term step that ought to be considered to ensure stability and clarity for contractors, subject to whether contracting continues to be used as an instrument of government action.

21 Victoria University of Wellington, 'Public Sector Advice Not Always "Free or Frank"', 13 August 2015, www.victoria.ac.nz/news/2015/08/public-sector-advice-not-always-free-and-frank (accessed 13 June 2016).

22 Thanks to a Bridget Williams Books reader for making this point.

23 Richard Mulgan, 'What Future for Free and Frank Advice?', Address to Institute of Public Administration New Zealand, 30 May 2012, www.ipanz.org.nz/Folder?Action=View%20File&Folder_id=84&File=IPANZ%20Distinguished%20Lecture%2030%20May%202012.pdf (accessed 13 June 2016).

24 See Victoria University of Wellington, 'Public Sector Advice Not Always "Free or Frank"'.

25 Geoffrey Palmer, 'The Constitution and the Public Service', speech to the Public Service Associaion, 28 November 2016, www.psa.org.nz/assets/Uploads/The-Constitution-and-the-Public-Service.pdf (accessed 19 March 2017).

26 William Renwick, 'Beeby, Clarence Edward', Te Ara – the Encyclopedia of New Zealand, www.teara.govt.nz/en/biographies/5b17/beeby-clarence-edward (accessed 14 June 2016). Beeby is also the subject of a documentary in production at the time of the writing of this book.

27 See Global Centre for Public Service Excellence, 'From New Public Management to New Public Passion: Restoring the Intrinsic Motivation of Public Officials', 2015, www.undp.org/content/dam/undp/library/capacity-development/English/Singapore%20Centre/NotesPSE1_PublicPassion.pdf (accessed 14 June 2015).

28 See Hamish Rutherford, 'Public servant numbers climb', Stuff, 5 December 2014, www.stuff.co.nz/national/politics/63849330/public-servant-numbers-climb (accessed 14 June 2016).

29 Adam Bennett, 'Civil Servants Told to Show Their Colours', New Zealand Herald, 11 May 2011, www.nzherald.co.nz/nz/news/article.cfm?c_id=1&objectid=10644152 (accessed 14 June 2016).

30 One matter that is not discussed in this chapter, but which requires further debate, is the physical design and layout of New Zealand's Parliament. The current Parliament is austere, old-fashioned and distinctly British in design. While symbolic change is only part of the change to parliamentary processes that is needed, there could be further discussion about how Parliament might jettison symbols and rituals that serve only to alienate the public, and better incorporate aspects of New Zealand's bicultural and multicultural traditions.

31 See Holly Walker, 'Feminism and Silence', in Morgan Godfery (ed.), The Interregnum: Rethinking New Zealand, Bridget Williams Books, 2016, p.112.

32 Ibid., pp.121–22.

33 I saw this done in Adelaide, South Australia, under the premiership of Mike Rann, while I worked there as an intern in early 2008.

34 Max Harris and Marek Sullivan, 'How a "Politics of Listening" Could Change Britain', 19 February 2016, The Staggers (The New Statesman Online), www.newstatesman.com/politics/staggers/2016/02/how-politics-listening-could-change-britain (accessed 20 June 2016).

35 Ibid.

36 Ibid.

37 In 2011, right-leaning lobbyist Barrie Saunders was appointed to the board of TVNZ. In 2012, former National Party chief of staff Richard Long was appointed to the board of TVNZ. The National-led government also appointed Stephen McElrea, John Key's electorate chair in Helensville, to the board of NZ on Air. These are but three examples. Labour-led governments of the past have also made political appointments in this area.

38 Mel Bunce, a UK-based New Zealand academic, made this point to me in conversation.

39 Some sports rely on private TV rights for funding, as Mel Bunce noted to me in conversation. Decisions would have to be made carefully, in light of this. More explanation is also needed about how free-to-air sports coverage builds community. One argument is that free-to-air sports coverage makes sports viewing easier, increasing the number of those able to watch sports, making it more likely that groups of people can watch sport together, and providing a common experience that can be the basis for friendship or at least conversation.

40 New Zealand music writer Alaister Moughan has argued compellingly that NZ on Air is caught between commercial and public interest imperatives in the way it funds New Zealand music; it is arguable that this tension might be resolved through situating NZ on Air squarely within a new public broadcaster. See Alaister J. Moughan, 'Reflecting and Devolving Identity and Culture: Is New Zealand's Public Music Funding Model "Making Tracks" Achieving its Objectives?', New York University Master's Thesis, 2015, www.scribd.com/doc/277214707/Reflecting-and-Developing-Identity-and-Culture-Is-New-Zealand-s-Public-Music-Funding-Model-Making-Tracks-Achieving-its-Objectives (accessed 27 June 2016).

41 See p.5 of: McGuinness Institute, *Proceedings of the Civics and Media Project: A Report on Three Workshops Held in 2015*, May 2016.

42 Farrar supported a version of the proposal in 2009, though he would include NZ On Air and 'maybe' Māori TV: David Farrar, 'Bye Bye Charter', *Kiwiblog*, 10 December 2009, www.kiwiblog.co.nz/2009/12/bye_bye_charter.html (accessed 27 June 2016).

43 New Zealand First, 'Policy: Broacasting and ICT', http://nzfirst.org.nz/policy/broadcasting-ict (accessed 27 June 2016).

44 Mihingarangi Forbes, 'Navigating the Waters of Māori Broadcasting', *The Pantograph Punch*, 26 June 2016, http://pantograph-punch.com/post/navigating-the-waters-of-maori-broadcasting (accessed 27 June 2016).

45 Andrew Dean, *Ruth, Roger and Me: Debts and Legacies*, Bridget Williams Books, 2015, p.36.

46 Ibid., p.37, citing Karen Nairn, Jane Higgins and Judith Sligo, *Children of Rogernomics: A Neoliberal Generation Leaves School*, Otago University Press, 2012, pp.167–68.

47 Henry A. Giroux, 'Neoliberalism, Youth, and the Leasing of Higher Education', pp.30–53, in Dave Hill and Ravi Kumar (eds), *Global Neoliberalism and Education and Its Consequences*, Routledge, 2009, p.40 (citing Tannock, 2006, p.49).

48 Charlotte Frank, 'Germany's Scaling Back of National Service Leaves Voluntary Sector Confused', *The Guardian*, 22 November 2010, www.theguardian.com/commentisfree/2010/nov/22/germany-national-service-changes-voluntary-sector (accessed 27 June 2016).

chapter 12

1 See Morgan Godfery (ed.), *The Interregnum: Rethinking New Zealand*, Bridget Williams Books, 2016.

2 Nancy Fraser, 'The End of Progressive Neoliberalism', *Dissent*, 2 January 2017, www.dissentmagazine.org/online_articles/progressive-neoliberalism-reactionary-populism-nancy-fraser (accessed 13 January 2017).

3 'New Labour Because Britain Deserves Better', Labour Party Manifesto, General Election 1997, www.politicsresources.net/area/uk/man/lab97.htm (accessed 14 January 2017).

4   Mandelson acknowledged making these comments, and resiled from them, in 2012: Shiv Malik, 'Peter Mandelson Gets Nervous about People Getting "Filthy Rich"', *The Guardian*, 26 January 2012, www.theguardian.com/politics/2012/jan/26/mandelson-people-getting-filthy-rich (accessed 14 January 2017).

5   See Duncan Walker, 'How Prisons Became So Busy', BBC News, 3 April 2006, http://news.bbc.co.uk/1/hi/uk/4841938.stm (accessed 20 September 2016).

6   See, for example, Radio New Zealand, 'PM Says Job Losses Reflect Flexible Labour Market', 14 February 2013, www.radionz.co.nz/news/political/128098/pm-says-job-losses-reflect-flexible-labour-market (accessed 20 September 2016).

7   Cited in: Neal Ascherson, 'Is it Dead or Only Sleeping?', *The Independent*, 22 September 2006, www.independent.co.uk/voices/is-it-dead-or-only-sleeping-1364483.html (accessed 20 September 2016).

8   Tony Blair and Gerhard Schroeder, 'Europe: The Third Way/Die Neue Mitte (Working Documents No. 2)', Friedrich Ebert Stiftung, 20 February 1998, p.2, http://library.fes.de/pdf-files/bueros/suedafrika/02828.pdf (accessed 20 September 2016). My thanks to Jan Bakker for drawing my attention to this document.

9   David Farrar made this point trenchantly when I spoke with him at the Aspiring Conversations event in Wanaka in April 2016.

10 Tony Judt, *Ill Fares the Land*, Penguin, 2011, p.181.

11 Ibid., p.180.

12 Thanks to the late Tony Atkinson for prompting my thinking on whether New Zealand is a 'unique case' or whether it can be an example for other countries.

13 My thanks to Akif Malik for this point.

14 Blair and Schroeder, 'Europe: The Third Way', p.3.

15 Ibid., p.8.

16 Judt, *Ill Fares the Land*, pp.162–63.

17 'Social insurance' – along with the phrase 'freedom from want' – is the key phrase in the Beveridge Report, responsible for consolidating the UK's welfare system: Sir William Beveridge, 'Social Insurance and Allied Services', H. M. Stationery Office, 1942, partial copy http://news.bbc.co.uk/1/shared/bsp/hi/pdfs/19_07_05_beveridge.pdf (accessed 28 September 2016).

18 W. B. Sutch, *The Quest for Security in New Zealand*, Oxford University Press, 1966, p.157.

19 Judt, *Ill Fares the Land*, p.176.

20 A variety of activists and writers have worked with these terms, with 'the under-commons' referring in particular to black responses to the exclusionary nature of the commons. For two examples of websites dealing with these concepts, see: www.onthecommons.org/about-commons and www.autonomedia.org/node/181 (both accessed 28 September 2016).

21 The term has been popularised by Paul Mason, *PostCapitalism: A Guide to our Future,* Penguin, 2015.

22 Sue Goss, *Open Tribe*, Lawrence & Wishart (in association with Compass), 2014.

23 See David Marquand, *Mammon's Kingdom: An Essay on Britain, Now*, Penguin, 2015.

24 Scott Hamilton, 'The Missing Intellectuals: Review of Roger Horrocks' *Re-inventing New Zealand: Essays on the Arts and Media*', *Landfall Review Online*, 1 October 2016, www.landfallreview.com/the-missing-intellectuals (accessed 29 October 2016).

25 One useful repository of kaupapa Māori resources is 'Hei Hauhake Whakaaro: A Resource for Kaupapa Māori

Researchers', www.hauhake.auckland.ac.nz (accessed 30 October 2016).

26 New Zealand History, 'Ernest Rutherford: Biography', https://nzhistory.govt.nz/people/ernest-rutherford (accessed 3 January 2017). My thanks to Maarten Wevers for drawing my attention to this quotation.

27 The 'Overton window' is a concept that was first developed by Joseph Overton in his work for the Mackinac Center for Public Policy in the mid-1990s.

28 Robin D. G. Kelley, *Freedom Dreams: The Black Radical Imagination*, Beacon Press, 2002, p.198.

29 Ani Mikaere, *He Rukuruku Whakaaro: Colonising Myths, Māori Realities*, Huia Publishers and Te Tākupu, Te Wānanga o Raukawa, 2011, p.274.

30 Ibid., pp.274–75.

31 Ibid., p.109. John Ralston Saul has told a similar story about the importance of indigenous values for Canadian politics in: John Ralston Saul, *A Fair Country: Telling Truths About Canada*, Viking, 2008.

32 A similar point is made in the Australian context in the concluding chapter of: Macgregor Duncan, Andrew Leigh, David Madden and Peter Tynan, *Imagining Australia: Ideas for our Future*, Allen & Unwin, 2004.

33 William Pember Reeves, *The Long White Cloud: Ao Tea Roa*, Horace Marshall & Son, 1898, p.323.

34 Courtney Sina Meredith, 'Va Space Va'a Ship', in Godfery (ed.), *The Interregnum*, p.iii.

acknowledgements

I'm grateful to Sir John Vickers, Warden, and the Fellows of All Souls College, Oxford, for financial support, accommodation and other assistance during the writing phase of this book. I am also very appreciative of a grant awarded by the New Zealand Law Foundation towards costs, research flights to New Zealand and my research trip to Norway. I am grateful for a Rhodes Scholarship, which first brought me to Oxford; I want to acknowledge in particular the personal support of Mary Eaton at Rhodes House.

A great number of people have contributed to the ideas in this book. It is the result of conversations, exchanges, and friendships, which in some case go back many years. I am especially indebted to Philip Tremewan and Gregor Fountain. Philip supported me in the development of the concept at the outset, invited me to share work on the book at Aspiring Conversations in Wānaka, read multiple chapters, and provided important high-level feedback. Gregor strengthened my interest in progressive ideas when he taught me history (and coached me in debating) at Wellington College, suggested interviewees, read the entire manuscript and offered cogent suggestions and corrections. I also want to acknowledge Sian Elias and John McDougall: two people who, in their own ways – one as a judge for whom I worked, the other as my primary school teacher – inspired me to think more deeply about values.

I was so lucky to have others read lengthy portions of the book, especially Andrew Dean, Louis Chambers, Tai Ahu, Stephen Parry, Tara Paterson and Toby Moore. Others who offered significant feedback on the book include: Akif Malik, Ralph Hall, Julia Spelman, Lewis Mills, Kinley Salmon, Kingi Snelgar, Kiri Toki, members of Sandy Fredman's Oxford human rights research group, and members of the All Souls-based crime and politics discussion group. Other people with whom I had important conversations that sparked or strengthened my thinking for the book, or who helped out with arranging interviews, or supported me in other ways, include: Max Rashbrooke, Morgan Godfery, David Hall, Nomfundo Ramalekana, Philip McKibbin, Sarah St John, Marek Sullivan, Jenny Harding, Tony Spelman, Heather Anderson, Claudio Sopranzetti, Kathy Errington, Finn Smith, David Taylor, Genevieve Taylor, Michael Littlewood, Margo Picken, Ted Thomas, Julia Whaipooti, David Baragwanath, Tess Little, David Williams, Shelagh Noble, James Bonifacio, Jorgen Rennemo, Lizzie

Peacocke, Mads Andenas, Lana Doyle, Zachariah Sammour, Robin Congreve, Tracey Taylor, James Bonifacio, Robbie Tilleard, Alaister Moughan and Eirik Bjorge. I want to thank all individuals I interviewed for the book, many of whom offered constructive suggestions on the manuscript in draft. I also want to thank a Los Angeles taxi driver – and Mahoney Turnbull – for rescuing my phone, and the audio from all of my interviews, in 2015.

I want to express my deep gratitude to Bridget Williams Books. They took a chance on me with this project, a decision reflective of Bridget Williams's brave and brilliant faith in the voices of young New Zealanders. They then worked closely with me through to publication. David Cohen gave me the benefit of his superb editing skills, improving the style and substance of the book, and always interacting with me with patience and respect. In particular, he had a good eye for the parts of my book that lacked fresh language, and a great ear for new turns of phrase that could add dynamism to the writing. I learned a lot from working with him. David Hall arranged particularly useful reader feedback, and many anonymous readers have saved me from errors and misjudgements, while also suggesting useful additions. Julia Wells and Barbara Graham helped with permissions, further feedback and general editing. Julia offered particularly incisive feedback on Chapters 2 and 10. And Tom Rennie was an outstanding publisher. He backed my vision and imagination, supported me where I expressed doubt, and helped to nudge me away from my worst ideas. He put up with overly optimistic predictions of when I would complete the writing. I could not have hoped for a better person to work with.

Finally, all that is best in the book comes from my family. They have given me the love, encouragement and laughter that made me secure enough to try to put together this project. My brother has kept me grounded and provided interesting perspectives that have indirectly fed into this book's content. My sister has discussed many of the ideas of this book with me, rightly dissuading me from pursuing some lines of inquiry and encouraging me when I've needed it. My Mum and Dad stirred my interest in learning, pushed me to think big, and read the entire manuscript. When I write about 'care' in the book, I think of the care they've given me. I owe them, and love them, so much.

index